Upholstery Conservation: Principles and Practice

Butterworth-Heinemann Series in Conservation and Museology

Published titles:

Artists' Pigments c.1600–1835, 2nd Edition (Harley)
Care and Conservation of Geological Material (Howie)
Care and Conservation of Palaeontological Material (Collins)
Chemical Principles of Textile Conservation (Tímár-Balázsy, Eastop)
Conservation and Exhibitions (Stolow)
Conservation and Restoration of Ceramics (Buys, Oakley)
Conservation and Restoration of Works of Art and Antiquities (Kühn)
Conservation of Brick (Warren)
Conservation of Building and Decorative Stone (Ashurst, Dimes)
Conservation of Earth Structures (Warren)
Conservation of Glass (Newton, Davison)
Conservation of Historic Buildings (Feilden)
Conservation of Historic Timber Structures: An Ecological Approach to Preservation (Larsen, Marstein)
Conservation of Library and Archive Materials and the Graphic Arts (Petherbridge)
Conservation of Manuscripts and Painting of South-east Asia (Agrawal)
Conservation of Marine Archaeological Objects (Pearson)
Conservation of Wall Paintings (Mora, Mora, Philippot)
Historic Floors: Their History and Conservation (Fawcett)
A History of Architectural Conservation (Jokilehto)
Lacquer: Technology and Conservation (Webb)
The Museum Environment, 2nd Edition (Thomson)
The Organic Chemistry of Museum Objects, 2nd Edition (Mills, White)
Radiography of Cultural Material (Lang, Middleton)
The Textile Conservator's Manual, 2nd Edition (Landi)
Upholstery Conservation: Principles and Practice (Gill, Eastop)

Related titles:

Concerning Buildings (Marks)
Laser Cleaning in Conservation (Cooper)
Lighting Historic Buildings (Phillips)
Manual of Curatorship, 2nd edition (Thompson)
Manual of Heritage Management (Harrison)
Materials for Conservation (Horie)
Metal Plating and Patination (Niece, Craddock)
Museum Documentation Systems (Light)
Risk Assessment for Object Conservation (Ashley-Smith)
Touring Exhibitions (Sixsmith)

Upholstery Conservation: Principles and Practice

Kathryn Gill and Dinah Eastop

BUTTERWORTH
HEINEMANN

OXFORD AUCKLAND BOSTON JOHANNESBURG MELBOURNE NEW DELHI

Butterworth-Heinemann
Linacre House, Jordan Hill, Oxford OX2 8DP
225 Wildwood Avenue, Woburn, MA 01801-2041
A division of Reed Educational and Professional Publishing Ltd

A member of the Reed Elsevier plc group

First published 2001

British Library Cataloguing in Publication Data
A catalogue record for this book is available from the British Library

Library of Congress Cataloguing in Publication Data
A catalogue record for this book is available from Library of Congress

ISBN 0 7506 45067

Composition by Scribe Design, Gillingham, Kent
Printed and bound in Great Britain by The Cromwell Press, Trowbridge, Wiltshire

This book is dedicated to
Karen Finch, DLitt, OBE, FIIC,
Founder of the Textile Conservation Centre,
and its Principal from 1975 to 1986

Contents

Foreword

It would never happen today, when curators are appointed to specific posts in museums, specially advertised in newspapers and journals. But in 1954 I was put in the Department of Textiles in the Victoria & Albert Museum, after the dust from a staff reshuffle had settled and the vacancy I was finally asked to fill was in that Department. I spent eight years there and learned a great deal about textiles – a subject about which I had previously known nothing. I concentrated on seventeenth and eighteenth century materials because that was mostly the kind of expertise the public wanted when they brought things to the Museum for an opinion. It also allowed my boss and his deputy to continue with their studies of Oriental textiles, Elizabethan embroidery, tapestries and Mediaeval materials, all of which were more glamorous and important.

In 1962 I moved to the Department of Woodwork (mainly furniture, in fact) and soon became aware of how great a part textiles played in the appearance of furniture and especially of seat-furniture with its often very striking upholstery. It was not all 'brown wood' as we used to call it, and I began to try to convince people that upholstery actually mattered. It was not irrelevant and something one could send out to commercial upholsterers to do up as they thought fit – which was usually in the Victorian tradition, very well made but over-stuffed and quite wrong in style.

As you of course all know, upholstery can totally alter the silhouette of a chair and at many periods did so – look at engravings by Marot showing chairs with deep valances, so very different from so many actual Marot chairs today with their skimpy appearance, mean little seats and lack of fringes.

In the late 1950s I met a young curator – we were both young in those days and she is still a close friend – from Nordiska Museet in Stockholm. In 1961 Elisabet Hidemark published a little paperback on the covering of chairs (it is on my desk as I write: a larger and expanded edition came out in 1993) and it inspired me greatly. I could read Swedish. It was actually intended for ordinary people wanting to re-upholster their own chairs but it served museum curators very well, too. There was nothing else like it, certainly not in England.

At the V&A, however, we had been busy collecting information on the subject and now Temple Newsam at Leeds, the other chief repository of ancient furniture in our country, joined in the search. A key figure pursuing this new study was Karin Walton who was writing a thesis on eighteenth century upholstery in England (it finally came out in 1980) and she did most of the work in putting on an exhibition there already in 1973 where virtually all the pieces by then discovered were on show, and much information was also assembled and published in a small paperback catalogue (Walton 1973). That was a good start but it did not attract as much attention as one might have expected.

A major international turning point in the development of upholstery studies, however, came in 1979 when a Conference was held at the Museum of Fine Arts in Boston (Mass.). It was the first conference on the subject ever held. Elisabet Hidemark and Karin Walton were there and so were two hundred other people – curators, conservators, interior designers, collectors and historians. They were the pioneers of your movement and, in my initial address, I even quoted from *Henry V* the words about those not present thinking themselves 'accursed they were not here' at the Battle of Agincourt. That was a bit over the top, perhaps, but it caught the mood of the meeting and there was a great cheer because those present realised that this was an important occasion, it was something new.

Well, great things have sprung from that Conference (the papers unfortunately took nearly ten years to bring out (Cooke, 1987)) and gone are the days when I wanted to put up some curtains at Ham House, which I at that time ran for the V&A, and a Ministry of Works Official told me that 'we only spend thirty shillings a yard on curtain material, Mr Thornton'. He was deeply horrified as he was used to doing up offices every few years and knew nothing about long term requirements for which no money was in those days set aside. That was one of the reasons why we could not do things properly, even if we knew, or thought we knew, how it should be done. Those who are going to have access to the vast amount of information in the present book are to be envied by those of an earlier generation who did not have at their disposal the equipment, the new materials, and the techniques now available, let alone the funding and staffing now made possible.

Karen Finch, another Scandinavian with the determination and persuasiveness of so many women of that race, was already then working in the Textile Conservation Section at the V&A. What she has achieved during her years working in this field is truly remarkable and it has culminated in the fine Laboratory devoted entirely to textile conservation now standing on the Winchester Campus of the University of Southampton, where her successors carry on the exemplary tradition she established.

A further great stride was taken by Geoffrey Beard who in 1997 published his monumental tome on Upholstery in England. It is a mine of information and he deserves enormous credit for assembling it all. I wish Continental scholars would do something similar: there seems to be nothing like it coming from France or Germany. I do, however, urge British textile conservators 'to keep an eye on "abroad"', for so much that we have done in our country in the past in this field comes to us from across the waters.

I personally have learned an enormous amount from the close study of contemporary pictures (coeval is the more correct word). For they are the best evidence we possess of how things looked in the past, even if you have to make certain allowances. Most people think inventories reveal more but not about what furnishings actually looked like: they usually tell you of what they are made but, only if the descriptions are good, will they help you to guess their shape.

When you are faced with a piece of seat-furniture that is very old, it will not have been left untouched and you will have to undertake painstaking research, removing layer by layer, like archaeology, and recording everything. All this is explained at length in this book but I cannot stress sufficiently how important that research is. In my time commercial upholsterers stripped out a chair in a matter of minutes – and told you they had found nothing. I urged that one should take far longer to strip out a chair, that it should take as long as it would to rebuild the chair (and even that is nothing to what some of you are now doing with splendid results).

One of several key passages in the book (p. 93) stresses that 'textile and upholstery expertise is essential if informed deduction is to be drawn from [the] often scanty and confusing data' that one finds when one dismantles the upholstery of a chair. Read widely and study old pictures is what I recommend.

I am currently writing a book about Baroque interiors (north of the Alps) and am trying to illustrate it entirely with coeval pictures. It should complement the sort of work the authors are doing here. I am very pleased, as I write the book, to have lived long enough to see how splendidly the field of Textile Conservation has evolved from the small beginnings which I did what I could to urge it along back in the 1960s and 1970s.

One thing I have learned over the years, however, is that you must not think this book is the last word on the subject. Others will follow you and will develop new skills, even new ways of thinking. You must not be disappointed if what you have written, what you have done, is one day thought by the new Young Turks to be out-of-date or no longer appropriate. In the first place the same will happen to them later. But much of your work will probably still be valid half a century on or more. Either way this book marks a giant step forward in the history of your discipline.

I congratulate you all most warmly.

Peter Thornton, CBE, FSA
June 2000

Dedicatee's Preface

Hans Christian Andersen, the Danish storyteller, wrote a tale about a display cabinet inhabited by china figurines whose social hierarchy mimicked that of people of the day. One figurine, however pretty, was not acceptable to the rest because she had a tape measure in her back, and nothing that is useful can be art – a little bit like upholstered furniture. However well made or beautiful, upholstery has rarely been seen as an artform – an aspect that has contributed to the many hurdles in the path towards scientifically based upholstery conservation.

Conservation seeks to preserve all aspects of the original object, but this ideal can seldom be completely achieved with objects that are expected to fulfil their original function. In historic houses upholstered furniture is normally displayed in open room settings with the inevitable danger of unintentional use – or even planned use for special occasions. These were issues that needed to be addressed before conservation treatments could be devised.

I first learnt about the traditions of British upholstery workshops from Doris Bradley, who worked with me in the early days (1960s) in my Ealing studio and eventually left her tools to the Textile Conservation Centre (TCC). Doris had trained at the Royal School of Needlework and worked with several distinguished interior designers. She spoke about chairs having to stand up to use as well as look right. Therefore re-upholstery always began by discarding the old and unfashionable covers, including the webbing on the frame. Any re-usable materials became the perquisite of the upholsterer.

That conservators would have to work against this destruction of the original was also brought home to us by Karin Walton of Bristol Museum and Art Gallery. Karin came to the TCC to tell our students about her research into early upholstery. She explained how upholstery probably began with loose cushions, which, when they came to be fixed to the woodwork, drew on the skills of saddlers and coach makers. She also gave us an introduction to the kinds of materials used, such as webbing, tied springs and horsehair for moulding the shapes. She described the problems of tracing the historic development of upholstery due to scarcity of original material to study. This was caused not only by the conventions of stripping old upholstery, but because even when repaired and retained, old covers were usually remodelled into more fashionable shapes using new materials and often new techniques.

These observations confirmed my own: the technical history of upholstery was being lost along with each bit of material discarded. I began to think about how to deal with these diverse problems, which to my advisers seemed insoluble and best left as they were. It was then that the London College of Furniture offered to teach us how the tools left by Doris Bradley would have been used and how to apply this craft knowledge to 'read' any evidence left by past upholsterers. I persevered with getting funding to start a new course while realising that we would first have to reconcile the current position of upholstery in museums and historic houses with the basic precepts of conservation and the discoveries made by practical research on surviving intact upholstery.

Building on earlier research, explored in the 'Upholstery Bay' at the Victoria & Albert Museum and the Museum Room at Ham House, the training course in upholstery conservation that evolved arose from collaboration between colleagues at the Victoria & Albert Museum, the London College of Furniture and the Textile Conservation Centre itself. Parallel developments in establishing the discipline of upholstery conservation in the USA, included initiatives at Colonial Williamsburg, Winterthur and SPNEA (Society for the Preservation of New England Antiquities). A research climate was formed which allowed significant additions to be made to long-established practices of traditional re-upholstery, for example, tack-free solutions to re-upholstery.

Historically based upholstery conservation is now well established in both the UK and USA. Internationally accepted standards in the care and conservation of upholstery have now been developed. The symbiotic quality of the overlapping fields of practical and historical studies is now understood. This book reflects such cooperative research and is a major contribution to this increasingly important subject.

Karen Finch OBE, DLitt, FIIC
March 2000

Series Editors' Preface

The conservation of artefacts and buildings has a long history, but the positive emergence of conservation as a profession can be said to date from the foundation of the International Institute for the Conservation of Museum Objects (IIC) in 1950 (the last two words of the title being later changed to Historic and Artistic Works) and the appearance soon after in 1952 of its journal *Studies in Conservation*. The role of the conservator as distinct from those of the restorer and the scientist had been emerging during the 1930s with a focal point in the Fogg Art Museum, Harvard University, which published the precursor to *Studies in Conservation, Technical Studies in the Field of the Fine Arts* (1932–42).

UNESCO, through its Cultural Heritage Division and its publications, had always taken a positive role in conservation and the foundation, under its auspices, of the International Centre for the Study of the Preservation and the Restoration of Cultural Property (ICCROM), in Rome, was a further advance. The Centre was established in 1959 with the aims of advising internationally on conservation problems, co-ordinating conservation activators and establishing standards of training courses.

A significant confirmation of professional progress was the transformation at New York in 1966 of the two committees of the International Council of Museums (ICOM), one curatorial on the Care of Paintings (founded in 1949) and the other mainly scientific (founded in the mid-1950s), into the ICOM Committee for Conservation.

Following the Second International Congress of Architects in Venice in 1964 when the Venice Charter was promulgated, the International Council of Monuments and Sites (ICOMOS) was set up in 1965 to deal with archaeological, architectural and town planning questions, to schedule monuments and sites and to monitor relevant legislation. From the early 1960s onwards, international congresses (and the literature emerging from them) held by IIC, ICOM, ICOMOS and ICCROM not only advanced the subject in its various technical specializations but also emphasized the cohesion of conservators and their subject as an interdisciplinary profession.

The use of the term *Conservation* in the title of this series refers to the whole subject of the care and treatment of valuable artefacts, both movable and immovable, but within the discipline conservation has a meaning which is distinct from that of restoration. *Conservation* used in this specialized sense has two aspects: first, the control of the environment to minimize the decay of artefacts and materials; and, second, their treatment to arrest decay and to stabilize them where possible against further deterioration. Restoration is the continuation of the latter process, when conservation treatment is thought to be insufficient, to the extent of reinstating an object, without falsification, to a condition in which it can be exhibited.

In the field of conservation conflicts of values on aesthetic, historical, or technical grounds are often inevitable. Rival attitudes and methods inevitably arise in a subject which is still developing and at the core of these differences there is often a deficiency of technical knowledge. That is one of the principal *raisons d'être* of this series. In most of these matters ethical principles are the subject of much discussion, and generalisations cannot easily cover (say) buildings, furniture, easel paintings and waterlogged wooden objects.

A rigid, universally agreed principle is that all treatment should be adequately documented.

There is also general agreement that structural and decorative falsification should be avoided. In addition there are three other principles which, unless there are overriding objections, it is generally agreed should be followed.

The first is the principle of the reversibility of processes, which states that a treatment should normally be such that the artefact can, if desired, be returned to its pre-treatment condition even after a long lapse of time. This principle is impossible to apply in some cases, for example where the survival of an artefact may depend upon an irreversible process. The second, intrinsic to the whole subject, is that as far as possible decayed parts of an artefact should be conserved and not replaced. The third is that the consequences of the ageing of the original materials (for example 'patina') should not normally be disguised or removed. This includes a secondary proviso that later accretions should not be retained under the false guise of natural patina.

The authors of the volumes in this series give their views on these matters, where relevant, with reference to the types of material within their scope. They take into account the differences in approach to artefacts of essentially artistic significance and to those in which the interest is primarily historical, archaeological or scientific.

The volumes are unified by a systematic and balanced presentation of theoretical and practical material with, where necessary, an objective comparison of different methods and approaches. A balance has also been maintained between the fine (and decorative) arts, archaeology and architecture in those cases where the respective branches of the subject have common ground, for example in the treatment of stone and glass and in the control of the museum environment. Since the publication of the first volume it has been decided to include within the series related monographs and technical studies. To reflect this enlargement of its scope the series has been renamed the Butterworth-Heinemann Series in Conservation and Museology.

Though necessarily different in details of organisation and treatment (to fit the particular requirements of the subject) each volume has the same general standard, which is that of such training courses as those of the University of London Institute of Archaeology, the Victoria & Albert Museum, the Conservation Center, New York University, the Institute of Advanced Architectural Studies, York, and ICCROM.

The authors have been chosen from among the acknowledged experts in each field, but as a result of the wide areas of knowledge and technique covered even by the specialised volumes in this series, in many instances multi-authorship has been necessary.

With the existence of IIC, ICOM, ICOMOS and ICCROM, the principles and practice of conservation have become as internationalised as the problems. The collaboration of Consultant Editors will help to ensure that the practices discussed in this series will be applicable throughout the world.

Editors' Preface

Upholstery Conservation: Principles and Practice presents one stage in the development of upholstery conservation. The book's preparation is timely because the ground-breaking publication *Upholstery Conservation* (Williams, ed., 1990) is no longer in print. Much interesting work has been undertaken in the intervening period. Building on *Upholstery Conservation*, this book aims to complement another in Butterworth-Heinemann's Conservation and Museology series: *Conservation of Furniture and Wooden Artefacts* (Rivers and Umney, eds, forthcoming).

The case histories show the interdisciplinary nature of much upholstery conservation; they demonstrate an increasingly reflective approach to the conservation of upholstered furniture, and the importance attributed to documentation. Each case history demonstrates the complexities of acting to conserve and present upholstered furniture, where preservation of information, both material and contextual, may be as important as the maintenance of function and the conservation of the artefact itself. We hope this book will contribute to a further understanding of upholstered furniture and to upholstery conservation.

Kathryn Gill and Dinah Eastop
Winchester, June 2000

Acknowledgements

This book is like a top cover stretched over a complex understructure. It is supported by traditional upholstery practice, historical and technical research, innovation and international collaboration. We would like to thank everyone who contributed to the book and supported its creation.

Our greatest debt is to the contributors, who responded to our invitation with enthusiasm, and to our editorial queries with great patience and sensitivity to deadlines. We were pleased when Karen Finch, to whom we dedicate this book, offered her thoughtful perspective, published as the Dedicatee's Preface. We felt especially honoured when Peter Thornton accepted our invitation to write the Foreword.

Custodians of the many collections represented here could not have been more helpful. We thank colleagues at the Brooklyn Museum of Art, New York, USA; the Cleveland Museum of Art, Cleveland, USA; the Detroit Institute of Arts, Detroit, USA; English Heritage, Brodsworth Hall, South Yorkshire, UK; the Geffrye Museum, London, UK; Houghton Hall, Norfolk, UK; the Metropolitan Museum of Art, New York, USA; Raby Castle, County Durham, UK; Victoria & Albert Museum, London, UK; William Morris Gallery, Walthamstow, London, UK; Winchester Cathedral, Winchester, UK.

We acknowledge the support provided by the University of Southampton and by a research grant from the British Academy.

We also acknowledge the support of colleagues at the Textile Conservation Centre, University of Southampton, notably Nell Hoare, Mary Brooks and Amber Rowe, who were encouraging in both word and deed. The final stages of assembling the text and illustrations would have been much harder without the help of Vivienne Martin, Ann Morrice, Sylvie Tye and Mike Halliwell.

We benefited from the interdisciplinary collaboration manifested at the one day forum: The Conservation and Restoration of Upholstered Furniture: Reviewing the Issues held at West Dean in December 1998. We thank particularly David Leigh, Pat Jackson and Norbert Gutowski of West Dean.

We would also like to acknowledge the advice given by Andrew Oddy, as Series Editor, and staff at Butterworth-Heinemann. We thank Bob Smith and David Goldberg for their support, and William Smith for his unflagging enthusiasm for *The Adventures of the Wishing Chair* (Blyton, 1937).

Kathryn Gill and Dinah Eastop,
Textile Conservation Centre,
University of Southampton
June 2000

List of Contributors

Derek Balfour
Retraining (in the late 1970s) as an upholsterer led to contacts with textile conservators dealing with upholstered objects. This involvement resulted in a period of conservation training, specialising in upholstery, on the RCA/V&A Joint Course gaining an MA in Conservation in 1993. This was followed by contracts in the V&A Textile Conservation Section and The Metropolitan Museum of Art, New York. Derek was appointed Senior Conservator (Upholstery), of the Victoria & Albert Museum Textile Conservation Section in 1995. AMUKIC.

Nancy Britton
Nancy Britton is the Associate Conservator for Upholstered Works of Art at the Metropolitan Museum of Art in the Sherman Fairchild Centre for Objects Conservation where she has been since 1991. She received her Master's of Science degree from the University of Rhode Island. Previously, she had worked in the Upholstery Conservation Laboratory at the Society for the Preservation of New England Antiquities Conservation Center in Waltham, MA.

Frances Collard
Frances Collard is Acting Deputy Curator in the Department of Furniture and Woodwork, Victoria & Albert Museum. Her specialist areas are British nineteenth-century furniture and the history of upholstery. Her publications include *Regency Furniture*, published by the Antiques Collectors Club, 1985 (reprinted 1996).

Sherry Doyal
Sherry Doyal trained as an upholstery conservator after an initial training as an objects conservator. She is committed to 'fusion' conservation, that is, cross-specialist discipline collaboration for the conservation of mixed material objects. Her current portfolio of employment combines a part-time position as The National Trust Regional Conservator for Devon and freelance conservation of plant collections, plant material ethnography and conservation teaching.

Dinah Eastop
Dinah Eastop is Senior Lecturer at the Textile Conservation Centre, University of Southampton. She had in-service training in textile conservation with Dr Karen Finch, OBE, FIIC and with Dr Mechtild Flury-Lemberg at the Abegg-Stiftung, Switzerland. She has worked at the Textile Conservation Centre since 1976 as Conservator, Tutor and as Director from 1988 to 1991. She was Assistant Coordinator of the Textiles Working Group of ICOM-CC, 1990–3 and 1996–9, and was elected a Fellow of IIC in 1993. She was an appointed member of the Expert Panel set up by the Museums and Galleries Commission (UK) for *Standards in the Museum Care of Costume and Textiles*, 1995–8. She is active in developing the scholarly foundations of textile conservation. She is co-author with Dr Agnes Timár-Balázsy of *Chemical Principles of Textile Conservation*, 1998 and is Deputy Editor of UKIC's journal *The Conservator*. Her current interests are in material culture, expanding the social sciences base of textile conservation, and promoting practice-based research. AMUKIC.

Nicola Gentle
Nicola Gentle trained as a painter at Winchester School of Art (Diploma in Art & Design, Fine Art, 1973). In 1978 she joined the staff of the Conservation Department (Textiles Section) of

the Victoria & Albert Museum, London, and as Senior Conservator (1988–94) was in charge of the Osterley Textile Studio, specialising in the conservation of textile furnishings. Since 1994, she has worked as a freelance Conservation Consultant, based in Devon. AMUKIC.

Kathryn Gill

Kathryn (Kate) Gill is Senior Conservator and Lecturer at the Textile Conservation Centre, University of Southampton. She specialises in the conservation of textiles and upholstery; she also teaches, and supervises postgraduate projects. She has worked on both sides of the Atlantic and has played a key role in developing upholstery conservation at the Metropolitan Museum of Art, New York and in the UK. Her aim has been to enhance the standard of upholstery conservation and documentation, while maintaining craft knowledge and skills. She has published widely, and is co-author (with Sherry Doyal) of the upholstery sections in *Conservation of Furniture*, edited by Nick Umney (forthcoming). She recently led the Upholstery Conservation Forum and Course at West Dean, Sussex. AMUKIC.

Maria Hayward

After taking a history degree, Maria Hayward trained and worked as a textile conservator at the Textile Conservation Centre, Hampton Court Palace, working in both the general and tapestry departments. Between 1993 and 1997 she studied for a PhD on the possessions of Henry VIII and then returned to the TCC, as a member of the teaching staff. She has published several articles drawing on this research and an edition of the 1542 inventory of the palace of Westminster should be published this year. Maria is currently working on a project looking at liturgical textiles at the time of the reformation in England. This will combine a study of archival sources and surviving textiles from the period. AMUKIC.

Elizabeth Lahikainen

Elizabeth Lahikainen is a Historic Upholstery Conservator in private practice and is associated with the Peabody Essex Museum in Salem, MA. After a BS in Textiles (Syracuse, 1972) she narrowed her career focus from textile conservation to upholstery after receiving a Kress Fellowship for Advanced Study in 1985. She has been an active participant in the field of upholstery conservation for more than a decade, developing new techniques to upholster museum quality furniture that will not destroy historic materials in the process and at the same time create historically correct presentations. Her credits include being an organiser for the first Upholstery Conservation Symposium at Williamsburg in 1990.

Simon Metcalf

Simon Metcalf began his career working in various metalworking disciplines, mainly jewellery, silversmithing, blacksmithing and allied crafts. A long-term interest in historic metals and technology prompted a move into the world of conservation. He trained in conservation while working at The Wallace Collection, before moving on to work in the Conservation Department of the Royal Armouries at the Tower of London. In the past five years he has worked in the Metals Section of the Conservation Department at the Victoria & Albert Museum. AMUKIC.

Crosby Stevens

After graduating from Cambridge in 1983 with a history degree, she gained a Diploma in Textile Conservation from the Textile Conservation Centre Courtauld Institute, in 1987. After working as a Assistant Textile Conservator for the National Trust, 1987–9, she then worked as a freelance textile conservator between 1989 and 2000, gaining a Doctorate from the University of Sheffield in nineteenth-century cultural history during this time. From 1999 involvement at Brodsworth Hall included various textile conservation and curatorial projects, and from 2000 she is Curator of Art & Furniture for English Heritage. AMUKIC.

Lesley Wilson

Lesley Wilson studied Sociology at London University, Furniture Production and Design at the London College of Furniture and Science for Conservators at Hammersmith & West London College. She works for public and private collections as an independent conservator specialising in upholstery and the historic development of upholstery techniques and materials. AMUKIC.

Introduction: Upholstery conservation as a practice of preservation, investigation and interpretation

Dinah Eastop and Kathryn Gill

Upholstery conservation is a complex practice, encompassing processes of preservation, investigation and interpretation. The principles and practices of upholstery conservation are illustrated with case examples to show both ethical and technical problems. This book does not aim to be comprehensive nor to advocate one practice over another. Rather it is an attempt to demonstrate how conservation principles have been applied recently to the documentation and treatment of upholstered artefacts. We have deliberately adopted a wide definition of upholstery, extending the term, like the eighteenth-century upholderer (upholsterer), to cover beds and carriages, as well as seat furniture. We have also deliberately encompassed the preservation and creation of knowledge as well as artefacts. Our concern is to demonstrate the complementary nature of material, pictorial, textual and experiential evidence for an understanding of upholstery and its conservation.

Traditional seat upholstery often consists of a decorative cloth top cover nailed over a resilient, many-layered understructure to a wooden chair frame. Like an iceberg, much of the material normally remains concealed. The many organic and inorganic materials that make up upholstery are subject to deterioration, some more rapidly than others. Upholstery conservation often necessitates gaining access to parts that are normally concealed, as in the temporary removal of a top cover to examine and treat underlying layers. The conservation of the multi-media, many-layered, functional artefacts that constitute 'upholstery' is the subject of this book.

1 Upholstery conservation as preservation

The decision to conserve upholstered furniture is predicated on the assumption that something (the upholstered thing) requires conservation. Before undertaking interventive investigation or treatment, decisions must be made about what is to be preserved. The significance of the item's materials, construction, form and function need to be assessed.

1.1 Preservation of the designer's intentions

As in fine art conservation, treatments intended to reveal or restore the original appearance of an artefact are common in upholstery conservation. It is therefore not surprising that 'restoration' approaches are chosen for artefacts that are valued as the work of an artist or designer, rather than an upholsterer. In such cases, priority is usually accorded to interventions which allow for the preservation of the designer's (presumed) original intentions over preserving evidence of subsequent use, such as repairs, alterations and signs of wear. Well-documented examples include the treatment of the settee designed by the artist Alma-Tadema in c.1884 (Kathryn Gill, Chapter 2) and an important chair designed by Robert Adam and made by Thomas Chippendale in c.1764–5 for Sir Lawrence Dundas (Balfour *et al*., 1999).

The treatment of the Mermaid chair (Sherry Doyal and Dinah Eastop, Chapter 3) was determined by the wish to reflect the intentions of its Victorian designer, the architect William Burges. However, both the material and archival evidence suggested uncertainties about his intentions. Burges' original design was clearly for a chair with rush seating: what remains unclear is whether the later covering of the rush seating with plush upholstery reflects a change in the taste of Burges himself, or of a later owner. The conservative approach adopted for the treatment and presentation of the Mermaid chair allows decisions to be reviewed as and when more conclusive evidence becomes available. It also allows for evidence of changing tastes to be preserved and presented. It is now more widely accepted that a single object may have multiple histories (Eastop, 2000).

1.2 The treatment of surviving components

Having decided what role an upholstered artefact is to serve (Eastop, 1998), and therefore what is to be given priority in terms of preservation and presentation, decisions must be made about how the upholstery is to be conserved. There is a great range of possibilities, encompassing differing degrees of intervention, from documentation only at one end of the spectrum to restoration at the other. Four categories of conservation can be distinguished: restoring to presumed original appearance; introducing new materials, either by integrating them with the old materials, or using new materials to substitute (either temporarily or permanently) for damaged or missing originals; treating original materials only; and restricting 'intervention' to investigation and documentation only. These categories can be hard to distinguish, and are not mutually exclusive. Many upholstery conservation treatments will involve all of them. The subtle adaptation and integration of each type of intervention often characterises best practice in upholstery conservation.

The temporary removal of original components is not uncommon in upholstery conservation. Top covers may be temporarily released to allow access to underlying structures that require treatment. They may also be removed so that they can be cleaned and/or supported prior to being reinstated (Kathryn Gill, Chapter 1; Nicola Gentle, Chapter 6). Where top covers require extensive remedial treatment, this is undertaken by textile conservators, although the covers are often removed by upholstery specialists (Lesley Wilson, Chapter 8). The overlapping specialisms of textile conservation and upholstery conservation are recognised in the recent advertisement for a furniture upholstery conservator: applicants were required to have 'good knowledge of the underlying principles of textile conservation and a keen interest in traditional furniture upholstery' (Anon., 2000).

The choice of support fabric for top covers that are to be reinstated is very important. In the case of very damaged components, the remaining parts may be supported onto new fabric which both camouflages holes and infills larger areas of loss. This was particularly important in the treatment of the carriage trimming, where significant parts of the severely damaged elements were missing. These parts needed to be reinstated, both to preserve and present the original form of the trimming, and because the carriage may be required for occasional use (Nicola Gentle, Chapter 6). As well as supporting the material and camouflaging areas of loss, support fabrics must not interfere with the re-upholstery. A very thin support fabric was selected for the stamped plush top cover on the Mermaid chair, to ensure that it added as little bulk to the top cover as possible, thereby allowing the folds to be reinstated during the re-upholstery (Sherry Doyal and Dinah Eastop, Chapter 3).

1.3 Integration of new and old materials, or substitution of new for old

The careful integration and/or substitution of new materials for old is sometimes necessary. In the case of two French eighteenth-century chairs the entire seat and back upholstery was missing, the chairs having presented for treatment as bare frames (Elizabeth Lahikainen, Chapter 7). It was therefore necessary to recreate the missing elements. In this case the missing seat and back upholstery was replaced with polyethylene foam inserts covered in new silk top covers. This established technique is characterised as minimally interventive, because it involves little or no damage to the frames caused by the nailing of traditional (re-)upholstery. This foam-based, non-intrusive approach was recently introduced into the Victoria & Albert Museum for the treatment of the Dundas chair (Balfour *et al.*, 1999).

The treatment of the Denon chairs, also undertaken at the Victoria & Albert Museum, involved an unusual application of the minimally intrusive approach (Derek Balfour *et al.*, Chapter 4). Damage to the bare frames was avoided by fitting each chair with a thin, detachable, metal shell. Once covered in cloth the shell formed the basis for new upholstery. Rather than replacing the missing upholstery with carved foam components, the reconstruction was effected with traditional upholstery materials and techniques. This achieved a compromise between the objective of preserving evidence on the frame, and the objective of restoring the upholstery in a traditional way. Seat furniture on open display can be at risk of being sat upon; the metal shell could accommodate the weight of a sitter.

The creation of an upholstery profile with expanded polyethylene foam is a reductive process, in that the foam is cut and carved away to achieve the desired shape. In contrast, traditional upholstery is a process of addition, where one layer is built up on top of another. The choice of one technique over another may reflect the skills of the practitioner; someone with a background in traditional upholstery is more likely to be skilled in building up than someone skilled in, say, wood carving who is more likely to adopt a cutting down approach.

The integration of original and replica materials is sometimes necessary. The treatment of the blue state bed from Hampton Court, Herefordshire, UK provides an excellent example of such integration (Nancy Britton, Chapter 5). The treatment of the 'Heron' chair designed by Race in c.1955 involved the re-incorporation of original materials in a novel way (Kathryn Gill, Chapter 1). Several of the polyurethane foams used in the original upholstery had deteriorated to crumbs. Samples of this foam debris were collected and sealed between archival quality, transparent sheets. The encapsulated foam crumbs were incorporated with the new upholstery materials added to replace and/or supplement the missing and compressed foams. In this way the original shape and profile of the chair were re-established, and the degraded foam samples stay with the chair, and remain available for further investigation.

1.4 Documentation

The systematic recording of upholstered furniture is an important but often overlooked part of upholstery conservation. It ensures that information revealed during investigations and treatments is not lost, but remains accessible to later researchers without unnecessary handling or disturbance to the object. A guide to the documentation of upholstered furniture is included here (Sherry Doyal, Appendix I). X-ray plates can provide a record of internal structure and materials without the need for interventions. Although X-ray opaque materials, such as metals, are well known to show up clearly in X-ray plates, it is also possible for details of organic materials to be revealed (e.g. Buck, 1991; Javér *et al.*, 1999). Close inspection of the X-ray plates of the Brooklyn chair revealed the individual layers of upholstery, including webbing and a suggestion of a loose filling (Kathryn Gill and Sherry Doyal, Appendix III).

The analysis of upholstered objects, in combination with information from other sources (e.g. archives, accounts and paintings) can be very revealing about upholstery practice. Although very little seat furniture from the court of Henry VIII survives, and those chairs that have been preserved appear to have undergone changes, a comparative analysis of accounts, inventories and visual sources proved very informative (Maria Hayward, Chapter 9). When considered together, these sources and the x-frame chair associated with Mary Tudor at Winchester Cathedral provide a vivid impression of luxury furniture at the Tudor court. Comparing the data allowed the findings from one source to be evaluated in relation to evidence from another. So, for example, a manuscript illustration shows Henry VIII (1491–1547) seated on a blue chair, but only a very small percentage of chairs in the king's possession at his death were that colour. Such comparisons encourage a more critical approach to sources, which may corroborate or refute one another. The technical and stylistic comparison of twelve Massachusetts State House chairs provides an excellent model of what careful documentation alone can reveal (Buck, 1991).

An investigation of the textile furnishings of a bedroom in Brodsworth Hall, Yorkshire, UK, provides a fascinating insight into the way decorative schemes are changed (Crosby Stevens, Chapter 11). Surviving textiles and textile-covered furniture were compared with evidence from accounts and photographs. Together they demonstrate the economic and social value of textiles. The many covers present on a single chair or headboard manifest the widespread practice of re-upholstery, preserved like an 'archaeology' of decorative schemes. The survival of many case covers testifies to the careful house-keeping practices recently revived by bodies such as the National Trust (Lloyd, 1997; Sandwith and Stainton, 1991 [1984]).

The documentation of conservation treatments is also very important, as this book aims to demonstrate. Bringing together both technical and cultural issues means that decision-making processes are made more transparent and therefore readily accessible for professional scrutiny. Conservators, custodians and curators in the future will be better able to understand not only what interventions were carried out but also why they were undertaken (Appelbaum, 1997; Eastop, 1998).

2 Upholstery conservation as revelation and investigation

One feature of upholstery conservation is the temporary exposure of parts that are normally concealed. The documentation, preservation and interpretation of this material evidence is an essential feature of the specialism.

2.1 Preserving evidence of workshop practices

Evidence of maker's workshop practices can be revealed. For example, the conservation of the carriage trim exposed writing on the linen covers of the seat pads, which had been temporarily removed for treatment. It became obvious that the trimmer had not followed the initial pattern of tying which had been marked out in pencil on the linen scrim. A crudely stitched gash in the hind back squab was initially interpreted as a later attempt to supplement fillings, which were presumed to have become crushed or missing. However, archival research revealed that loosely stuffing a squab and then cutting it open to insert more stuffing as required, may have been a standard part of trimming practice (Nicola Gentle, Chapter 6). Pencil markings were also discovered on the Tadema settee when the modern top covers were removed; pencil lines marked the location and width of the missing original decorative panels (Kathryn Gill, Chapter 2).

The presence of maker's marks on the base of the suite of furniture in the Octagon Room, Raby Castle, County Durham, UK was documented as part of the conservation project (Lesley Wilson, Chapter 8). The name of the upholsterer, G.J. Morant, is stamped on the underside of the furniture, on the bottoming, webbing and base cover. Embroidered labels, worked on the detachable, tight-fitting covers and on upholstery understructures of the green velvet chairs at Houghton, have been recorded by Beard (1997: Plate 183). They must have helped to ensure that the covers were fitted on the correct chairs. The use of cords fitted with metal aigulettes to secure the detachable covers on the red velvet suite at Houghton may widen the interpretation of these finds. Aiguillettes found under floorboards in the ducal palace of Urbino are recorded as being items of dress (Lopez, 1997: 96–7). Given the covers at Houghton, they may be evidence of the history of upholstery rather than dress.

In outward appearance, with its steel rod frame, Race's 'Heron' chair is an icon of modern furniture design (Kathryn Gill, Chapter 1). However, the temporary removal of the top covers revealed a combination of both traditional and innovative upholstery techniques (Gill, 2000). For example, the single continuous strip of rubberised webbing was attached to the frame in a novel way, using a series of metal clips. In contrast, the jute cloth base, on which the polyurethane foam was adhered, was secured under tension to the frame with hand stitching in a traditional manner. Further evidence of workshop practices was gained by interviewing an upholsterer who had worked as an apprentice in the workshop of 'Race Furniture Limited' in the 1960s (Kathryn Gill, Chapter 1, Report A).

Documenting evidence of the actual physical practice of upholstery is difficult, though photographic techniques provide a means of recording characteristic body movements and positions. The computer modelling of movements for the design of robots may have potential for recording upholsterers' practice. An extremely useful record of contemporary upholstery practice is provided in the photographs, line drawings and videos of David James. His long experience as an upholsterer and teacher of upholstery techniques has led him to create a vivid record of his practice (e.g. James, 1990, 1994, 1997).

2.2 Preserving evidence of use

Most seat furniture is designed to be sat on, although the design of chairs commissioned by Baron Denon also demonstrate his recently acquired knowledge of ancient Egypt, as well as the wealth and taste necessary to commission exquisite inlay (Derek Balfour *et al.*, Chapter 4).

The explicit preservation of evidence of the social practice of sitting is unusual. It is particularly noteworthy that, not withstanding the complex demands of the Raby Castle project, the upholstery conservator remained sensitive to the need to preserve even the most subtle signs of use (Lesley Wilson, Chapter 8). The understructure of one of the sofas had shifted in a characteristic way, and care was taken not to correct this evidence of prolonged use. The deformations resulting from thirty years of use (and degradation of the constituent materials) posed problems in presenting the 'Heron' chair and footstool now at the Geffrye Museum (Kathryn Gill, Chapter 1). The foam filling and webbing had become permanently deformed, which means that the profiles of the cushions from the chair and footstool no longer follow the shapes intended by their designer.

There is a growing interest in the study of body praxis, about how a person's very body and his/her movements are constrained by social forces. For example, the way social norms were embodied in Algeria and France has been analysed (Bourdieu, 1977, 1984); and Elias (1978) has studied what constitutes 'good manners' in the history of Western Europe. The references to close stools in sixteenth-century court records reveal a lot about Tudor attitudes and facilities (Maria Hayward, Chapter 9). The way a contemporary Western teenager 'sits' on a chair or who occupies a 'shared' arm rest on public transport reveals much about current social practice. An upholstered armchair used almost exclusively by one person soon takes on the shape, and pattern of wear and tear, characteristic of the sitter.

2.3 Preserving evidence of the 'social biographies' of upholstered objects

Although upholstery conservators are often required to preserve the designer's or maker's original intentions, there is an increasing awareness of the possibilities of conserving evidence of an artefact's subsequent history. This reflects changing attitudes: whereas production was once the primary focus of study, the consumption of goods is increasingly recognised as being significant (e.g. Miller, 1987; Medlam, 1993). Upholstered furniture, because of its intimate contact with humans, often in domestic contexts, provides vivid material evidence of social life, as analysed for instance by Grier (1988).

Analysing the way suites of furniture are dispersed and modified is very revealing. In discussing the relative roles of the upholsterer and the architect in fashioning domestic interiors, Thornton emphasises that the 'occupants of rooms also change things all the time. They move things around, they add items and remove others' (1993 [1984]: 12). This is evident in the analysis of textile furnishings at Brodsworth Hall (Crosby Stevens, Chapter 11) and the chairs from the Massachusetts State House (Buck, 1991).

The conservation strategy developed for the Mermaid chair designed by Burges was an explicit attempt to conserve two stages in the 'life' of the chair: evidence of both its original form and later changes (Sherry Doyal and Dinah Eastop, Chapter 3). When the eighteenth-century state bed at Uppark,

Sussex, UK, was 'resurrected' after the devastating fire of 1989, it was agreed that the 1930s repair work 'should be allowed to remain, as an important part of the history of the bed' (Wylie and Singer, 1997: 121). Interventions required to preserve the upholstered interior of a carriage manifested significant changes to the form of the vehicle. It may have started life as an open chariot, which was later altered to form the current closed carriage (Nicola Gentle, Chapter 6).

Changes in the Mermaid chair, the Uppark bed and the chariot/carriage can be usefully analysed by adopting a 'biographical approach' to mapping the social life of objects (Kopytoff, 1986). A recent attempt at plotting the 'social biography' of an eighteenth-century embroidered thangka now in the collections of the Victoria & Albert Museum provides an excellent model of what can be revealed by adopting this approach to documenting such material and contextual data (Bacchus, 2002).

3 Upholstery conservation as interpretation

Many upholstery conservation interventions involve an element of interpretation. Even when founded on thorough research such interventions are never purely objective, but are inevitably subjective in character. They also involve compromise, often due to resource constraints or to incomplete or insufficient data (Balfour *et al.*, 1999). This explains the priority given to re-presentation techniques that are reversible and minimally intrusive.

3.1 Interpreting designers' intentions

Presenting a designer's original intentions is usually a matter of interpretation rather than certainty. Only in the case of modern furniture is there likely to be a sufficient quantity and variety of evidence (material, visual, archival and experiential) for the curator and conservator to be reasonably certain what effect the designer was really after. The abundance of evidence about Race's designs, materials and manufacturing arrangements helped in the conservation of the Geffrye Museum's 'Heron' chair and footstool (Kathryn Gill, Chapter 1). Similarly, decisions about the re-presentation of the Tadema settee were facilitated by sale catalogues, photographs and paintings. A curtain from the Tadema suite was discovered after the replication of the covers. This material evidence helped in evaluating the effectiveness of the top cover replication and presentation of the settee (Kathryn Gill, Chapter 2).

There is usually less information about a designer's intentions, and reliance is often placed on the interpretation of other primary sources, such as contemporaneous paintings. They provided evidence for re-establishing the seat profiles of two French eighteenth-century chairs, of which only the bare frames remained (Elizabeth Lahikainen, Chapter 7). The minimally intrusive method chosen for these chairs allows for other interpretations and presentations in the future, without jeopardising the evidential value of the chair frames themselves. This case history demonstrates how a modern inert polyethylene foam, when modelled with great sensitivity and skill, and according to carefully selected historic sources, can replicate the appearance of traditional upholstery. An alternative approach to minimally intrusive re-upholstery was adopted in the case of the Denon chairs, as outlined above (Derek Balfour *et al.*, Chapter 4).

The challenges of interpretation are evident in the reconstruction of the top cover for the magnificent inlaid ebony settee designed in c.1884 as part of a large suite of furniture for the Music Room of Marquand's Mansion, New York City, by Alma-Tadema (1836–1912). When the settee was bequeathed to the Metropolitan Museum of Art, New York, in 1975, it had recently applied striped top covers. Extensive research was necessary to deduce the design of the original top covers, and a replica printed top cover was made of the embroidered original. Five years after the settee was fitted with the replica top cover, a curtain from the Music Room was found. This provided an opportunity to compare the replica panels of 1991 with embroidered panels on the surviving curtain of c.1884. The comparison revealed that the recreated design and handling of the motifs closely resembled the embroidered curtain, albeit with colour variations.

The desire to present upholstery in its original form does not necessarily lead to success, because the available evidence is often incomplete and open to a variety of interpretations.

Analysis of twelve chairs from the Massachusetts State House revealed that at least five different top covers (black haircloth and red, brown, green and black leather) had been considered authentic at different times and by different people: 'The twelve chairs reflect different approaches and interpretations of the proper historic upholstery form and materials' (Buck, 1991: page unnumbered).

The treatment of the 1697 blue state bed from Hampton Court, Herefordshire, UK demonstrates the wide range of knowledge and skills required to integrate replicas with original materials (Nancy Britton, Chapter 5). When the bed was selected for long-term display at the Metropolitan Museum of Art, New York the condition of its various textile and non-textile components was assessed. The textile-only components, i.e. the curtains, upper and lower valances, tester cloth and head cloth, were considered too weak to withstand long term open display. It was therefore decided to put the original textile-only components into study-storage and to display the bed with replica hangings. The replicas were made of reproduction fabric, which was required to duplicate the features of the original blue silk damask as accurately as possible. In commissioning the damask, great care was taken, not only in replicating the pattern, weave, handle, weight and colour, but also in achieving the colour variations, called strie, which are characteristic of old damask. Similar care was taken in drawing up and meeting the specifications for the reproduction passementerie, and in replicating the cut and construction of the various components. The original method of attaching the valances was not adopted for the replicas, for which a non-intrusive clamping system was developed. The success of this conservation-cum-display project rests on the carefully co-ordinated collaboration of different specialists, both within the museum sector and with the manufacturers of the reproduction materials. The commissioning and manufacture of the reproduction damask and passementerie were fundamental to the effective presentation of this magnificent state bed.

3.2 Restoring decorative schemes

The desire for authenticity in the restoration and re-presentation of historic interiors is well established and has fostered the material and contextual research that underpins scholarly upholstery conservation. Ground-breaking research on seventeenth-century furnishings has been undertaken (Thornton, 1978), notably for the re-presentation of Ham House, UK (Thornton and Tomlin, 1980). The recreation of the royal apartments at Hampton Court Palace, UK after the fire of 1986 (Fishlock, 1992) has also promoted important research (Westman, 1994). Presenting an interior so that it is true to a particular period can pose problems in upholstery conservation. The significance of alterations, 'later accretions' (Thornton, 1993 [1984]: 13), and the needs of a single object in relation to the needs of the overall decorative scheme must be assessed. Compromises may be required to protect 'the identity of the composite work of art' while meeting the needs of individual artefacts (Thurley, 1997: 21).

In addition to reflecting a designer's original intentions or a particular period, it is also often necessary to treat seat furniture so that it can fulfil its original function of providing support and comfort to the sitter. Simply put, seat furniture needs to look 'right' and feel safe to sit on. Treatments undertaken to preserve and restore a carriage's trimming for occasional use demonstrate the subtle compromises necessary to achieve both objectives (Nicola Gentle, Chapter 6). Developing practical solutions to the conservation problems encountered in a working collection was identified as a key role for the post of furniture upholstery conservator within the Master of the Household's Department, Windsor (Anon., 2000). Meeting the demands of both form and function may be particularly significant where social relations may be ambiguous in character. For example, meeting the needs of distinguished guests at a royal palace, or welcoming fee-paying delegates/guests at a reception hosted in a historic house.

Meeting these demands, without loss of evidence, can be very difficult. The refurbishment of the Octagon Room at Raby Castle demonstrates the skill and sensitivity necessary to reconcile potentially conflicting demands (Lesley Wilson, Chapter 8). Here the conservators had three main aims: re-upholstery of the furniture as part of the restoration of the room's overall decorative scheme; restoration of the seat furniture for occasional use; and preservation of evidence of original design, materials and techniques, and use.

The authentic domestic interior may be characterised by a lack of homogeneity, such as that proudly exhibited at Brodsworth Hall (Crosby Stevens, Chapter 11). Also, grand rooms and treasured furniture would not have been open to daily scrutiny and use (Thurley, 1997: 23). Most seat furniture would have been protected with case covers (Swain, 1997; Balfour *et al.*, 1999: 23). The conservation and reproduction of such covers is an important part of upholstery conservation (Lesley Wilson, Chapter 8).

4 Upholstery conservation as process

Upholstery conservation encroaches on the domains of the fine and applied arts, social and economic history, materials science and technology, and current social practice. It exemplifies the inherent tensions of preserving and presenting both the form and function of artefacts and decorative schemes. Scholarly upholstery conservation arises from a cycle of investigation, analysis, intervention (preventive and interventive) and interpretation, when rooted in an ethos and practices of assessment and re-assessment. Each case history demonstrates part of such a cycle or indeed repeated cycles of intervention, assessment and interpretation. The ethical and practical difficulties of upholstery conservation explain the importance given to investigation and documentation, interdisciplinary collaboration, minimally intrusive conservation treatments, and the management of upholstery conservation as phased rather than fixed projects. The case histories presented here demonstrate the value of object-based research and the cycle of investigations, interventions and interpretations that constitute best practice in upholstery conservation.

References

Anon. (2000) Advertisement placed for a Furniture Upholstery Conservator within the Master of the Household's Department, Windsor Castle. *Grapevine Supplement*, January 2000, **66**, 4.

Appelbaum, B. (1997) Some thoughts on conservation literature and the publication of treatments. *AIC News* **22** (6), 1–2.

Bacchus, H. (2002) Single image, changing contexts: understanding a rare 18th century Chinese embroidered thangka [working title]. In: M.M. Brooks and M. Hayward (eds), *Textile styrands: Images and Values in Textiles*. Edited papers from the Textile Strand of the Association of Art Historians' annual conference, 'Images and Values', held at the University of Southampton, 1999. (forthcoming)

Balfour, D., Metcalf, S. and Collard, F. (1999) The first non-intrusive upholstery treatment at the Victoria and Albert Museum. *The Conservator* **23**, 22–9, 46.

Beard, G. (1997) *Upholsterers and Interior Furnishings in England, 1530–1840*. London and New York: Yale University Press.

Bourdieu, P. (1984) *Distinction: A Social Critique of the Judgement of Taste*. London: Routledge.

Bourdieu, P. (1977) *Outline of a Theory of Practice*. Cambridge: Cambridge University Press.

Buck, S.L. (1991) A technical and stylistic comparison of twelve Massachusetts State House chairs. In: AIC, *Wooden Artefacts Group Preprints*. Washington, DC: American Institute for Conservation, 22pp.

Eastop, D. (1998) Decision making in conservation: determining the role of artefacts. In: A. Timar-Balazsy and D. Eastop (eds), *International Perspectives on Textile Conservation*. London: Archetype Press, pp. 43–6.

Eastop, D. (2000) Textiles as multiple and competing histories. In: M.M. Brooks (ed.), *Textiles Revealed: Historic Costume and Textiles in Object-based Research* [working title]. London: Archetype Press (in press).

Elias, N. (1978) *The Civilising Process. The History of Manners*. Oxford: Basil Blackwell.

Fishlock, M. (1992) *The Great Fire at Hampton Court*. London: The Herbert Press.

Gill, K. (2000) A 1950s upholstered chair: combining the conventional and the innovative in both manufacture and conservation. In: *Tradition and Innovation: Advances in Conservation*. Summaries of the Posters at the 18th International Congress of IIC, Melbourne 2000, p. 11.

Gill, K. and Eastop, D. (1997) Two Contrasting Minimally Interventive Upholstery Treatments: Different Roles, Different Treatments. In: K. Marko (ed.), *Textiles in Trust*. Proceedings of the Symposium 'Textiles in Trust' held at Blickling Hall, Norfolk, September 1995, pp. 67–77.

Grier, K.C. (1988) *Culture and Comfort. People, Parlors, and Upholstery 1850–1930*. Rochester, NY: The Strong Museum in association with the University of Massachusetts Press.

James, D. (1990) *Upholstery: A Complete Course*. London: The Guild of Master Craftsman Publications.

James, D. (1994). *Traditional Upholstery Workshop*. Part 1: *Drop-in and Pinstuffed Seats*. Part 2: *Stuffover Upholstery*. London: The Guild of Master Craftsman.

James, D. (1997) *Upholstery Restoration*. London: The Guild of Master Craftsman Publications.

Javér, A., Eastop, D. and Janssen, R. (1999) A sprang cap preserved on a naturally dried human head. *Textile History*, **30** (2): 135–54.

Kopytoff, I. (1986) The cultural biography of things: commoditization as process. In: A. Appadurai (ed.), *The Social Life of Things*. Cambridge: Cambridge University Press, pp. 64–91.

Lloyd, H. (1997) The role of housekeeping and preventative conservation in the care of textiles in historic houses. In: K. Marko (ed.), *Textiles in Trust.* Proceedings of the Symposium 'Textiles in Trust' held at Blickling Hall, Norfolk, September 1995, 40–53.

Lopez, M.G. (1997) *Urbino Palazzo Ducale. Testimonianze inedite della vita di corte.* Urbino: Soprintendenza per i Beni Artistici e Storici delle Marche.

Medlam, S. (1993) The decorative art approach: furniture. In: D. Fleming, C. Paine and J.G. Rhodes (eds), *Social History in Museums. A Handbook for Professionals.* London: HMSO, pp. 39–41.

Miller, D. (1987) *Material Culture and Mass Consumption.* Oxford: Blackwell.

Sandwith, H. and Stainton, S. (1991 [1984]) *The National Trust Manual of Housekeeping.* London: Penguin Books.

Swain, M. (1997) Loose covers, or cases. *Furniture History* (The Journal of the Furniture History Society), Vol. **XXXIII**, 128–33.

Thornton, P. (1978) *Seventeenth-Century Interior Decoration in England, France and Holland.* New Haven, CT and London: Yale University Press.

Thornton, P. (1993 [1984]) *Authentic Decor. The Domestic Interior 1620–1920.* London: Weidenfeld & Nicolson.

Thornton, P.K. and Tomlin, M.F. (1980) *The Furnishing and Decoration of Ham House.* London: The Furniture History Society.

Thurley, S. (1997) A conflict of interest? Conservation versus Historic Presentation, a Curatorial View. In: K. Marko (ed.), *Textiles in Trust.* Proceedings of the Symposium 'Textiles in Trust' held at Blickling Hall, Norfolk, September 1995, 20–4.

Westman, A. (1994) Splendours of state. The textile furnishings of the King's Apartments. *Apollo,* Vol. **CXL**, No. 390 (New Series) August 1994, The King's Apartments Hampton Court Palace (William III 1689–1702), pp. 39–45.

Wylie, A. and Singer, P. (1997) The Resurrection of the Uppark State Bed. In: K. Marko (ed.), *Textiles in Trust.* Proceedings of the Symposium 'Textiles in Trust' held at Blickling Hall, Norfolk, September 1995, 118–27.

Part One

Object Treatment: Case Histories

1

The Ernest Race 'Heron' chair and footstool, designed c.1955: an example of conserving foam-filled upholstery

Kathryn Gill

1.1 Introduction

This case history illustrates the wide range of organic and inorganic materials that can be present in a single upholstered object, and demonstrates the importance of understanding the properties of these component materials and original construction techniques when formulating conservation strategies.

The objects in this instance are a chair and footstool designed by Ernest Race in c.1955, and which were in production in England from 1955 to 1965 (Figure 1.1).[1] The chair and footstool are rare surviving examples of the work of one of England's leading designers of the mid-decades of the twentieth century and reflect many of the material and technical innovations in furniture design and construction of this period. A Race Furniture Limited advertisement of 1962 (Figure 1.3) states that the 'Heron' chair and footstool have 'a welded steel rod frame upholstered in plastic foam supports reversible latex foam seat and backrest cushions on a resilient webbing base. Legs, of square section steel and fitted with Armstrong quads, are stove enamelled satin aluminium.'

In 1945, Ernest Race co-founded Ernest Race Limited, a firm that became well known for exploiting the potential and development of 'non-traditional materials' for new furniture designs[2] (Wilson and Balfour, 1990). In 1955, as Design Director, he created the 'Heron' chair and footstool (Figure 1.3). The design was very innovative in combining a frame of welded steel rod (Figure 1.2), a material that Race had been exploiting in the development of furniture construction for over nine years (Conway, 1982: 48–57), with rubberised hair, pincore latex foam and two materials relatively new to the market, rubberised webbing[3] and polyurethane foam sheet (Murphy, 1966: lxxxii). As a result, he produced an upholstered chair of modern design for the domestic market that was not only light in weight and delicate in shape, but also with upholstery reduced in volume but not in comfort.[4,5]

Although innovative in design and in the use of recently developed materials, the 'Heron' chair and footstool relied upon skilled workers to hand-build the frames and upon experienced upholsterers who were prepared to adapt conventional upholstery hand techniques to accommodate the different working properties of these new materials.[6] For example, the pincore cushion pad construction required both hand-tailoring and adhesion of foam sheets, and the rubberised webbing required a novel means of attaching and securing it to the metal frame, while the jute cloth base was hand-stitched to the frame in a traditional manner.[7] Consequently, the chair and footstool reflect modern design achieved with a combination of traditional and new materials, adapting techniques used in conventional hand-built upholstery structures.

Figure 1.1 The 'Heron' chair and footstool designed by Ernest Race c.1955 (Geffrye Museum number 1/1993/1 & 2), three-quarter front view, before treatment. The degraded inner foam structure has caused the top cover to sag, particularly noticeable along the wings, arms and front seat rail of the chair

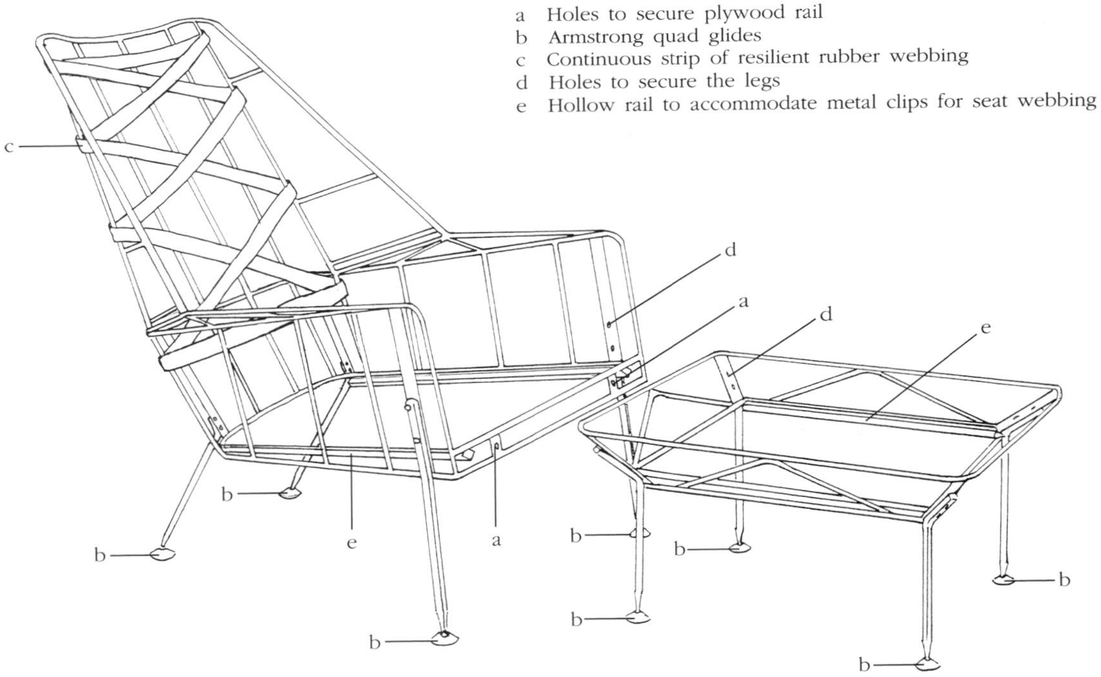

Figure 1.2 Line drawing of a three-quarter front view of the 'Heron' chair and footstool designed by Ernest Race c.1955 to show the construction of the welded steel rod frames. Since nailing into the frame was not possible, alternative methods of attaching upholstery had to be designed. For example, holes in the front seat rail accommodated nuts and bolts for an upholstered plywood rail (a), a hollow end to each steel rod leg accommodated the pronged ends of the Armstrong quad glides (b). The resilient rubberised webbing (c) was interlaced across the inner face of the back

Figure 1.3 A Race Furniture Ltd promotional leaflet for the 'Heron' and 'Flamingo' chairs, which were both in production by 1957. The company name, its address and reference to the 1962 budget increase suggest the leaflet was produced just before the company moved to the Isle of Sheppey. The advert describes the 'Heron' chair as having 'plastic foam ... reversible latex foam seat ... on a resilient webbing base' ... 'legs of square section steel and fitted with Armstrong quads, are stove enamelled satin aluminium'. The company also promoted the removable legs and nesting frames for export packing. The headrest cushion was an optional extra. (Reproduced by kind permission of Race Furniture Limited)

1.2 Role

The chair and footstool now form part of the collection of the Geffrye Museum, London, to which they were donated in 1993 (mus. nos. 1/1993/1&2).[8] This museum is well known for its display of English domestic interiors.[9]

The Heron chair and footstool were acquired in the late 1950s or early 1960s for a London home, where they stayed until 1993 at which point they were added to the museum's collection.[10] The chair and footstool were briefly displayed outside the museum's 1950s period room soon after their acquisition by the museum. However, the condition of the pieces was giving cause for concern as the top covers were soiled and the rubberised webbing was misshapen, stiff, cracked and disintegrating. Some of the foams were in an advanced state of deterioration, either hard, cracking and powdery, or compressed and sticky. Therefore, due to the unstable condition of the chair and footstool, they were removed to storage. During the building of an extension to the Geffrye Museum in 1998 it was proposed that the chair and footstool be treated to allow them to be on open display in the museum's 1950s period room.

The chair and footstool are thought to retain all of their original upholstery materials.[10] This makes the chair and footstool rare survivals considering two major factors: the first, that they were in use until 1993 in a domestic setting, and the second, the inherently unstable nature of the majority of upholstery materials comprising the upholstery structure.

1.2.1 Treatment objectives

The conservation treatment initiated by the Geffrye Museum had two primary aims. The first was to meet the requirements of preserving the integrity of what appears to be virtually untouched original upholstery. The second was to identify and implement appropriate remedial and preventive treatments that would involve no more intervention than was absolutely necessary to the top covers, understructures and each frame. The treatment objectives were to enhance the long-term preservation of both pieces, whilst facilitating their role as exhibits on open display in a period room setting. Other aims included the characterisation of materials and construction techniques, and determining the causes of the deterioration noted in the webbing and the foams.

1.3 Preliminary investigation

The upholstered chair and footstool have frames of metal onto which are attached strips of rubberised webbing, a support layer of jute cloth and a variety of foam fillings. There are also two loose seat cushions, a lumbar cushion and headrest pad comprising a variety of fillings. Both pieces of furniture, including the cushions, have top covers of matching beige woven cloth, not dissimilar in texture and tone to that covering the chair illustrated in the upper section of a company advertisement c.1962 (Figure 1.3).

1.3.1 Frames

The frames are made primarily of welded steel rod sections and hollow steel.[11]. Holes through various points in the frame accommodate detachable elements (see Figure 1.2). For example, each leg is attached with two screws, the plywood seat rail is held with two nuts and bolts, and the seat webbing is secured with wire clips. The Race advert of c.1962 notes 'Legs removable and frames nest for export packing' (Figure 1.3). The steel rod is coated with a light grey finish, the hollow steel with a light brown finish (both enamelled[?]). The finish on the square section steel metal legs of the chair and footstool look most similar to those described and illustrated in the inset photograph of the same company advert showing the chair upholstered in a dark fabric against the lighter-toned stove enamelled satin aluminium or satin matt chromium.[12] The legs are tipped with 'Armstrong quads'™, which are black plastic swivel glides.

1.3.2 Webbing

Hooked into sections of hollow steel welded to the front and rear of the frame are wire clip hooks which support the seat webbing. The seat webbing arrangement comprises a single strip of light-grey-coloured resilient rubber webbing stretched back and forth across the width of the seat well and threaded through a series of wire clips. A wire bar on the first and last clip secure the webbing in place.

Laced across the back upright section of the chair frame, encased between two base layers of jute cloth, is another single strip of rubberised webbing; this webbing is not visible, but can be felt between the jute cloth. This webbing arrangement (including location and method of application to the back as illustrated in Figure 1.2) is similar though not identical to that noted on another 'Heron' chair recently studied (Wilson, 1999: 22).[13] The method of application of the rubberised webbing in a single strip was probably the precursor of the individual strip systems in use today.[14]

Base panels of jute cloth are stretched across the back, each wing, arm and arm rest of the chair frame and the four rectangular sections of the footstool frame (Figure 1.4, numbers 3, 8 and 10). The panels are held to the frame with a single row of lock stitches executed in a waxed linen[?] stitching twine (Figure 1.5). A combination of adhesives, metal fasteners and hand and machine stitching has been used in the attachment of the upholstered elements to the frame.

1.3.3 Filling

With the exception of the upper section of the outer back, each panel has a filling comprising a single layer of pre-cut, sheet foam. In all, five, possibly six types of either polyurethane or latex sheet foam of varying density, thickness and colour have been used (Table 1.1). In addition, the arm rest is partially filled with rubberised hair (see Figure 1.4, number 3). Most foam layers are glued directly to the base cloth. An additional upholstery structure layer, in the form of a small triangular panel of black card, is located between the base cloth and the filling of each arm rest.

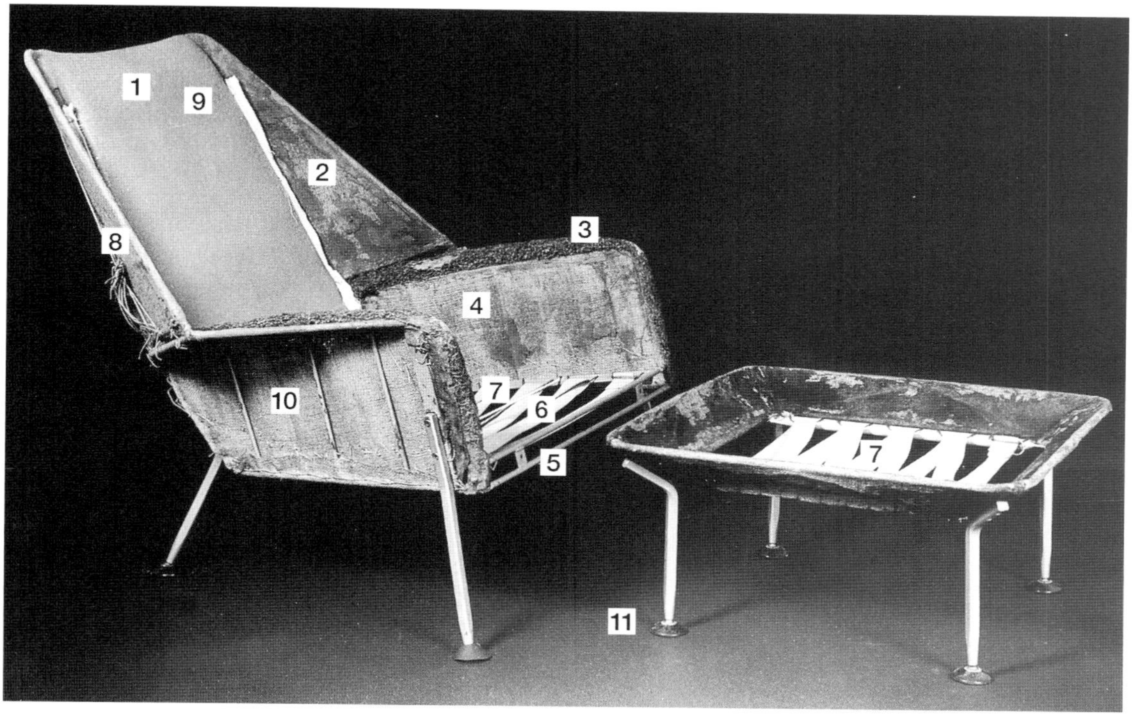

Figure 1.4 Treatment in progress on the 'Heron' chair and footstool. The top cover and loose cushions have been removed revealing what has survived of the upholstery understructure. Traditional and new materials are combined using techniques adapted from more conventional hand-built upholstery structures; for example, the jute base cloth is wrapped around the frame and held with locking stitches (10). The hand-built foam sheet filling is glued to the base cloth (1, 2, 4, 10). The continuous strip of resilient rubberised webbing is threaded through fasteners clipped to the seat rail of the chair and the footstool (6). The webbing illustrated in Figure 1.1A is concealed between two layers of jute cloth behind the foam sheet (1)

1 Inner back covered by yellow polyurethane foam sheet filling (largely extant and retaining foam structure)
2 Inner wing covered by orange polyurethane foam sheet filling (largely missing, only foam residues extant)
3 Arm rest supporting strip of rubberised hair (largely extant and retaining structure)
4 Inner arm covered by orange polyurethane foam sheet filling (largely missing, only foam residues extant)
5 Detachable plywood based front seat rail temporarily removed, exposing metal frame and holes through which bolts are screwed
6 Single strip of resilient rubberised webbing, threaded through metal clips attached to side rails of seat
7 Plastic-coated helical tension wire through which top cover fabric (extending from front seat rail under loose cushion) is threaded
8 Outer wing revealing jute cloth base through which is threaded the stitching twine which holds the wood dowels (9) to the inner back
9 One of the two cotton-covered wood dowels
10 Outer wing revealing jute cloth base wrapped around frame from the inner to outer face and anchored under tension by a row of locking stitches. A row of locking stitches can be seen along the lower edge of the horizontal seat rail
11 Armstrong™ quad glides

With the exception of the feather-filled headrest cushion, which has a cover of downproof cotton, there are no filling cover layers present in the entire understructure of the chair and footstool (Figure 1.6).

1.3.4 Top cover

The top covers of the chair, footstool and all four loose cushions are of the same fabric, a beige-dyed, plain weave wool/acrylic[?].

Figure 1.5 Line drawing of the lock stitch used to secure the jute base cloth to the steel rod frame of the 'Heron' chair and footstool

A Steel rod
B Jute base cloth
C Needle
a Slip knot
b Formed locking stitch
c Stitching twine enters base cloth
d Threaded needle re-enters base cloth
e Stitching twine wrapped around needle as needle leaves base cloth

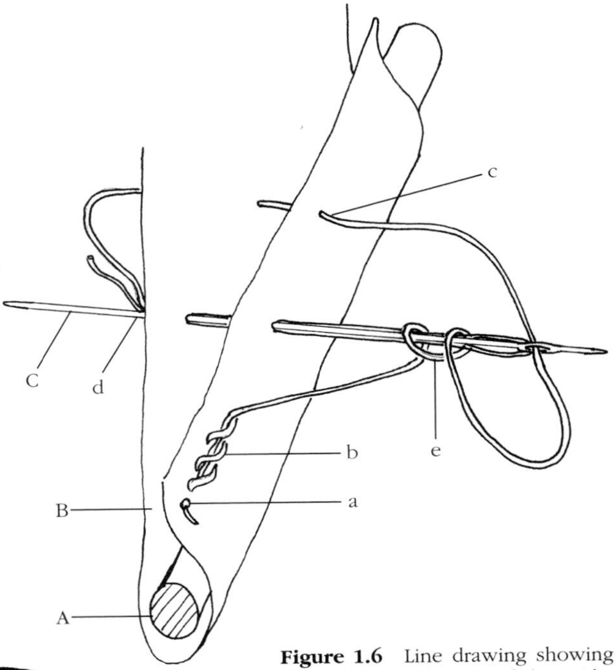

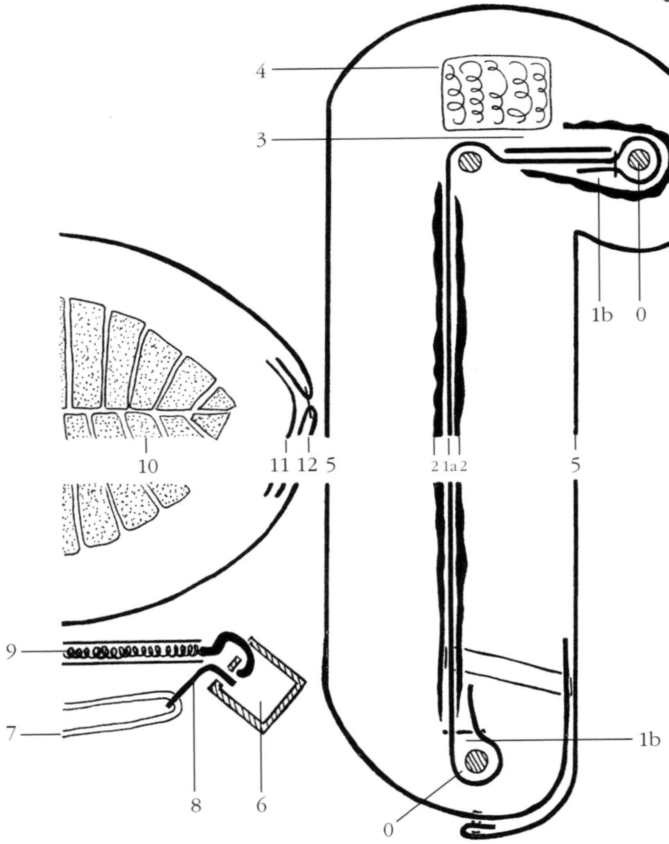

Figure 1.6 Line drawing showing a cross-sectional view of the mid point of the arm and seat frame of the 'Heron' chair at the Geffrye Museum to show the various upholstery layers – before treatment

Chair: Arm unit
0 Frame (welded steel rod)
1a Base cloth (jute) held to frame with locking stitches (1b)
1b Locking stitch
2 First filling (only traces remaining – top surface treated with a consolidant)
3 Second base (black card)
4 Second filling (rubberised hair)
5 Top cover

Seat unit
6 Frame (hollow enamelled metal rail)
7 Webbing – single strip of resilient rubberised webbing
8 Webbing fastener – metal clip through which webbing is passed
9 Front seat rail top cover fastener (plastic coated helical tension wire)

Loose cushion
10 First filling (latex pincore sheet foam) treated with a consolidant
11 Seam reinforcement strip of adhesive coated cotton
12 Top cover

1.3.5 Assembly of component parts

All the main seams of the top covers are machine-stitched. All raw edges of the component panels are machine-overlocked. The seams of the seat cushion and the lumbar cushion top covers are flattened out and reinforced with strips of adhesive (PVA)-impregnated cotton fabric heat-sealed to the seam allowances after machine-stitching of the seams. When turned right sides out, the reinforced strips would have prevented the seam allowances from shifting during insertion of the cushion pads. Since there was no filling cover between the foam pad and the top cover, the seam re-enforcements would also have prevented dislodged crumbs of foam from working their way through the machine-stitched seams.

The headrest cushion is counterweighted by a metal plate enclosed in a cloth extension which hangs over the back of the chair. The weight holds the cushion in place and allows the position of the cushion to be adjusted by the sitter.

The opening of all cushion covers, including the pocket accommodating the metal plate, was stitched closed with a heavy upholstery stitching twine executed in hand-worked slip stitches. The top cover of the footstool and chair are secured to the upholstered frame with large crudely executed hand stitches of the same stitching twine used to close the cushion cases.

The system devised to secure the top cover close to the inner back of the chair involves a wood dowel and linen ties which work in the following way. A narrow cotton fabric sleeve (long enough to accommodate a 400 mm length of wood doweling) has been machine-stitched to the reverse face of the inner back panel at the juncture of each back and wing section. Before the cover was positioned on the upholstered chair a dowel was inserted into each sleeve and secured by knotting a length of twine to the encased dowel. One piece of twine is located towards the top of the dowel in line with the upper horizontal bar of the wing section and the other in line with the lower horizontal bar of the wing section, in line with the arm rest. The twine was stitched through the jute cloth at these two points on the left and the right side of the chair and pulled firmly and tied off around the rigid metal frame. This system places even tension on the entire length of each vertical section of the inner back cover by drawing it into the upholstery filling and holding it in the correct position without the need for adhesives.

1.4 Identification of component materials

The woven fabrics of the chair and footstool, including the filling cover from the headrest pillow, top covers and those making up the understructures were investigated. Fibre identification was undertaken by microscopy and was confirmed by stain and/or solubility tests. Natural fibres were recognised by their characteristic morphology in longitudinal section. The identification of the man-made (semi-synthetic and synthetic) fibres was on the basis of their interference colours when viewed between cross-polars at 45 degrees (i.e. between extinction positions) through a first-order red plate.

As expected, the undyed warp and weft threads of the base cloth were identified as jute,[15] the undyed warp and weft threads of the filling cover were identified as mercerised cotton. The beige weft yarn of the plain-weave top cover fabric was identified as a blend of wool and fine strands of a leaf fibre having the characteristics of sisal. The beige warp threads were a blend of wool, leaf fibre (probably sisal) and synthetic fibres; tests for the latter proved inconclusive, although, based on their visual appearance under magnification and bearing in mind the fibre blends that were popular in 1950s and 1960s furnishing textiles, they are probably acrylic.

The machine stitching used to attach the cotton sleeve to the top cover fabric and to seam the main panels together are of cream-coloured cotton[?] yarn. The hand stitching used to close seams and to secure the jute cloth to the frame is of unbleached linen[?], possibly waxed. The stitching yarn used to slip-stitch the seam in the headrest cushion was not sufficiently accessible for examination or sampling.

The headrest cushion pad filling was not accessible for examination but was presumed to be feathers. The filling had the texture and feel of a feather and down mix, and one feather was sticking out from the filling cover top and through the cover. The label machine-stitched into the side seam of the head cushion is printed with the following words:

'GUARANTEED TO
CONTAIN ONLY
Fogarty
FILLINGS'

The Race Furniture Limited advertisement of 1962 (Figure 1.3), referred to above, states that the 'Heron' chair and footstool have 'a welded steel rod frame upholstered in plastic foam supports reversible latex foam seat and backrest cushions on a resilient webbing base. Legs, of square section steel and fitted with Armstrong quads, are stove enamelled satin aluminium'. Materials identification of metals, glides, foams and adhesives, could corroborate (or refute) the manufacturer's data. The metal components could be identified by *in situ* electrolytic tests (Tímár Balázsy and Eastop, 1998). The plastic of the four black Armstrong glides could be identified using an infrared transmitting microscope attached to an FTIR spectrometer (Mucci, 1997).

The foamed plastics from the seat cushions and lumbar cushion and the rubberised hair, webbing and adhesive were sampled for possible identification. Some of these samples are undergoing analysis in an attempt to characterise their composition and their deterioration.

The adhesive used to attach the foam to the jute cloth was not identified, but tests showed that it was soluble in acetone and industrial methylated spirits. Investigation into typical materials used at the time suggested that the adhesive was most likely to be a rubber-based solution similar to that found on a contemporary coat (Stoughton-Harris, 1993; Tímár Balázsy and Eastop, 1998, 139–43).[16]

It is hoped that the adhesive and various foams will be identified using a spectrometer with special attachment for powdered samples[17] and perhaps by using pyrolysis-gas chromotography (P-GC). The presence of various inorganic compounds, often added to rubber-based foams to modify their properties, could be identified by Energy Dispersive X-Ray analysis (EDX). It is likely, for example, that the grey-brown coloured foam (located in the outer back and footstool) contains carbon black fillers.

At the time of preparing this account, the test results were not available; however, other sources have facilitated materials identification. For example, information acquired on the foams as a result of examining the chair during removal of the top cover and discussions with an upholsterer who served his apprenticeship for Race Furniture Limited in 1962 (Appendix, Report A) was compared with information provided by a retired product development manager for a leading foam manufacture (Appendix, Report B) and other sources. Material identification is summarised in Table 1.1. In time, this information will be compared to results obtained from the proposed analysis of foam samples.

1.5 Condition assessment

Initial examination of the chair and footstool confirmed that the legs were scuffed and distorted in areas, that the profile of the upholstery was distorted and that the top cover fabric was discoloured and stained.

1.5.1 Frames

The exposed sections of the frame were generally soiled and had some surface scratches. However, there were no signs of corrosion products on the metal components, even those in direct contact with the rubber-based adhesive and foams. This is most likely due to the presence of the protective enamelled coating on metal elements. Structurally the metal frame was sound although the proper left rear foot was severely bent preventing the chair from sitting level on the floor.

With the exception of the plywood section of the front seat rail, which is peppered with holes created by tacks and staples securing the various upholstery layers, the two main techniques used to attach the individual upholstery layers (wrapping and hand-stitching around the metal frame and bolting and clipping of metal fasteners through pre-drilled holes) have imposed little or no damage to the metal frames.

1.5.2 Foams

The condition of the foamed plastic upholstery fillings varied greatly. This variety was attributed to a number of factors, including location, function (degree of exposure to mechanical abrasion and the environment), density, thickness and chemical composition. The large number of different foams present, and the variability in their decomposition was unexpected. This range of condition probably reflects the experimental approach adopted to the use of the polyurethane foams newly available to Ernest Race Limited in the period 1955–65, when the 'Heron' chairs and footstools were in production.

The foam fillings from the inner back (yellow-coloured foam-type 1),[18] the lumbar cushion (yellow-coloured pincore foam-type 6)[19] and the yellow/orange-coloured rubberised hair filling (type 3)[20] from the arm rests appeared to be in fair condition and still retained their resilient structure. The blue-coloured pincore seat cushion pad foams (type 7) were less degraded than their appearance suggested. The entire surface of each pad (to a depth of approximately 5–10 mm) was in an advanced stage of degradation (the foam structure was completely lost and resembled grains of sand), but the majority of the foam pad (approximately 90%) directly below this degraded surface layer appeared to be structurally quite sound. The dry and powdery surface of the cushion pad had changed colour from light blue-green to a light yellowish brown. The original structure and colour of the foam was preserved in the rear section of seat pad foam resting between the lumbar cushion and the webbing. It was equally well preserved below the degraded foam layer in the remaining sections of the seat cushion. This suggests that the main factor in the degradation of the foam may have been photo-oxidation and airborne pollutants, rather than inherent instability alone.

As anticipated, the dark grey-brown-coloured foam filling (type 4) in the front seat rail was in an advanced stage of degradation; none of it retained its original foam structure. The majority of this layer of foam was dry and granular, although those areas still adhered to the wood were slightly more sticky. This may indicate that the sticky foam was in a less degraded state, that the foam was combined with a possible adhesive layer or the foam had been affected by contact with the wood (e.g. by acids given off by the wood).

The dark grey-brown foam (type 5) in the outer arms, wings, lower back of the chair and all surfaces of the stool were also found to be in an advanced state of degradation.[21] However, unlike the dry and granular degraded foam in the majority of the front seat rail and seat cushion pads which filtered through the weave of the top cover, the degraded foams in these other areas were soft and sticky and had a slightly glistening surface characteristic of polyester urethane.[22] These residues had become embedded into the reverse face of the top cover panels. The orange-coloured foam (type 2) in the inner wings and inner arms was also in an advanced state of degradation; it had become soft and sticky, and was embedded into the reverse face of the top cover panels (see Table 1.1).

The adhesive layer that originally held the seat foam to the jute cloth remained attached to the jute cloth. Foam residues covered the top layers of the adhesive layer. The webbing was considerably stretched and distorted; this was mainly attributed to the weight imposed by the loose cushion and, when in use, the sitter. Although somewhat flexible, the webbing had become dry and brittle around the metal hooks, and in some areas small splits and cracks were appearing.

The jute base cloth appeared to be structurally sound.

The feather-filled-headrest cushion pad appeared to be in good condition. Although structurally sound, the filling cover was stained with the brown spots characteristic of iron stains. The feathers were inaccessible for examination but to the touch through the top cover appeared to have retained some resilience and loft.

1.5.3 Top covers

The beige top cover fabric was discoloured, ranging from grey tones through yellow to light pinkish tones. Four main contributing factors were identified: surface soiling and the colours of the foams (orange, yellow and dark grey-brown). The coloured foams, located directly beneath the relatively loosely woven

Table 1.1 A summary of foam types in the 'Heron' chair and footstool

Object location	**Colour** Exposed areas Geffrye chair and footstool	**Colour** Protected areas Geffrye chair and footstool	**Colour** Chair and stool as recalled by Race apprentice (Appendix, Report A)	**Colour** Chair and stool comments from techn. director (Appendix, Report B)	**Surface characterisation** Geffrye chair and footstool	**Likely material** Geffrye chair and footstool
Chair: inner back	Yellow, uniform	Yellow	Blue	Uniform colour suggests it is polyether urethane	Matt, foam structure extant	Type 1
Chair: inner wing	Orange-red	Orange	—	Uniform colour suggests it is polyether urethane	Matt, foam structure not extant, soft and sticky	Type 2
Chair: inner arm	Orange-red	Orange	—	Uniform colour suggests it is polyether urethane	Matt, foam structure not extant, soft and sticky	Type 2
Chair: arm rest	Orange-yellow	Orange-yellow	—	Vulcanised liquid latex sprayed onto short staple hair	Open structure well preserved	Type 3
Chair: seat rail	Dark grey-brown	—	—	—	Glistening, foam structure not extant, soft and sticky	Type 4
Chair: outer wing	Dark grey-brown	—	—	—	Glistening, foam structure not extant, soft and sticky	Type 5
Chair: outer arm	Dark grey-brown	—	—	—	Glistening, foam structure not extant, soft and sticky	Type 5
Chair: outer back	Dark grey-brown	—	—	—	Glistening, foam structure not extant, soft and sticky	Type 5
Chair: lumbar cushion	Yellow	Cream	—	Most likely white when new	Matt, surface dry and cracking	Type 6
Chair: seat cushion	Light yellow-brown	Light blue-green	—	Most likely white or grey-blue when new	Matt, surface dry and granular	Type 7
Footstool: seat cushion	Light yellow-brown	Light blue-green	—	Most likely white or grey-blue when new	Matt, surface dry and granular	Type 7
Footstool: inner face	Dark grey-brown	—	—	—	Glistening, foam structure not extant, soft and sticky	Type 4
Footstool: outer face	Dark grey-brown	—	—	—	Glistening, foam structure not extant, soft and sticky	Type 4

Likely material Another 'Heron' chair and footstool	**Material type** As described in Company advert. 1962	**Material type** As recalled by Race apprentice (Appendix, Report A)	**Material type** Comments from techn. director (Appendix, Report B)	**Material structure** Geffrye chair and footstool
Type 1	Plastic foam	Polyether urethane	Polyether urethane poss. 'Kay foam™' now 'Vitafoam™'	Foam sheet approx. 30 mm thick
(Type 5)	Plastic foam	Polyether urethane	Polyether urethane poss. 'Kay foam™' now 'Vitafoam™'	Foam sheet approx. 20 mm thick
(Type 5)	Plastic foam	Polyether urethane	Polyether urethane poss. 'Kay foam™' now 'Vitafoam™'	Foam sheet approx. 20 mm thick
Type 3	—	Rubberised hair poss. 'Hairlock™' or 'Vitafoam™'	Rubberised hair, poss. 'Hairlock™' or Harrison and Joan'	Sheet of rubberised hair, approx. 20 mm thick: vulcanised liquid latex sprayed onto layer of hair
—	Plastic foam	—	Polyether urethane	Foam sheet approx. 10 mm thick
Type 2	Plastic foam	Polyester urethane	Polyether urethane	Foam sheet approx. 10 mm thick
Type 2	Plastic foam	Polyester urethane	Polyester urethane	Foam sheet approx. 10 mm thick
Type 2	Plastic foam	Polyester urethane	Polyester urethane	Foam sheet approx. 10 mm thick
—	Latex foam	Latex foam, pincore, poss. 'Dunlopillo™'	Latex foam, pincore (natural/synthetic mix)	Foam sheet approx. 40 mm thick 2 layers adhered together
—	Latex foam	Latex foam, pincore, poss. 'Dunlopillo™'	Latex foam, pincore (natural/synthetic mix)	Foam sheet approx. 60 mm thick 2 layers adhered together
—	Latex foam	Latex foam, pincore, poss. 'Dunlopillo™'	Latex foam, pincore (natural/synthetic mix)	Foam sheet approx. 60 mm thick 2 layers adhered together
—	Plastic foam	Polyester urethane	Polyester urethane	Foam sheet approx. 10 mm thick
—	Plastic foam	Polyester urethane	Polyester urethane	Foam sheet approx. 10 mm thick

beige top cover, created tonal differences amongst the various panels. Another factor was the strongly coloured sticky foam residues which penetrated through to the top surface and latched on to the weave interstices. The most influential factor was probably the acid fumes given off by the degraded foams (their pH range was as low as 2.5–3.0) which could have resulted in yellow discoloration of the wool due to acid hydrolysis (Tímár Balázsy and Eastop, 1998: 342).

There were also signs of wear to the top cover at the crest rail, front seat rail and the horizontal plane of each arm.

The adhesive bond holding the seam reenforcement strips to the inner face of the cushion covers was failing; the strips were detached in many areas and had become creased.

1.6 Previous treatment

Extra tack holes were observed in the wood frame section of the front seat rail. However, there was insufficient evidence to draw any firm conclusions about these additional tack holes. They might indicate that the present top covers were not original to the frame or that the first attempt at tacking the existing top covers had to be undone. Comparing the construction and materials of the Geffrye Museum chair with another thought to retain its original materials strongly suggests that the upholstery is either original to the frame, or the chair was perhaps recovered at a later date by the original manufacturer.[23]

1.7 Treatment issues

Given the clearly identified role of the chair and footstool at the Geffrye Museum, and its significance in the history of design and technology, four treatment objectives were identified: first, the removal of acid soiling from the top covers to reduce the risk of further discoloration of the dyes in the top cover and to reduce the risk of further hydrolysis of the fibres; secondly, to reduce the source of acidic gassing from the upholstery understructures; thirdly, to support weak areas and components, and to re-distribute the weight load on particularly vulnerable areas; finally, to reduce distortions to the upholstery profile.

A number of key issues were discussed and various treatment options were considered. Since the most unstable element of the complex 3-d mixed media structure was the concealed inner filling, the main concern in treating this object was to consider the degree of intervention appropriate in this case.

If the chair and footstool were to be left untreated the degraded acidic foam residues would continue to filter through, both abrading and contaminating the top cover and causing unsightly marks. Without treatment both the chair and the footstool would be insufficiently stable for display and transport.

Some treatment would be possible with only minimal intervention. For example, a reversible support system for the webbing which would also take some of the cushion weight by distributing it more evenly across the webbed seat area. However, further treatment would require highly interventive treatment. Temporary removal of the cover could perhaps have been justified on the grounds that the filling layers requiring most attention would be accessible for effective stabilisation and isolation. However, such interventive treatments raised ethical issues: first, loss of information and evidence by undoing the original construction; secondly, loss of support to the understructure by removing top covers; thirdly, not being able to replace all loose/detached materials; finally, not knowing the extent of treatment until work has started, by which point it is often too late to be able to stop treatment.

Other issues regarding treatment and the future role of the chair and footstool were addressed, including striking the appropriate balance between how the object looks now and the designer's original intention. The upholstery profile has become deformed, but how much new material, if any at all, should/could be introduced to bring back some of the original appearance? In fact, in the case of both loose seat cushions, which were originally fully reversible, not only had the cushions become permanently deformed, so had the webbing, and adjusting their shape without the introduction of new materials was not possible. Consequently, retaining the deformed shape of the seat cushions became critical, in order that they match exactly the contours of the webbing.

By far the biggest challenge within the treatment of these objects was identifying appropriate techniques and materials to stabilise the degraded foam residues. It was not felt appropriate to discard the degraded foam on ethical grounds, therefore a consolidation treatment of the foam was devised. Concerns about the consolidant included the type of consolidant, the effect of the consolidant on the foam, the purpose and the expectations of the consolidant.

1.8 Treatment undertaken

Photographs were taken before, during and after treatment. To facilitate comparison of the designer's objectives, the staging of the photographs was arranged to mimic the 1962 advert (Plate 1.1 and Figures 1.1, 1.3, 1.4 and 1.7). Diagrams were made (Figures 1.2, 1.5 and 1.6) and samples were taken.

1.8.1 Top cover panels

Loose soils were removed from all exposed surfaces of the upholstered frames using a low powered vacuum cleaner with special mini-tool attachments. All removed soils were retained.

In order to gain access to the unstable upholstery fillings it was necessary to release top cover panels from the chair and stool frame and the loose cushions. This was achieved by clipping rows of hand stitches holding the covers to the understructure, and the two rows of machine stitches holding the wood dowels to the inner back panel. Care was taken to document construction details prior to releasing the various elements.

Once removed from the frames and cushion pads, the top cover panels were turned inside out. The degraded foam impregnating the weave interstices was removed with a combination of a low powered mini-vacuum cleaner, small bristle brush and fine tweezers. Samples were retained. The covers were quite soiled and stained and therefore further cleaning was considered. Wet cleaning was not a suitable option since there was a risk that the panels would undergo dimensional changes. The majority of the soiling also appeared to be of a greasy nature. Therefore, following tests, a decision was made to use an organic solvent (Perchloroethylene™ (tetrachloroethylene), widely known as Perklone™).

Since the panels appeared structurally very sound it was proposed that cleaning be undertaken at a commercial dry cleaners with whom the Textile Conservation Centre staff had worked for a number of years. The closed, charged system could be adjusted to an appropriate cycle, and the amount of solvent used and the temperature setting would be pre-set and monitored throughout the cleaning procedure.[24]

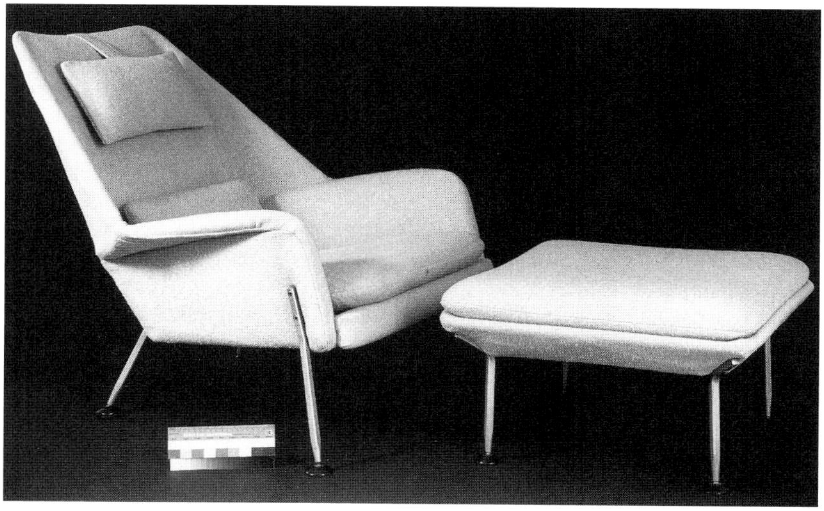

Figure 1.7 The 'Heron' chair and footstool after treatment. Compare the subtle difference in profile with Figure 1.1 (before treatment) now that the surviving filling materials have been supported and losses rebuilt; compare also with the advertisement illustrated in Figure 1.3

In preparation for solvent cleaning the covers were supported and protected by padding out and encasing in a soft nylon net. As a result of solvent cleaning a considerable amount of soiling was removed. The panels looked much brighter and were less harsh to the touch. One of the two dark grey stains on the chair was successfully removed, although the second stain (located at the mid-front of the chair seat cushion) was only slightly reduced. Further spot tests were carried out on this area, with industrial methylated spirits (IMS), IMS/water (50:50) and acetone (n-propanone). However, none of these proved to be an effective solvent for this stain and no further cleaning was attempted.

All raw edges of the top covers surrounding the leg sockets, and other vulnerable raw edges were protected and supported with a stitched patch overlay of a colour-matched nylon net, secured with polyester multi-filament thread (Skala™).

Each cotton sleeve encasing the wood dowels of the chair cover was temporarily removed for treatment. Each sleeve was protected and re-enforced by covering with a layer of scoured, fine weave downproof cotton held in place with a row of running stitches. The sleeves were then re-attached to the inner back panel of the top cover with a row of back stitches following the original line of machine stitching. In each case the thread used was polyester (Gütermann™ 403 no. 70).

Creases in the partially detached seam re-enforcement strips of cotton were eased via a contact humidification treatment. This process involved laying the cotton strips onto a layer of dry acid-free tissue paper over a layer of blotting paper moistened with de-ionised water in order that the moisture could be gently introduced into the creased cotton and assist in relaxing the creases. Before and after humidification treatment, tests carried out to reactivate the thermo-plastic adhesive on the cotton strips with heat proved unsuccessful. Therefore, the detached sections of the strips were not re-adhered but were stitched to the cushion covers with colour-matched fine cotton lace thread.

1.8.2 Understructure

During removal of the top covers, where possible, the foam fillings were temporarily supported *in situ* with nylon net and panels of polyester film (Melinex™) in an attempt to disturb as little as possible of the original, extremely degraded, structure. The most stable sections, the inner back of the chair and the pads from the chair seat cushion and the footstool cushion, could be treated *in situ*.

Following tests, the degraded top surface of the foam sheet fillings of the chair's inner back and seat cushion and the footstool cushion were consolidated with an acrylic adhesive to hold the unstable foam layers in position. A butyl methacrylate based resin was selected: Lascaux 360HV and 498HV (1:3 dispersion in de-ionised water, two coats sprayed on). This conservation grade adhesive was selected as it had a pH between 8 and 9, could be applied finely and evenly in dispersion with water using an air brush. Tests indicated that two coats created a near continuous film over the entire surface, sufficient to consolidate the crumbling surface and to hold the unstable foam layers in position.

It was not possible to consolidate those sections that no longer retained any of their foam structure, in particular those positioned vertically on the frame. Therefore, in an attempt to keep evidence of the filling with the chair, quantities of the foam from the inner and outer arms were collected and encased in custom-made archival Melinex™ envelopes sealed with Tyvek™ tape (the trade mark for Dupont's group of bonded (non-woven) sheets of polyethylene) with the intention of re-incorporating the filling samples into the understructure and making available material for future analysis (Figure 1.8, item C).

It was not possible to use the envelope system to reincorporate the detached degraded foam from the chair's inner wings and seat rail or from the footstool without putting strain on the top cover or adversely effecting the chair's profile. Therefore, the foam was packed and labelled in preparation for storage with the object record and the treatment report at the museum.

Each consolidated cushion pad was encased in two fitted panels of finely woven, down-proof cotton to provide an external support to reduce the risk of further profile distortions. The panels were hand-seamed using a polyester thread. The supported cushion pad was covered entirely in a layer of (adhesive-free) polyester

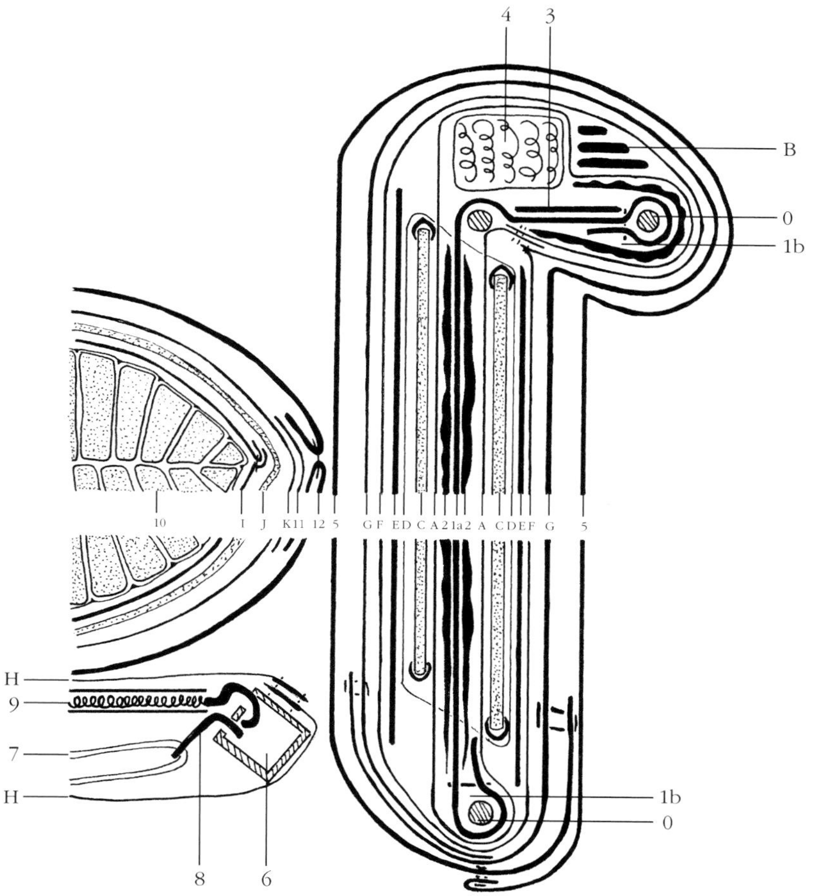

Figure 1.8 Line drawing showing a cross-sectional view of the mid point of the arm and seat frame of the 'Heron' chair, showing the various upholstery layers after treatment

Chair: Arm unit

0 Frame (welded steel rod)
1a Base cloth (jute) held to frame with locking stitches (1b)
1b Locking stitch
2 First filling (only traces remaining – top surface treated with a consolidant)
3 Second base (black card)
4 Second filling (rubberised hair)
A Support layer for first and second layer (dyed nylon net)
B Infill 1 for first filling (polyester felt)
C Storage envelope for detached portions of first filling (Melinex sealed with Tyvek™ tape)
D Polyester thread which holds storage envelope (C) to netted base cloth (1)
E Infill 2 for first and second filling (polyester wadding)
F Support layer for upholstery understructure layers (nylon net)
G Barrier layer for upholstery understructure layers (downproof cotton)
5 Top cover

Seat unit

6 Frame (hollow enamelled metal rail)
7 Webbing - single strip of resilient rubberised webbing
8 Webbing fastener - metal clip through which webbing is passed
9 Front seat rail top cover fastener (plastic coated helical tension wire)
H Support layer for webbing and loose cushion (semi-transparent, polyester, leno weave fabric)

Loose cushion

10 First filling (latex pincore sheet foam) treated with a consolidant
I Support layer for first filling (downproof cotton)
J Infill for first filling (polyester wadding)
K Support layer for upholstery understructure layers (nylon net)
11 Seam reinforcement strip of adhesive coated cotton
12 Top cover

wadding to compensate for loss of foam and therefore of height. This was followed by a layer of nylon net which was stitched in place. The net provided further support and held the wadding layer in position during reapplication of the top cover.

The base cloth layer of the inner and outer arm sections of the chair frame was covered in panels of nylon net to provide a protective layer prior to attaching the foam-filled archival envelopes. The envelopes were attached to the netted base cloth by stitching.

The upholstery of the chair frame and the footstool frame were supported and missing elements were rebuilt with conservation grade materials in the following way. The losses of foam filling were re-built with layers of polyester felt and polyester wadding. This was followed by a layer of nylon net which provided support to the conserved layers and assisted in holding the wadding layers in position. This was followed by an additional layer of finely woven, down-proof cotton to provide further support and a barrier layer between the degraded foam and the cleaned top cover.

The rubberised webbing was surface cleaned using vacuum suction in combination with a small sable hair brush to dislodge loose particulate soils. In order that the overstretched section of webbing towards the rear of the chair did not hang so close to ground level its positioning was gradually re-adjusted by temporarily releasing the wire clamp fastener and applying body heat and gentle pressure through gloved fingertips. The body heat allowed the webbing to be gently manipulated without causing the rubber to crack further. Each unit of webbing was encased in semi-transparent polyester crepeline (Stabiltex™, leno weave), the edges of which had been previously hemmed and re-enforced with cotton tape. The crepeline provided support and a protective barrier for the webbing, and helped to support and distribute the weight of the loose cushion.

The top covers were reapplied to the frames. They were attached with stitches (worked in polyester thread) to the underlying upholstery layers. Where possible the original stitching threads were left in the top cover panels.

1.8.3 Legs

Following discussions with various specialists in metal conservation and the client about the bent metal rod of the rear proper left leg which prevented the glide ('Armstrong quad') from reaching the floor, it was agreed that the risk of damaging the rod by attempting to straighten the leg would be too great. Therefore a decision was made not to straighten or replace the rod. A 5 mm deep disk of black expanded polyethylene sheeting (Plastazote™) was prepared and positioned under the glide providing support to the glide and returning the chair to a position level with the floor. (Spare disks were prepared and are stored with the foam samples.)

The metal components of the legs were lightly cleaned with lint-free tissue paper moistened with IMS to remove surface soils. The plastic glides were lightly cleaned with a bristle hairbrush and vacuum suction to remove soil build-up from the creviced areas. A light protective coating of micro-crystalline wax (Renaissance Wax™) was applied to the cleaned legs.

A dust cover was made for each piece of furniture. Each cover comprised an outer layer of Tyvek™, fully lined with a polyester voile to reduce friction between the dust cover and top cover fabric. The Tyvek™ (bonded (non woven) sheet polyethylene) was rinsed first to remove the anti-static finish (potassium dibutylphosphate) which is reported to have a deleterious effect on metals (Walker, 1986: 23). Ties attached to each corner of the dust cover provided a means of securing the covers to the chair and stool legs.

Preventive conservation advice was supplied; this included the recommendation that each piece of furniture should be carried by two people at all times, by the legs and not the upholstery to avoid applying pressure to the fragile foam filling.

1.9 Treatment evaluation

The chair and footstool responded well to treatment (see Figure 1.7). The top covers are considerably cleaner and better supported on the three-dimensional form. Although more intervention to the understructure was required than initially planned, nearly all of the original materials remain with the chair frame. Individual layers and the upholstered frames as a whole are more stable and well supported as a result. The webbing is less vulnerable to damage that could have occurred from normal handling or from the weight of the cushions. The profile of the upholstery more closely resembles the form intended by the designer, as seen by comparing the furniture (Figure 1.7) with the 1962 advertisment (Figure 1.3).

Samples of the degraded foams have been retained in order that further analysis can be undertaken (by Gill and Wyeth, University of Southampton).

The 'Heron' chair and footstool combine material and technical innovation of furniture design and construction, with conventional materials and technical features (Gill, 2000). Similarly, conservation treatment of the chair and the footstool in 1999 as outlined in this case study, combined established upholstery conservation techniques with innovative treatments.

Notes

1 According to Conway (1982: 53), production of 'Heron' and 'Flamingo' lines ceased in 1961 when the company (which at the same time changed its name from Ernest Race Limited to Race Furniture Limited) moved from South London, UK to the Isle of Sheppey (1982: 66). However, promotional material from the company of Race Furniture Limited (Figure 1.3), suggests that production continued into 1962. Eric Fuller, who commenced his apprenticeship with the company in 1962, remembers the occasional 'Heron' chair being brought back to the factory after production ceased for recovering or complete reupholstery (personal communication with K. Gill, April 1999; see Appendix, Report A). According to Ian Finlator, Director of Race Furniture Limited, production ceased in 1965 (personal communication with K. Gill, November 2000).

2 This was partially out of necessity given the British Government's restrictions on the use of certain materials between 1939 and 1952 when the Utility Scheme was in operation.

3 Rubberised webbing was first produced in Britain by 'Pirelli' in 1948 (Wilson, 1990: 146).

4 Four years later Race's 'Flamingo' chair, c.1957 (with a design and construction basically the same as the 'Heron' chair, but with wood legs and fixed seat rather than loose cushion) was chosen for a Design Centre Award, in part because its 'skilful use of up-to-date materials (steel frame and foam sheeting) help to give it an interesting form' and having the 'unusual advantage of being comfortable however you sit in it – straight backed or sprawling' (cited in Conway, 1982: 53). Both chair designs were advertised together by Ernest Race Limited in 1962 (Figure 1.3).

5 Race was not alone in exploring new materials for such purposes. In 1951 the 'Lady' chair, designed by the Italian Marco Zanusso, was one of the first chairs to be produced by Arflex, a company set up by Pirelli to develop the use of foam rubber and rubberised webbing in upholstered furniture (Fiell and Fiell, 1997: 737; Gill, 1990: 307, 319). In common with the 'Heron' chair, the upholstery layers of the 'Lady' chair were hand-built.

6 When the company moved to the Isle of Sheppey in 1961 it left many of its skilled upholsterers behind. Conway reports that 'Production had to be revised to suit the new conditions' (1982: 66).

7 Pre-formed latex foam units had been in use in seat furniture since the early 1930s and 1940s. However, due to high costs involved in producing the moulds this technique was only feasible for mass production (Murphy, 1966: lxxxi).

8 TCC ref. no. 2473.

9 The Geffrye Museum, London, set in the former eighteenth-century almshouses of the Ironmonger's Company, 'presents the changing style of the [English] domestic interior. The displays lead the visitor ... through time, from the 17th century ... to 20th century modernity' (Museum information leaflet, February/April 1999, pages not numbered).

10 The chair was in the donor's sitting room, which was the best room and rarely used. This is perhaps one of the main reasons why the upholstery (which, according to the donor, is unchanged from the time of the donor's purchase in c.1960) has survived in such good condition (Museum archive, notes taken during telephone conversation with donor 14/7/98 by Eleanor John, Assistant Keeper of Collections, Geffrye Musem).

11 Interestingly, the hollow metal welded to the seat section of the chair frame is of square cross-section in contrast to that on the stool which is round. This may be a technical requirement to do with the weight load of the sitter on the chair being much greater than that on the footstool; however, it is more likely to be due to the relatively small size of the company. Race furniture was not mass-produced, and

therefore the makers likely as not used what was available, and worked and – responding to performance of early models – made adaptations and developments to original construction.

12 Graphite finish was also available, as illustrated and described in the Race Furniture Limited advertisement featured in *House and Garden*, April 1961 and in the company advertisement of 1962 (Figure 1.3).

13 Lesley Wilson (upholstery conservator, see this volume, owns another 'Heron' chair and footstool. Photographs taken of the original upholstery materials of her chair, as it was being stripped down, reveal various differences between the two sets of chair and footstool. For example, the Geffrye Museum chair and footstool have grey webbing, whilst Wilson's chair had brown webbing. The system used to attach the webbing differed between the two sets of furniture. The fastening system used to secure the inner back of the Geffrye Museum chair could not be determined due to the inaccessibility of this area. The webbing of Wilson's chair and footstool is wrapped around the frame, the ends being joined with a square metal link, in contrast to the Geffrye Museum footstool and chair seat webbing which feeds through wire clips on the frame and is secured with a fine wire bar in the first and last clip. This difference was interpreted as a development of the original construction to improve its function (personal communication with Lesley Wilson, March 1999).

Anne Bruce (upholsterer specialising in 1950s–60s furniture) is of the opinion that the headrests were introduced later, as illustrated in the company advert appearing in *House and Garden* in 1961. All of the above observations suggest that the Geffrye Museum chair was produced in the late 1950s/early 1960s, rather than in 1955. Wilson's chair may be closer to that of 1955.

14 To compare this technique to present day practices, refer to D. James' book *Upholstery: A Complete Course*, which provides an informative and a well illustrated section on structure and current day application of resilient webbing to metal and wood frames (James, 1990:159–64).

15 Confirmed by the twist test in the following way: fibres were held with tweezers and in front of the observer, face front, and wetted out with a drop of de-ionised water while examined under magnification. This enabled detection of the direction of the natural twist the fibre has upon drying. A clockwise direction indicates either flax or ramie; a counterclockwise direction denotes either hemp or jute.

16 Tightbond™ adhesives (Personal communication with Eric Fuller, April 1999; Appendix, Report A).

17 Personal correspondence with Mucci, December 1999.

18 The uniform colour of the yellow foam used to pad the inner back (especially in its degraded state) suggests that it is a polyether urethane (Personal communication with Bob Ludman, December 1999; Appendix, Report B).

19 All pincore foam was of latex, always a combination of natural and synthetic. Pincore for upholstery had a higher content of less resilient synthetic latex to make it more resistant to photo-degradation. Latex foam used for mattress production had a much higher content of natural latex to increase resilience required. Although natural latex was the more light-sensitive product, this was not necessarily a problem in mattress construction as the foam pad was always covered with various additional upholstery layers and bedding, and was more protected from light. This information suggests that the relatively well-preserved pincore pad of the lumbar cushion and the seat cushion pad in the 'Heron' chair (concealed only by the top cover) are likely to have been made of a foam with a higher percentage of synthetic latex.

Pincore manufacture required the inclusion of a mould release agent; in the early days this was probably a soap solution, but in later years it was replaced with silicone. This is something to bear in mind when interpreting analytical data from degraded (and new) foams and assessing contributing factors to degradation. The matt appearance of the orange foam of the inner wings and arms, even in its degraded state, suggests that it is a polyether urethane. This polyurethane foam was produced by a company called 'Kay Foam', now part of 'Vitafoam' which is part of 'Vita Group' (Personal communication with Bob Ludman, December 1999; Appendix, Report B).

20 The two leading manufacturers of rubberised hair were 'Hairlock' of Bedford and Harrison and Joan from Bolton or Halifax (Personal communication with Bob Ludman, December 1999; Appendix, Report B).

21 The first polymer to be foamed was polyester, but it was found to deteriorate rapidly under exposure to ultra-violet radiation. Polyether, the second polymer to be foamed, was a more stable product, chemically resistant and having better mechanical resistance (Personal communication with Bob Ludman, December 1999; Appendix, Report B).

22 In contrast the 'grinning' (glittery) effect on the degraded foam from the outer wing, arms and back of the chair, suggest that it is a polyester polyurethane ('grinning' effect is due to the polyester being a harder polymer) (Personal communication with Bob Ludman, December 1999; Appendix, Report B).

23 Notes made during discussion with Lesley Wilson (March 1999), owner of another 'Heron' chair, during viewing of original upholstery materials taken by her during stripping down of her chair. Her chair had retained its original materials; however, they had to be removed for hygiene reasons when the chair was flooded by contaminated water. Since Gill's investigation of the Geffrye Museum chair and footstool, Wilson has published findings of her chair (Wilson 1999: 21–3).

24 The dry cleaning machine was set on the 'delicate' cycle. Adding the solvent took 5 minutes and solvent evacuation and drying (at approx. 30°C) took approximately 20 minutes. The cleaned items were aired for 2 hours initially and then left under acid-free tissue paper in the workroom for a further five days by which time solvent fumes were not noticeable.

Appendices

Report A

Interim Report on Oral History Account of Race Apprenticeship. The Textile Conservation Centre, University of Southampton.

The following notes were made by Kathryn Gill during a telephone conversation with Eric Fuller on 23 April 1999. Eric Fuller is an upholsterer who was an apprentice with Race Furniture Limited during the early 1960s. Mr Fuller recalls 'Heron' chairs being worked on, possibly re-upholstery of earlier pieces. Speaking from memory, Mr Fuller thought the following materials were used on the 'Heron' chair:

Location	*Material*
Lumbar cushion	latex foam, possibly manufactured by 'Dunlopillo'?
Inner back	a blue-coloured foam
Outer arms and outer wings	'Polyester' (polyester urethane)
Inside back	'Polyether' (polyether urethane)
Arm rests	black fibre board
Chair seat and back	continuous strip of webbing
Footstool	continuous strip of webbing
Chair back	two layers of hessian on the back (12 oz jute)
Arm rest	rubberised hair (likely suppliers 'Hairlock' or 'Vitafoam'
Adhesive	Tightbond™ adhesives

Mr Fuller also recalled that the inner back covers were held in position against the upholstered form by means of calico sleeves stitched to the back covers which were in turn slipped over wood rods (dowels) and secured to the frame by tying off under tension to the adjacent horizontal bar on wing of the metal frame. He was also of the opinion that tacks or staples could have been used to secure the top covers to the front seat rail but it would have been unusual for both types of metal fasteners to have been used in combination.

Report B

Interim Report on Oral History Account of Foam Production. The Textile Conservation Centre, University of Southampton.

The following notes were made by Kathryn Gill during a meeting on 2 December 1999 with Mr Robert Ludman. Mr Ludman was asked about the manufacture and visual characteristics of early polyurethane foams and latex foams as they were in the 1960s and 1970s when he was the Technical Director of Dunlopillo and Aerofoam respectively. His observations are noted below:

The uniform colour of the yellow foam used to pad the inner back of the 'Heron' chair (especially in its degraded state) suggests that it is a polyether urethane.

All pincore foam was of latex, always a combination of natural and synthetic. Pincore for upholstery had a higher content of less resilient synthetic latex to make it more resistant to photo-degradation. Latex foam used for mattress production had a much higher content of natural latex to increase resilience required. Although natural latex was the more light-sensitive product, this was not necessarily a problem in mattress construction as the foam pad was always covered with various additional upholstery layers and bedding, and was more protected from light). This information suggests that the relatively well preserved pincore pad of the lumbar cushion and the seat cushion pad in the 'Heron' chair (concealed only by the top cover) are likely to have been made of foam with a higher percentage of synthetic latex.

Pincore manufacture required the inclusion of a mould release agent; in the early days this was probably a soap solution, but in later years it was replaced with silicone. This is something to bear in mind when interpreting analytical data of degraded (and new) foams and assessing contributing factors to degradation. The matt appearance of the orange foam of the inner wings and arms, even in its degraded state, suggests that it is a polyether urethane. This polyurethane foam was produced by a company called 'Kay Foam', now part of 'Vitafoam' which is part of 'Vita Group'.

The two leading manufacturers of rubberised hair were 'Hairlock' of Bedford and Harrison and Joan from Bolton or Halifax.

The first polymer to be foamed was polyester, but it was found to deteriorate rapidly under exposure to ultra-violet radiation. Polyether, the second polymer to be foamed, was a more stable product, chemically resistant and having better mechanical resistance.

In contrast the 'grinning' (glittery) effect on the degraded foam from the outer wing, arms and back of the chair, suggest that it is a polyester urethane ('grinning' effect is due to the polyester being a harder polymer).

Acknowledgements

The author would like to thank the Geffrye Museum and the Textile Conservation Centre for permission to publish this work. Thanks are also due to Anne Bruce, upholsterer, and Ian Finlator, Stuart Finlator and Eric Fuller, Race Furniture Limited, Bourton Industrial Park, Bourton-on-the-Water, Gloucestershire for archival information; Elenor John, Geffrye Museum, Derek Balfour and Frances Collard, Victoria & Albert Museum; and Lesley Wilson for access to information on Race Furniture; Robert Ludman, Cellular Polymer Consultant, for information on early polyurethane foams; Paul Wyeth, chemist, Textile Conservation Centre, and Peter Mucci, Department of Mechanical Engineering, University of Southampton, for advice on analysing degraded foam samples.

References

Conway, H. (1982) *Ernest Race*. London: The Design Council.

Fiell, C. and Fiell P. (1997) *1000 Chairs*. Köln: Taschen.

Gill, K. (1990) Approaches in the treatment of 20th-Century upholstered furniture. In: M.A. Williams (ed.), *Upholstery Conservation Symposium Pre-prints*. New Hampshire: American Conservation Consortium Ltd, pp. 305–22.

Gill, K. (1999) *Interim Report on Oral History Account of Foam Production*. Unpublished report, The Textile Conservation Centre, University of Southampton.

Gill, K. (2000). A 1950s upholstered chair: combining the conventional and the innovative in both manufacture and conservation. Poster presented at IIC Congress 2000, *Tradition and Innovation: Advances in Conservation*. IIC Melbourne, 2000 (forthcoming, p. 11).

James, D. (1990) *Upholstery: A Complete Course*. London: The Guild of Master Craftsman Publications.

Kerr, N. and Batcheller, J. (1993) Degradation of polyurethanes in 20th century museum textiles. In: D. Grattan (ed.), *Saving the Twentieth Century: The Conservation of Modern Materials*. Proceedings of the Symposium '91, Ottawa, Canada, pp. 189–212.

Mucci, P.E.R. (1997) Rapid identification of plastics using external beam mid-infrared spectroscopy. In: *Proceedings of the Royal Society of Chemistry Symposium. Chemical Aspects of Plastics Recycling*. University Manchester Institute of Science and Technology, Manchester (1996). Cambridge Royal Society of Chemistry Information Services, pp. 53–70.

Murphy, E.A. (1966) Some early adventures with latex. *Technology* **39**, 3 June 1966, lxxiii–lxxxiv.

Stoughton-Harris, C. (1993) Treatment of 20th-century rubberized multimedia costume: conservation of a Mary Quant raincoat (ca. 1967). In: D.W. Grattan (ed.) *Saving the Twentieth Century: The Conservation of Modern Materials*. Ottawa: CCI, pp. 213–221.

Tímár Balázsy, A. and Eastop, D. (1998) *Chemical Principles of Textile Conservation*. Oxford: Butterworth–Heinemann.

Walker, S. (1986) Investigation of the properties of Tyvek, pertaining to its use as a storage material for artifacts. *IIC-CG Newsletter*, September 1986, 21–25.

Wilson, L. (1999) Foams in upholstered furniture. In D.A. Rogers and G. Marley (eds), *Modern Materials – Modern Problems*. Postprints of the Conference, Modern Materials, Modern Problems, organised by the UKIC, 17 April 1999. London: UKIC, pp. 19–25.

Wilson, L. and Balfour, D. (1990) Developments in upholstery construction in Britain during the first half of the 20th century. In: M.A. Williams (ed.), *Upholstery Conservation Symposium Pre-prints*. New Hampshire: American Conservation Consortium Ltd, pp. 136–48.

2

The Lawrence Alma-Tadema settee, designed c.1884–85: the challenges of interpretation and replication

Kathryn Gill

2.1 Introduction

This case history concerns the treatment undertaken on the upholstery of a magnificent late nineteenth-century inlaid ebony settee from the collection of the Metropolitan Museum of Art (Figure 2.1). The settee is part of a well-documented suite designed by the Dutch-born English painter Sir Lawrence Alma-Tadema (1836–1912) and was made by a British (London) firm, Johnstone, Norman and Company, between 1884 and 1885. It was commissioned by the art patron Henry G. Marquand (1819–1902) for the music room of his new mansion in New York City.

Unlike the rest of the suite (including a piano and stools, chairs, long and short settees and curtains), which was sold at auction (in 1903, 1927 and 1980), the settee remained in the possession of the Marquand family until 1975, when it was bequeathed to the Metropolitan Museum of Art by Elizabeth Love Godwin (MMA acc. no. 1975.219) (Kisluk-Grosheide, 1994).

2.2 Role

In 1991 the European Sculpture and Decorative Arts Department proposed that the settee would be placed on long-term display in the Metropolitan Museum's new Iris and B. Gerald Cantor Galleries of Nineteenth Century European Sculpture and Decorative Arts. However, it was recognised that the settee no longer retained its original outer covers and trimmings. The covers in place when the settee was acquired in 1975 were thought to be recent applications, and were not considered to be of any historic significance (Figure 2.1). The discovery of a black and white photograph of a smaller settee from the same suite with its original top covers (Figure 2.2) showed how far removed the 1970s upholstery was from the designer's original intention. As a result of this discovery the curatorial department suggested that the settee should be recovered to more closely resemble the original appearance.

2.3 Preliminary investigation

Once the proposal had been made to remove the 1970s covers and replace them with more authentic looking covers and trimmings, the extent of treatment (if indeed any at all) as well as the type and degree of replication were dependant upon the nature and extent of information assembled by the curator, Danielle O. Kisluk-Grosheide, Associate Curator, European Sculpture and Decorative Arts, during her research into the suite, room and house from which the settee came.

Curatorial research unearthed much information about the suite of furniture, including contemporary black and white photographs of several views of the Music Room with the suite

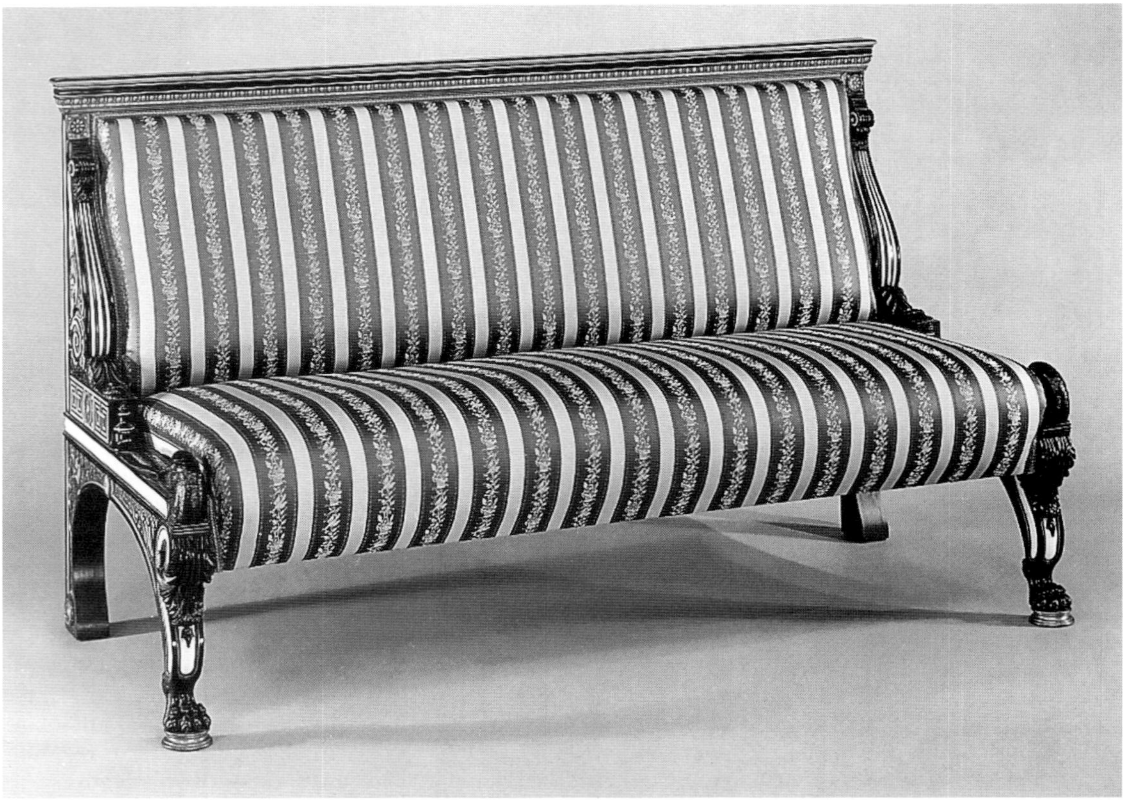

Figure 2.1 Settee before 1991 treatment. The settee is part of a large suite designed by Sir Lawrence Alma Tadema (1836–1912) and executed by Johnstone, Norman and Company, for the music room in the Marquand residence, New York, USA. English, 1884–5; ebony, box wood, sandalwood, cedar and ebonised mahogany, ivory, mother-of-pearl and brass; maximum dimensions 902×1480×711 mm. (The Metropolitan Museum of Art, 1975.219, bequest of Elizabeth Love Godwin, 1975)

in situ (Kisluk-Grosheide, 1994). Unfortunately, none of the photographs appeared to have the Museum's settee in view. Written descriptions of the suite were found in contemporary journals (*The Building News & Engineering Journal*, July 1885a: 122) and later auction sales catalogues (American Art Association, 1903; American Art Association, 1927: 145). For example, the September 1885 issue of *Cabinet Making & Upholstery* states that:

> The couches, chairs and stools are upholstered in silk of a beautiful shade of pure grey, transversed by bands of exquisite embroidery in colours which are rich, but carefully subdued, as one sees them in Mr. Tadema's pictures. The ground of the embroidery is also silk, the colour being precisely that of the bloom of a ripe plum. Upon this the tints of gold and orange, blue, red and brown, with slender curved lines of pure white, giving peculiar delicacy to the whole form a beautiful scroll pattern. A rich trellis fringe of mingled grey and gold runs along the edges of the couches, and beneath it is a deep silk fringe of the plum-bloom colour, which does not show, except in the effect of depth and richness it imparts to one upper fringe. (Anon. 1885: 104)

Several pieces of the suite were located, including one of the tub chairs now in the collection at the Victoria & Albert Museum (Mus. ref. W.25.1980) (Figure 2.3). Unfortunately this chair had also been recovered. The Victoria & Albert Museum had undertaken an investigation of the tub chair when it was acquired in 1980

Figure 2.2 Small settee from the same suite as the Metropolitan Museum's settee (1975.219). This settee has its original top covers with embroidered decorative panels, and deep tasselled fringe. The small settee has a curved back unlike the settee at the Metropolitan Museum, which has a straight back. Note also the configuration of geometric and floral decorative panels, and compare them with Figure 2.6, the museum's settee after the 1991 treatment. (Sale catalogue, *American Art Association*, 1927: 145, illus. no. 742)

(Thomerson, 1980). This investigation revealed fragments of the original top covers, comprising a green-dyed silk rep top cover fabric and a contrasting black-purple silk satin weave central panel on which the embroidered design was assumed to have been executed.[1]

On the basis of the information assembled by the curator (Kisluk-Grosheide) and conservator (Gill), a joint decision was made to proceed with a preliminary examination and investigation of the composite upholstered units and individual layers of the Metropolitan Museum settee. It was recognised that the

Figure 2.3 Tub chair from the same suite as the Metropolitan Museum of Art's settee (1975.219). This chair displays non-original top covers and trimmings applied in 1981 following an investigative examination in the same year. The investigation revealed large fragments of the original green-dyed silk and black-purple silk satin top covers. None of the embroidery or the trimming survived. During re-upholstery in 1981 the embroidered panel was not recreated. (©The Board of Trustees of the Victoria & Albert Museum, mus. no. W25-1980)

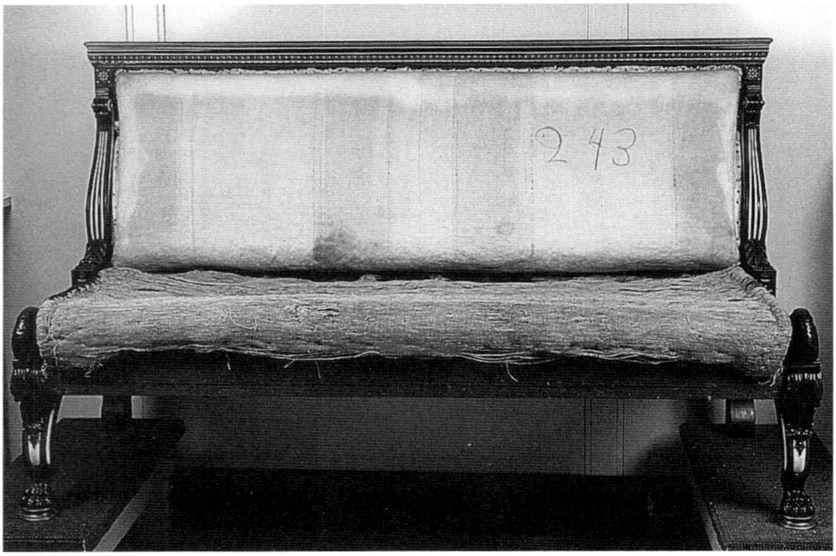

Figure 2.4 Front view of the settee, 1991 – treatment in progress. The modern top covers have been removed to reveal the original understructure materials. The location and width of the original decorative panels (now missing) are clearly visible on the inner back upholstery, denoted by pencil lines and discoloration of the cotton filling cover. (Reproduced by kind permission of the Sherman Fairchild Center for Objects Conservation, The Metropolitan Museum of Art, New York)

nature and extent of treatment would be influenced by information revealed by this investigation of the settee's composite upholstery units and individual layers.[2]

The modern top cover and trimming were removed from the Metropolitan Museum's settee to allow investigation of the understructure. Examination revealed that nearly all the original understructure material was in place and intact. Discoloration of the cotton filling cover layer revealed the location and width of the decorative panels on the settee (Figure 2.4). Small fragments of the main top cover and decorative panels, including some embroidery threads and traces of embroidery stitches, were also uncovered.

All of the original back upholstery understructure appeared to be intact and the majority of the original seat understructure appeared undisturbed and intact. This was largely due to the fact that when the original webbing and base cloth had been removed and replaced with new, the overlying understructure upholstery layers had been released from and reapplied to the frame as one unit, rather than as individual layers. No attempt had been made to secure the unit directly to the new webbed base. Instead, it was held in place only by the new top cover, which had been stretched over the unit and tacked to the frame.

The results of the preliminary examination are given in Appendix II, and summarised in the accompanying Figures II.1–II.4.

2.4 Condition assessment

Overall the frame was structurally very sound. As expected, the inner back upholstery understructure unit had sagged and some of the filling had migrated slightly to the lower section. There was some soiling and staining, otherwise the inner back unit appeared to be structurally sound (see Figure 2.4).

The outer back layers appeared to be structurally sound, with the exception of the outer back top cover which, because of its very fragile condition, had been documented, removed and prepared for long-term storage in 1981.[3]

The replacement jute webbing and base cloth in the seat were quite degraded and the fibres brittle to the touch. The web support had stretched and was insufficiently stable to take the weight of the heavy seat unit. The original filling cover was quite brittle and there was some fibre loss along both roll edges, around stitches and along the lower front edge. The stitched edge and overall shape of the stitched first filling were well preserved in their original form. In contrast, the uneven distribution of the second filling, shorter staple length of the individual curled hairs and the distribution of tiny fragments of top cover and cotton fibres, suggested that this layer of hair had been re-teased. The hair appeared to have retained a considerable amount of loose particulate soiling. The second filling cover was missing.

2.5 Treatment options/proposals

It was reassuring to discover that all textile fragments identified as being original to the settee frame matched those revealed on the Victoria & Albert Museum tub chair in 1981. What was not revealed from either the Metropolitan Museum or the Victoria & Albert Museum investigation was the full range of colours, or the range of thread types or embroidery stitches used in the decorative panels. Also, no further information was revealed about the number of different designs or design details of the decorative panels.

Nevertheless, a decision was made to proceed with a partial reconstruction based on the information revealed by this preliminary investigation. It was proposed that all extant original materials should be stabilised and missing elements should be rebuilt so that the settee would more closely resemble its original appearance, as deduced from research to date.

The stages of treatment would involve permanent removal of remaining non-original upholstery materials, stabilisation of original materials (possibly involving temporary removal of some of the material for treatment), and 'rebuilding' of missing elements around the conserved materials using conservation grade materials.

The aim of treating extant materials was to make them stable enough to support their own weight on the wood frame, in order to facilitate long-term display in the museum galleries. It was proposed that treatment would be carried out in a manner that would cause minimum disruption to the frame and to the upholstery elements. Therefore, where possible the textile elements were to be secured to the frame using stitching techniques rather than metal fasteners. It was proposed that this would be achieved by attaching narrow strips of acid-free card, covered in a fine, tightly woven, cotton fabric, to the frame with staples. (It was estimated that over 10 per cent fewer metal fasteners would be required using staples rather than with tacks and conventional techniques.) The conserved upholstery and the new materials would be stitched to the cloth-covered card strips.

Even though the quantity and quality of information revealed by the preliminary investigation were considerable, the range of stitching techniques, threads and colours of the embroidered panels remained largely unknown. Consequently, because of this lack of information and other factors (including time and budgetary constraints), it was recognised that some compromises would be necessary in the reconstruction of the decorative panels. The following compromises were anticipated.

The first compromise would be made in the recreation of the design of the decorative panels. Some of the details of the design could not be deciphered from the 1927 black and white photograph (see Figure 2.2). Therefore missing details would have to be deduced. It was decided to copy motifs present in the carved and inlaid panels of the tub chair, piano and two settee frames, because they too reflected Tadema's designs (Figure 2.5). A letter written by W.C. Codman records that

> all drawings and designs of details for woodwork inlays, carving, embroidery, were made by me under the supervision of Mr L. Alma Tadema, R.A. (*Building News and Engineering Journal*, 1885b: 188)

Furthermore, enough of the floral decorative panels was visible in the black and white photograph to show that the designs on the seat differed from those on the back (Figure 2.2). However, not enough of the designs was visible for them to be copied in full. Therefore, it was proposed that for the reconstruction, the designs for the seat panel and the back panel would be identical.

In comparison, the design of the narrow decorative panels, of a familiar geometric, symmetrical pattern, was much easier to reconstruct. This design was also located in a number of nineteenth-century pattern books (e.g. Jones, 1856, plate XXII, nos. 22, 27).

Figure 2.5 Initial design for the replacement decorative panels. The design is based on the inner back panel seen in the black and white illustration of 1927 (*American Art Association*, see Figure 2.2). Details that could not be deciphered from this image were copied from well-preserved images from the wood frames of the piano, tub chair and settees. This line drawing records the sources of the individual motifs.

Frame source of the individual design motifs in the decorative panel:

a Tub chair frame
b Tub chair frame
c Piano frame
d Long settee frame
e Piano frame
f Long settee frame
g Long settee frame
h Short settee frame
i Piano frame
j Piano frame
k Tub chair frame
l Short settee frame
m Piano frame
n Long settee
o Piano frame
p Piano frame
q Piano frame
r Short settee frame
s Piano frame
t Long settee frame
u Tub chair frame
v Short settee frame

Another compromise involved the technique of the decorative panels, which were known to have been embroidered originally. There was neither enough information on the original techniques and threads to replicate the embroideries, nor sufficient funds to cover the cost of custom-made embroidered replicas.

What was known about the decorative panels was that there had been a total of six panels, three on the back and three on the seat. The dimensions and original position of each back panel were also known. Each panel was known to have been of black-purple satin, although the exact shade of the 'ripe plum' colour was not known (Anon., 1885: 104).

There was much discussion at this stage of the decision-making process about how far to go in the re-creation of the decorative panels. Two options were considered. The first reflected a more conservative approach – to prepare six black-purple dyed silk satin weave panels of the same dimensions as the original and apply them to the settee back and seat in line with the location of the original panels. This would certainly assist in the interpretation of the designer's original concept. This is the approach adopted by the Victoria & Albert Museum in 1981 when recovering the tub chair.[4,5] However, in the case of the settee there was one other factor to consider. The tub chair and consequently its two decorative panels were considerably smaller than the settee and its panels. The settee's decorative panels covered over 50 per cent of the surface area of the top covers, approximately four times the area covered by the tub chair panels. With or without the floral patterning, the impact of the panels upon the overall design of the settee would be considerable.

It was generally felt by the curator and conservator that to leave the panels plain would perhaps be too far from the original design concept of the piece since the colours and floral pattern were integral to the overall appearance of the settee. Therefore, a joint decision was made to go one step further and to introduce pattern and colour to the plum-coloured panels. However, since the range of stitching techniques and thread types was unknown, a compromise was proposed – embroidery would be substituted with printing. Hand-printed, silk-screened adaptations of the floral patterns were chosen to suggest the missing embroidered panels.

This decision led to another compromise concerning the number and distribution of colours within the floral and geometric panels and within the deep trellis fringe. It was proposed that the colours of the silk screened design would be matched directly with the few found in the embroidered fragments, discovered in the second filling layer of hair in the seat of the settee and with those colours used in the carved inlaid frames. The tonal values of the embroidered panels in the black and white photographs would also be taken into consideration. Colour selection and distribution for both the panels and trellis fringe were also influenced by descriptions of the suite when it was first exhibited after completion in 1885, and when presented for auction in 1903 and 1927. These accounts include that in *Cabinet Making and Upholstery* (Anon., 1885: 104) quoted earlier and the following:

> silvery grey silk embroideries ... The colours of the embroidery are Greek red and warm white, used in patterns copied from Classic examples. (*Building News and Engineering Journal*, 1885a: 122)

> silk richly embroidered ... (Moyr Smith, 1889: 95)

> Objects are upholstered in a silk of ashen olive embroidered with panels, either of floral scrolls or of the Greek wave design, contained within narrow borders of repeated circles. (American Art Association/Anderson Galleries, 1903)

> upholstered in olive-grey silk with bands of silk embroidery and tendril motifs ... (American Art Association, 1927: 145)

Owing to budgetary constraints, it was decided that the plum-coloured trellis fringe for the lower edge of the front seat rail would be constructed with a reduced number of tassels (57 originally and 33 in the replacement). Since neither the construction nor the colour of the narrow braid that originally trimmed the remaining edges of the top cover panels was known, it was proposed to use a plain, unobtrusive braid, colour-matched to the main top cover fabric for the 1991 recovering.

Owing to budgetary and time constraints it was also decided that the fabric for the outer back would not be re-woven. Instead, it was proposed that the same fabric as used on the inner back would be used.

2.6 Treatment undertaken

2.6.1 Recreating the missing elements

The recreation of the missing elements was dependent on a number of other specialists who were briefed at various stages of the project by the conservator (Gill), working in close collaboration with the curator (Kisluk-Grosheide). The specialists were provided with designs, technical drawings, and fabric and colour swatches where appropriate. Once samples had been approved by the conservator and curator the specialists proceeded with the various projects. Where necessary the conservator visited the individual studios to monitor the work in progress.

The material selected for the top cover was a new silk fabric of the same weave and approximate thread count as the original green silk (see Appendix II). It was custom-dyed to match the original colour by the dyeing department of Scalamandré, NY.[6]

The decorative panel designs were carried out as proposed. The draft designs compiled by the conservator were finished off by an accomplished textile designer and printer who transferred them to screens and hand-printed them on to white satin weave silk.[7]

The deep fringe comprised a black–purple bullion behind a knotted trellis of green silk threads and yellow and green silk wrapped wooden beads. The deep fringed braid was custom-made by Scalamandré based on Gill's interpretation of the information illustrated in Figure 2.2.[8]

As proposed the narrow braid selected was a plain weave warp-faced silk braid which was custom dyed to match the top cover fabric.[9]

2.6.2 Frame preparation, stabilisation of original elements and application of recreated elements

The original seat unit was lifted from the frame and temporarily put aside. The non-original base cloth and webbing were removed and replaced with a polypropylene mesh,[10] an inert material which would provide full, even support for the upholstery unit without putting undue strain on the frame and the upholstery. The mesh was covered on one side with scoured linen stitched in place to prevent the loose filling from falling through the polypropylene mesh and to provide a stitching ground for all subsequent layers of upholstery. The mesh was attached to the top of the seat rail with Monel (copper and nickel alloy) metal staples (13 mm crown, 13 mm depth).

Acid-free cardboard strips were encased in fine cotton fabric and stapled to the tacking rails of the settee frame, to provide a stitching ground for the support materials, reproduction top covers and trimmings.

After a thorough surface clean using a hand-held vacuum cleaner to remove loose particulate soils, the seat unit was re-positioned on the frame, supported by the new structure. The second filling was temporarily removed to allow the main seat unit to be encased in custom-dyed, colour-matched nylon bobbin net. The net was arranged to follow the contours of the roll edge, and was held in position with a single row of large running stitches worked through the layers of upholstery, close and parallel to the row of top stitches. The net was extended over the sides of the seat unit and was stitched to the linen support base with stranded cotton thread.

The seat's second filling of curled horsehair was gently teased to even out lumps, and re-positioned on the main seat unit. The second filling was also held in position by covering it with a layer of colour-matched bobbin net. This net layer also served to protect and separate the original materials from the new. The net was stitched to the cotton-covered card strips. To provide a smooth clean surface for the recreated top cover, the seat above the net layer and the inner back above the filling cover layer were covered in a thin layer of polyester needle-punched felt,[11] followed by a layer of scoured, brushed cotton. The outer back was also covered in a new layer of brushed cotton. All layers were stitched to the cotton-covered card strips.

The green dyed silk top covers were then applied by stitching to the fabric-covered card.

The 'replica' decorative satin weave panels were slip-stitched directly onto the top cover (Figure 2.6).

The raw edges of the green top cover panels were concealed by a colour-matched braid. Owing to limited access, stitch attachment of the braid with the precision and tension control required, was not possible. Attaching with metal fasteners was not considered since the fasteners could not be concealed. Therefore, adhering the braid was the most appropriate option. Thermoplastic adhesives requiring heat application were considered, however, because of the restricted access to the area combined with the uneven bonding surface (comprising overlapping raw edges of nylon net and the silk replica fabric on a cotton covered card ground) an adhesive that could also act as a consolidant to bond all layers to the cotton ground was required. Sodium carboxy methyl cellulose (SCMC) was considered as it has been used in the past in paper and textile conservation (Tímár-Balázsy and Eastop, 1998: 304, 313, 323; Horie, 1987: 129). It also creates one of the strongest bonds, although least flexible bonds of cellulose-based group of adhesives (Gill and Boersma, 1997: 11, 12). Tests showed that SCMC in a dispersion of 13 ml de-ionised water, 1 g SCMC, would create a sufficiently viscous gel which would not spread when applied directly to the textile ground and therefore reduce the risk of staining. The adhesive was applied sparingly and directly in 40 mm long sections to the reverse side of the braid with a small bristle stencil brush. The section of braid was then carefully positioned

Figure 2.6 Settee after the 1991 treatment and on display in 1992 in the Iris and B. Gerald Cantor Galleries of Nineteenth Century European Sculpture and Decorative Arts, The Metropolitan Museum of Art, New York. (Reproduced by kind permission of the Department of European Sculpture and Decorative Art, Metropolitan Museum of Art, New York)

with tweezers onto the top cover and gentle finger pressure was applied for about one minute in order to create a sufficient bond. All the braid was attached in this fashion.

In contrast, access to the front face of the seat rail enabled attachment of the fringe by stitching the heading tape to the cloth-covered card.

2.7 Discussion

2.7.1 Initial evaluation

This partial reconstruction project was considered as success because its aims were realised. The original elements of the Metropolitan Museum's settee were conserved and its appearance now more closely resembles its presumed original form (compare Figures 2.2 and 2.6).

However, this resemblance was achieved via a series of compromises, albeit, carefully considered compromises, and it is reasonable to consider what effect this combination of compromises has had on the overall appearance of the settee. By far the most significant compromises concern the decorative panels, e.g. in the selection of colours and their distribution within the panels, and the substitute technique selected for the original embroidery. A silk screen print, no matter how accurate the colour match, will never have the same qualities, such as depth, texture and movement created by the interaction of light with an embroidered surface, as silk embroidery. Is the interpretation more misleading than its 1970s appearance before treatment (Figure 2.1) or does it just 'mislead' in a different way?

The issue of interpretation emphasises the importance of documentation and informative exhibition labelling, explaining the evidence and basis on which decisions are made. Where possible such reconstructions can be accompanied by an illustration to show what the object on display looked like originally.

2.7.2 Re-evaluation of treatment following the discovery of original curtains

A pair of the original curtains from the Music Room of the Marquand Mansion was discovered in 1996, five years after this project was finished. One of them is now in the Metropolitan Museum's collection (MMA acc. no. 1996.330).

This exciting discovery provided a unique opportunity to compare the overall appearance of the embroidered panels on the curtains from the same room with the replica panels of the 1991 treatment. Furthermore, the design and colours selected for the silk screen print could be compared to embroidered areas of the curtain (Plates 2.1, 2.2, 2.3). The green silk ground fabric and the black-purple panel fabric selected for recovering the settee could also be compared to the original textiles of the curtains.

Comparison revealed that the scale and handling of the recreated design closely resembles that of the original. The distribution and range of colours are remarkably close to the original. The colours of the embroidery on the curtain appear slightly subdued in tone compared to those of the printed reconstruction. However, this contrast is less marked when the reconstruction panels are compared with unfaded areas of the curtain embroidery, which have retained the brighter colours.

While the settee's embroidered trellis designs were worked on black-purple satin, the trellis design on the curtain is worked on green-dyed rep. Consequently, the impact of the colour contrast is different; the original effect of the trellis design on the settee probably more closely resembled that observed in the embroidered repeat border design on black-purple satin, located in the curtain's lower section (Plate 2.3).

As anticipated, the subtle textures and light qualities of the embroidered surface are not replicated in the silk screen print panels. However, there is now enough information to commission embroidered panels to replace the printed reconstructions, should funds and priorities permit.

Notes

1 The author was given access in 1991 by Frances Collard, Deputy Curator, Department of Furniture and Woodwork, to the Victoria & Albert Museum's files on this chair and viewed the chair (with Collard) after Thomerson's re-covering.

2 This preliminary investigation was undertaken by Kathryn Gill, when Associate Conservator in charge of upholstered works of art 1984–91.

3 Metropolitan Museum file notes – in 1981: outside back removed, old braid removed by Charles Anello (when Museum's in-house upholsterer), washed and replaced. Old cambric removed from base. The outside back is now stored in the Museum's Antonio Ratti Textile Center.

4 Personal communication with Collard, 1991.

5 'The "silvery grey" silk covering described by the *Building News* in 1885(a), proved on investigation to have been a pale ribbed grey/grey-green. This was copied in recent upholstery, but embroidery in "Greek red and warm white" was not attempted' (Jervis, 1983: 201).

6 The silk was custom-dyed by an accomplished dyer at Scalamandré, NY. A good colour match was achieved by eye – the recipe was adjusted during the dyeing process until the correct colour and depth of shade was achieved. Ciba Geigy acid dyes were used.

7 Silk screen panels were executed by Gwenlin Goo from designs complied by Kathryn Gill.

8 The trellis fringe was custom-made by hand, by the trimming and dyeing departments of Scalamandré, NY based on technical drawings and colour swatches compiled and prepared by Kathryn Gill. The interpretation of the fringe technique and colour selection was based on information illustrated in Figure 2.2 and the description in *Cabinet Making and Upholstery* (Anon., 1885: 122).

9 The braid was custom-dyed by Kathryn Gill using Giba Geigy acid dyes.

10 Internet Inc.XN.-1672 MSF 521 lb.

11 Polyfelt™, UK; Pellon®, USA.

Acknowledgements

The author would like to thank the Metropolitan Museum of Art for permission to publish this work and the museum's curatorial and conservation staff who were involved at various stages of the treatment of the settee, in particular Danielle Kisluk-Grosheide, who also alerted me to the discovery of the embroidered curtain, and Tom Campbell, Curator of Textiles, for access to the curtain. I am grateful for discussions with Frances Collard, Victoria & Albert Museum, and for access to museum files.

Bibliography

American Art Association/Anderson Galleries (1903) New York, 23–31 January 1903, Marquand sales catalogue.

American Art Association (1927) *Sales Catalogue*. New York, 15 October 1927.

Anon. (1885) Furniture for New York millionaires, from London Truth. *Cabinet Making and Upholstery* (New York), September, p. 104.

Aslin, E. (1962) *Nineteenth Century English Furniture*. London: Faber and Faber.

The Building News and Engineering Journal (London) (1885a) **49**: 24 July.

The Building News and Engineering Journal (London). (1885b) **49**: 31 July.

Gill, K. (1991) *Report on the treatment of the Alma-Tadema settee*. Unpublished treatment report, Sherman Fairchild Center for Objects Conservation, The Metropolitan Museum of Art, accession number 1975.219.

Gill, K. and Boersma, F. (1997) Solvent reactivation of hydroxypropyl cellulose (Klucel G) in textile conservation: recent developments. *The Conservator,* **21.{??8}**

Horie, C.V. (1987) *Materials for Conservation: Organic Consolidants, Adhesives and Coatings*. London: Butterworths.

Jervis, S. (1983) A painter as a decorator. [USA] *House and Garden,* November, 142–7, 201 and 206.

Jones, O. (1856) *The Grammar of Ornament*. London: Messrs Day & Son.

Kisluk-Grosheide, D.O. (1994) The Marquand Mansion. *Metropolitan Museum Journal,* **29**: 151–81.

Montgomery, F.M. (1984) *Textiles in America, 1650–1870*. New York: Norton & Co.

Moyr Smith, J. (1889) *Ornamental Interiors Ancient and Modern*. London.

Swanson V.G. (1990) *The Biography and Catalogue Raisonne of the Paintings of Sir Lawrence Alma-Tadema*. London: Garton & Co.

Thomerson, C. (1980) *Report on the investigation of the tub chair. Mus. ref. W. 25. 1980*. Unpublished investigation report, Dept. of Furniture and Woodwork, Victoria & Albert Museum.

Tímár-Balázsy, A. and Eastop, D. (1998) *Chemical Principles of Textile Conservation*. Oxford: Butterworth-Heinemann.

3

William Burges' Mermaid chair, c.1870: conserving both original materials and later adaptations

Sherry Doyal and Dinah Eastop

3.1 Introduction

Recognizing and establishing the significance of alterations made to upholstered furniture is an important aspect of upholstery conservation. In this case, investigation by one of the authors (S.D.) identified that the current seat upholstery was added over a rush seat. Archival research confirmed that the rush seat was part of the original design. The conservation strategy adopted for the chair aimed to document the chair in its presenting form, to preserve each type of seat upholstery, and to facilitate study of both the rush seat and the later plush upholstery.

3.2 The Mermaid chair

This small upright chair (Figure 3.1) was designed as one of a pair by the architect/designer William Burges (1827–81). It gets its name from the mermaid painted on the outside back. She is depicted holding up tresses of her hair in one hand and a mirror in the other (Figure 3.1). Mermaids figured frequently in Burges' designs. For example, similar mermaids appear on the pottery basin he designed for Lord Bute's bathroom at Cardiff Castle (Mordaunt Crook, 1981b: 41), on the metal Mermaid bowl (Mordaunt Crook, 1981a: Figures 234 and 235) and, most dramatically, on the Mermaid chimneypiece of his own bedroom at Tower House (Mordaunt Crook, 1981b: 65; Pullan, 1885: Plate 26). The pair to the Mermaid chair is decorated with a merman holding a club and a shield, and wearing a helmet of shell. Sketches for merman and mermaid chair backs are found on sheets 27 and 30 of Burges' *Furniture Album*, now in the Victoria & Albert Museum, London (93.E.8).

The framework of both chairs is painted a deep red (blood red) with gold-coloured bands on the legs and uprights. These bands have been described erroneously as gilding (Mordaunt Crook, 1981b: 86). The appearance of gilding is due to a coloured varnish, which coats the painted wood; the varnish gives the underlying white metal foil its gold colour and darkens the overall appearance of the red paint. Bands of decorative painting in black lie over bands of metal foil on the legs and uprights.

The top covers of the seat and inside back panel of the Mermaid chair have a design of stylised leaves stamped into a dark pink wool, pile-weave fabric, known as plush (Hodgkins and Bloxham, 1981; Cornforth, 1992). The top covers are attached to the chair frame by a single line of close nailing, arranged so that the decorative heads touch one another. The nails are machine-made and have brass heads and steel shanks. The seat cover is fitted at the front corners in a series of pleats (Figure 3.2); at the back, the velvet is cut and folded back around the uprights. When presented for treatment in 1982, a piece of plywood, nailed to the underside of the seat frame, served as the 'bottoming' for the chair (Figure 3.3).

Figure 3.1 The Mermaid chair, as received for treatment in 1982, showing the mermaid painted on the outside back panel. Painted, leafed and varnished wood, with upholstered seat and backrest covered in 'Utrecht velvet', wool plush; height 812 mm, width 430 mm, depth 380 mm. (TCC neg no. 82-005, 21a)

Figure 3.2 Seat of the Mermaid chair before treatment, showing the slit in the wool plush top cover. (TCC neg no. 82-005, 23a)

Figure 3.3 Underside of the Mermaid chair, showing the plywood 'bottoming'. (TCC neg no. 25a)

The treatment requested for the chair was 'cleaning and repair of upholstery'. A slit in the top cover was of particular concern, because the previous patch repair was failing, and the cut edges of the slit were lifting up to reveal the two adhesive-coated, silver-coloured insulation type tape patches below.

3.3 Condition assessment

3.3.1 The wooden frame

The wooden chair frame was structurally sound, but the paint work was scratched and chipped in a manner consistent with sustained use. Examination of these damaged areas revealed the bright red colour below the varnish and the areas of white metal foil.

3.3.2 The top covers

The top cover on the backrest was in good condition, but some light soiling was evident. The seat cover was in poor condition. It was heavily soiled and worn in a manner consistent with use. Much of the pile on the plush at the proper right front edge was missing, apparently worn away. A slit, approximately 155 mm in length, ran diagonally across the seat top cover. An attempt had been made to repair this slit using adhesive-coated tape; the tape appeared to have been slipped through the slit, with the adhesive side uppermost. The tape had become brittle and was pulling away from the edges of the slit, making it wider and further damaging the plush fabric. Small slits were present along the folds in the plush at the front corners of the seat; one had been repaired with stitching in pink linen thread (see Figure 3.2).

3.3.3 Bottoming

Remains of a dark-brown bottoming fabric were evident underneath the decorative tacks but the underside of the seat was hidden by a piece of plywood. It had been cut to approximately the correct shape, fitted to the underside of the seat and nailed to the chair frame with seventeen nails. The plywood had warped so that in some places it was possible to see areas of rushing on the underside of the seat. The museum curator was alerted to the presence of the rushing. The plywood was considered to be a later addition of little or no historical significance, and the decision was therefore made to remove the plywood bottoming in order to assess the extent and condition of the rushing. The plywood proved quite difficult to remove because it had warped and it was possible to move it only 50 mm or so down each leg. It was a tight fit and was the most likely cause of the scratches on the inside of each leg. To remove the plywood bottoming the chair was inverted to increase access to the plywood, and to reduce the risk of damaging the rushing. Cutting either side of the plywood, with a hacksaw, for a distance of 70–80 mm allowed the plywood to be bowed enough so that it could be passed between the front uprights without causing further damage to the painted surface of the chair legs.

3.3.4 The rush seating

With the plywood removed, it was clear that the rushing extended across the entire seat (Figure 3.4). It had broken away from the front seat rail, but was otherwise intact. The knotted rushes untwisted below the seat are a mark of English (as opposed to Continental) rushing and do not indicate amateur workmanship.[1] The rushes were dry, brittle and heavily soiled.

Removal of the plywood also revealed other features. The upholstery understructures were not attached directly to the wooden chair frame, as had originally been assumed, but were secured to extra timber which had been attached to the chair rails. This timber added approximately 10 mm around the inner seat frame. At the front seat rail the thickness was built up by two layers of plywood, each 6 mm wide. The timber had been split by the nails which secured the plywood bottoming. The original whittled and unpainted chair rail was also exposed. This indicated that the rushing was the original form of the seat, because seat rails were shaved down to prevent their otherwise sharp edges from cutting into the rushes.

Further fragments of the closely woven, dark brown material found under the decorative tacks were revealed. This suggested that the brown fabric was indeed the remains of a previous bottoming fabric. Fragments of a red woollen [?] material were found under two

Figure 3.4 Underside of the Mermaid chair after plywood 'bottoming' was removed, revealing the original rush seating. (TCC neg no. 82-006, 19)

nails in the rushing at the proper right-hand corner. This find suggested that the present plush was not the first cloth top cover.

3.4 Role

The discovery of the rushing raised various questions. Was the rush seating original? Was the plush upholstery considered to be a significant part of the history of the object? Was one objective of the conservation treatment to re-establish the design and proportions originally intended by the designer for the chair (Doyal, 1982a, 1982b)?

The chair is preserved as an important example of 'Pre-Raphaelite' furniture design and Burges' *oeuvre*. Burges held strong views about furniture, and protested at the 'enormities, inconveniences, and extravagances of our modern upholsterers' (1865: 69). He advocated the use of 'medieval style' painted furniture because it 'not only did duty as furniture, but spoke and told a story' (1865: 71). Burges was particularly interested in the use of tin foils to embellish painted furniture and he investigated medieval precedents of the technique (Wainwright, 1981: 68). Such painted furniture did not prove popular and Handley-Read states that it was mainly for Burges' own use, both at his rooms in Buckingham Street and later at Tower House, the house he built for himself between 1875 and his death in 1881 (1963: 496). The Mermaid chair is said to be recorded in photographs taken by the architect Pullan of Tower House (Mordaunt Crook, 1981b: 86). In the introduction to the album of these photographs Pullan records that Tower House was 'a model residence in the style of the thirteenth century' to which 'Mr Burges devoted all the resources of his great genius' (1885).

The Mermaid chair now forms part of the collection of the William Morris Gallery, Walthamstow, England, UK (Acc. no. G24). The 'Utrecht velvet' used for the top cover was produced by William Morris and Co. (Mordaunt Crook, 1981b: 86). After consultation with the curator, the view taken was that both the rush seating and the later plush covers were significant aspects of the chair, and both should be preserved.

3.5 Treatment

After removal of the plywood bottoming, the chair was given a temporary bottoming of nylon monofilament screening to help prevent damage and loss of the dry rushing. The head-to-head nails were eased out, temporarily

Figure 3.5 Removal of the top cover in progress, revealing its unpatterned underside and showing the previous adhesive tape repairs to the slit in the wool plush. (TCC neg no. 82-006, 26)

removed and labelled so that each could be replaced in its previous position. The wool plush top cover was removed, and was found to measure 490 mm×490 mm approximately. The following layers were revealed under the top cover: a wadding layer immediately below the plush top cover, then a layer of plain-weave cotton (calico) (Figure 3.5), then a layer of plain weave jute cloth, over a horsehair-filled pad. This lay directly on the rushed seat.

3.5.1 Cleaning

The wool plush, wadding and calico layers were surface-cleaned (with low-powered suction) to remove ingrained dust and rush fibre residues. The two tape patches and adhesive residues on the underside of the top cover were removed in a spot cleaning treatment, using the solvent amyl acetate and absorbent pads. Wash tests confirmed that the stamped pattern in the wool plush would be disfigured by a wet treatment. The plush fabric was therefore 'dry cleaned' by immersion in four successive baths of the organic solvent Arklone™ (trichloro trifluoroethane). This was effective in removing soiling without damaging the stamped pattern. The calico was wet cleaned before being replaced.

3.5.2 Support

The plush seat cover was given a full, stitched support of ready-dyed brown, plain-weave, polyester crepeline ('Stabiltex'™), worked in threads drawn from the crepeline. The support fabric was attached using an irregular pattern of support lines of running stitch with an occasional back stitch. The two sides of the long slit across the seat cover were drawn together, but the slit could not be closed completely because the plush had become permanently distorted; the edges of the slit were secured to the crepeline with stab stitches. Polyester crepeline was selected as a support fabric because it is smooth, fine and strong. Its fineness meant that the supported top cover did not become too bulky; this was particularly important at the corners of the seat where the plush cover had to be re-gathered to ease it back into position during the reapplication.

The original layer of wadding on the chair was no longer performing its function (of preventing hair from protruding through to the cover). A new layer of wadding was therefore laid over the original. This was overlaid with wool fabric dyed to a colour that camouflaged the slit in the plush of the seat cover. In dyeing this fabric, the colour was chosen so that the combined effect of the brown polyester crepeline and the wool fabric below blended with the overall colour of the plush, so as to minimise the effects of the still open slit. The dyed fabric was slip-stitched to the upholstery.

3.5.3 Reapplication

The supported seat cover was then reapplied with the nails. A length of dyed tape was laid

Figure 3.6 Underside of the Mermaid chair after treatment, showing the tape-edged, transparent mesh in place. (TCC neg no. 83-0001, 23a)

between the nails and the plush to give a good line and to prevent the nails from cutting into the plush. Some of the nails had to be repaired before replacement. Heads and shanks were re-soldered to make them strong enough to take the hammer blows required to replace them. The temporary bottoming was removed and replaced by nylon monofilament screening, cut to shape and edged with red-dyed cotton tape. The timber was too weak to withstand hammer blows, so the screening was secured with brass thumb-tacks pressed into the wood. This transparent bottoming allows the original rushing to be viewed, while helping to prevent further loss of the rushes, and allowing access to the base for occasional surface cleaning (Figure 3.6).

3.6 Discussion

Archival research indicated that Burges' original design was for a chair with rush seating (Burges, n.d., 27), suggesting that the plush upholstery was a later addition. Although Pullan's photographs of Tower House show similar chairs, none of the plates shows either the Mermaid or Merman chairs, as has been suggested (Mordaunt Crook, 1981b: 86). The painted chair next to the Mermaid fireplace in Pullan's photograph of Burges' bedroom is similar to the Mermaid chair, but it has a backrest of four turned spindles (1885: Plates 26 and 27; and Mordaunt Crook, 1981b: 65). However, it does have rush seating. Pullan's photograph of Burges' dressing table (1885: Plate 30) shows an upholstered painted chair, very similar to the Mermaid chair, but with a leather top cover and spaced decorative nailing. Another chair is shown in Plate 23 of Burges' wardrobe (Pullan, 1885); it is also similar to the Mermaid chair, but it has rush seating, no decorative banding and the backrest is not upholstered.

From the evidence of Burges' drawings and from the photographs of Tower House, it appears that the Mermaid chair was originally intended to have rush seating. This view is endorsed by Norah Gillow, Keeper of the William Morris Gallery, Walthamstow, who recently reported[2] that another example of the chair with rush seating came to light in 1995. It is identical in style to the Mermaid and Merman chairs at the William Morris Gallery, but with dark green, instead of red, paintwork and without the paintings of the mermaid and merman.

However, further archival research (D.E.) revealed that 'medieval style' chairs with upholstered top covers were in use in Burges' house on the Strand. For example, a photograph taken in 1876 of Burges' office/sitting room at 15 Buckingham Street, Strand, London shows a small upright chair (Mordaunt Crook, 1981a: Figure 166). Like the Mermaid chair, this chair has decorative banding, but it has a cloth top cover; nine decorative nails secure the top cover to the chair frame along the proper left edge. Another photograph, taken at the same time, shows two chairs flanking Burges' 'Architecture Cabinet'. The two chairs are both painted in Burges' 'medieval style'. They have been carefully arranged so that outside back of one, painted with a winged mythical beast, is visible. (An engraving of this composition also survives: Handley-Read, 1963: 497). The seats of both these chairs are upholstered in a very similar manner to the chair photographed in Burges' office; for example, there are nine nails along the proper left side of the chair with the winged beast on the outer back. The office chair appears identical to the two shown with the 'Architecture Cabinet'. They could be three matching chairs, or perhaps there were only two chairs, and one was moved around to accommodate the needs of the photographer.

3.7 Conclusion

The material evidence of the Mermaid chair itself and research into Burges' designs allowed the following deductions to be made. The chair had been manufactured with a rushed seat, following Burges' original design. Sometime after the chair was made, an upholstered seat was added. It consisted of layers of horsehair and stitched hessian secured to the added timber, and probably had a top cover of the red wool fabric. Later the red wool top cover was replaced with the present top cover of stamped plush, close-nailed to the painted frame, and the dark-brown bottoming fabric was added. Whether Burges instigated alterations to his original chair design is not known. The presence of several chairs with upholstered seats at Tower House, as noted above, suggests that he was not averse to upholstery with decorative nailing. The seat covers preserved on the Mermaid chair may provide evidence for changes in Burges' own designs for 'medieval style' furniture.

At some point, perhaps when the rushing and bottoming fabric began to degrade, the plywood was added to the front seat rail and as a 'bottoming' layer. (A photograph published in 1967 shows the Mermaid chair with a solid (presumably the plywood) bottoming: Watkinson, c. 1979: Plate 40). It was in this state that the chair was received into the museum's collection.

The conservation treatment was considered successful in that the plush seat cover was cleaner, softer to the touch, less vulnerable to loss and damage, and the slit was less disfiguring. The treatment was also effective in preserving evidence of the various forms of the seat, by making the original rush seating visible, while at the same time preserving the later upholstery.

Notes

1 Personal communication with Derek Balfour when upholstery tutor at the London College of Furniture, 1982.
2 Keeper's letter to Kathryn Gill of 9/3/2000.

Acknowledgements

We are pleased to acknowledge Norah Gillow, Keeper, William Morris Gallery, Walthamstow, UK, for her help and advice, and Nell Hoare, Director, Textile Conservation Centre, for permission to publish.

References

Burges, W. (1865) Furniture. In: W. Burges, *Art Applied to Industry: a Series of Lectures.* Oxford and London: John Henry and James Parker, pp. 69–82.

Burges, W. (n.d.). *Furniture Album.* Victoria & Albert Museum, Prints and Drawings Department, Album 93.E.8.

Cornforth, J. (1992) Velvet stamp duty. *Country Life*, 1 October 1992, pp. 76–7.

Doyal, S. (1982a) Daybook. Unpublished records. Property of the author.

Doyal, S. (1982b) Conservation Report 0432a. Unpublished Report, The Textile Conservation Centre.

Handley-Read, C. (1963) Notes on William Burges's painted furniture. *Burlington Magazine*, **CV**: 496–509.

Handley-Read, C. (1966) Aladdin's Palace in Kensington. *Country Life*, 17 March, pp. 600–4.

Hodgkins, V. and Bloxham, C. (1981 [1980]). *Banbury and Shutford Plush.* Oxford: Banbury Historical Society/ Oxford Museum.

Mordaunt Crook, J. (1981a) *William Burges and the High Victorian Dream.* London: John Murray (Publishers) Ltd.

Mordaunt Crook, J. (ed.) (1981b) *The Strange Genius of William Burges, 'Art-Architect', 1827–1881.* A catalogue to a Centenary Exhibition organised jointly by the National Museum of Wales, Cardiff, and the Victoria & Albert Museum, London. Cardiff: National Museum of Wales.

Pullan, R.P. (ed.) (1885) *The House of William Burges*, ARA. London.

Wainwright, R. (1981) Pre-Raphaelite furniture. In: J. Mordaunt Crook (ed.) *The Strange Genius of William Burges, 'Art-Architect', 1827–1881.* A catalogue to a Centenary Exhibition organised jointly by the National Museum of Wales, Cardiff, and the Victoria & Albert Museum, London. Cardiff: National Museum of Wales, pp. 67–70.

Watkinson, R. (c.1979) *William Morris as Designer.* London: Studio Vista.

4

Developments in untacked re-upholstery: the Denon chairs project

Derek Balfour, Simon Metcalf and Frances Collard

4.1 Introduction

This chapter explains how a pair of early nineteenth-century French chairs were re-upholstered using conventional techniques and materials but without tacking into the original frames (Figure 4.1). The adoption of this non-intrusive approach allows the use of historically appropriate upholstery methods to create the upholstery as well as to protect historical information on the frames. In this way two, often opposing, objectives are reconciled. The essential elements of the treatment were to minimise damage to the frames, to re-

Figure 4.1 The Denon chairs after treatment, with the removable upholstery *in situ*. (Victoria & Albert Museum)

create upholstery that was removable so that further study of the frame would be possible without too much difficulty, and to make the upholstery appear as authentic as possible by using conventional upholstery techniques and materials on detachable 'shells'.

This case history explains the choice of materials and techniques, the processes involved and how the desired aims were realised. The necessary research by curators and conservators is also included.

4.2 The Denon chairs

The Denon chairs, in an Egyptian Revival style, were designed by Baron Dominique Vivant Denon (1747–1825), the influential and self-proclaimed champion of the Egyptian Revival style in France (Denon, 1802). Denon is known to have owned two examples of the chairs and a day bed *en suite*, made by the firm of Jacob-Desmalter in Paris, all described in detail in the catalogue for the sale of his property after his death (Dubois, 1826: 189–90). Denon's furniture has not yet been traced but the catalogue description refers to silver inlay on the chairs. The two chairs that are the subject of this case history have gilt-bronze inlay and were also made by Jacob-Desmalter. The firm's name, as used between 1803 and 1813, is stamped into the seat frames, which gives a clear date for their manufacture.

These two chairs were sold to a foreign buyer by Christie's on 16 November 1995, lot 344. As a result of the temporary deferral of the export licence, the chairs were purchased jointly by the Victoria & Albert Museum (W.6-1996) and by the National Museums and Galleries on Merseyside (Walker Art Gallery WAG-1996.64) in 1996. This joint acquisition of highly important examples of the Egyptian Revival style by two national museums attracted a great deal of interest and it was decided that the chairs should be upholstered in the same manner at the Victoria & Albert Museum, where the necessary curatorial and conservation expertise was available. The deadline for the project was the public display of the two chairs in their newly upholstered form in the Victoria & Albert Museum in January 1997.

Curators from both museums collaborated on the historical research necessary for the re-upholstery of the Denon chairs; such research is an essential feature of any successful upholstery conservation project. Although French sources were thoroughly investigated, the only contemporaneous reference found to chairs of the same design was that to Denon's own pair. No details of the upholstery were given in the 1826 sale catalogue of his collection (Dubois, 1826). However, the inventory of his collection, on which the catalogue was based, lists the chairs as having been in his bedroom and includes a description of the curtains and hangings as '*drap gris*' (grey drap), drap being a finely woven wool (Anon., 1825). In the absence of any other clues to the original upholstery, a grey wool with a smooth warp-faced weave was chosen for the new top covers with a simple matching braid.

To date, the earliest English reference found to Denon's Egyptian Revival furniture is dated 1819. The novelist Maria Edgeworth visited Deepdene, Surrey, the home of Thomas Hope (1769–1831) in 1819 and described 'a bed made exactly after the model of Denon's Egyptian bed, a sofa bed wide enough for two aldermen' (Colvin, 1971: 197). Hope, a renowned connoisseur and collector who visited Paris in 1803 and in 1815–17, is known to have admired Denon's designs and may therefore have acquired a day bed and chairs similar to those belonging to Denon. Although the day bed described by Maria Edgeworth has not been traced, a pair of chairs were included in the sale of the Hope Heirlooms at Deepdene in 1917, when they were acquired by the noted Regency collector Edward Knoblock (Christie, Manson and Woods, 1917, lot 140). In 1922 the chairs were covered with a striped silk fabric (Jourdain, 1922: 223, fig. 339; 260, fig. 426). At the sale of Knoblock's collection in 1946 the chairs were acquired by another collector, Ian Phillips, and subsequently sold by his executors at Christie's in 1995 and are the chairs that are the subject of this case history.

When sold in 1995 the 'Hope' chairs were covered in a different striped yellow silk fabric, probably applied during the post-Second World War period. They had been upholstered in a manner that obscured their

Empire origins. Wooden extension frames had been added to the front rails to accommodate springs and under-upholstery. Between the 1995 sale at Christie's and the joint acquisition by the V&A Museum and NMGM all the existing upholstery, none of it original, was removed and repairs to the frame and minor repairs to the woodwork and the gilt-bronze inlay were carried out by a firm of restorers for the overseas buyer. The upholstery that had been removed during the restorations was acquired with the chairs and remains in each of the museums' collections.

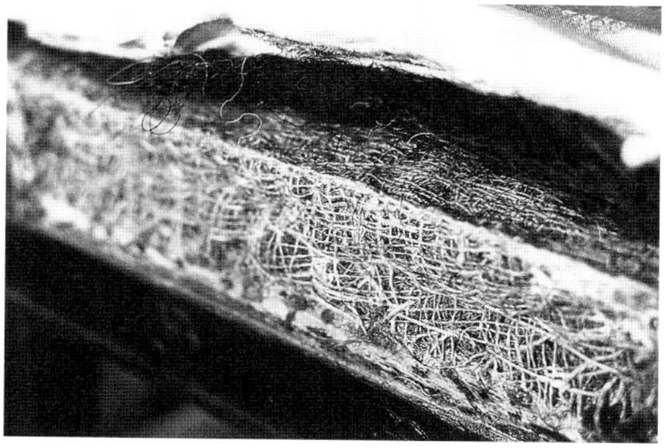

Figure 4.2 One of the chairs made by Jacob that retains its original upholstery structure and shows the upholstery stitching that helps to form the profile of the seat

4.3 Preliminary investigations

When received at the V&A Museum in 1996 the chairs lacked any upholstery, and it was therefore possible to examine the frames thoroughly for evidence of textiles that might relate to the original or subsequent covers. Unfortunately, the only fibres found related to the top covers that had been removed prior to the chairs coming to the V&A. The tacking pattern for webbing on the drop-in seat was inconsistent with the French practice of interweaving wide webbing without spaces. Instead the upholsterer appeared to have used narrow webbing with wide spaces between each, in the English manner. Although the chairs are known to have been made in France, the webbing pattern on the drop-in seat suggests either that the chair frames were exported and upholstered in England, or that the present drop-in seat frames are not original, even though (like the chair frame) they have been upholstered several times.

4.3.1 Upholstery constructions and profiles

It was necessary to establish what profiles the original upholstery might have had, and a set of furniture[1] made by the Jacob workshop and now in the V&A collection was a logical starting point for this investigation. Although their overall design is very different, the seats have a similar curved front rail and crisp vertical sides to the upholstery that was considered applicable to the Denon chairs. Part of the set was investigated and the seat structure of two of the chairs[2] was found to be intact. The upholstery retained the original very open-weave scrim enclosing curled horsehair. Linen twine upholstery stitching worked through the sides of the stuffing produced the crisp vertical profiles. The twine upholstery stitches closely matched the yarn of the open scrim, making it very difficult to trace the exact form of the stitches; basically they appeared to follow the simple looped stitch characteristic of Continental and English upholstery of the early nineteenth century (Figure 4.2). The design and structure of the backs of these chairs is very different from the scroll crest rail on the Denon chairs. However, a chair of a slightly earlier date but with a scroll crest rail, and possibly by the Jacob family, is illustrated in *World Furniture* (Philp, 1980: 142). The illustration shows the profile of the inside back to be quite flat with seams down each side creating crisp lines. This square stitched edge (*a tablet*) for seats and backs was particularly favoured in France in the late eighteenth and early nineteenth century. It was therefore decided to reupholster the Denon chairs with crisp vertical sides on the seat, and a flat profile on the inside back, with a crisp line at each side.

4.3.2 Mock-up for the upholstery profiles

The team of conservators and curators agreed that a mock up of the upholstery should be produced, using cardboard, expanded polyethylene foam (Ethafoam™),[3] polyester wadding and calico. This gave the appearance of upholstery but it was possible to alter its thickness and gradient, especially on the inside back and over the top of the crest rail, and to work out details of the finish. Positions of seams in the top cover were plotted, as were positions and width of trimming. Placing fabric samples on the mock-up enabled visualisation of the finished upholstery at an earlier stage than would otherwise have been possible. The mock-up, together with lessons learned on a previous non-intrusive upholstery treatment (Balfour *et al.*, 1999), enabled the team to work out the practical details of the project and finalise the treatment proposal.

4.4 Treatment proposal

It was agreed:

- that the re-upholstery should be based on the information found during the historical research;
- to base the upholstery on what was already known about techniques and materials of the period and the information found on the Jacob chairs in the collection of the V&A Museum;
- that the upholstery should not be tacked directly on to the frame in order to eliminate damage to the chairs;
- that the re-upholstery should be made removable to allow further study of the frames.

The idea behind such re-upholstery is simple. A birch-ply[4] frame (secondary frame) is made to fit within the original frame of the chair. Metal plates, shaped to follow the contours of the parts of the frame that have to be upholstered, are attached to the plywood secondary frame. Strong cotton fabric is used as a binding around the outer edges of the metal plates; the textile layers used to create the upholstery are stitched onto this binding fabric (Figures 4.3 and 4.4).

For ease of reference the following terms were assigned to the various parts of the removable upholstery structures:

- module: the new structures, complete with their upholstery;

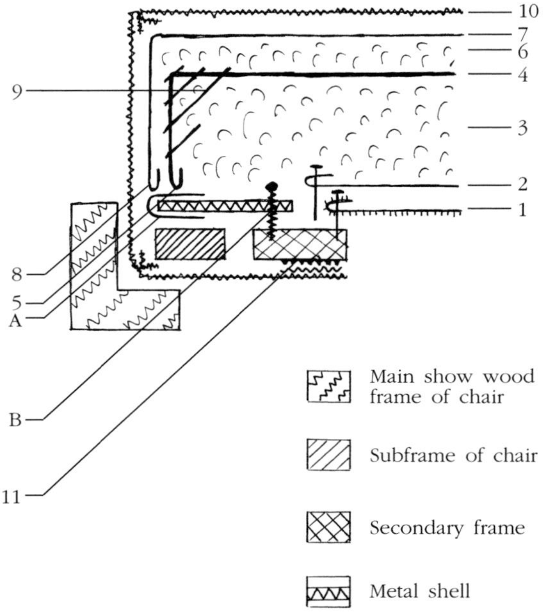

Figure 4.3 Diagram illustrating the cross-section of one seat after the re-upholstery

A Cotton binding stitched to the edge of the metal shell
B Screw attaching the metal shell to the secondary frame (plywood)
1 Webbing tacked to secondary frame
2 Base cloth tacked to secondary frame
3 First filling (horsehair)
4 First filling cover (linen scrim)
5 First filling cover stitched to metal shell binding
6 Second filling (horsehair)
7 Second filling cover (linen)
8 Second filling cover stitched to cotton binding on metal shell
9 Linen twine forming upholstery stitches
10 Top cover of grey wool
11 Top cover held onto secondary frame with hook and loop fastening (Velcro™), loop side stitched to top cover, hook side stapled to secondary frame

- secondary frame: the wooden part of the module that sits within the original chair frame and to which the shell is attached;
- shell: the metal parts of the module that cover the tacking areas of the chair frame and to which most of the textile layers of the upholstery are stitched;
- cotton binding: the strong cotton fabric that covers the edges of the shell and to which the textile layers of the upholstery are stitched.

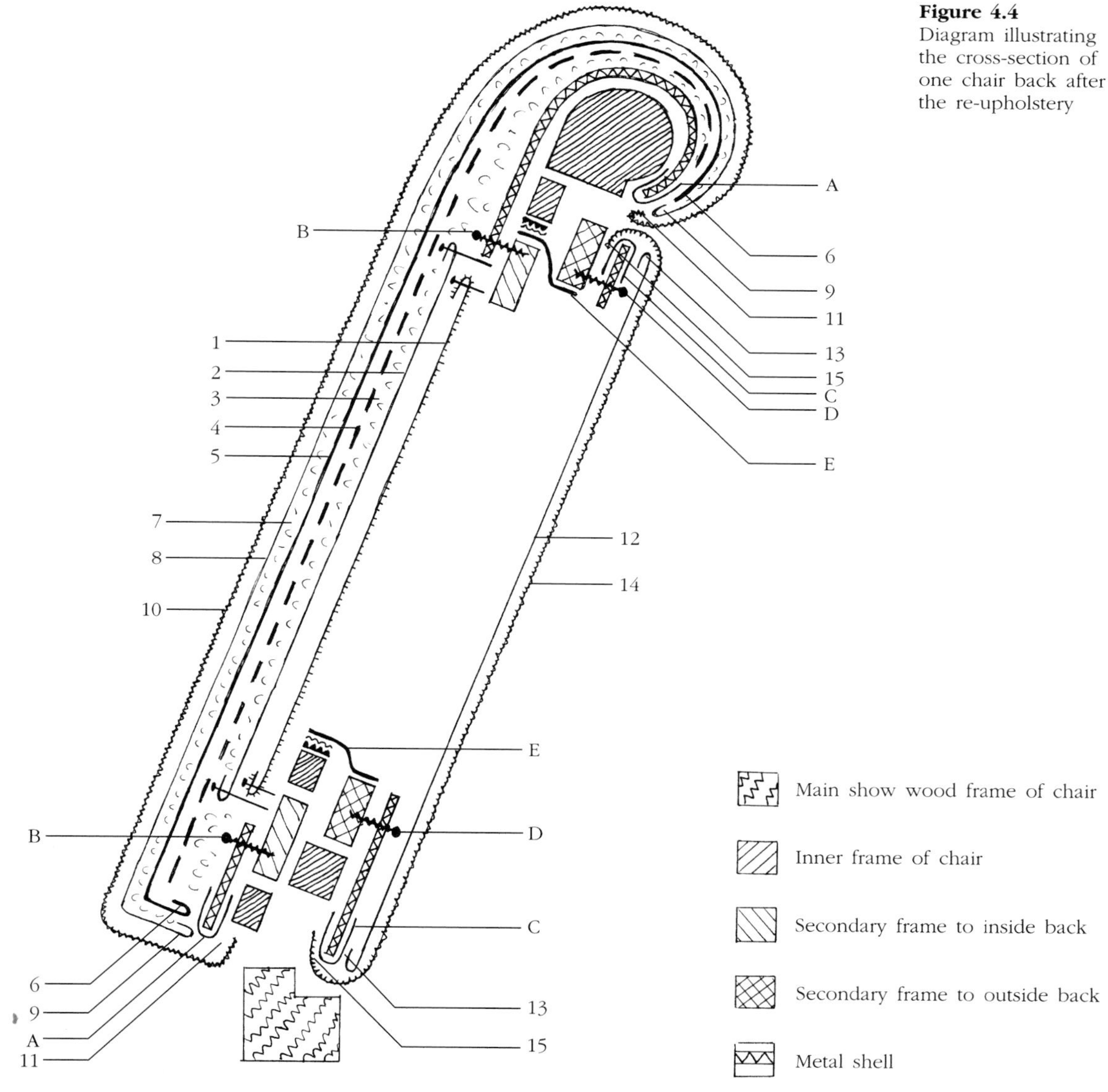

Figure 4.4
Diagram illustrating the cross-section of one chair back after the re-upholstery

A Cotton binding stitched to the edge of the metal shell
B Screws attaching the metal shell to the secondary frame (plywood)
1 Webbing tacked to secondary frame
2 Base cloth tacked to secondary frame
3 First filling (horsehair)
4 Linen twine upholstery stitches
5 First filling cover
6 First filling cover stitched to cotton binding on metal shell
7 Second filling (horsehair)
8 Second filling cover (linen)
9 Second filling cover stitched to cotton binding on metal shell
10 Top cover (grey wool)
11 Top cover stitched to cotton binding on metal shell

Outside back
C Cotton binding stitched to the edge of the metal shell
D Screws attaching the metal shell to the secondary frame (plywood)
E Tab holding the secondary frame onto the chair with hook and loop fastener (Velcro™)
12 Lining (cotton)
13 Lining stitched to cotton binding on metal shell
14 Top cover (grey wool)
15 Top cover stitched to cotton binding on metal shell

4.5 Design requirements

The positioning of the modules on the chair frame had to be uncomplicated so that they could be removed with the help of straightforward written instructions. It was therefore decided the seat module had to drop into the chair frame, the inside back module had to hook over the crest rail, and the outside back module had to fit within the back of the chair (Figures 4.5 and 4.6).

The seats and inside backs were to be fully upholstered (as they had been originally) but the outside backs had to appear as simple flat pieces of top cover fabric with trimming around the edge. The seat module had to incorporate the existing drop-in seat frame but the frame had to be accessible (Figure 4.7).

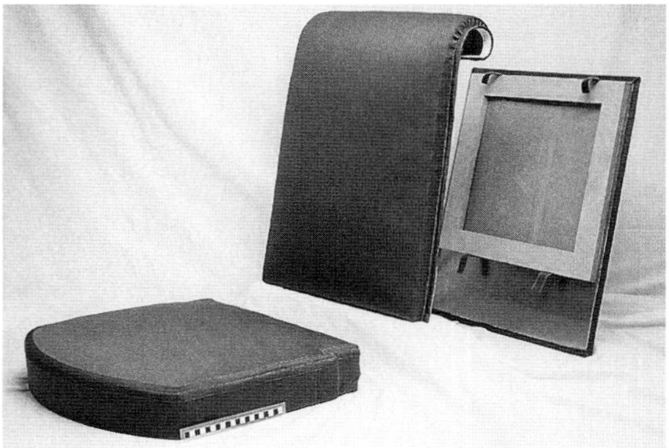

Figure 4.6 A set of completed modules before being positioned on one of the chairs (*left*: seat module; *middle*: inside back module; *right*: outside back module). The outside back (*right*) shows the secondary wooden frame, part of the stainless steel shell, and the hook and loop (Velcro™) tabs, which hold it onto the chair

Figure 4.5 One of the Denon chairs before treatment. The repair work undertaken by the firm of restorers before the chairs were acquired by the two museums is visible on the back. The drop-in seat frame is also visible. Despite close examination, no traces of original textile fibres were found

Figure 4.7 One of the seat modules, viewed from the underside. Two of the Velcro™ edged flaps of the top cover have been folded back, revealing the existing drop-in seat frame

4.5.1 Selecting materials and making the modules

Before work started on constructing the metal shell the following aims were set:

- to minimise the possibility of corrosion of the metal shell which supported the non-intrusive upholstery;
- to keep the manufacture of the metal plates as simple as possible;
- to avoid the use of adhesives that will deteriorate, in order to increase the longevity of the treatment.

With these aims in mind the search for the best metal for the shell of the chair was begun.

Whatever type of metal was to be used for the treatment it had to have the key properties listed below:

- be as chemically stable as possible;
- have the correct mechanical properties, e.g. it would have to be capable of being shaped to the required form using the equipment available in the Conservation Department; and be rigid enough to not distort when the upholstery was constructed over the shell;
- be thin enough so that the shell was invisible under the new upholstery.

Stainless steel was researched as a possible material due to its reputation for corrosion resistance. Avesta Sheffield, a major stainless steel manufacturer in the UK, was consulted to find out if stainless steel would be suitable. It was found that L316 grade stainless steel of 1 mm thickness had all the required properties, the only disadvantage identified being that the metal's toughness would make it difficult (but not impossible) to shape by hand. It was concluded that this drawback was outweighed by the steel's other advantages.

The shape of the Denon chair carcasses meant the metal plates forming the shell were required to be mostly flat, making the manufacture relatively simple. However, the crest rail presented major difficulties because of the tight curve that the metal plate had to be shaped to follow (Figure 4.8). To make the shell follow the shape of the chair, accurate templates were crucial. These were made using a combination of card, polyester film (Melinex™) and 5 mm diameter plastic-coated electrical wire (for curved areas). These templates were then used to mark out the required plates for the shell on the stainless steel sheet, using an indelible marker.

The toughness of stainless steel made it impossible to cut out large plates with hand shears, therefore mechanical shears had to be employed. Even with electrically powered shears this part of the process was difficult and potentially hazardous. As each plate was cut the metal tended to distort, and the freshly cut edges were very sharp. After roughly cutting out each plate they were finely adjusted to fit the chair frame using hand files. The curved crest rail plate was formed using conventional metal-shaping techniques, with a rawhide mallet and metal working stakes.

(a)

(b)

Figure 4.8 The metal shell and the secondary frame when in position on the inside back of a Denon chair: (a) front view; (b) rear view. The tight curve of the steel around the crest rail is evident. The front view also shows how the shell is screwed to the secondary wood frame. Also visible along one side of the shell are the holes to which the upholstery was stitched

Holes 2 mm in diameter were drilled at 10 mm intervals at a constant 10 mm from the edge. The idea was adapted from the construction of historic armour (Blair, 1958; Ffoulkes, 1988 [1912]), where textile linings had to be attached to metal plates (Figures 4.9 and 4.10). The use of holes and stitching as a way of joining the upholstery to the shell has several advantages. The holes avoid the need to use adhesives. Also the option to change the upholstery at a later date if desired is made possible: cutting the stitches securing the upholstery would release the upholstery,

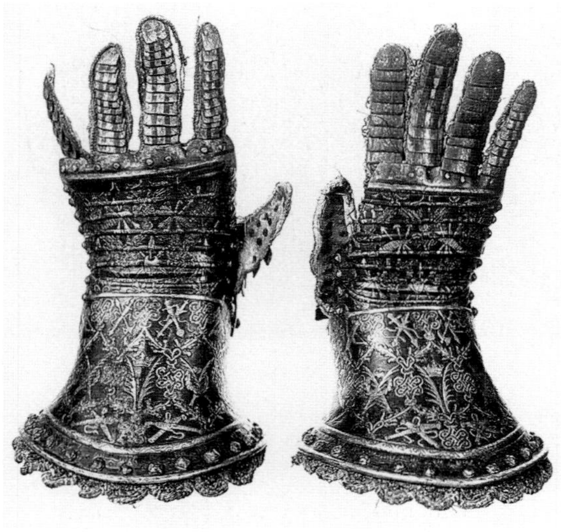

Figure 4.9 A pair of gauntlets c.1614 from armour ordered by Phillip III of Spain, now in the V&A's collection (1386.a-1888). The original textiles are still *in situ*. The fabric around the cuffs is held in place by being stitched to a leather binding strip, which is riveted to the metal through a series of holes. (Victoria & Albert Museum)

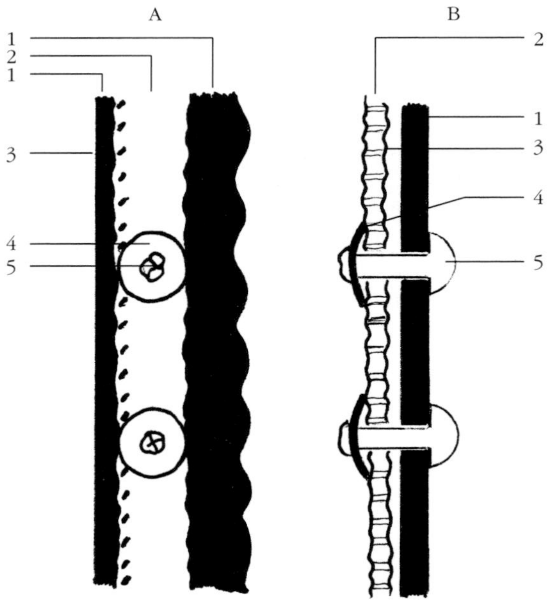

Figure 4.10 Typical construction method used in historic armour for attaching textile linings. A cloth or leather strip is riveted to the armour plate. The textile linings are then stitched to this binding strip and can, therefore, be replaced without dismantling the armour

A: plan view of the inside surface
1 Armour plate
2 Cloth or leather binding strip on the inside of the armour
3 Stitching holes where the textile lining would be sewn
4 Iron washer
5 Iron rivet

B: cross section
1 Armour plate
2 Cloth or leather strip
3 Stitch holes
4 Washer
5 Rivet

allowing re-use of the base part of the module. The optimum size of the holes for easy drilling and stitching on of the binding tape was found to be 2 mm. Sharp edges were removed by chamfering with a hand file and then countersinking each hole from both sides. Removing all sharp edges avoids the danger of stitching being cut. To avoid future corrosion of the stainless steel it is important to use clean tools and to avoid contamination of the stainless steel (e.g. by filings generated from using dirty files or wire wool) which can lead to rusting.

When each shell was completed it was marked with the year of the conservation treatment. The metal sheet was dated using steel number punches and a hammer, before being cleaned with acetone. Where possible modern parts or materials added to an historic object are physically marked with the year the part was added and/or a V&A logo. This is done in addition to recording details in a treatment report. Date stamping of new parts provides future curators and conservators with an obvious and permanent record of what has been added on the actual object and when this addition was made. The individual plates of the shells were then attached to the secondary frame using stainless steel screws. The use of stainless steel screws avoids the possibility of galvanic corrosion occurring in the future, which can result if differing metal alloys are in contact with each other.

The plywood secondary frames were made by a member of the V&A's Furniture Conservation staff.[5] They were made to fit within the original chair frame with a small allowance of approximately 2 mm for movement and to allow for any dimensional change in the original frame due to fluctuations

Figure 4.11 The shell for the inside back, showing the cotton binding stitched onto the edge of the metal shell

Figure 4.12 One seat module sitting on one of the existing drop-in seat frames. The completed under-upholstery is shown before the addition of the top cover. The cotton binding on the edge of the metal shell is visible as a thin white line. Also illustrated is the hole damage to the existing drop-in seat frame, resulting from upholstery tacks. Un-tacked re-upholstery methods avoid causing more of this type of damage

in relative humidity. After the wood and metal elements were screwed together the cloth binding was applied.

White cotton ticking, which has a tight herringbone weave, was used as the binding material around the edge of the metal shell. The edges of the ticking were turned under on both surfaces and sewn in place, using polyester thread, through the holes in the metal plates. This made a strong, neat surface to which the upholstery layers were sewn (Figure 4.11).

4.6 Recreating the upholstery

It is general practice in upholstery and textile conservation to scour new materials to remove undesirable finishes incorporated during the manufacturing process. Some materials become very soft and elastic after scouring; this is not advantageous where they have to support and restrain new upholstery filling. The fabrics used in this re-upholstery were not scoured and the finishes were not identified.

Webbing and a heavy linen fabric were attached to the plywood secondary frames to support the horsehair filling. The upholstery profiles were created by applying curled horsehair on top of the linen base cloth; the horsehair was then enclosed in linen scrim (an open-weave linen cloth) which was tucked under the horsehair and stitched to the cotton binding. Linen twine was used to form large stitches through the filling; the stitches pass from the sidewalls, through the filling, to the top surface of the pad. They help to create the profile and also hold the filling in place. Following conventional upholstery practice, to add the final sharp line to the profile a row of blanket stitches was formed around the top edge of the seat and down each side of the inside back. The top surface of the pad has another, but thinner, layer of hair added and the whole is then enclosed in fine linen. Again this is turned under around the edge and stitched to the cotton binding (Figure 4.12). The upholstery for both the seat and the inside back modules was created in this way.

4.6.1 Top cover and trimming

The top seat cover was made with a border seamed around the top edge to help retain the sharp profile to the curve of the seat. The existing drop-in seat frame was incorporated into the seat module, and remains removable. The underside of the cover is held in place by four flaps that wrap over the drop-in frame and are attached to the plywood secondary frame with hook and loop fastener (Velcro™), holding the existing frame in place (see Figure 4.7). Silk trimming is stitched to the top and sides of the seat upholstery; together they outline the shape of the seat. The inside back top cover has seams down each side and these help to emphasise the upholstery profile. Trimming is applied down each side at the junction of the cover and the show-wood. In conventional upholstery the trimming hides the tacks attaching the cover to the frame.

The module to the outside back was not stuffed, but was simply lined with cotton fabric. In this case the top cover was wrapped around the edges of the module and sewn to the cotton binding on the reverse. The trimming was sewn to the top cover, around all four sides, so that it butted against the show-wood of the frame when the module was in position. The module was fixed into the chair with tabs of hook and loop fastener (see Figure 4.6) that were stapled to the new internal parts of the frame, thus avoiding damage to the original chair structure.

4.7 Evaluation of treatment

Although time-consuming, but close to the estimated hours, the treatment met all the objectives that had been agreed at the beginning of the project: the original structure of the chair frame remains accessible for investigation because the upholstered elements are easily removed: the re-upholstery incorporates appropriate techniques and materials, and the top cover and trimming can be replaced easily.

4.8 Conclusion

This conservation treatment represents only the second un-tacked re-upholstery project undertaken at the Victoria & Albert Museum and an advance on the first project. The stability of stainless steel, the birch ply and durability of the textiles ensures the longevity of the treatment. The upholstery appears to be tacked to the frame in a conventional manner, demonstrating that it is possible to re-upholster seat furniture with appropriate materials and techniques without tacking into the frame. In this way, the approach adopted here reconciled the opposing objectives of re-creating authentic upholstery profiles while protecting vulnerable frames from damage.

Notes

1 The accession numbers of the chairs investigated are W.3:a and b-1978. W.7:b-1987.
2 The museum numbers of the two chairs found to have their seat structure still intact are W.5b and W.8b-1978.
3 This expanded polyethylene foam is a rigid inert carvable material.
4 Birch ply was used because of its stability and availability while taking into account the adhesives used in its manufacture. In this instance there are no original or earlier textiles to be taken into account.
5 The wooden secondary frames were made by Timothy Hayes, Senior Conservator, V&A Furniture Conservation Section.

Acknowledgements

We would like to thank the Victoria & Albert Museum and the National Museums and Galleries on Merseyside (Walker Art Gallery) for permission to publish, Nicola Gentle for her drawings and suggestions on the diagrams, and Timothy Hayes for his work on the chairs. Thanks are also due to curatorial and conservation colleagues for their help and support during this project.

References

Anon. (1825). Inventaire après le décès de M. le Baron Denon. *Archives Nationale, Paris.* MN Etude VC 1541.

Balfour, D., Metcalf, S. and Collard, F. (1999) The first non-intrusive upholstery treatment at the Victoria and Albert Museum. *The Conservator,* **23**: 22–9, 46.

Blair, C. (1958) *European Armour.* London: B.T. Batsford Ltd.

Christie, Manson and Woods (1917) *Catalogue of Objects of Art Porcelain Old English and Other Furniture being a Portion of the Hope Heirlooms Removed from Deepdene, Dorking* (Sale: 18 July). London: Christie, Manson & Woods.

Colvin, C. (ed.) (1971) *Maria Edgeworth: Letters from England 1813–44.* Oxford: Clarendon

Denon, D.V., Baron (1802) *Voyage dans la Basse et la Haute Egypt, pendant les campagnes du Gënëral Bonaparte.* Paris: P. Didot.

Dubois, L.J.-J. (1826) Description des objets d'art qui composent le cabinet de feu M. le Baron V. Denon: estampes et ouvrages à figures, par Duchesne âiné. In: L.J-J. Dubois (ed.), *Monuments antiques, historiques, modernes; ouvrages orientaux, etc.,* Vol. III. Paris: Imprimerie d'Hippolyte Tilliard.

Ffoulkes, C. (1988 [1912]) *The Armourer and his Craft.* New York: Dover Publications.

Jourdain, M. (1922) *English Furniture of the Later XVIIIth Century.* London: B.T. Batsford Ltd.

Philp, P. (1980) The Empire style. In: N. Riley (ed.), *World Furniture.* London: Octopus Books, pp. 141–59.

5

Reconciling conservation and interpretation: strategies for long-term display of a late seventeenth-century bed

Nancy C. Britton

5.1 Introduction

The renovation and re-installation of the Aitken Galleries in the European Sculpture and Decorative Arts Department at the Metropolitan Museum of Art initiated the possibility of conserving one of the two 1697 state beds from Hampton Court in Herefordshire, UK for exhibition in the new galleries. Conservation planning began in 1992 with the opening scheduled for 1995. The initial approach was to assess the condition of both state beds in the collection: the red damask bed (68.217.2), which has a flying tester, and the blue damask bed, with four posts (68.217.1). After selecting the blue bed, the documentation and evaluation of the condition of its various components was undertaken, a treatment plan was developed and implemented, and finally, the re-assembly and installation of the bed took place in the galleries (Plate 5.1).

This chapter focuses on the complex problems posed in conserving the textile components of the blue bed, and the influences bearing upon the decisions made. The final treatment included the use of reproduction textiles. Issues arising from the use of reproduction textiles, the selection and manufacture of appropriate reproduction textiles, the fabrication of missing components and the non-intrusive attachment system developed for the bed are discussed. Other aspects of the textile conservation treatment of the blue bed, the wood conservation or the careful orchestration of the many conservators and specialists that contributed to the project are not discussed here. Also, general issues arising from the integration of replica components within a conservation treatment have been discussed elsewhere (e.g. Oddy, 1994) and are not covered here.

5.2 Treatment goals

The many factors that shape the wide range of possible treatment choices can be divided into two broad categories: external and internal. For the state bed the most important factors were the exhibition space, exhibition design, object interpretation, information on the object, object provenance and object condition. The first three issues are external considerations related to exhibition and environmental concerns. The latter three are internal considerations arising from the object itself.

Internal object considerations largely guided the selection of the blue bed rather than the red one. The blue state bed had been put in storage in an attic at Hampton Court early in the nineteenth century, thereby exempting it from the subsequent restorations that the red bed, which remained in constant use, had been subjected to. With the exception of some clearly identifiable early twentieth-century post-discovery restoration, such as the stitched stabilisation of splits and tears in the original curtains and valances, the inaccurate reconstruction and placement of other parts, and the loss of the original coverlet and foot curtains, the blue bed's remaining textiles were in a surprisingly intact and stable condition.

External factors narrowed the treatment choices. The exhibition space was designed to replicate the approximate dimensions of a room in a seventeenth-century English country house. The exhibition design aimed to maintain a room-like ambience by the use of low, unobtrusive platforms to display the furniture, the absence of barriers and the careful placement of furniture. The blue state bed – dimensions 365.7 cm (12 ft) high, 152 cm (5 ft) wide and 198 cm (6.5 ft) long – fills the far end of the gallery opposite the main visitor entry, accentuating the magnificence of this object. From a conservation point of view it was important to recognise that the exhibit design would allow the visitor an easy reach to the foot curtains. Additionally, the 'permanent' status of these galleries required long-term exhibition of these objects. This resulted in long-term conservation treatment concerns and a long-term care plan.

5.3 Preliminary investigations for condition and risk assessment

The preliminary investigation of this large, complex object suggested three categories of media within the state bed, wood-only, textile-on-wood and textile-only[1]. The wood-only substructure included the bed rails, and head and foot posts; the textile-on-wood components consisted of the cornice frames, cartouche, headboard and base moldings; and the textile-only components consisted of foot and head curtains, cantoons[2] (two short curtains hanging on iron forks at the side/foot juncture of the tester cornice), the headcloth, upper inner and outer valances, lower or base valances, mattress sack cloth and the tester. Conservation specialists were assigned to each of the three categories, and separate treatment proposals were developed accordingly.

The textiles-on-wood components were deemed to be in a sufficiently stable condition overall to withstand the demands of long-term exhibition. They were supported by the wood substrate, and were shown to have a satisfactory pH ranging between 4.7 and 5.5. Some sections of the adhered textiles had detached and required reattachment. Protruding areas of the carved and damask-covered wood motifs had suffered abrasion with resulting losses. In other areas there were breaks in the underlying wood; this necessitated temporary lifting of textile sections to allow the wood conservator access to the substrate for stabilisation treatments.

Assessing the condition of the silk hangings was of primary concern. Water marks on the lower edge of the proper left head curtain and the base valances indicated water damage, which had resulted in the weakening of the silk damask in these areas with occasional splits and losses. Some of these splits had been repaired early in the twentieth century. The unlined silk curtains were found to have a pH between 4.4 and 4.7, and the silk in the protected and lined inner valances ranged between pH 5.0 and 5.5. This surprising difference between the free-hanging unlined silk's lower pH and the adhered silk suggested that the hide-glue might have behaved as a buffer between the wood and the textile. Additionally, the free-hanging silk with its unlined construction probably functioned as a filter for passing air currents, trapping contaminants that lowered the pH. All these observations suggested that, although the textile-only elements appeared to be in a good and stable condition, they were in fact more fragile than they appeared initially.

The bed's proximity to visitors and the fact that it was to be on 'permanent' display increased the risks for the textile-only components. The selection of the blue bed on the basis of its value as a relatively well-preserved document heightened the concern for the safety of the textiles. Initial options had included a stitched stabilisation treatment or the use of an adhesive treatment for the textile-only hangings. However, all of the concerns noted above led to the decision to abandon the option of treating and displaying the original textile-only components and to consider an alternative option: that of putting the original textile-only components in study-storage and displaying the bed with hangings made of reproduction fabric. Preparing specifications for the reproduction textiles became an important element in the overall conservation and exhibition strategy.

5.4 Issues in using reproduction fabric and trims

The decision to use a reproduction fabric is a complex one requiring careful consideration of a spectrum of issues. Primary among them for the state bed were the aesthetic considerations of integrating a contemporary reproduction textile with aged original textiles, and the conservation concerns of documenting and identifying contemporary materials and keeping them discernible from original materials. From the perspective of the exhibition, the bed could not have been interpreted back to its original presentation without the introduction of some reproduced textile-only components due to the loss of some original parts. This raised the issue of how to present an interpretation that included reproduction textile components to the viewing public.

To eliminate possible confusion between the original damasks and the reproduction damask, the use of the reproduction fabric was restricted to only two areas of the bed. The entire textile-only component category, consisting of the upper and lower valances, curtains, tester cloth and headcloth, were replaced with replicas fabricated from the reproduction textile. In the case of the textile-on-wood components, infills using the reproduction textile were limited to covering only the large expanses of newly carved wood replacement motifs. This eliminated the scattering and mingling of small infills in the reproduction damask throughout the original damasks on the cornices and headboard (Figure 5.1).

To address the aesthetic concerns, the reproduction textile was required to duplicate precisely the original textile, not only in colour and weave structure but also in fibre, twist, sett, beat and surface sheen. By reproducing the latter characteristics it was hoped that it would be possible to duplicate the drape and hand of the original damask. The quality of the new reproduction fabric also had to reflect the three hundred years of age of the original textiles and the irregularities inherent in hand production.

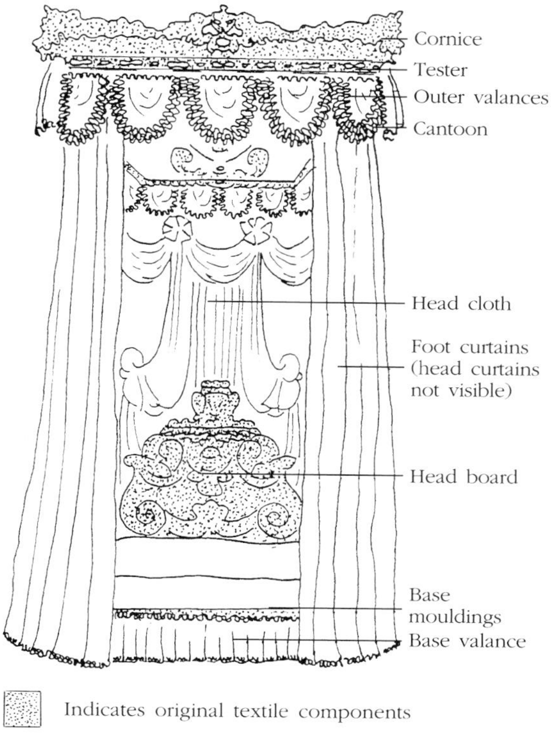

Figure 5.1 Diagram of the state bed after installation at the Aitken Galleries at the Metropolitan Museum of Art, New York, showing the original and reproduction components. (Collection of the Metropolitan Museum of Art, New York. Gift of Mr and Mrs William Randolph Hearst Jr, 1968. 68.217.1.) (Line drawing by Kathryn Gill)

The reproduction process requires the manufacturer to understand the period processes and to translate these hand manufacturing techniques into a contemporary manufacturing setting, which is generally predicated on quantity and standardisation using sophisticated machinery. Furthermore, the satisfactory replication of a textile requires carefully controlling the entire gamut of textile production, from the quality and denier[3] of the fibre to the amount of twist and doubling, through to the dyeing processes, the weave structure and finishing processes.[4]

Identifying an appropriate manufacturer was crucial to the success of this project. A manufacturer was sought whose manufacturing technology closely approximated to that of the period in question, or who had the flexibility and capacity to replicate such period technology.[5] A willingness to work and communicate closely during every process was also essential. Fortunately, in the current high-end silk weaving industry a small number of manufacturers actually retain nineteenth-century hand-operated equipment which can be adapted to produce the effects of seventeenth-century drawloom production and who are willing to accommodate the demands of this type of project.[6]

5.5 Documentation and reproduction of the damask

5.5.1 Pattern and weave analysis

Two variations of a single damask pattern were found on the blue bed: they were identified as Design 1 and Design 2. The pattern is a well-known damask design which has been in almost continual production since the mid-seventeenth century. Design 1 was used more widely in the bed, with Design 2 present only in the fabrication of the tester cloth. The components requiring replication, except the tester cloth, had been made in Design 1; the most expedient and economical decision was to commission the replica fabric only in this design.

The original damask structure of Design 1 was analysed as a five-end satin weave in the warp and a five-end sateen in the weft with 188 ends per cm (480 per inch) and 44–5 picks per cm (112–14 per inch). The repeat length was 117.45 cm (46.24 in) and the width was 50.8 cm (20 in). Design 2 has a shorter vertical repeat of 39 in. The manufacturer commissioned to make the replica damask was already producing three other variations of this well-known damask pattern, but Design 1 on the blue state bed was the longest repeat he knew for this pattern.[7]

For the design to be precisely copied, one of the narrow head curtains was sent to the manufacturer. This curtain was chosen for three reasons: it was flat and relatively small in size, and could be rolled for packing and shipping; it was in sound enough condition to withstand the transatlantic journey to the manufacturer in the UK; and it had a full-length, selvage to selvage, repeat. The original seventeenth-century fabric was woven on a drawloom, but the reproduction damask would be woven on a nineteenth-century hand-operated loom with a Jacquard attachment and a production rate of about two metres per day. The design had to be redrawn and the cards cut for the Jacquard. The draughtsmen who redrew the design carefully retained the characteristics of seventeenth- and eighteenth-century drawloom-woven fabrics, such as the uneven 'stepping' at the satin and sateen interstices. At two picks per card, 2,636 cards were cut for the vertical repeat.

5.5.2 Silk thread preparation

Analysis of the seventeenth-century damask revealed that both its warp and weft were silk filaments; the organzine[8] warp was dyed a dark blue and the tram[9] silk of the weft was a somewhat lighter blue.

Reeled silk filament was procured from China for the reproduction fabric; each filament was composed of seven to eight reeled cocoon ends having a combined denier of 20/22. This filament was used to make both the warps and the weft for the reproduction fabric. To make the warps, the reeled silk warp thread received 6.2 Z twists per cm (16 per inch) during a process known as throwing.[10] Two Z twist threads were then ringdoubled at 5.6 S twists per cm (14 per inch). The resulting thread was then steamed to set the twist, and reeled into skeins ready for dyeing. Threads for the tram wefts of the reproduction fabric were made as follows: six of the 20/22 denier silk filaments were Z twisted at 1.77 twists per cm (4.5 per inch) on the ringdoubler. This small amount of twist is called a 'holding twist'. The higher twist in the organzine imparted the strength required in the warp yarn for it to withstand the loom tension. Having less twist in the weft yarns maximised the impact of the silk's lustre in weft floats.

The amount of twist in the yarns can be used to modulate the quality of the hand, drape and lustre of silk damask. The characteristic feature of damask is the contrast between the figure and the ground in the design. In the original damask, the ground was formed of the more tightly twisted organzine in the higher sett of the warp, while the figure was rendered in the more loosely twisted, lower count tram weft silk (which was therefore more lustrous). Dyeing the warp and weft in different hues or shades can further heighten the ground/figure contrast, as was present in the original damask. These factors were carefully considered when evaluating the samples of reproduction damask, in order to ensure that the desired properties were appropriately replicated in the reproduction fabric, as will be explained further below.

5.5.3 Dyeing

The blue silk damask of the state bed exhibited a colour effect known as strie, which was considered to be a significant feature of the original damask. Strie is a colour change either along the same thread or within a block of contiguous threads and is frequently present in aged silk textiles. Several explanations are given for this inadvertent characteristic of older textiles: irregular dye application techniques, variable and/or mixed dye lots, particular methods used in the winding or warping processes, and irregular colour degradation.

In the case of the blue state bed damask, which had been dyed with indigo, the most likely explanation is the dyeing technique. Indigo is a vat dye whose water-insoluble colourant is applied to the yarn in a leuco (water-soluble) solution and then oxidised on the fibre to achieve its former state as a water-insoluble colourant. An early method of applying indigo was via a 'hanging skein' dyeing technique in which the skein was suspended over the dye vat partially submerged. The submerged yarn absorbs the indigo dye; when the submerged portion of the skein is rotated out of the dye liquor, the indigo oxidises and another portion of the skein is submerged into the dye bath. The newly submerged yarn is in a dye bath with a lower dyestuff concentration because the previously submerged portion of the skein absorbed some of the dyestuff. The 'hanging skein' dyeing method has several advantages, for example, allowing the dyeing of large quantities at one time and preventing the skeins from tangling. However, as a hand process it is almost impossible to achieve an even colour throughout the skein. Since the state bed damask exhibited colour change within single threads rather than blocks of threads, the colour variations were probably due to this 'hanging skein' dyeing technique.

The strie was an important visual characteristic and the manufacturer was asked to duplicate this effect. The manufacturer was able to accommodate this request because he has a fully integrated production system; for example, all the production processes take place on his premises. This manufacturer's dye process was immersion skein dyeing, currently a less frequently used method than package dyeing[11] but more flexible. However, the manufacturer routinely uses acid dyes, not vat dyes. The application of acid dyes is different from that of vat dyeing as outlined above for indigo. In the case of acid dyes, the yarn must remain immersed during the full dyeing cycle if the yarn is to absorb the dye. The manufacturer adapted his standard milling acid dyeing method to dye half a skein at a time rather than rotating the yarn. The dye was prevented from wicking up the skein by tying a 'choke' at the skein's entry point into the dye bath. In this manner, a colour change was achieved within each individual thread (Plate 5.2).

Multiple tints and shades, essential to the varied effect and an important aspect of the visual success, were easily achieved in this way. The reproduction fabric was extremely effective in reproducing the strie effect; the new damask did not exhibit any of the mechanical qualities indicative of post-industrial processes. The final effect was an outstanding replication of the original textile's multiplicity of tones.

5.5.4 Colour matching

Several factors affect the matching of colours between an original and a reproduction textile: the hue translation between two dye classes; the colour mixing of the warp colour with the weft colour when each are different; the distance of the viewer from the object; the object's distance from the light source; the direction and diffusion of the light source (ambient or spot); the intensity of the light (lux or footcandles); the nature of the light source; and, the colour temperature of the light that the object is viewed in. In an exhibition gallery, these factors are interrelated, difficult to separate and hard to control.

Some hue shift should be anticipated when attempting to match colours dyed by different dye classes, in this case the change from the indigo vat dye to the milling acid dye. The colour temperature of the light bulbs and the type of light bulb used, e.g. fluorescent, incandescent, halogen or 'natural light' type, varies this disparity. To help avoid the effects of such metamerism, before attempting to assess the dyed samples and the original, a simulated gallery space was set up with the selected light bulbs, to reproduce the intensity, distance and light quality that would be achieved in the final gallery space. The gallery lighting is a combination of halogen and incandescent at a general ambient light level on the bed of 50 lux (5 footcandles). Spot lighting was limited. The manufacturer was asked to view his samples in a similar lighting condition prior to sending them for our approval.

In a damask, the weave structure and the mix of the warp and weft colours is distributed in such a way that the warp, being denser, nearly covers the weft completely. The result is that the ground of the design is the warp colour. The weft colour is seen in the figure, but the greater proportion of the exposed warp modulates the colour more. The first colour sample assessment was therefore primarily concerned with the selection of a warp colour. The manufacturer wove simple figure/ground stripes so the warp colour, sett, beat and surface quality could be assessed. Once the warp colour was selected, a colour 'blanket' was sent; the blanket was warped with the warp colour chosen, but now with the figure/ground design drawn in and woven with five differently coloured wefts.

This last colour blanket, made to aid choice of the weft colour, was hung in the simulated lighting gallery next to one of the curtains in the original damask. The matches were assessed at the closest visitor viewing point of 4 ft (1.25 m approx.), and then at several increments back to 50 ft (15 m approx.), the longest visitor viewing point. The final choice was achieved with only two sets of woven samples passing between the Metropolitan Museum of Art and Richard Humphries, the UK manufacturer of the reproduction damask.

5.5.5 Reproduction of drape and hand

In addition to precisely reproducing the yarn and weave structure of the original textile, and matching its colour and strie, a less definable quality of the damask had to be achieved in the reproduction textile, namely the drape and hand of the original. The working of the pipe-organ pleats in the headcloth and the drape of the curtains and valances required a damask of a crisp hand. Additionally, a low lustre to the surface quality was desired in the replicated textile to match and blend with the aged surface quality of the original damask. Many of the factors that affect the hand and drape of a textile also affect the lustre. Adjusting the amount of twist imparted to the warp and weft yarns, reducing the length of the floats by increasing the number of interstices and/or using a closer sett and tighter beat in the weave structure, and partial degumming of the silk filaments reduce the lustre and create a crisper hand and stiffer drape.

Important to the structure was the replication of the original five-end satin/sateen in the new fabric. Most reproduction damasks today are woven with an eight-end satin/sateen, which increases the sheen because of the reflectance from longer floats. Both the reduced float size and the greater number of interstices per inch of the five-end satin/sateen contributed to a crisper hand of this reproduction damask. In addition, it is normal practice for the gum on silk filaments to be removed prior to dyeing, but in the case of the replacement damask the gum removal was deliberately left incomplete, thereby contributing to its lower lustre and crisper hand. Finally, the amount of twist inserted into the tram weft was increased slightly, as compared to the weft in the original. The higher twist also decreased the lustre and contributed to the desired crisper hand.

5.6 Weaving the passementerie

Reproduction of the passementerie was equally demanding, and commenced with identification of each style and recording their locations on the blue state bed. Measurements were taken and total yardage for each style was calculated. Nine different styles of passementerie, categorised as seven tasseled trims and two flat trims, were identified. The two flat trims appeared only on the textile-on-wood areas. The remaining seven trims (which were labelled A–G) fell within three groups based on three lengths from header to tassel – a short stubby trim averaging 0.75 in (20 mm), a medium trim averaging 1.5 in (40 mm) and long trims averaging 2.75 in (70 mm). There were two variations within these three groups: one woven with a tassel attached to the header and one without (a plain header) (Figure 5.2).

The thread and weave structure of each textile component of the bed's passementerie was documented in detail. The trims in all groups had woven headers with three to five centred paired floats, generally floating over three wefts. All of the groups exhibited a wide variation in colour within the threads of the header and tassels. The colour shift also occurred in segments of a trim as a result of light exposure over an area. In addition, the trims exhibited a wide variation within each style in terms of number of centre floats, and the number of ends and picks per inch. The entire group of trims exhibited a low twist in the warp and spun silk[12] was used in the two-ply wefts rather than reeled silk filament. Combined with a highly irregular beat and loose weave construction, the trims had a limp hand and drape with a dimensionally flat quality to the headers.

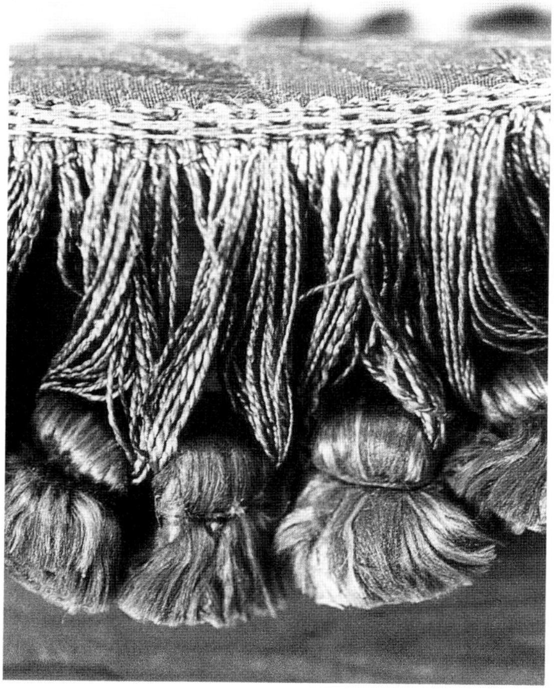

Figure 5.2 Detail of original passementerie, trim type A, one of the two trims with plain woven headers

The three groups of trims based on the header-to-tassel length exhibited considerable variation in the number of wefts that each tassel was made over, even within a single trim. The header-to-tassel length is determined during the weaving by the distance beyond one selvage edge of the woven header that a plied yarn is allowed to extend to create the loop onto which the tassel is secured. A pre-determined number of extended plied wefts were grouped together to form the hanger for each tassel. Once the wefts were grouped, the silk filaments that were to form the tassel were inserted through the weft loops, and folded over, and the head of the tassel was secured onto the wefts with a burnished metal wire. The manufacturer of reproduction passementerie pointed out how rare it was at this period to encounter an exposed wire, i.e. wire that had not been wrapped in dyed silk thread. It was also noted that none of the trims had the arched or crested gimp (a linen core thread wound with silk) forming a decorative edge along the top of the trim.

The manufacturer of the reproduction passementerie was chosen on a similar basis as the damask manufacturer, with communication, flexibility, compatible technology and knowledge of historic production techniques being foremost considerations.[13] In addition, the ability to work closely with the damask weaver was important, because the damask manufacturer was commissioned to dye the silk for the passementerie to the colours of the reproduction damask.

The flatness, loose beat and weave irregularities were considered important qualities of the passementerie, as was the colour variation within the threads. However, the weave structure variations within each style, probably the result of having been woven on different looms, were not considered significant when it came to specifying the reproduction because such variations would be inefficient to reproduce. Allocating a slightly different centre paired float variation to each style ordered achieved variations. Each style could then be woven in one piece on a single loom to accommodate the cutting plan. So in the case of the reproduction trims, rather than the weave variations occurring within each style, the variations were all present but in a single style and woven throughout that style.

Obtaining the colour variations within the trims was deemed important, but the flat trims were handling differently than the tasselled trims. A decision was made to order the two reproduction flat trims undyed, with the intention that they would be custom-dyed as needed in the conservation laboratory. Replicating the variation in the colour of the tassels and woven headers began with the dyeing of several different shades of blue and grey filaments prior to spinning. The six blues and greys that worked best with the replica damask were selected. The warp and weft yarns for the woven header were spun and plied with different combinations of the selected colours, resulting in a varied group of headers ready for the addition of the tassels.

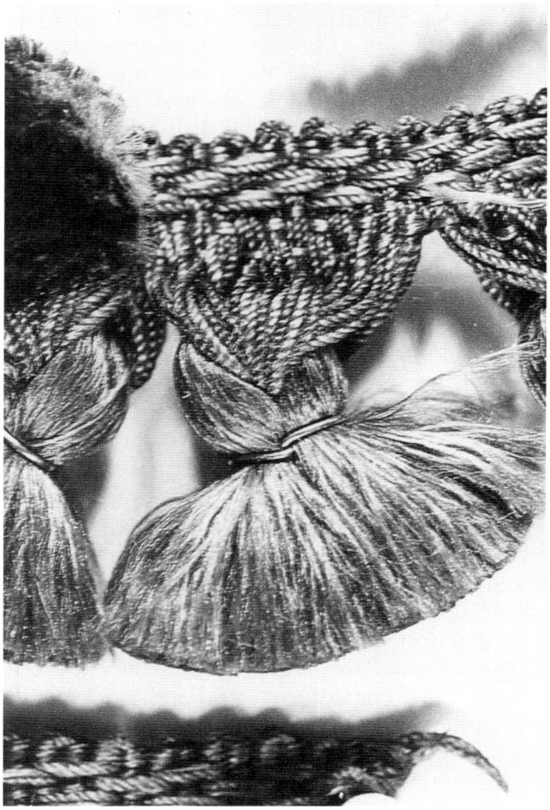

Figure 5.3 Detail of reproduction passementerie, trim type D, showing the exposed metal wire of the tassel

Preparing and attaching the tassels was the final step in fabricating these trims. The goal was to achieve colour variation within each tassel as well as to achieve variations from tassel to tassel. Tassels are not made individually, but are cut from a prepared warp. The size required for the reproduction tassels was achieved by winding the six-thread tram silk into 400 thread warps. The colour variations were accomplished by winding each 400 thread warp of random quantities of varying combinations of four of the six variously coloured filaments. The tassels made up from these four colour combinations and randomly tied onto the trim created the desired random appearance (Figure 5.3).

5.7 Construction of the reproduced components

Replicating the cut and construction techniques was also considered essential to reproduce precisely the hang and drape of the textile elements. As the damask had been reproduced precisely, it was possible to place the damask motifs in exactly the same place as on the original. To begin the sewn construction of each piece, the original textile-only components were documented for their shape, dimensions, the placement of the damask design, their cut and seam construction, fibre and construction of stitching threads, type and length of stitch used (Figure 5.4). The resulting detailed drawings were later used to develop the 3 mm Mylar® (transparent polyester film) patterns used to cut the damask fabric. For easy reference and clarity of information during the sewing construction phase, trim style locations were documented on another set of drawings.

The original construction of the headcloth included a coarse linen ground fabric, to which the pipe organ pleats were sewn. A

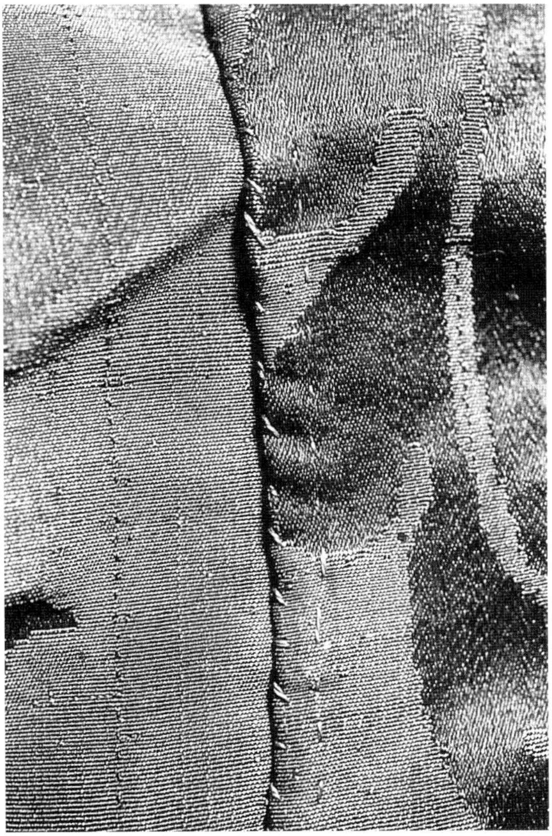

Figure 5.4 Detail of the original inner back valance, showing the seam construction and hand stitching. (Collection of the Metropolitan Museum of Art, New York. Gift of Mr and Mrs William Randolph Hearst Jr, 1968. 68.217.1)

blue-dyed linen fabric lined some of the original textile components, such as the base valances, the tester's outer valances and portions of the headcloth elements (pipe organ pleats and swags). The reproduction linings were obtained from standard commercial suppliers. The new coarse ground linen was purchased undyed and the blue linen lining was dyed by a custom-dyer in New York.[14] The two-ply, blue-dyed linen thread used to sew the original together was not reproduced; stitching of the reproductions was completed with Gütermann's 100 per cent polyester cordonnet, a buttonhole or topstitch weight sewing thread. Although linen thread of similar weight and quality was available, it required custom-dyeing and the polyester thread selected had the advantage of clearly and easily distinguishing original parts from reproduction parts without altering their drape or appearance.

5.8 Non-intrusive attachment: developing the clamp system

Once installed in the gallery, the large wood frame of the state bed would not be able to be disassembled, nor moved. As the structure and frame support issues were being addressed, a long-term maintenance plan was developed for the textile-only components. This involved modifying their method of attachment, in order to enable their removal independent of the frame assembly. The original attachment system for the inner and outer valances required tacking through a linen tape (sewn to the rear of the valances) to the wooden tester and cornice frames.

The upholstery conservation principle of non-intrusive or low-interventive systems of attachment was used to develop a fastening system for the reproduction textile-only elements. Tacking produces a tight, flush appearance that was desirable for the non-intrusive system to emulate. The option of a hook and loop fastener (Velcro™) system was eliminated as too bulky, and stitched systems were judged too time-consuming for easy removal and re-installation for maintenance and cleaning. Alternative attachment methods were therefore sought. In the case of the attachment of the inner and outer valances to the tester and cornice frames, a clamp system was proposed. Not all upholstery substructures can accommodate clamp systems as three sides of the structure must be available with space allotted on one side for the clamping mechanism, but the tester frame met these conditions.

Several ideas were developed and prototypes of the clamp and valance attachment system were fabricated and tried. The final system required sewing a 1.25 in wide strip of .05 mm polyethylene into the linen tape on the top back of each valance. A narrow three-sided 'C' clamp with a slotted 'L' bracket was positioned on the tester and cornice frames. To hang and attach the valances, the polyethylene strip sewn to the rear of the valance was

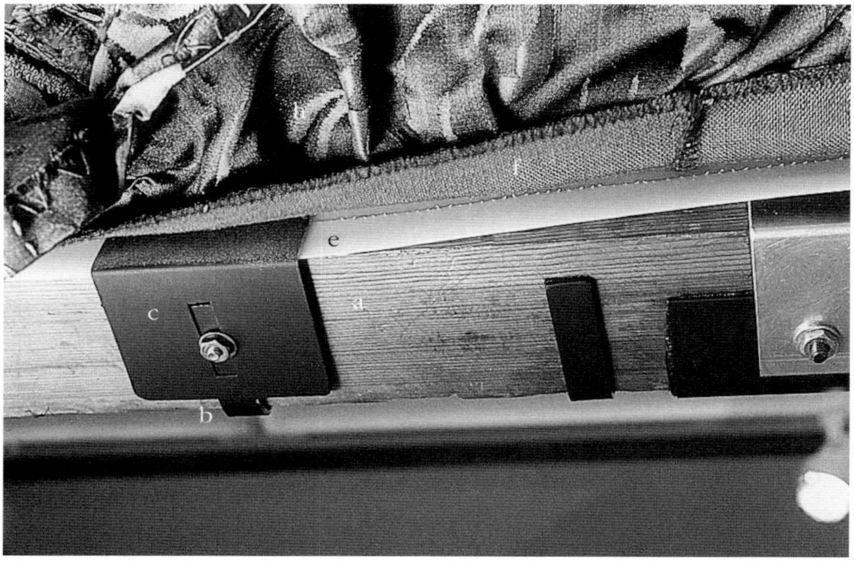

Figure 5.5 Close-up of the clamp system (viewed from below) showing the stiff white polyethylene strip (sewn to the underside of the valance) clamped to the tester frame. (The reproduction valance has been temporarily turned back to expose the clamping system.) (Treatment photograph, Sherman Fairchild, Center for Objects Conservation)

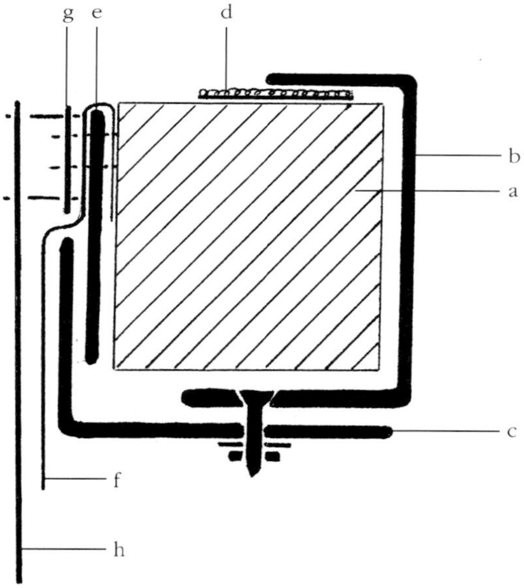

Figure 5.6 Cross-section of the clamping system to show how the valance and tester cloth are attached to the tester frame. (Line drawing by Kathryn Gill)

a Tester frame
b 'C' clamp
c Slotted 'L' clamp
d Velcro™ loop
e Polyethylene strip
f Muslin skirt
g Tape
h Valance

'seated' into the sliding two-piece clamp. Once the valance was 'seated', the clamp was tightened and screwed closed (Figures 5.5 and 5.6).

The added advantage of the top set of clamps was that it also provided a means of attaching the tester cloth. Hook tape fastener (Velcro™) embedded in a stiff polyester strip was added to the outer valance cornice frame on the top surface of the wooden tester frame. A matching length of soft loop tape was sewn around the perimeter of the reproduction tester cloth. The reproduction tester cloth was then attached to the frame by means of the hook and loop fastener, rather than being tacked in place as in the original fastening system (Figure 5.6).

5.9 Discussion

This case history has focused on one part of the treatment of the blue state bed, namely the decision-making process related to commissioning reproduction textiles (damask and passementerie), the fabrication of replica components using hand stitching techniques, integrating reproduction components with original textiles, and their attachment to the bed frame. The use of reproduction components within a textile object can serve many purposes encompassing a range of issues, from interpretation to conservation. In the case of the blue state bed, the primary concern was the conservation of the original textiles whose safety and longevity was jeopardised by exhibition conditions and requirements.

The decision to reproduce an original textile is complex and not all reproductions can be as detailed and precise as that of the blue bed's damask. Some projects and objects may require a greater degree of compromise for varying reasons, yet successfully accomplish the conservation and interpretation goals.

Many factors were important in contributing to the success of this complex project. A thorough understanding of the original processes and their translation into current manufacturing processes determined where compromises could be made and how these will affect the precise replication of the textile. The technology manufacturers use and their ability to understand the needs of the museum's project and adapt their production to these requirements inform the selection of an appropriate manufacturer to meet the textile specifications. Essential to the success is a thorough and complete analysis of the original object, detailed documentation, a clear sense of how the reproduction is to be used within the object, and the ability to predict the final appearance and integration of these reproduced elements. Knowledge of other comparable objects to inform the object being worked on enriches the treatment and confirms decisions. All of the processes of the reproduction must be closely attended to, from the quality of fibre through the finishing choices (if any) and including the cut and stitching techniques in the final fabrication. Close communication with manufacturers, at times daunting due to the considerable geographical distances, is essential. Finally, sufficient time must be allotted for these time-consuming liaison phases; such investment is essential and may not involve any more time commitment than other treatment options.

5.10 Conclusion

The use of the reproduction textiles in the blue state bed was successful from both the visual aspect and in addressing the conservation concerns. The visual success pivoted on the ability of the conservators to convey their needs to the manufacturer and the manufacturer's ability to address these concerns. The clearly defined role of the reproduction textiles in the treatment plan allowed the conservation concerns to be successfully addressed.

Notes

1 Nicola Gentle served as consultant at this point in the process. The Victoria & Albert Museum's Melville bed was constructed within five years of the MMA's Hampton Court beds and was an invaluable comparable object that we used heavily as a reference at many junctures.

2 The Oxford English Dictionary defines canton (with the pronunciation of can'toon) as 'to divide (land) into portions; or to divide (a part), or cut (it) out of a whole; to separate, sever by division' (Simpson and Weiner, 1989, v.II: 849).

3 '[D]enier – An important international direct numbering system for describing linear densities of silk and manufactured filament yarns and fibers other than glass. Denier is equivalent numerically to the number of grams per 9,000 meters length of the material' (Tortora and Merkel, 1996: 168).

4 '[F]inishing – sequence of treatments (excluding coloration) worked on greige fabric intended for sale to consumers or downstream users prior to that sale' (Tortora and Merkel, 1996: 220). A useful resource for accessing the silk processing literature of the first half of the twentieth century with some historic references is Howitt's *Bibliography of the Technical Literature on Silk* (1948), listed in the Bibliography.

5 The manufacturer of the reproduction damask for the blue state bed was Humphries Weaving Company, UK. Richard Humphries and John Minors oversaw the project and Richard Humphries provided the details of the spinning, dyeing and weaving processes in his operation. Humphries had purchased the Jacquard handlooms his weavers work on from Warner's. Warner's had the looms built specifically for high-end silk production over 180 years ago.

6 We have also found that handweavers are a resource for the reproduction of less complex cloths.

7 Humphries Weaving Company produces the 'Fairstead 21 inch Damask', Archive #358 at 39 in; the 'Fairstead Damask', Archive #418 at 45.5 in; and the 'New Hampton Court Damask', Archive #542, at 39 in.

8 '[O]rganzine – raw silk yarns made of two or more twisted singles that are then doubled and

twisted in the reverse direction in the ply. The number of turns per inch in singles and ply is generally from ten to twenty. Generally used as a warp' (Tortora and Merkel, 1996: 397).

9 '[T]ram – 1. Raw silk yarns doubled and twisted with a low number of turns per inch; generally used as filling (ASTM). 2. French term for filling' (Tortora and Merkel, 1996: 586).

10 '[T]hrowing – The operation used to make a twisted yarn from reeled silk or to put an additional twist into filament yarns of manufactured fibres. In some cases, this is done by combining and twisting two separate yarns into one plied yarn. Texturing by the FALSE TWIST method also is done extensively by THROWSTERS' (Tortora and Merkel, 1996: 577).

11 '[P]ackage dyeing – a process of dyeing yarn that has been wound into packages. The yarn is wound loosely on a perforated cylinder or spiral spring covered with a protective fabric material. Next, a large number of these packages are placed on fixed perforated spindles, and an assembly of several spindles loaded into each dyeing machine. Then the dye solution is forced alternately from the outside of the package inward and from the inside out, under pressure' (Tortora and Merkel, 1996: 402).

12 Tortora and Merkel (1996) define spun silk (590), waste silk (623) and Schappe (496) silk similarly. All are short silk fibres that either could not be reeled from the cocoons or were damaged in the reeling process. Schappe silk was further defined as waste silk that had been only partially degummed. Ephraim Chambers in his 1738 *Cyclopaedia; or, an Universal Dictionary of Arts and Sciences* also describes this short fibred silk and called it 'floretta'. He further describes it as being carded or spun from a distaff on a wheel and that it 'makes a tolerable silk' (no page numbers).

13 Wendy Cushing of Wendy Cushing Ltd, was the manufacturer of the passementerie and provided the details of her manufacturing processes. Ms Cushing's business is over one hundred years old and includes an archive. Her weavers and passementeurs work on nineteenth-century handloom equipment.

14 Linen was purchased from Hamilton Adams, P.O. Box 465, 107 High Street, Gordonsville, VA 22942. The dyer was Jean Mignola, Inc., 59 West 19th St, Suite 6-D, NewYork City, New York, 10019.

Acknowledgements

Conservators: Derek Balfour, Senior Conservator (Upholstery), Victoria & Albert Museum, London, UK; Nicola Gentle, Textile Consultant, UK; Lynda Hillyer, Chief Textile Conservator, Victoria & Albert Museum, London, UK; Irin Von Myer, Furniture Conservator, Museum für Kunstgewerbe, Hamburg, Germany; Gwen Spicer, Conservator in Private Practice, USA; Susan Wellnitz, Associate Conservator, Textile Conservation Center at the American Textile Museum, Lowell, MA, USA.

Curator: William Rieder, Curator, European Sculpture and Decorative Arts Department, Metropolitan Museum of Art, New York.

Manufacturers: John Buscemi, Classic Revivals, Inc., Boston; Wendy Cushing, Wendy Cushing Ltd, UK; Richards Humphries, Humphries Weaving Company, UK; John Minors, UK.

Object Conservation Installers, Metropolitan Museum of Art, New York: Nancy Reynolds, Senior Installer; Sandy Wolcott, Senior Installer.

Stitchers: Susan Asmundson; Alice Blohm; Molly Hope; Ata Tassart; Agnes Wnuk; all New York.

Bibliography

Anon. (1911) Furniture of the XVII & XVIII Centuries: Furniture at Hampton Court, near Leominster – I. *Country Life* (18 November), **30**: 750–3.

Anon. (1911) Furniture of the XVII & XVIII Centuries: Furniture at Hampton Court, near Leominster – II. *Country Life* (25 November), **31**: 788–91.

Beard, G. and Westman, A. (1993) A French Upholsterer in England: Francis Lapiere, 1653–1714. *The Burlington Magazine,* August, **CXXXV**: 515–24.

Brooks, M. (1990) The conservation of a textile covered bed cornice from Harewood House. In: A. French (ed.), *Conservation of Furnishing Textiles.* London: UKIC Textile Section, pp. 49–57.

Chambers, E. (1738) *Cyclopaedia; or, an Universal Dictionary of Arts and Sciences,* 2nd edn, 2 vols. London: D. Midwinter, J. Senex *et al.*

Clinton (White), L. (1979) The State Bed from Melville House. *Victoria & Albert Museum Masterpieces,* Sheet 21.

Cornforth, J. (1973a) Hampton Court, Herefordshire – I. *Country Life* (22 February), pp. 450–3.

Cornforth, J. (1973b) Hampton Court, Herefordshire – II. *Country Life* (1 March), pp. 518–21.

Cornforth, J. (1973c) Hampton Court, Herefordshire – III. *Country Life* (8 March), pp. 582–5.

Cornforth, J. (1986) British state beds. *Magazine Antiques* (February), pp. 392–401.

Davies, V. and Doyal, S. (1990) Upholstered mattress construction and conservation. In: A. French (ed.), *Conservation of Furnishing Textiles.* London: UKIC Textile Section, pp. 58–67.

Digby (Wingfield), G.F. (1939) Damasks and velvets at Hampton Court. *Connoisseur* (January–June), **103**: 248–53.

Flury-Lemberg, M. (1988) Hangings of a state bed. In: *Textile Conservation and Research.* Berne: Abegg-Stiftung, pp. 148–53.

Howitt, F.O. (1948) *Bibliography of the Technical Literature on Silk*. London: Hutchinson's Scientific and Technical Publications.

Oddy, W.A. (ed.) (1994) *Restoration: Is It Acceptable?* London: British Museum.

Simpson, J.A. and Weiner, E.S.C. (eds) (1989) *Oxford English Dictionary*, 20 vols. Oxford: The Clarendon Press.

Tortora, P.G. and Merkel, R.S. (eds) (1996) *Fairchild's Dictionary of Textiles*. New York: Fairchild Publications.

White, L. (1982) Two English state beds in the Metropolitan Museum of Art. *Apollo* (August), pp. 84–7.

6

Documentation and conservation of carriage trimming: the treatment of a nineteenth-century carriage interior

Nicola Gentle

6.1 Introduction

The construction of upholstery *(trimming)* which lines a carriage is relatively undocumented in the study of furnishing textiles.[1] Methods, materials and even terminology[2] used by the carriage *trimmer* differ from those used by the upholsterer of a piece of furniture. Conservation of carriage trimming is also a relatively unexplored area.[3]

The treatment of a nineteenth-century carriage being conserved for a private client has provided an opportunity to observe the traditional trimmer's craft, and to evolve conservation methods for a specialised type of upholstery.[4]

This case history will discuss the need to understand the construction of such an object and the problems of access to its interior. The past neglect of this particular carriage and the current requirement for it to be made presentable for a private owner, who wished to display it to full effect in his coach house, influenced the conservator's approach. The necessary removal of a large proportion of the trimming from the interior for appropriate conservation treatment, revealed fuller information about the carriage, its history and its making.

6.2 The carriage

In 1996, selected contents came up for auction at Hall, a grand house belonging to the Chichester family near Barnstaple in North Devon (UK); the carriage (see Figure 6.11) was among them. It was described as an early nineteenth-century enclosed coach[5] built by Pettle of Barnstaple, whose name appears on the hub caps of the wheels. Based on the design of fashionable coaches of the time, the Hall carriage seems to display some idiosyncrasies of the regional builder, such as the U-shaped window in the front quarter panels, and for this reason it was seen as an interesting survival. One or two irregularities can be noted in the trimming; in particular, the upper lace *(vallens)* has a step and join where the front area meets the rest of the carriage (Figure 6.1); this lace would more usually continue in one smooth line all around the top of a coach. Overall, however, the trimming is consistent with, and the construction and materials typical of, those used c.1850 (Figures 6.1, 6.2 and 6.3).

6.3 Description of materials and construction of the trimming

Although not of the grandest quality, the materials used in the textile trimming are none the less of good quality and the making shows a very sound standard of craftsmanship. In such a coach, not only were the seats upholstered and furnished with textiles, but the interior 'walls', the doors and the roof were totally lined, while the floor was covered with

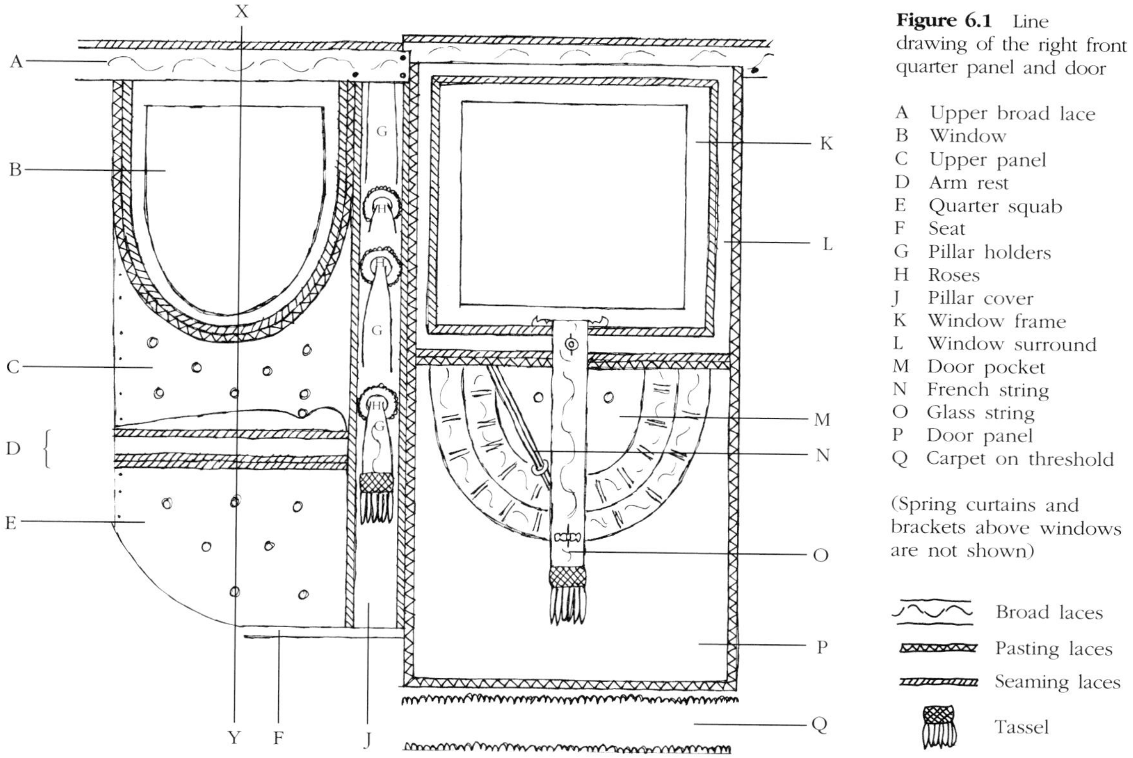

Figure 6.1 Line drawing of the right front quarter panel and door

A Upper broad lace
B Window
C Upper panel
D Arm rest
E Quarter squab
F Seat
G Pillar holders
H Roses
J Pillar cover
K Window frame
L Window surround
M Door pocket
N French string
O Glass string
P Door panel
Q Carpet on threshold

(Spring curtains and brackets above windows are not shown)

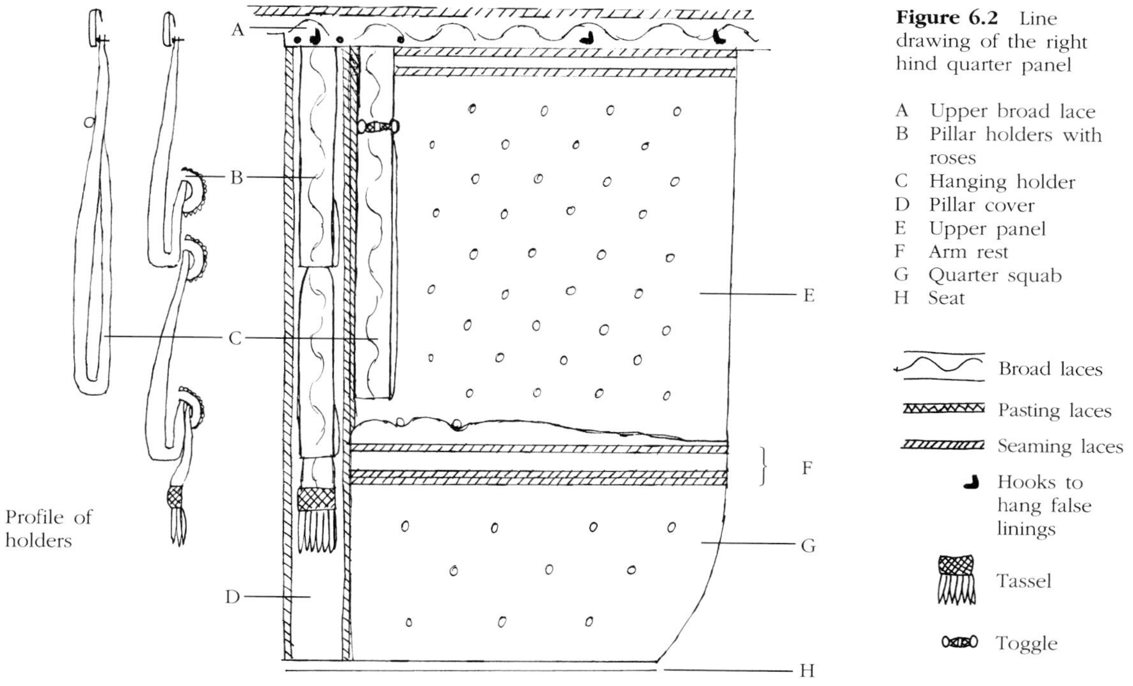

Figure 6.2 Line drawing of the right hind quarter panel

A Upper broad lace
B Pillar holders with roses
C Hanging holder
D Pillar cover
E Upper panel
F Arm rest
G Quarter squab
H Seat

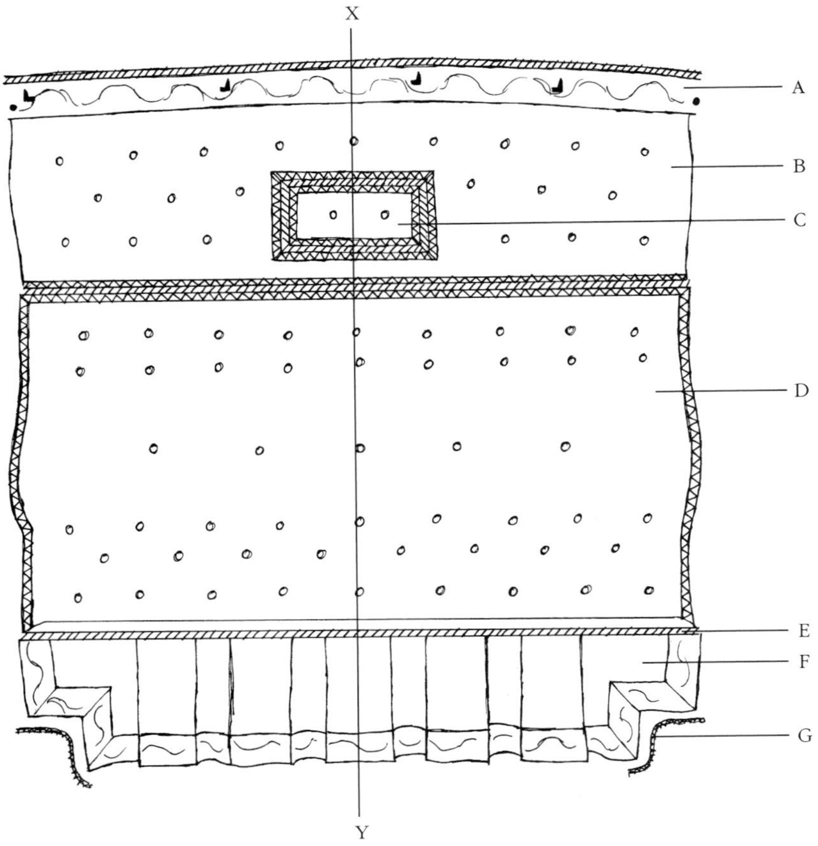

Figure 6.3 Line drawing of the hind panel

A Upper broad lace
B Upper panel
C Hind window flap
D Back squab
E Seat roll
F Seat fall
G Carpet on thresholds

Broad laces
Pasting lace
Seaming lace
Hooks to hang false linings

carpet. Everyday use of a carriage – climbing in and out, motion, abrasion from outdoor clothing and boots, exposure to external environment – meant the textiles and threads employed were required to be more hard-wearing than those chosen to cover a piece of domestic furniture.

In the Hall carriage, the main show covers are of a cream-coloured watered textile of silk warp ribbed with a cotton weft (hereafter referred to as *moiré*), and a heavier beige woollen cloth with plain weave made thicker by fulling (hereafter referred to as *woolcloth*).

Moiré is used for the *upper panels*, *arm rests* and *back squabs*. These items were constructed as independent units prior to being fitted into the interior: a linen base cloth, curled hair stuffing, calico stuffing-cover and moiré top cover are buttoned through with rounded tufts of cut wool yarn *(daisies)*. The moiré presumably also covered the loose *seat squabs* (or cushions), which were missing from the carriage when it was presented for conservation.

Woolcloth is used for the *quarter squabs* (lower quarter panels) and the *door pockets*, also pre-constructed as independent units, consisting of a linen base cloth (lined with moiré for the pockets), curled hair stuffing (but with no stuffing-cover), woolcloth top cover, buttoned through with wool tufts.

The base cloth linen of the pre-constructed units shows slashes for extra stuffing to be introduced, with the opening somewhat roughly but soundly closed by lacing together with linen thread (Figures 6.4 and 6.5). This addition of stuffing was thought, at first, to be a later refurbishment, but reference is made in Farr's *Handbook of Coach Trimming* (1998 [1888]) to suggest that this was, in fact, standard practice during the original construction.[6] The items were made up on a frame outside the

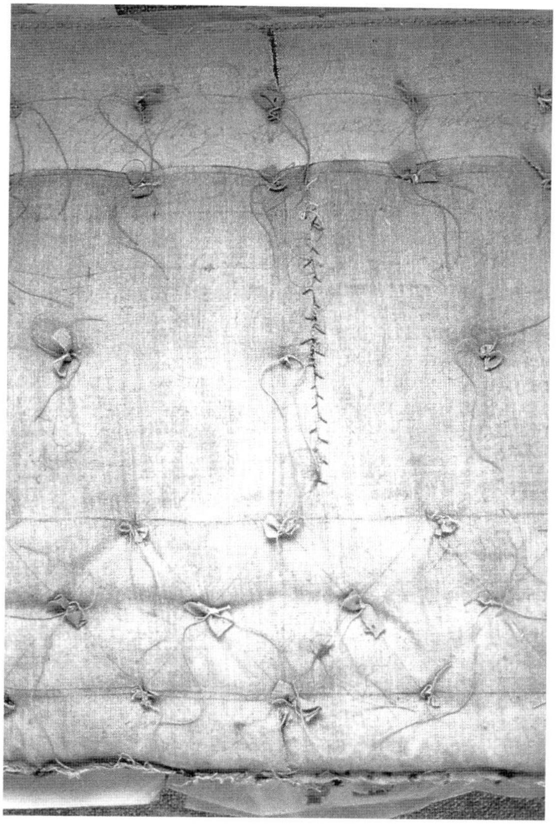

Figure 6.4 Hind back squab (D in Figure 6.3 and detail Figure 6.5), with slash where extra stuffing was introduced

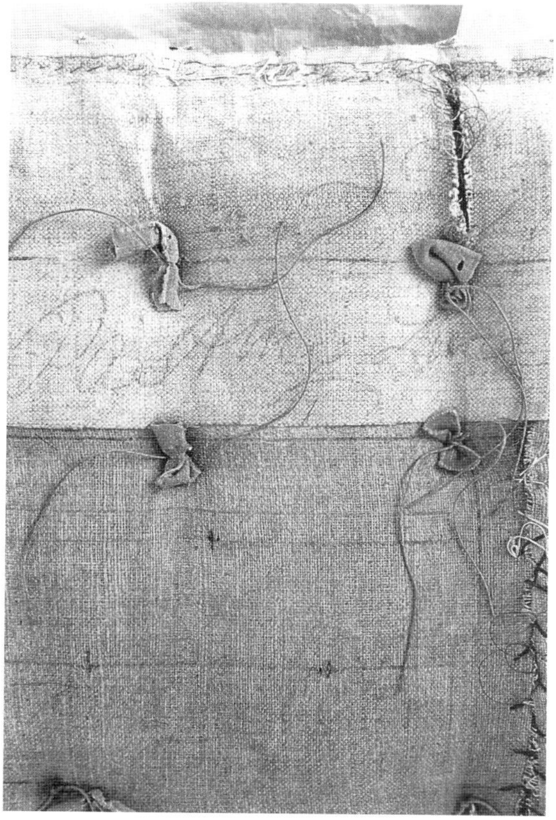

Figure 6.5 Hind back squab (D in Figure 6.3); detail of the reverse side once removed from the carriage. The trimmer's pencil markings can be seen on the linen base cloth: the design for buttoning has been adjusted in the making; the inscription reads *Pasting lace except along bottom*. The squab has had extra stuffing added, during the original making, through the central upright slash which is roughly laced back together with thread. The 'butterflies' of the buttoning ties appear to be a mix of originals reused and new ones added during refurbishment

carriage; their edges had to be finished with stitching before the stuffing could be finally adjusted and the buttoning completed.

The stuffing of the buttoned items is curled horsehair, sometimes found to contain fragments of cloth, thread and string. Felton (1996 [1794–5]) mentions the re-use of old stuffings for making new squabs. A vegetable fibre filling (possibly coir fibre added at a later date) is present in the panel recess behind the quarter squabs.

Elsewhere in the carriage, the woolcloth is used flat to line the roof, the window surrounds (where it is pasted with starch paste to the carriage body), and the lower face of the arm rests. With curled hair filling, it covers the *door panels* and *pillars* (the uprights either side of the doors) and, with short hair, the edge *roll* of the seats. Unlined, it hangs as a pleated *fall* (valance) at front of each seat.

The *laces* (the term used for braid and piping 'passementerie' in carriages) are also of a durable yet luxurious nature. Woven on a strong warp and basic weft of cotton, a secondary warp of worsted creates the decorative motif in uncut pile; the more ornate broad lace and the pasting lace have also a ground weft of silk.

Broad laces (here 55–58 mm wide) are used as a decorative as well as a functional element.

Sometimes woven with a plain cotton tape flange which folds behind the decorative width (thus known as *binding lace)*, broad lace trims the upper panels (the flange is stitched to the upper seaming lace and they are back-tacked together over the edges of the roof lining). Also with a flange, it is used to bind the seat falls, stitched with a linen thread.

Woven without a flange, it is utilised for its strength. Lined with moiré and filled with curled hair, broad lace forms the *pillar holders* (or hand holders) which aid entry and exit of passengers, and the *hanging holders* (or swing holders) through which the passenger's arm can be rested during travel. The ends of the holders pass through circular holes cut in the pillar cover and are tacked onto the framework. The circular holes (three to each pillar) are strengthened and decorated with a *rose*, a leather ring wrapped alternately with wool and silk yarn and surrounded with an ornament of silk-wrapped metal wire (see Plate 6.2).

Lined with woolcloth, broad lace also makes the *glass strings*, used to raise and lower the window panes, tacked to the bottom of the pane frame. When the pane is raised, an eyelet hole at the top of the glass string is fitted onto an ivory stud on the carriage framework: the lower end of the glass string is retained by a *French string*. The French string can be made of a narrow lace, but in the Hall carriage it consists of a substantial cord of wool yarn. A decorative ivory toggle at the end is pushed through a lower eyelet hole in the glass string and held in place by an ivory ring behind.

The lowest pillar holders and the glass strings are finished with a large flat tassel. The heading of the tassel is of parchment and metal wrapped with silk yarn and faced with netting; the hanging fringe is silk-covered cotton and wool bullion.

Seaming and *pasting laces* play a role in attaching the items of trimming to the carriage body. Seaming lace, similar to piping, has a decorative rounded fold (14 mm wide) stitched around a cord of twisted paper. The plain cotton tape flanges at either side are tacked to the carriage body, providing an edge to which other items of trimming are attached by stitching in heavy linen thread. It is also used as a piping, stitched into the seams of squabs or cushions.

Pasting lace has a flat decorative width (14 mm) with a plain cotton tape flange folded behind. It is used to bind the edges of trimming items; the folded edge can then be blind-stitched to the seaming laces tacked to the carriage framework. Pasting lace can also be used to 'finish' items which are tacked to the framework with their edges unbound: the flange is back-tacked over the item's edge and then the decorative width of the lace is pasted down with starch paste to cover up the tacks.

At each of the windows – two in the front panel, one in each front quarter panel and each of the doors – is a *spring curtain* (roller blind) of silk taffeta of magenta pink colour. The curtain is rolled over a metal barrel covered with two layers of twill weave cotton and containing a spring with ratchet mechanism to lower or raise the curtain. The lower edge of the curtain is weighted by a *curtain stick* stitched into the hem of the taffeta. The stick has metal eyelets at either end to run up and down on fixed lines of cord, steadying the curtain when the carriage is in motion.

The thresholds and bottom of the carriage are covered in Brussels carpeting of linen warp and weft, with a looped wool pile patterned in a simple repeated blue and black flower on beige ground.

There are metal hooks spaced around the upper broad laces for the hanging of *false linings* (case covers). The linings themselves are missing. They would most likely have been made of linen or glazed cotton, and could have had edges bound with a border in imitation of lace.[7]

6.4 Condition

In latter years, the Hall carriage had suffered extreme neglect. It was discovered in 1996 in an outbuilding where it had been abandoned, and was used as a chicken house (see Figure 6.6).

Despite neglect, much of the trimming could be seen as complete and in surprisingly sound condition. In the hind half of the carriage, the upper panels and laces in particular, and the back squab (when later uncovered) still conveyed the splendour and luxury

Figure 6.6 Front half of the carriage interior on first examination, December 1996. Straw on the seats bears witness to its use as a chicken house

of this totally upholstered interior (Plate 6.1). Long exposure to a damp environment, however, had resulted in the presence of mould throughout. More specific damage associated with dampness had occurred to the front half of the carriage, particularly to the left quarter where wet conditions resulted in long-term saturation. (Corresponding damage was evident in the carriage body and exterior paintwork.[8]) Here the textiles of the upper panel and arm rest, parts of the back squab and seat fall were degraded beyond reasonable presentation. Only a few unidentifiable fragments of the quarter squab remained.

The other major factor to deterioration – infestation by moth (white-shouldered house moth, *Endrosis sarcitrella*) – was particularly evident throughout in the woolcloth and horsehair. Hidden away in the dark and damp conditions, the larvae had eaten away holes throughout and destroyed the lower edge and concealed side of the quarter squabs, leaving characteristic debris within the stuffings (Figure 6.7).

Carpeting remained on the two thresholds but the length across the carriage bottom had been cut away and discarded in the past, perhaps when it became too worn. The fragments on the thresholds showed damage owing to moth and damp and were extremely fragile.

Pieces of taffeta from the spring curtains, torn from their rollers, were lying loose on the seats and carriage bottom, crumpled, soiled and stained. The taffeta appeared to have been saturated during the period of neglect; this had caused migration of the already faded pink dye, resulting in mottled unevenness of colour. Deep pink staining was evident on the front seat fall, against which some of the curtains had rested.

It was obvious that the carriage had been well used in its working lifetime. The moiré of the pillar holders and the back squabs was abraded and in places worn away by handling and rubbing. There were patterns of soiling associated with use: for example, where hands clasped onto the holders, heads rested against the upper panels, and boots rubbed against the seat falls.

6.5 Past refurbishment and repair

There was evidence of the carriage having been cared for in the past, with one major refurbishment: the abraded moiré of the hind back squab had been re-covered with woolcloth held by buttons in place of the original tufts. The wool used was of inferior quality and the metal buttons had subsequently rusted and stained their silk coverings, but this refurbishing appeared to have been carried out by a professional trimmer.

Some other repairs had disfigured and damaged the textiles. On the most worn pillar holders, the moiré backing was badly split with areas of loss. Here the moiré had been roughly folded together and held with unsightly stitching in thick cotton thread;

stuffing that had dropped out had not been replaced.

6.6 Access and assessment

In 1996 the carriage was acquired by a private owner. Happily, he not only wished to keep it in Devon, but he also respected the nineteenth-century making of the trimming and wanted this preserved as far as possible rather than replaced with new. By good fortune, the nearby National Trust Carriage Collection at Arlington Court could offer not only the necessary curatorial advice, but also the facilities of an established conservation unit to house the coach and a team of conservators with some prior experience of this type of object (Nicholson, 1997).

Necessary initial examination of the textile trimming had to be made from outside the vehicle which, at that stage, was too unsafe to enter. Carried out at a distance, with limited aid of a torch and angle-poise lamp, the extent of degradation was not initially apparent. Even when closer examination was possible, it was difficult to fully realise the condition of the trimming before conservation work started. Unlike a piece of furniture, where a representative section of the under-upholstery would be more immediately visible or easily accessible, in a piece of carriage trimming, the stuffing and base cloth, frame and tacking are all completely hidden. Also their condition may vary greatly from one panel to another. In the Hall carriage, for example, it was only on the removal of a hind quarter squab, significantly moth-damaged but apparently otherwise sound, that the extreme devastation to stuffing and base cloth resulting from a mouse nest was revealed. Nor is it easy to assess problems that might lie behind the trimming in a carriage body. Mould growth found on the wood framework and interior panels once some squabs were removed confirmed in this case that it was necessary to check behind other items of the trimming.

The degree of difficulty in removing tacks from the trimming was not anticipated. Corrosion was found throughout, but in places this was so severe that tack heads had become ingrained in the textile, leaving nothing to lever against when attempting to lift out the shank.

6.7 Conservation policy

For such a complex object, where only a sequential assessment of condition is possible, it is necessary to establish a policy for treatment within which methods can continue to evolve.

The current *role* of the object was established as a showpiece for display in private surroundings, thus presentable from every viewpoint. The disfiguring or total loss of some items, which in a *museum* display might be compensated for by careful angle of viewing, here needed to be addressed by a combination of conservation and reproduction techniques.

Overall objectives were discussed and agreed with the owner.[9] First, to use a conservation approach wherever possible. Secondly, to use a combination of conservation and replication, when an item is too disfigured, unsound or missing. It was agreed that anything that remained of the original should be preserved and incorporated into a reconstruction of the item, following the trimmer's way of making.

Removal of the refurbishment to the hind back squab could be justified. The replacement woolcloth was of inferior quality and now in bad condition; its pale orange colour was inconsistent with the rest of the interior; the re-buttoning had corroded causing disfigurement and damage. The original moiré was preserved at an early stage of deterioration beneath the refurbishing; this presented a good impression of how the carriage interior looked when the trimmings were new. Reconstruction of the missing seat squabs would be essential.

The vulnerability of the textiles, even after conservation, was stressed. For example, a facing overlay of Stabiltex could give excellent durable support to the moiré as a display piece, but would not adequately protect it from the soiling or abrasion associated with handling and use. Minimal handling and display in a stable environment and low light levels were advised.

6.7.1 The removal of the trimming from the carriage

It is always hoped that items may be adequately treated with minimum disturbance, but in this carriage it became clear with closer observation that even the relatively sound panels of trimming needed to be partially released both to check them more fully and also the bodywork behind them. Decisions of whether, by how much and then exactly how to remove items have to be allowed to evolve within increasing knowledge of a complex object as a whole.

The need to remove or partially release most items was regrettable in terms of the loss of fixings, but was paramount to the continuing preservation of the object in its new role. This necessary but apparently radical approach was of benefit to the conservator by providing an opportunity to fully examine and document the construction of such an object. It was interesting, for example, to discover the trimmer's pencil markings on the linen base cloths, setting out the pattern of buttoning and instructions for finishing. The inscription on the hind back squab reads *Pasting lace except along bottom* (see Figures 6.4 and 6.5).

For the least disruption to the frame, it was decided that wherever possible the trimming would be removed or released by snipping stitching rather than lifting tacks. This was because the stitching could be most easily reconstructed later when the conserved items were reassembled in the carriage.

A piece of furniture can usually be approached from all angles, turned and lifted so that all sides can be reached. Access to the fixing of carriage trimming is not so straightforward. The need to work in the confined space of a carriage interior (average 1480 mm length by 1070 mm width) is in itself difficult. It was impossible to stand upright once inside the interior height of 1385 mm; much of the work around the upper areas had to be done from a stooped position and with arms stretched upwards. Lighting can best be gained from a small lamp, which can be angled towards the area being worked, not throwing too much light and heat onto the surrounding textiles, but it is not easy to avoid casting a shadow with one's hands. Positioning of tools is limited and an awareness of surrounding textiles has always to be kept in mind. Original attachment, both by stitching and tacking, was made to be hard-wearing and is thus not simple to remove. The extra time needed to remove carriage trim must be appreciated.

To remove or release the trimming most sympathetically and efficiently, methods and order of construction need to be fully investigated and understood.

Door panels and pockets

The carriage doors could be lifted off their hinges and laid flat; this allowed more easy access for partially lifting the laces and top covers of panel and pocket, which needed attention.

Carpet

The remaining fragments of carpet were removed to prevent further damage occurring when stepping over the thresholds. Their outside edges were seen to be tacked and finished with pasting lace tacked over and their cut edges had been tacked at a later date to the carriage bottom.

Spring curtains

When the pieces of taffeta were lifted out of the carriage and laid out, it was found that four almost complete curtains were present. A section of the fifth also remained but the sixth was totally missing. One curtain still had its stick hemmed into the lower edge. All but one of the rollers were extant; these were removed from their brackets above the windows. Several small tassels (silk-wrapped wood mould, silk-wrapped cotton cord hangers twisted around metal wire) were in place on the roller ratchets or found loose within the interior.

Back squabs and hind window flap

By the method of unpicking stitching, the two largest items which needed full conservation treatment could be removed. The front and hind back squabs, together with the little upholstered flap at the hind window, were unpicked from along their bound top edge and lifted out as self-contained units, leaving the seaming laces tacked in place, ready for stitching onto once conservation was complete (Figure 6.8).

Seats, edge rolls and falls

The wooden seat was covered with a cloth of twill-weave cotton tacked along the edges. This was worn thin and disfigured by

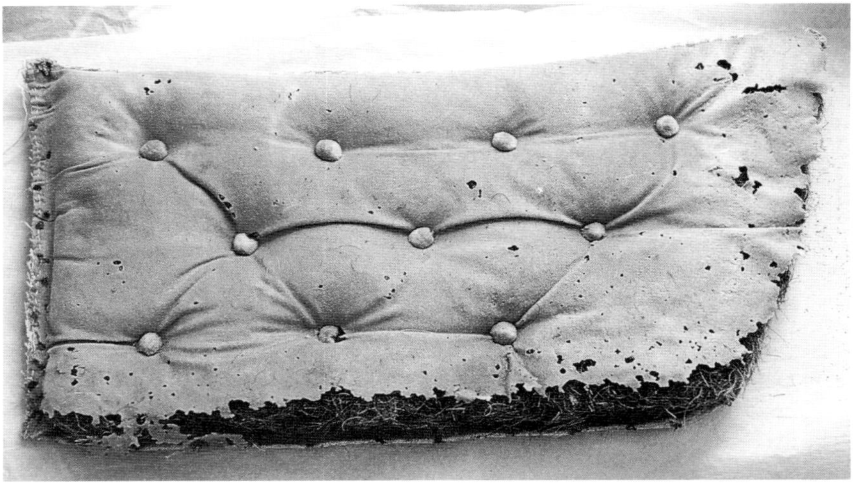

Figure 6.7 Right hind quarter squab (G in Figure 6.2) removed from the carriage. The extent of damage to the wool cloth top cover can be seen, particularly along lower edge and proper left side which have been tucked away under other squabs, providing ideal conditions for moth infestation

ingrained dust but could be left in place to be covered with new cotton fabric later.

The fall of pleated woolcloth was seen to be held along the front edge of the seat, on the upper surface. The edge roll cover, stitched to a length of seaming lace, is back-tacked over this, then taken over a loose stuffing of short hair, turned under and tacked along its inner edge (Figure 6.8). The roll cover and the fall were removed as one unit, still stitched together. Tack-heads were so corroded that it was necessary to lift each crumbled head with the textile, leaving its shank in the wood seat.

Pillar covers with 'roses', and pillar holders

All the pillar covers and pillar holders needed conservation. As the fixing of the pillar holders is so integrated with the pillar cover and its filling, the removal of all these elements was carried out as one operation. Filling of curled hair in the pillars is added section by section once each holder is fixed into place.

The pillar cover could be unpicked along each upright, with roses kept stitched in place. Releasing from the lower end upwards, each section of hair filling was lifted out, giving access in turn to the fixings of the holders. Where possible, the tacks, three to each fixing, were lifted out complete, but in places the corroded heads broke off and the textiles were eased over the remaining shank end.

At the top, where the pillar cover was held beneath the upper broad lace with two large tacks with heads decorated with ribbed silk fabric, the heads of these were again so corroded that some losses had to be accepted.

Quarter squabs

All three extant quarter squabs had to be removed for full conservation treatment. The lower edge of these squabs is first back-tacked to the framework; the sides are then held with tacks which would be hidden by the back squab on one side and the pillar seaming lace on the other, while the top of the squab, finished with stitched seaming lace, sits free below the arm rest (Figure 6.9). To release the squab on the outer (door) side, some of the pillar seaming lace had also to be lifted (Figure 6.10). Tacks from the inner side were accessible because the back squabs had been removed. The devastation resulting from damp and moth enabled easy detachment at the lower edge. Debris of what remained of the left quarter squab was cleared away.

Front quarter upper panels and arm rests

These items were in the very poorest condition. Removal from the left quarter proved easier as large areas of loss provided good access to the tacks; it was more difficult on the right quarter.

1 Edge of roof lining, turned under, tacked
2 Seaming lace tacked around window
3 Top edge of upper panel tacked
4 Lower edge of upper panel tacked
5 Edges of upper panel (bound with pasting lace) around window, stitched to seaming lace
6 Window flap (bound with pasting lace), stitched to seaming lace along top edge only
7 Upper broad lace stitched to seaming lace, back-tacked over roof lining edge. Lower edge of broad lace stitched to upper panel
8 Pasting lace, with flange opened out below, tacked over edge of upper panel. Top edge of pasting lace then stitched to panel
9 Seaming lace tacked over pasting lace flange
10 Seat cloth back-tacked
11 Lower edge of back squab back-tacked
12 Top edge of back squab (bound with pasting lace) stitched to seaming lace
13 Top edge of seat fall, tacked
14 Outer edge of seat roll, stitched to seaming lace, back-tacked
15 Seat roll: filled; inner edge turned under and tacked

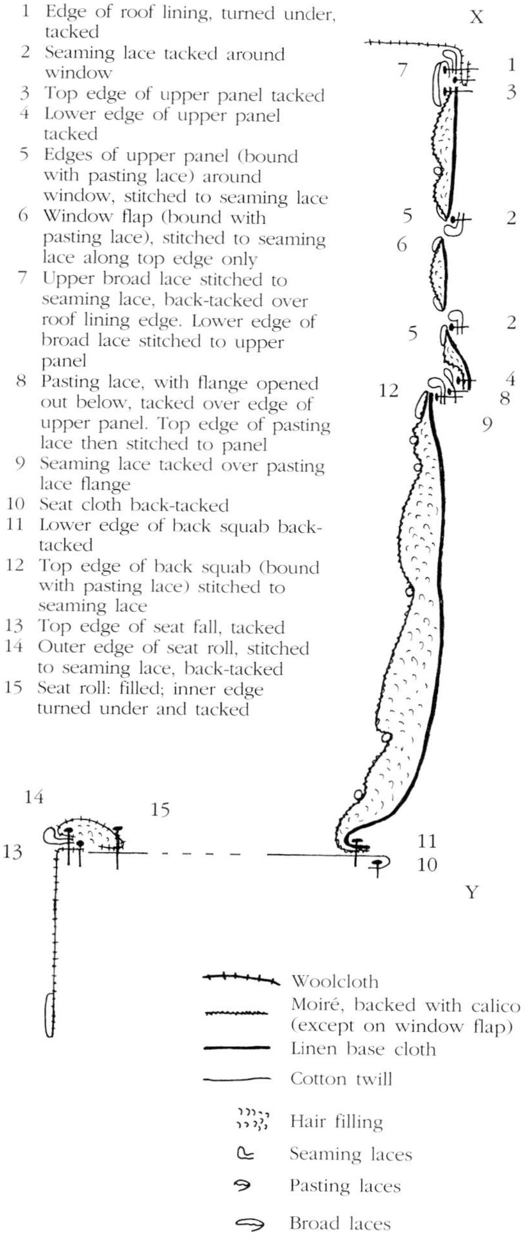

Figure 6.8 Line drawing of cross-section (X–Y on Figure 6.3) to show construction of the hind panel and seat and possible order of trimming

1 Edge of roof lining, turned under, tacked
2 Seaming lace tacked around window
3 Pasting lace tacked around window recess
4 Inner edge of arm pad tacked. Lower edge of upper panel back-tacked to arm frame
5 Edge of upper panel tacked around window and covered with pasting lace, tacked. Pasting lace stitched to seaming lace
6 Upper broad lace stitched to seaming lace, back-tacked over roof lining edge
7 Arm rest cover is preconstructed: moiré upright is seamed with seaming lace to arm pad on upper side and to wool cloth at underside
8 Extra filling added around arm frame
9 Inner edge of arm underside tacked
10 Side of seat cloth turned under and tacked
11 Lower edge of quarter squab back-tacked
12 Top edge of quarter squab (finished with stitched seaming lace) sits free, tacked only at corners

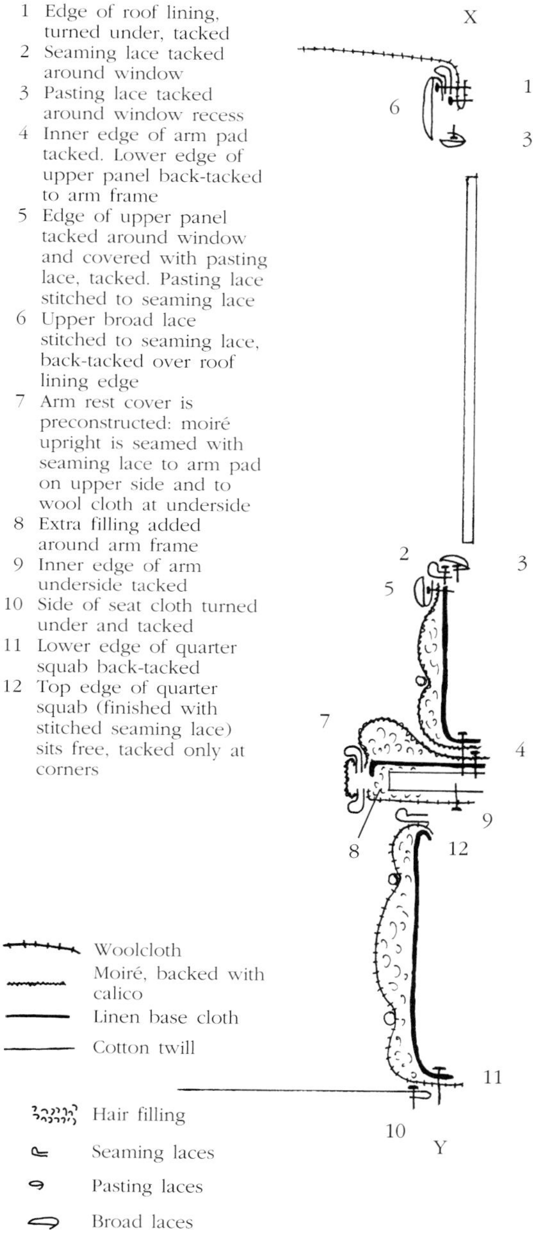

Figure 6.9 Line drawing of cross-section (X–Y on Figure 6.1) to show construction of the right front quarter panel and possible order of trimming

As with the quarter squab, the upper panel is tacked along each upright side. To release these meant another section of the pillar lace had to be lifted (Figure 6.10), though a substantial section at the top could be left *in situ*. The top edge of the panel is held by tacking, finished with a length of pasting lace, which also had to be lifted. The lower edge is back-tacked to the arm frame over the top cover of the arm pad; the fullness of the arm rest stuffing made it very difficult to reach these tacks (Figure 6.9). Soiling of the arm rest made it impossible to understand its construction; it therefore seemed wise to lift this out complete without destroying evidence of its making.

Once the sides and top of the panel were released, also the underside cover and buttoning of the arm, access could be gained to the arm frame. By slowly working along from the near end, the arm pad and lower edge of the panel were lifted together. With the arm rest trimming removed, its construction could be investigated more closely and documented as invaluable information for future work.

Hind upper panels, arm rests and hanging holders

The hind upper panels, arm rests and hanging holders could be adequately treated *in situ*, but the panels required lifting to check conditions behind them. Unpicking stitching rather than disturbing tacking would be considered the ideal approach in this case.

Roof lining

Removal of the roof lining was the most difficult operation of all, but this had to be undertaken as much debris and frass had collected above it and a number of the small wooden blocks which strengthen the roof had become detached and fallen onto it. The lining is tacked around to the very top of the front, hind and side panels, the edges then being covered with seaming lace and broad lace, stitched and tacked together.

Brackets for the spring curtains and hooks for the false linings are fitted to the framework through the upper broad lace. Rather than disturb these fixtures and possibly cause damage both to them and to the lace by trying to remove them, it was decided to release the fixing of the broad lace only along its top edge. This gave access to the tacks holding the upper seaming lace and then the edges of the roof lining.

To hold the roof lining in position before tacking, across its centre is a line of stitches linking it to a flange of cloth (wool) tacked to the central cross beam of the roof; it is then similarly held across the front and hind halves of the carriage. Only a few of these link stitches remained intact on the centre beam and these were now snipped so that the lining could be removed from the carriage.

6.8 Previous history of the carriage and dating of the present trimming

The removal of the roof lining revealed a pencil inscription on the underside of the roof planks: *Richard Jackson, Trimmer 1850*. The similarity in this handwriting to that on the squab base cloths suggests that all the present trimming was constructed and fitted at this date.

It had been noted during the removal of the trimming that there were old tack holes, now unused, in parts of the framework. It was therefore considered that the present trimming could be an early refurbishment within the carriage's lifetime as a family coach.[10]

With the roof structure now exposed, it could be seen that the Hall carriage had undergone a more radical reconstruction altogether.[11] The foremost section of the roof is clearly an addition; the beams, planks and strengthening blocks differ from the rest of the roof. This explains the awkward step in the roof lining and the join in the upper laces at this junction. The idiosyncratic window and the unusual construction of the framework (Figure 6.10) might also be explained. It appears that the carriage was once a *chariot* (with only one seat facing forwards), possibly dating from the 1830s or earlier, and all of the front section has been added some time later (compare Figures 6.11 and 6.12). The evidence of this earlier construction had to be fully documented before the conserved items of the present trimming could be replaced in the carriage interior.

6.9 Conservation treatment

6.9.1 Cleaning and dismantling the items of trimming

General cleaning and removal of debris was carried out from the interior and then from the visible surfaces of the trimming while still *in situ*, using a soft brush to sweep into the flow of a vacuum-cleaner. As the items were removed from the carriage they were given further attention in this manner now all their surfaces could be reached.

The textiles of these items needed total support, thus much of their construction had to be dismantled. Although it was regrettable to lose original stitching and buttoning, the degree of degradation made this unavoidable. Representative areas of construction, both stitching and tacking, were allowed to remain in the carriage.

The dismantling of items also ensured more thorough cleaning. Obverse and reverse sides of the textiles were now thoroughly vacuum-cleaned with controlled suction. Moth-casings were carefully lifted using a spatula; debris, frass and mould could be cleared from stuffings. Where there might be traces of mould spores left, the textiles and stuffings were laid on blotting paper and swabbed with cotton wool pads dipped in IMS (industrial methylated spirits) to remove the soiling and deter further growth of mould.

Particularly soiled areas of the moiré were likewise swabbed with IMS. The most stained and degraded pieces of the moiré, calico and linen were to be wet-cleaned. Although this could result in dimensional change, these textiles were to be covered in a reconstruction fabric; the cleaning would make them stable and allow them to be kept within their particular item of trimming. However, a trial of wet-cleaning the woolcloth and lace of the seat rolls indicated that wet-cleaning would be of little benefit, so this treatment was taken no further.

The taffeta pieces from the spring curtains were washed, using a non-ionic detergent, Synperonic N. Although this treatment caused slight shrinkage in the curtains' width, the benefit of reducing creasing and removing soiling (in particular, bird droppings) was seen to outweigh this disadvantage. Some of the deeper stains remained and the overall colour was still very uneven.

In places where the broad laces had been exposed to airborne dust (especially the upper areas of the holders around the doors), the worsted pile was heavily ingrained. Good results were obtained using natural rubber sponge to lift this soiling (Figure 6.13). Small cubes of the sponge, held in tweezers, can be stroked over the raised pile without disturbing the more delicate ground yarns of the lace. Any remaining traces of rubber are removed afterwards by vacuum cleaning.

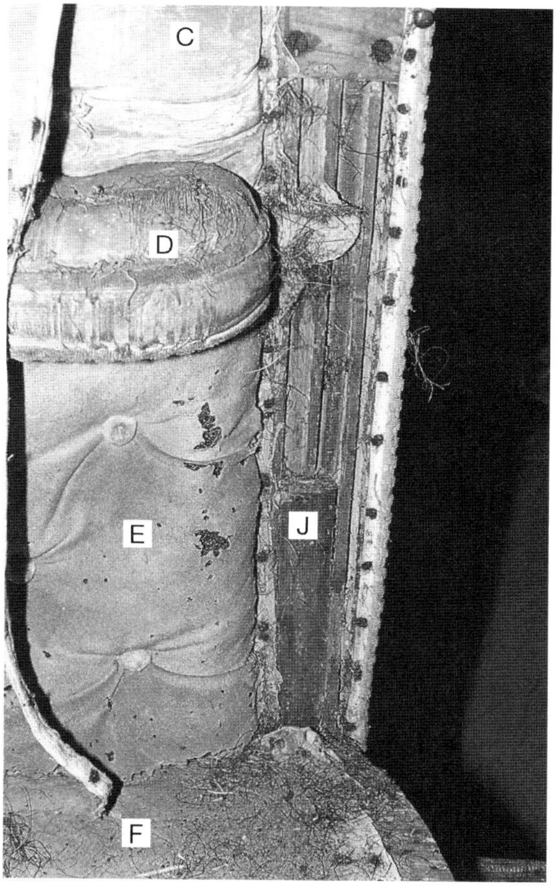

Figure 6.10 Detail of the right front quarter panel during removal of the trimming (refer to Figure 6.1 for Key to labels). The pillar cover (J) has been unpicked leaving its seaming lace *in situ* along the door edge. On the inner edge, the seaming lace has been lifted to reach the tacks along the upper panel and quarter squab. The close fit of the upper panel over the arm rest can be seen. (Removal of the pillar cover and stuffing reveals an unusual construction in the framework – grooves for lowering windows and shutters – which suggests an earlier history of the carriage as a *chariot*)

6.9.2 Support and reconstruction of the materials of the trimming

A consistent approach to supporting each category of textile and type of construction was established and was followed through the carriage.

The moiré

Where the moiré needed conservation it was totally supported on a backing of dyed cotton lawn, held by laid-couching stitching in fine polyester thread, and faced (overlaid) with fine plain-weave polyester Stabiltex, ready-dyed. The facing minimised the stitching required and also gave added protection for open display and use.

Stabiltex was chosen for its durability since the moiré occurred in places most vulnerable to possible rubbing and handling. Its visual qualities helped to re-establish the sheen and the watered effect of the textile.

This method was used on the hind back squab (once the refurbishment was removed), the window flap and the linings of the pillar holders (once the old repairs had been removed) (Figure 6.13). The hind arm rests, left *in situ*, were simply faced with the Stabiltex.

Where the moiré was very disfigured and degraded, it was supported on the cotton lawn then covered with a softly ribbed silk before being faced with the Stabiltex. Thus the original top cover was preserved within the trim, while the combination of ribbed silk and Stabiltex provided the appropriate appearance and durability. This approach was taken throughout the front half of the carriage, creating a unity of appearance to balance with the better preserved hind half.

Figure 6.11 Carriage undergoing treatment in 1999. A comparison with Figure 6.12 shows the extent of alterations made to convert the c. 1810 chariot into the carriage

Figure 6.12 Line drawing of a chariot (after Adams 1971 [1837]: opp. p. 225)

The woolcloth

The woolcloth needing conservation was supported on a backing of dyed calico, couched with fine polyester thread, and faced with nylon tulle (net of 20:40 denier), also suitably dyed. The calico was of sympathetic weight and weave to support and to camouflage loss of the textile. Its matt appearance was not disturbed by the nylon tulle, which, although less durable than Stabiltex, would be placed in areas unlikely to be handled, such as door panels and pockets, pillars, quarter squabs (Figure 6.14) and roof lining. The hind seat fall was complete enough not to need facing with tulle.

Where the woolcloth was neither visually acceptable nor strong enough in terms of the present role of the object, it was supported with a grid of stitching onto nylon tulle, then covered with a cotton 'moleskin'.[12] Here the more weighty and opaque fabric was needed on the obverse, the tulle giving sufficient support to the reverse. Dyed to match the original, the moleskin gave a perfect imitation of the texture of the woolcloth. More hard-wearing than wool, it would also be less attractive to further insect infestation. Both edge rolls, the front seat fall and all the glass string linings were treated in this way. The missing quarter squab was also reconstructed using cotton moleskin.

Linen base cloths

Most of the base cloths were in very poor state. It was decided to keep these within the trim but cover them on the outer face with a strong new linen 'duck' (plain-weave fabric). Where the base cloths were only minimally damaged at the edges, a patched support was given. Thus a representative sample of their construction, including the trimmer's drawing

Figure 6.13 Pillar holders before and after conservation. On the right, the worsted pile at the top half of the lace has been cleaned using natural rubber sponge. Old repairs in the lining have been removed and the moiré awaits support; the stuffing is removed to facilitate treatment. On the left, the moiré lining has been supported between cotton lawn and Stabiltex; the holder has been reconstructed as originally

and notes and the slashes made during stuffing, could still be studied.

Stuffing and buttoning, construction

Original hair stuffings were reused, augmenting loss with new curled horsehair. The vegetable fibre, which was in very poor condition, was removed, and a sample retained. The missing quarter squab which was reconstructed in new materials was filled with polyester wadding.

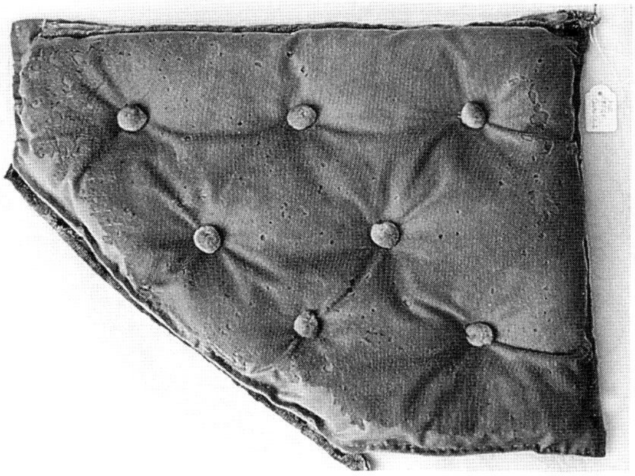

Figure 6.14 Right front quarter squab (E in Figure 6.1) after conservation

Buttoning tufts removed to facilitate conservation were re-employed, tying off with linen thread around new 'butterflies' of cotton fabric at the reverse side of the trim. Very moth-damaged or missing tufts were remade using dyed wool yarn tied with linen thread. All the corroded refurbishment buttons of the hind back squab were replaced with new tufts.

Laces

Broken sections in the laces were supported and 'filled in' by an appropriately dyed ribbed cotton, which was visually sympathetic in weave. The most obvious loss of broad lace was on the front seat fall and the missing glass strings. Here, the dyed ribbed cotton, painted with the original design, was thought acceptable, perhaps until a good reproduction could be woven.

'Roses' and tassels

The metal wire decoration of the 'roses' was corroded and most of the silk wrapping discoloured or lost. Corrosion products were cleaned off using acetone (n-propanone) on swabs, but there seemed no point in re-wrapping these hardly visible wires. Wrapping with new silk and wool yarns over the leather ring was, however, successful in stabilising and filling in for original wrapping yarns (Plate 6.2).

For the flat tassels, deteriorated or missing, the heading was reconstructed with acid-free card appropriately wrapped, and the fringing augmented or reproduced using new wool bullion fringe.

The small tassels missing from the spring curtains were replaced with replication of the originals.

Spring curtains

The four almost complete curtains were supported, after wet cleaning, between two layers of silk crepeline. Dyed to a mid shade of pink, the overlays helped to unify the uneven colour of the taffeta while not attempting to reproduce the original deeper magenta which would look too vibrant within the now more muted colours of the interior as a whole.

The fullness and the stitching of the overlays had to be worked carefully so that the three layers could be rolled comfortably together on the curtain barrel. It was advised that these curtains should be kept rolled up, being too fragile to be pulled up and down or to be exposed to light coming through the windows. Hems of new taffeta were added to carry new curtain sticks. The two missing curtains (those for the door windows) were reconstructed with new taffeta dyed to match the muted pink of the conserved curtains.

Two covering layers of twill cotton fabric were removed from the curtains' metal barrels. The outer one had intact, in places, the thread link-stitching the curtain to the barrel; this was pulled out as a continuous thread where possible. Corrosion produced from the metal barrel, exacerbated by adhesion with starch paste, had destroyed the inner layer of cotton beyond further re-use.

After cleaning the metal barrel, a layer of Tyvek™ was first rolled to isolate the metal and to replace the inner layer of cotton cover.[13] The original outer layer of cotton fabric was then reinstated for the curtain to be stitched onto. Link-stitching was remade where possible with original thread but augmented throughout with a new thread of polyester.

Carpeting

There was sufficient evidence in the remaining fragments of the carpet to be able to have this reproduced in structure and pattern.

6.9.3 Reattaching the trimming

Methods to reattach the trimming into the carriage needed to be least interventive to both trimming and framework. Stiff strips – of card or Nomex® – covered with calico could be held by staples or screws to the carriage body, isolating the remaining shank ends and providing a surface on which to stitch the trimming items in place. Where the original seaming laces had been left in situ, tackheads were isolated, with a layer such as Nomex, before the trimming was stitched back to them.

6.10 Assessment of treatment

Although at the time of writing work on the carriage interior is not yet complete, the conservation methods chosen for the items of trimming can already be seen to greatly improve their appearance and, more importantly, to benefit and stabilise their condition.

Construction of the present trimming has been thoroughly investigated, documented and reproduced. Although some items have been reconstructed, the integrity of the object has always been respected and any remaining original fragments will be preserved within the item. The treatment overall will help to recreate the experience of luxury and comfort of such a totally upholstered interior dating from 1850.

The necessity to remove a large proportion of the trimming for appropriate treatment has uncovered information about the history of the carriage which otherwise would have remained unknown. The conservation of the Hall carriage has given an insight into the extent of refurbishment that could be carried out in the mid-nineteenth century, not only to the trimming but also to the design and construction of a carriage as a whole.

Notes

1 A most informative source is Farr and Thrupp (1998 [1888]). There are also sections in Adams (1971 [1837]), Burgess (1881), and Philipson (1994 [1897]). Especially interesting are sections in Felton (1996 [1794–5]: 147–72 and supplement 37–43).

2 Felton (1996 [1794–5]), *A Treatise on Carriages*, appears to distinguish the term *linings* (for the items of upholstery and interior textiles) from the term *trimmings* (for the laces, fringes, tassels etc. which ornament the linings). By the time Farr and Thrupp (1998 [1888]), *Handbook of*

Coach Trimming was written, *trimming* has come to refer both to the upholstery *and* the ornament. Terminology used in this paper for the individual items of carriage trimming is taken from Farr (1998 [1888]), and Felton (1996 [1794–5]). I should like to acknowledge the advice of Patricia Stout, curator of the National Trust Carriage Collection, Arlington Court.

3 Sources include Calnan (ed., 1991), and Nicholson (1997). Felton's, *A Treatise on Carriages*, lists the repairs available for linings and trimmings in the late eighteenth century, with treatments itemised in detail and individually priced (1996 [1794–5], supplement 37–43).

4 At the time of writing, this project is on-going. I thank the owner of the carriage, Garth Pedler, for his permission to publish, and acknowledge his understanding that such a complex treatment takes time to be established and carried out.

5 A coach has two seats inside, one facing forwards and one backwards, usually to hold two or three persons on each seat.

6 I am grateful to Heather Porter for discovering this reference and for her help in assessing the original construction of the trimming.

7 Felton (1996 [1794–5]: 163), describes 'false linings and linen linings, used to cover and preserve the others if good, or to hide them if bad'.

8 An account of the conservation of the Hall carriage body is given in Hobbs, 1999.

9 After initial discussion, a representative example of each treatment – conservation and replication – was carried out for agreement with the owner.

10 The supplement in Felton (1996 [1794–5]), concerning repairs and replacement of trimming items, suggests that re-furbishment of the carriage interior was common practice.

11 I should like to thank and acknowledge Steve Conway, who has conserved the bodywork of the Hall carriage, for his invaluable part in the discovery of this reconstruction; and also to stress the need for conservators, working on different media within a complex composite object, to discuss and co-ordinate the information each finds.

12 'Moleskin' is a heavy twill weave cotton fabric with a brushed nap giving it an appearance very similar to the original woolcloth. Supplier: John Lewis.

13 Rinsing Tyvek™ is recommended before use with metals because it has an anti-static finish (potassium dibutylphosphate) which is reported to have a deleterious effect on metals and organics (Walker, 1986: 23).

References

Adams, W.B. (1971 [1837]) *English Pleasure Carriages*. Bath: Adams and Dart.

Burgess, J.W. (1881) *A Practical Treatise on Coach-building*. London: Crosby Lockwood & Co.

Calnan, C. (ed.) (1991) *Conservation of Leather in Transport Collections*. Papers given at a UKIC conference Restoration '91, London in October 1991. London: UKIC.

Farr, W. and Thrupp, G.A. (1998 [1888]) *Handbook of Coach Trimming*. West Yorkshire: William Binns.

Felton, W. (1996 [1794–5]) *A Treatise on Carriages*. Mendham, NJ: Astral Press.

Hobbs, J. (1999) The 'restore or conserve' dilemma, *Old Glory*, no.113 (July) (Surrey: CMS Publishing).

Nicholson, C. (1997) The care of the National Trust's carriage collections. In: K. Marko (ed.), *Textiles in Trust*. Proceedings of the Symposium 'Textiles in Trust' held at Blickling Hall, Norfolk, September 1995. London: Archetype, 59–66.

Philipson, J. (1994 [1897]) *The Art and Craft of Coachbuilding*. Warwickshire: TEE Publishing.

Walker, S. (1986) Investigation of the properties of Tyvek, pertaining to its use as a storage material for artifacts. *IIC-CG Newsletter*, September 1986, 21–25.

7

Ethafoam® treatments for two eighteenth-century French chairs

Elizabeth G. Lahikainen

7.1 Introduction

Upholstered objects constitute an important sub-set of a large genre of artifacts that includes almost any type of object that has fabric attached. Most often, but not always, the object is some kind of seating furniture. These artifacts often bring status to their owners but they are also functional and intended to give physical rest to the sitter. As such, they have developed over time as a multi-layered 'upholstery' that also gives comfort. Conservation treatments to objects with historic upholstery are interdisciplinary achievements involving any number of varied materials from cellulose parts of linen and cotton, to protein materials such as curled hair filling (stuffing) and wool or silk finish fabrics. An endless possibility of ornament from dyes to metal threads for embroidery multiplies the number of issues and elevates the amount of intricacy involved in integrating treatment for an individual part into the larger conservation project.

Many upholstered objects have no historic upholstery materials retained on the frame so historical information specific to that frame is restricted to physical evidence of what was there rather than extant materials. This information can then be supplemented by related objects that do retain some original upholstery. In this way, the history of upholstery technology can be communicated through the contours and textiles of the treated object. In addition, written and pictorial materials from that era can further contribute to the historical and aesthetic accuracy in defining the presentation. The combination of hard evidence on the object plus social and materials' history from the period usually reveals enough information to draw informed as well as sensible conclusions.

Often seating furniture requiring upholstery treatment is missing all or most of its textile components. Conventional upholstery has many layers of textiles that are attached to the frame with tacks. Tacks introduce hundreds of holes into the wood frame of the furniture, a serious deterioration factor for the artifact. A conservation-wise solution to re-upholstery is to carve expanded polyethylene foam plastic to recreate a historically correct profile of the upholstered forms. Ethafoam® is the Dow trade name for this foam plastic and this type of treatment is sometimes referred to as an Ethafoam® treatment. An Ethafoam® treatment offers the advantage that it does not require metal fasteners. This modern technology method bypasses the step of using the tacks of conventional re-upholstery. The plastic imitation upholstery further sculpted by padding is covered with an appropriate top cover fabric and trim to present the object as a vision of its original splendour.

It is possible to carve Ethafoam® to imitate an appropriate historical upholstered profile successfully, but its use in upholstery conservation is not without controversy. To make a piece of historic seat furniture convincing in either conventional upholstery or one that is carved out of plastic requires training and practice. The subtlety of curves and proportion of finely executed upholstery in plastic is a new skill. The carver must not only become familiar with Ethafoam® but trained in the craft of upholstery, the history of upholstery technology and the artistic features of a textile surface. It is critical to a historically accurate profile that the subtle shaping characteristic of traditional technique is incorporated into the carved form so it does not appear flat, hard or out of scale to the frame. The final effect of the Ethafoam® upholstery is believable as a soft-sitting surface only when these elements are successfully captured into the carved form. The replacement textile is also an obvious component of how the completed object will read as an artifact. The replacement textile should be chosen for reasons of historical accuracy even though availability and/or costs might require some type of compromise. They also need to be applied with the mastery of a highly skilled craftsman so the ultimate presentation of the object coalesces the essential elements of quality upholstery. When the carver is armed with upholstery technology, the textiles represent the era of the object and they are applied with the skills of a master upholsterer, the end result of Ethafoam® conservation treatments is not only a fair representation of an historical truth, but can be an exquisite one.

Ethafoam® treatments are particularly suited for the re-upholstery of bare chair frames for museum presentation. Although seat furniture treated in this way can be sat on, this type of treatment was not developed for use on functional furniture because the Ethafoam® is not soft or even remotely comfortable. Only a most unusual situation regarding the condition of a frame or exceptional domestic requirements would prompt a recommendation for home use.

Polyethylene is a conservation approved plastic because it is chemically stable and does not cause deterioration to other materials. The construction of Ethafoam® is also stable, meaning it will not torque easily and the air pockets are closed cells so spores and bacteria are prevented from penetrating the interior, thereby eliminating the possibility of sustained biological life on the inside. Ethafoam® products are available in an assortment of types and weights and are used commercially for many different functions. Upholstery conservation projects usually employ the high-density weight or 9 lb (weight per cubic foot in a liquid state) that is sold in 8 ft planks (about 2.5 m). These can be purchased in 1 (25 mm), 2 (50 mm) or 3 inch (75 mm) depths. While lighter weight densities can be used, the highest density carves the most uniformly because it offers some resistance to the knife. Also, it will easily hold a screw and is the most resistant to denting so once it is on the frame it is less vulnerable to distortion from an accident.

7.2 Two mid-eighteenth-century French chairs

Two distinguished French chairs are used in this study to demonstrate the process and outcome of an Ethafoam® treatment. The natural wood finish chair frame from the Detroit Institute of Art (Acc. no. 60.89; c.1750), is attributed to Jean Baptist Tilliard I (Figure 7.1). The gilded wood armchair (Acc. no.

Figure 7.1 Armchair by Jean-Baptiste Tilliard I, (1723–98) French, 1750, beech, modern upholstery. (Gift of Anne and Henry Ford II, The Detroit Institute of Arts, Acc. no. 60.89.) The three-quarter view of this chair demonstrates the curves required for an Ethafoam® upholstery. This piece does not yet have its Nomex® edges. This chair (and the Cleveland chair) later received additional padding of batting/wadding to complete the profile

Figure 7.2 Armchair by Nicolas Heurtaut, French, 1720–71, c.1755, carved wood, 104.7 × 73 cm. (© The Cleveland Museum of Art, 1999, Gift of Mr and Mrs Severance A. Millikin, 1989.160.) This chair (seen here full front) demonstrates the shaped Ethafoam® 'upholstery' with Nomex® facings in the tacking margins. Notice the seat back section is screwed to the frame close to each corner, and how the Ethafoam® is shaped to overhang the wood frame

1989.160; c.1750), from the Cleveland Museum of Art, is attributed to Nicolas Heurtaut (Figure 7.2). Mid-eighteenth-century French furniture was chosen for this case study because the curvilinear reverse curves of this period are the most challenging to achieve. It is especially difficult to imitate these lines in another medium like plastic while accomplishing the look of upholstery. Both chairs are intended for exhibition in an art museum setting.

7.2.1 Examination

Structural treatment to the frame and finishes of both chairs had been addressed by the time of upholstery conservation. Light blue silk fibres were discovered on the seat rail of the Heurtaut chair. Unfortunately, these fibres were located in a tack hole of an unidentifiable era, so there is no way to determine with which generation of upholstery this blue colour is associated. There is also some evidence of decorative brass nailing, most evident along the seat rails. The holes caused by these shanks are placed well into the rabbet (rebate) of the tacking margin and are spaced one inch (25 mm) apart. The seat back has some fill in the holes of the tacking margins so historical evidence is obscured.

The Tilliard armchair is now in natural wood, the gilding or painted finish having been removed before acquisition into the Detroit Institute of Arts collection. It arrived for upholstery conservation in a 1960s salmon pink velvet with the edges held in place with modern brass nails. The design of this upholstery also featured an overstuffed, loose, down-filled cushion. These materials were examined layer by layer and, like the Heurtaut chair, were also determined to be modern and were removed. Red and turquoise fibres were found in several places on the seat rails of the Tilliard chair. A red sample seemed to be associated with a square hole. Square holes with no ferrous staining are assumed to be from eighteenth-century decorative brass nails. This implies the fibres come from an eighteenth-century presentation. These brass nail holes are more closely spaced than in the Heurtaut chair. The Tilliard chair also retained the shanks of some eighteenth-century brass nails in the tacking margins, as well as a few discernible decorative brass nail holes. The remaining eighteenth-century brass nail shanks plus holes where shanks had been removed provided enough evidence to reconstruct the nailing patterns. The information revealed by examining the rear posts of the chair, the tightness of the lower seat back rail to the seat rail and researching other examples, indicated that a tight fully upholstered seat was the likely form of the chair's original upholstery.

All materials were sampled for the files so future custodians will have hard evidence of a material's history. Careful assessment at this examination phase of treatment is very important. In this and any conservation treatment, caution is advised when it involves removing parts or all of the textile layers. Materials should not be removed or discarded without careful consideration as to what they are and their place in the history of the object. The structures inside the upholstery, including the secondary woods, are the elements that hold the history of the generations of fabrics

Plate 2.1 (left) The Alma-Tadema settee: Detail of one of the silk-screened decorative panels of 1991. The choice of colours was determined by the fragments of original embroidery and influenced by the colours of the carved and inlaid frames. In 1990 the information available was limited to the colours described in contemporary published accounts. The colours were distributed according to the tonal values of the original panels as depicted in Figure 2.2. (Reproduced by kind permission of the Sherman Fairchild Center for Objects Conservation, The Metropolitan Museum of Art, New York)

Plate 2.2 (bottom left) The Alma-Tadema settee: Detail of an embroidered curtain (Metropolitan Museum of Art, Rogers Fund 1996, 1996.330.) from the music room of the Marquand residence. The discovery of the curtain in 1996, five years after the 1991 treatment of the settee, provided a unique opportunity to evaluate the interpretation of the design and colours made in 1991. (Reproduced by kind permission of the Department of European Sculpture and Decorative Arts, The Metropolitan Museum of Art, New York)

Plate 2.3 (bottom right) The Alma-Tadema settee: Detail of the curtain's lower section showing the embroidered border design on black–purple satin. The embroidered floral design of the settee was also worked on the black-purple satin originally, unlike the embroidered floral design of the curtain which is worked on the green dyed rep (see Plate 2.2). Consequently, the impact of the colour contrast is different. The original effect of the floral design on the settee probably more closely resembled that observed in this plate rather than that observed in Plate 2.2. (Reproduced by kind permission of the Department of European Sculpture and Decorative Arts, The Metropolitan Museum of Art, New York)

Plate 5.1 The blue state bed, English, dated 1697, from Hampton Court in Herefordshire, UK, shown here as exhibited in the European Sculpture and Decorative Art's Department's Aitken Galleries at the Metropolitan Museum of Art, New York. (Collection of the Metropolitan Museum of Art, New York. Gift of Mr and Mrs William Randolph Hearst Jr, 1968. 68.217.1)

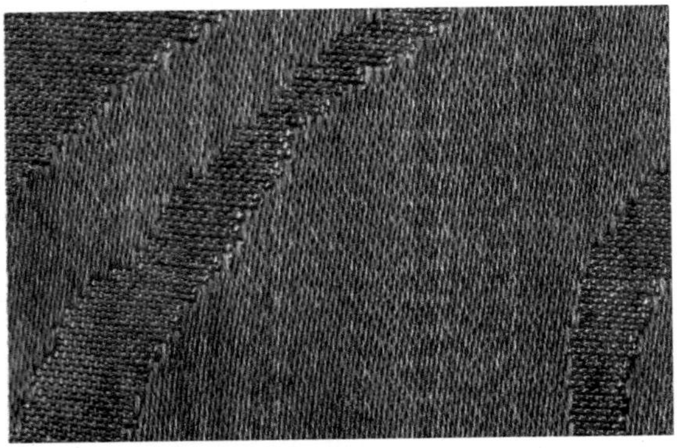

Plate 5.2 The blue state bed: Close-up of the reproduction damask, showing the strie effect. The manufacturer of the reproduction fabric achieved this effect adapting a skein-dyeing technique

Plate 6.1 The Hall carriage: Hind half of the carriage after initial cleaning. Although there are signs of wear and use, the original splendour of the totally upholstered interior is still evident. (The original moiré cover of the back squab has been covered over with a woolcloth in a later refurbishment)

Plate 6.2 The Hall carriage: Pillar covers and roses before and after conservation

Plate 8.1 The Octagon Room at Raby Castle, Co. Durham, UK after conservation and installation of the upholstered seat furniture, showing the corner sofa

Plate 10.1 Armchair (c.1715–20), Houghton Hall, Norfolk, UK: Part of a suite of four armchairs and eight side chairs. The carved gilt gesso frame displays its crimson Genoese velvet close-fitting removable cover. It provides an eighteenth-century model of minimally intrusive upholstery techniques

Plate 10.2 Detail of the gilt gesso armchair illustrated in Plate 10.1, showing lacing of the cover

Plate 10.3 Detail of the inner face of the front corner seat rail of the gilt gesso armchair illustrated in Plate 10.1. The lacing cords are threaded through pre-drilled holes in the seat rail and tied together

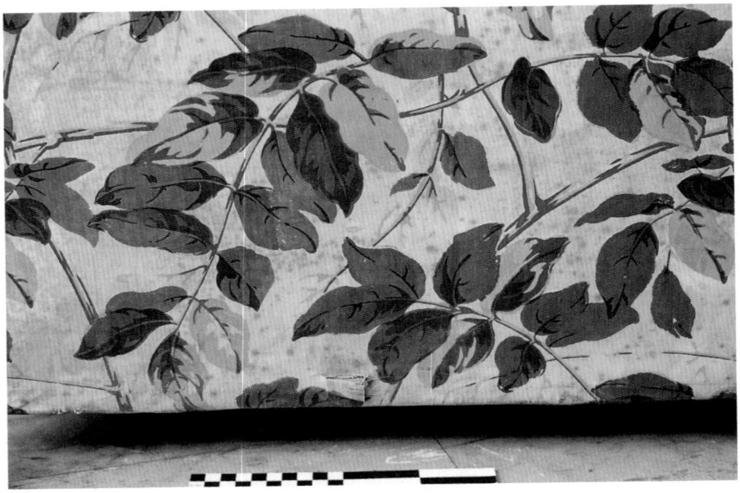

Plate 11.1 Textile furnishings at Brodsworth Hall, Yorkshire, UK: Detail of the fixed upholstery covering on an ottoman box (EHIN 9000 8226), showing the leaf design (Pattern 30)

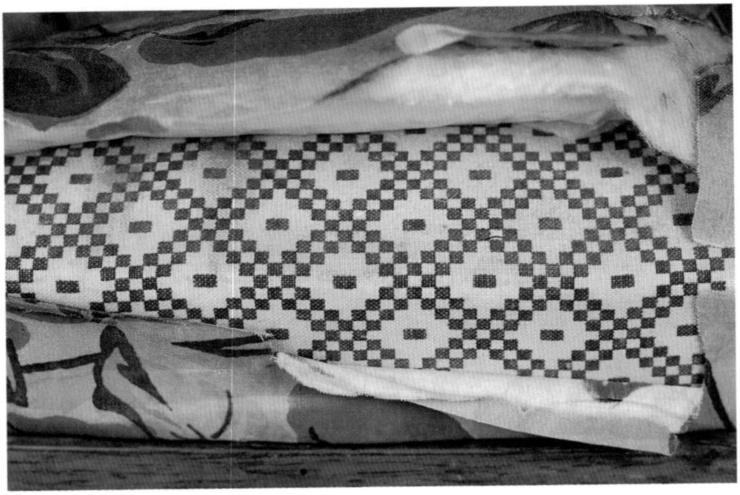

Plate 11.2 Textile furnishings at Brodsworth Hall: Detail of one of the drop-on seats from the set of rosewood side chairs showing the two layers of fixed upholstery coverings: the diamond design (Pattern 31) and the leaf design (Pattern 30)

Plate 11.3 Textile furnishings at Brodsworth Hall: Detail of a loose cover (EHIN 9000 5874) in the rose and phlox design (Pattern 6), probably supplied by Lapworth Brothers in 1863 for Bedroom 9 or 10

formerly attached to the frame as well as evidence of upholstery construction techniques that are indicators of the original profile. The materials retained on these structures and evidence of the materials once attached are not generally well understood and experience is required to document and decipher what is revealed. Textile and upholstery expertise is essential if informed deduction is to be drawn from this often scanty and confusing data.

7.2.2 Interpreting the evidence

In examining artifacts and in researching them, it can be difficult to distinguish between what we know and what we think we know. There are often conflicting opinions about what can be deduced from a certain type of evidence and specialists have their own orientation to information as well as their own expertise on any given issue. Considering the context of an artifact within the period it was made is very important for answering some presentation questions, such as: how luxurious should a piece look? Should it be the cutting-edge style of the period or express a less up-to-date style? Bringing together traces of data and the deductions arising from their study is key to distilling reasonable conclusions. This can be an arduous process. Integrating various materials' information about the wood, the metal components, the textiles and the often-ignored topic of upholstery technology, is essential in determining a sensible interpretation path as well as developing a treatment plan. When the upholstery conservator understands the individual details of the object and successfully integrates this with knowledge of the period, a clear rationale for re-interpretation can be evolved, facilitating effective decision-making. The closer the conserved artifact is to its own history, the more dynamic the visual statement is once treatment is complete.

These chairs present several issues concerning historical information that are as yet not fully understood. For example, the nailing pattern on the gilt chair is high off the rabbet edge and the nails are spaced about one inch (25 mm) apart. Since the decorative heads are not butted, it is not likely they had been used to hold the top cover fabric to the frame. Does this suggest there was trim under the nail heads? It is reasonable to assume that seat furniture was sometimes recovered within a generation of its production and the eighteenth-century evidence is from two upholsteries. It is clear that this chair had brass nails in the eighteenth century, but it is not clear if this was the only way this chair was upholstered within the period. How does this information impact on reinterpretation? For the interpretation of the chairs in this study trim was used to cover the fabric edge and no brass nails were used.

Revealing and recording information is not a mandate for re-using it in the reinterpretation, especially when its meaning is open to a number of interpretations. The role assigned to some artifacts or institutions means that custodians may have reasons for not including some historical knowledge in a particular presentation. However, caution is advised in developing a rationale for not using what is known to be true. Choices must go hand and hand with extant materials, evidence and historical knowledge. Inappropriately relying on personal taste, disregarding or biasing historical facts obviously defeats the fundamental purpose of interpretation. The treatment plan as well as the treatment report should explain the concepts behind interpretation decisions. All treatment reports for an artifact should in part be a record of hard facts, e.g., fibre evidence, the placement and type of holes as well as an account of deductions made from this evidence. Care should be taken so that the deductions are not represented as hard facts.

7.3 Treatment

In general, upholstery conservation projects have similar priorities to other areas of conservation:

1 to preserve historic materials relating to the object – this effort is usually centred around stabilisation and some type of cleaning;
2 to avoid any damage to the object in implementing the processes of treatment, which includes using conservation grade materials.

Pieces that retain historic textiles require some form of textile conservation to stabilise and preserve them. Pieces that undergo Ethafoam® treatments require new replacement textiles because no or very few textiles remain. In addition to meeting the above-mentioned goals, an Ethafoam® upholstery conservation project involves a reclamation of a period aesthetic by employing textiles that are not original to the furniture but represent the era of the re-presentation. As in most other Ethafoam® projects, in this case study treatment was designed to regain the historic profile by shaping Ethafoam® and reinstalling an historic aesthetic using historically correct replacement textiles. No textile conservation was required.

Presenting seating furniture without historically accurate upholstery makes it impossible to understand the object within its historical context or the frame's intended function and appearance. Setting the parameters for and choosing the replacement textiles are decisions that require knowledge in areas of style, aesthetics and technology of textiles. Information and expertise from curatorial resources and the textile industry are important factors in determining whether the textile choice is appropriate for the piece being treated. Making the chair or sofa 'look good' is not enough. Only a textile that truthfully represents the style, colour and scale of the period being presented will prove to be a lasting choice. Several historically correct options may be suitable and available for any given project and personal taste may play a role in making a choice from that pool of appropriate fabrics. However, fabric choices that illustrate personal taste alone demonstrate aesthetics of decades or centuries later than the object. Combining aesthetics developed in different periods can give a result that is pleasing to the eye, but presenting these combinations on period furniture diminishes what can be learned about the piece and the period in which it was made and/or used. In addition, it often results in the object looking out of context and it becomes vulnerable to being unsightly within a short amount of time, i.e., when today's fashion becomes yesterday's out-of-style statement.

7.3.1 Designing and installing Ethafoam® treatments

Both chairs in this study were ideal candidates for Ethafoam® treatments because neither one has historic textile materials larger than fragment size and the foam forms did not have to be integrated into existing shapes of historic textiles. The first step was to define the appropriate profile for the upholstered forms by finding a suitable prototype. For both chairs, the following prototypes were informative and helpful: the ceremonial armchair attributed to Nicolas-Quinibert Foliot by the architect Pierre Contant d'Ivry (c.1749) provided a useful model (Pallot, 1989: 1467). This was supplemented by paintings by Laurent Pechuex. Portraits of Marie-Louise (c.1765), daughter of Louise-Elisabeth (coincidentally the owner of the arm chair attributed to Foliot), Don Felipe (c.1765) and the Marquise de Pompadour (c.1764) were all used as primary guides for form and application of fabric and trims (Pallot, 1989: 144). Even though the Foliot chair chosen as the primary prototype is much more elaborate in carving and richness of textiles than either of the chairs in this study, it is the correct date and all original and, therefore, a very reliable form for an appropriate shape. The paintings are a few years later but have clear views of the details, such as arms and trims, and are more to the level of decoration as the chairs being treated.

The highest density Ethafoam®, i.e. 9 lb, is usually the best choice. It is the easiest to carve and has the most resistance to denting once the piece is put on display. The foam blocks are rough cut from measurements for each upholstered area and fitted to the frame. The seat back is laid in flat against the frame and cut large enough to fill the space of the seat back and rest on the rabbet of the tacking margin. The seat is keyed in between the back posts and at the front arm uprights. The breadth and shape of the seat together with the front arm uprights create a situation called lock out, meaning the seat form cannot be set into the space without cutting it in two pieces. Placing the join along the diagonal from the inside back of the arm upright to the near back post of the opposite side (Figure 7.3) enables the two halves to fit into the desired spaces of the frame. A diagonal cut creates a friction fit so there is very little opportunity for the pieces to shift.

The plastic forms are then shaped to imitate the furniture profiles on the historical prototypes using any number of cutting and filing tools from electric kitchen knives to palm sanders. The forms can also be comprised of several parts and fused together with hot-melt adhesive, such as Jet-melt® 3764 (a 3M product), an ethylene-vinyl acetate polymer with hydrocarbon resin, polyethylene, paraffin wax, antioxidant and vinyl acetate. This requires experience as it is necessary to work quickly before the adhesive sets and the adhesive must not be allowed to be so hot that the foam melts. The shape of the upholstered form evolves much as sculpture does from stone. At first, this step appears to be easy, but capturing the gentle curves of believable upholstery requires both skill and experience. Even an accomplished woodcarver might need a few tries before claiming to be a master.

Once the desired shape is achieved, the surface of the foam is sanded to smooth out any unevenness. The proportion of height to frame dimensions, and symmetry right to left and front to back, is evaluated and corrected at this time. The shape is further refined with shaped layers of polyester wadding/batting, which gives the form the appearance of conventional upholstery materials. Here again, experience and familiarity with upholstery techniques is essential so the padding becomes an integral part of the upholstery. Padding without a sense of the upholstered profile only makes it fatter, not shapelier or more believable as an upholstery. The fullness of the batting also provides the flexibility for final adjustments to the contours, so that characteristic features of upholstery can be presented rather than those of hard plastic.

The carved foam plastic defines and supports the basic profile, but the top cover fabric also needs a system of attachment. This system must grip the frame along the tacking margins so it looks as though the fabric is tacked down as it would be in a conventional upholstery. It also must be strong enough to retain tension on the top cover fabric to prevent waffling (similar to buckling of the fabric due to uneven tensioning). To avoid the deterioration that metal fasteners impose on the wood frame, an alternative to tacking must be created. In this study, the tacking margins were faced with a gluing edge to hold the fabric and trim. A sewing edge is another system that could be used. A good choice of materials for this edge is a stiff weight of Nomex®, a Dupont trade name for an Aramid polymer paper. The facings to the seat need to be cut wider than the margins of the wood frame so they can be glued or otherwise attached to the Ethafoam®. They require careful fitting to the sculpted tacking margins of the chair frame and should break at the joins of the seat foam pieces so the seat can be easily removed if necessary. Once they are properly fitted, they are lined on the outside edge with a narrow strip of sheet Beva® 371 adhesive (ethylene vinyl acetate copolymer with cyclohexanone resin and phthalate ester of hydroabietyl alcohol and petrolatum) for attaching the fabric. If they are being used as a sewing edge, they are covered with a fabric at this time. The facings can be attached to the Ethafoam® by pinning into place. For these chairs, however, they were set in place with a bead of hot-melt adhesive applied with a hot-glue gun. It is desirable to apply the facings so they angle toward the chair and carry the line of the fabric to the correct degree of slant to complete the shape of the upholstery. In this way, they then appear to be attached to the frame.

The seat back shape of Ethafoam® is backed with a full sheet of Nomex® that extends to the outside of the tacking margins. This sheet is used to hold the contrasting fabric seen from the outside back, as well as the decorative top cover fabric seen from the front. Once the Ethafoam® upholstery parts are in place, the top cover fabrics can be adhered to the Nomex® using a heat spatula to melt the adhesive. This appliance can be purchased at museum conservation supply houses and it should have a rheostat. The temperature recommended for sheet Beva® 371 is 150 °F (65 °C). Experience and skill are required to prevent either too much adhesive coming through the finish fabric or insufficient adhesive to hold the layers of fabric. Also, the temperature of the spatula needs to be compatible with the fabric to prevent scorching or over melting of the adhesive.

The seat back is held into place with brass plates (Figure 7.3) screwed to both the back of the Ethafoam® form and the rabbet of the

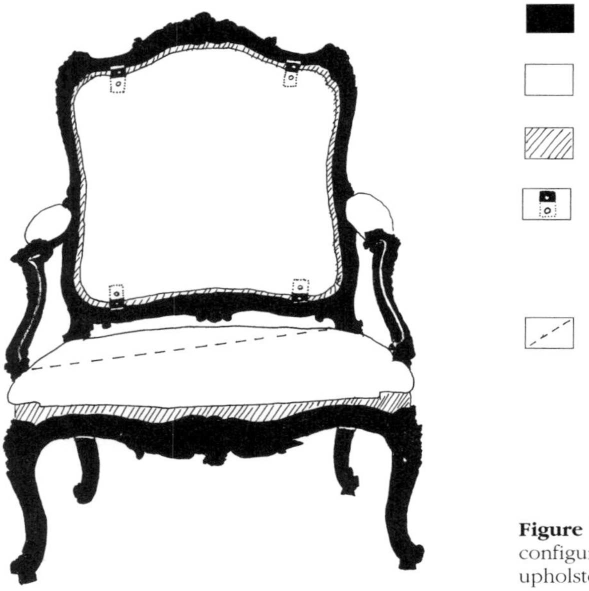
Wood frame
Ethafoam™
Nomex™ facings with Beva™ 371 adhesive applied to the edges
Brass plates hold the Ethafoam™ form to the frame with brass screws set into the Ethafoam™ from the back. The brass plates extend to the wood frame and screws are set into old holes in the tacking margin from the front.
The Ethafoam™ seat form is cut in two pieces to overcome "lock out" and the cut is made on the diagonal for a secure friction fit.

Figure 7.3 This construction diagram illustrates the configuration of the modern materials of an Ethafoam® upholstery

seat back frame. Brass is used because it will not rust and the hardware is readily available at a hardware store. The seat is held in place by gravity aided by the keying in around the back posts and front arm uprights. The arm pads are friction fit during treatment and spot glued to the frame with hot-melt adhesive once they are fully upholstered. A metal fastener through the fabric and Nomex® could also be used. It is not recommended these chairs go on view without anchoring the arm pads as it is possible they could disappear.

7.3.2 Finish fabrics and trim

Fabric chosen for the natural wood chair was a silk lampas that has a 42 inch (1070 mm) design repeat. The colours are gold and cream

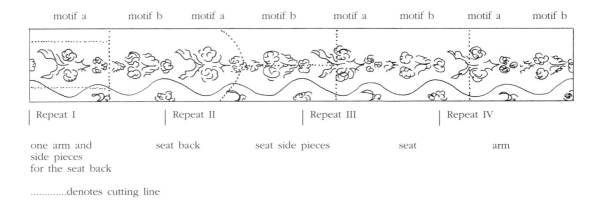

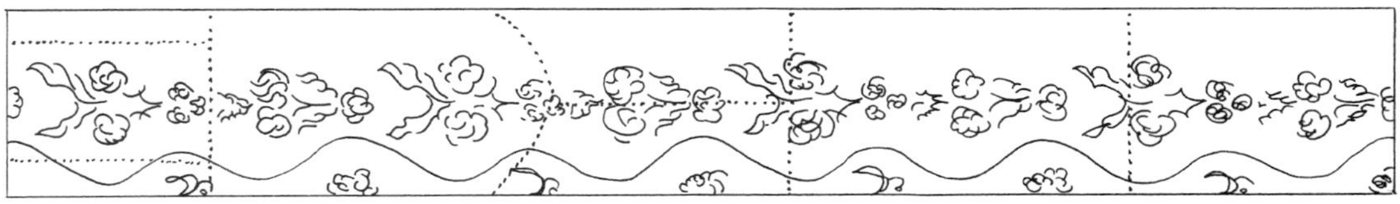

Figure 7.4 The amount of fabric required for a project is estimated by using the measurements of both the object and the design repeat of the top cover fabric. The chair from the Detroit Institute of Arts required four, 42 inch (1070 mm) repeats of silk lampas. This fabric has two major motifs in each repeat. They are similar but not interchangeable. Motif (a) was used for the seat back and Motif (b) was used on the seat. The fabric is 22 inches (560 mm) wide so both seat and seat back had to be widened with side pieces that matched in design. This plan makes enough yardage of Motif (a) available for use on the arms

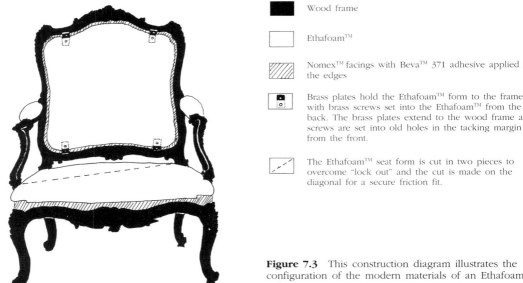

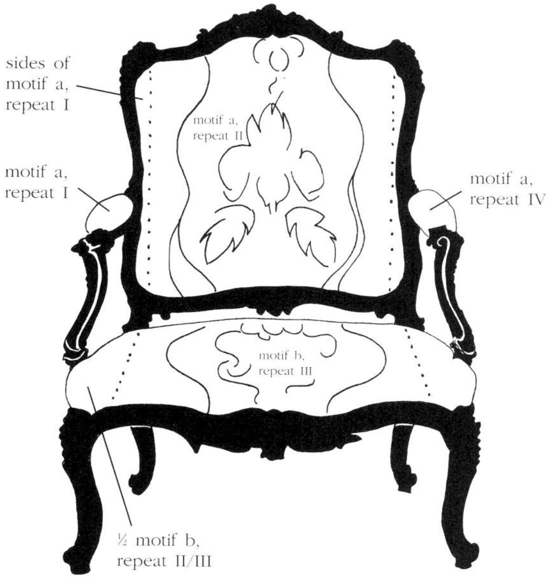

Figure 7.5 This diagram illustrates how the placement of the design motifs would appear on the chair using the cutting plan of Figure 7.4. Calculating the measurements can require accuracy to the centimetre but careful planning can save yardage and, therefore, money when use of the design is maximised

and turquoise (keeping with the eighteenth-century historic evidence). The repeat has two major motifs that are very similar but with slight differences so they cannot be interchanged. Lying out and cutting the fabric requires the conservator to be well versed in fabric design and in sewing. It becomes complicated to seam the same motif to the same motif for matching without loosing needed parts of the design in the seam allowance. Cutting the fabric always has to be carefully planned so one cut will not intrude on an adjacent motif making it too short to use and wasting expensive yardage (Figures 7.4 and 7.5).

The fabric for the gilt chair was not as complicated to lay out since it had only one major design motif. The repeat is 17 inches, shorter than the furnishing textiles usually used within the period, and is purple and grey silk damask. Both chairs were trimmed with a figured trim. Following the French tradition of incorporating several elements into the weave structure of upholstery trims, both these trims were configured with a decorative cord on one side and loops on the other (Figure 7.6). Brass nails were not used in these interpretations because of questions raised in evaluating the evidence of the nailing pattern. One strong advantage to this Ethafoam®/non-interventive treatment is that the decorative elements, such as fabric and trims used in a treatment, can be easily removed and replaced without interfering with the materials of the artifact should there be a need to do so in the future. When and if further evidence arises regarding the

Figure 7.6 The two French eighteenth-century chairs in 1999 after upholstery conservation treatments undertaken using Ethafoam®: on the left is the Heurtaut armchair, with a carved gilded wood frame (© The Cleveland Museums of Art, 1999; gift of Mr and Mrs Severance A. Millikin, Acc. no. 1989.160), on the right is the Tilliard I armchair, with a carved beech frame (Detroit Institute of Arts, Acc. no. 60.89)

decorative nailing pattern, the piece can be reinterpreted at a later date. It should be mentioned at this juncture that there is a considerable cost consideration when an object is presented with brass nails because the conservation expectation is that the brass heads be attached to the fabric rather than driving the shanks into the frame. Gluing on the nail heads protects the frame from the deterioration of another generation of holes but increases the time investment and, therefore, the cost.

7.4 Discussion

'Conservation treatment' is a term with specific meaning and, therefore, its use implies restrictions on how it should be used. The term conservation refers to the retention and preservation of historic materials, including evidence. Treatment is the implementation of the process of preserving the object-related materials. The intention of any conservation treatment is to stabilise original material and to reduce the effects of deteriorating factors, such as damaging or disfiguring repairs, corrosion products and dirt. When introducing new materials, it is of primary importance to use conservation grade supplies that are not likely to interact with the chemistry of the components of the artifact and accelerate the aging process. Adhesives that off-gas or plastics that turn brittle are examples of poor choices. Technique is another important part of the treatment process that has to be carefully thought out so problems are corrected and not amplified. Processes of treatment must be coordinated and implemented in a discernible way so that stabilisation treatment is not confused with being part of the original artifact and the records should bring definition and discussion to this point. These goals and conditions are served well by Ethafoam® treatments for upholstered furniture.

Judgements regarding presentation are a component of upholstery conservation because replacement textiles are often used and they are a high percentage of the visual dynamic and historical statement. When they are used there is the additional challenge of not only deciding what is appropriate, but also securing reasonable reproductions. The quality of the background information used to make interpretation decisions can be limited by the researcher's knowledge of upholstery and textile materials. If these areas of knowledge are not adequately pursued, the presentation suffers. Carving a hard plastic to look like something that is supposed to be soft and comfortable to sit on is also challenging. When the appropriate information and skills are utilised and integrated, this low-interventive method of upholstery conservation can satisfy the many issues that arise from scholarship and craftsmanship as well as meet the object's conservation needs.

7.5 Conclusions

Success can be measured by how well the multi-layered aspects of treatment come together. Ethafoam® treatments do not require many metal fasteners, if any at all. When Ethafoam® treatments are skilfully executed, the profile can sensitively reflect upholstery traditions as well as be historically accurate. The application of textile elements over the carved foam requires someone who is familiar with the craftsmanship and forms of conventional upholstery. When there is an appropriate, balanced interface between the object, current academic and technological knowledge of upholstery, textiles and the history of the artifact a splendid aesthetic result can be achieved. Ethafoam® treatments can meet very high upholstery conservation standards without compromising the object's interpretation. They provide elegant solutions to some very complicated and intricate problems because preservation and aesthetics are both well served.

Acknowledgements

I would like to thank both the Cleveland Museum of Art and the Detroit Institute of Arts for supporting the publication of treatments on their distinguished French chairs. I also thank the curators and conservators of those Institutions for their time and patience in this project. A special thanks to Tracey Albainy for her astute comments in editing. Thanks are also due to Marc Williams, David Mitchell, Scott Whitlow, Irena Calinescu, Carolyn Derrico and the Peabody Essex Museum and staff. The Detroit Institute of Arts would like to thank Francois Verzier of Maison Prelle and Jean Gourdon of Declercq Passementiers for their assistance in selecting appropriate fabrics and trims and Anne Charlotte and Edsel Ford for their generous support of this project.

Bibliography

Cooke, E.S. Jr (ed.) (1987) *Upholstery in America and Europe from the Seventeenth Century to World War I*. Paris: W.W. Norton & Company.

Ossut, C. (1994) *Le Siège et sa garniture*. Dourdan, France: Editions H. Vial.

Ossut, C. (1996) *Tapisserie d'ameublement*. Dourdan, France: Editions H. Vial.

Pallot, Bill G.B. (1989) *The Art of the Chair in Eighteenth-Century France*. Paris: ACR-Gismondi Editeurs.

Williams, M.A. (ed.) (1990) *Upholstery Conservation*. Preprints of a Symposium held at Colonial Williamsburg, February 2–4 1990. East Kingston, NH: American Conservation Consortium, Ltd.

8

Preserving a mid-nineteenth-century decorative scheme: conserving the Morant suite in the Octagon Room, Raby Castle

Lesley Wilson

8.1 Introduction

This study looks at the treatment of a large suite of giltwood, upholstered furniture carried out by a group of conservators over five years, 1992–1996. The treatment objectives are discussed and the planning, coordination and implementation are described.

Raby Castle in County Durham, UK, was built in the fourteenth century and underwent major changes in the eighteenth century.[1] In 1843 the architect William Burn[2] was invited to design a series of rooms on the south side of the castle, including the Octagon Room completed in 1848. His decorative scheme for this room included a highly ornamented ceiling, wall panels in yellow damask, three windows dressed in pink and gold, a great variety of cabinets and tables, and a large set of gilded furniture in a variety of styles, upholstered to match the curtains. The room has been described as having 'an eclectic style creating a romantic interior in harmony with its ancient historical surroundings' (Rogers, 1991) (Plate 8.1). The upholstery is of particular interest as it shows the work of a single upholstery company, G.J. Morant, London on a variety of pieces still in their original location. The Octagon Room is a rare survival of an entire decorative scheme of the mid-nineteenth century, with the textiles being the unifying features of the room.

The Octagon Room has been on open display during the summer months as part of a private collection open to the public for many years. During the winter months the room is in private use and is occasionally open for receptions. There is a permanent housekeeping staff and trained guides are stationed in the room.

8.1.1 The presenting problem

By the late 1980s the appearance of the room was causing concern due to the worn state of the textile furnishings, and much of the upholstered furniture was removed from display (Figure 8.1). In 1989 Lord Barnard, owner of Raby Castle, proposed restoring the Octagon Room. There were some bills for the 1840s works to the building but no other contemporary records have survived. An inventory of 1864 itemised the contents of the room, allowing identification of those pieces of furniture in store which were part of the early Victorian scheme. As this was the earliest surviving documentation for the Octagon Room, the 1864 inventory was used as the reference for its restoration.

Caroline Maude of the architects Donald Insall Associates, London, supervised the programme. The ceiling, walls and curtains were included in Stage One, and Stage Two included the Morant suite. The approach to

Figure 8.1 Corner sofa, before treatment. The sofa with the open serpentine back can be seen behind the corner sofa, also before treatment

treatment in Stage One had been to clean and conserve as far as possible, then reconstruct and restore where necessary to re-establish the unified appearance of the room. The ceiling had required cleaning only; the wall and curtain treatments combined conservation with reconstruction using rewoven silk and passementerie.

8.1.2 The brief

The initial brief for the treatment of the upholstery required that the furniture be suitable for occasional use and therefore that the seats be load-bearing. The architects were enthusiastic to reinstate those housekeeping practices which had been part of the castle routine in the mid-nineteenth century and which would help to protect the objects from further degradation. The rehanging of holland (linen) blinds at the Octagon Room windows to reduce light levels was in hand, and a set of case covers was commissioned for the Morant suite.

8.1.3 Investigation and planning

Initial investigation of the seat furniture was carried out at the Castle and started in 1992. Caroline Rendell, a textile conservator working in North-East England,[3] continued her work from Stage One and had reviewed which textile elements might be conserved. The upholstery was examined by the author (Lesley Wilson), who was later joined by Annie Ablett,[4] a gilding conservator, who investigated the finishes, and Jonathan Garrard,[5] a wood specialist, who assessed the condition of the beechwood frames. Pieces on display and in store were assembled outside the room for review; as it was not possible to see the furniture in its setting while the Stage One treatment of the ceiling and walls was in progress. The set was found to include six sofas and two pairs of armchairs and these were numbered for reference. The furniture was of various styles; all was gilded and most was covered in a pink/gold damask with a design of floral bouquets and garlands which matched the curtains. The complementary passementerie used two types of scroll gymp braid, cord, fringe and tufts. One sofa was covered in plain red silk damask. All the upholstered objects recorded in the 1864 inventory were brought together, including two sets of side chairs. All the objects were assessed and treatments were proposed, although the side chairs were not included in the Stage Two programme.

The investigation was undertaken with an open mind about the extent and nature of the treatment required. Small samples of silk top cover and passementerie were removed in order to test their response to cleaning, surface examination of the gilding was undertaken and the condition of the top cover and foundation upholstery was recorded. The suite was measured and the case covers associated with the suite were examined.

As is often the case, conditions on site were not ideal; for example, it was not possible to set up an inspection area with trestles or tables and good lighting. Objects were stored in a variety of locations throughout the castle; some were tightly packed together making access difficult. Also, short winter days and limited lighting reduced the quantity of detailed information that could be gathered during each visit. The gilding, wood and upholstery conservators carried out an assessment of each piece to evaluate its present condition and to propose a treatment for 'their part' of the object. Each conservator prioritised each object in the set based on the extent and difficulty of treatment. It soon became clear that the treatment of the gilding, wood and upholstery would inevitably be interconnected, requiring detailed planning and co-ordination between the specialists.

8.2 Condition assessment

All the frames were carved beechwood; they were mostly in excellent condition. Two chairs required major repair: one chair had a broken back rail and another had a broken front leg, which required partial gilding after repair.

Gilded upholstered objects are usually constructed in stages. New wood frames are supplied with a thin layer of gesso. The upholstery is built as far as the first stuffing (filling) cover when further layers of gesso are applied to those areas which are to be gilded. The object is then upholstered to the second stuffing cover when bole, gold leaf and a protective layer of size are applied before the top cover and passementerie complete the work. The majority of the Morant suite objects followed this pattern, although one piece was unusual in that it had been upholstered to the second stuffing cover, when all the remaining gilding stages were completed together.

The same high-quality gilding scheme was found throughout the set. Areas of wear exposed to view the three films of bole applied between the gesso and the gold leaf: first a brilliant yellow, second a pale red and topmost, only on the burnished areas, a blue bole. The original water gilded finish was intact and had not undergone any restoration, a rare find. The variation in condition of both the matt and burnished areas was mainly due to everyday wear and tear. The state of the gesso was more variable from piece to piece; in some cases the breakdown of the bond between the wood substrate and the gesso was causing delamination and some losses of gesso. This had implications for the upholstery treatment where vibrations caused by removing and reapplying fixings could affect the gilded finish.

The condition of the top covers was particularly distracting: the pink/gold silk covers were extremely degraded, with numerous splits and tears, and the silk hung in ribbons in some places. Many of the pink warp threads were abraded revealing the yellow weft threads. At this stage of the preliminary investigation the extent of the later treatment was not clear, although there were signs that some of the braid had been reapplied and extra layers of silk were found covering some pieces. The upholstery on the underside of the seats was intact, each piece carrying the stamp 'G.J. Morant, Upholsterer, 91 New Bond Street, London' (Figure 8.2). This was found underneath the seats, on the webbing and base cover and also printed onto the open weave, linen dust cover (bottoming fabric) fixed to the underside of the frame where springs had been used.

As might be expected, the pieces that appeared the most comfortable had the most displacement in their seats. Several findings suggested that the extant top covers were not original; for example, the additional top covers in the pink/gold silk and the reapplication of passementerie. Also, the sofa with an open serpentine back pad had a seat finished with a separate border and cord trim, while the matching pair of chairs had seat covers without borders or cord. On further investigation both styles were found to be original work, perhaps an example of poor communication between the craftsmen at G.J. Morant's workshop, or a lack of concern about consistency.

Figure 8.2 Detail of linen bottoming on sofa with central back pad, showing the Morant stamp

8.3 Treatment objectives

The aim of the conservation and restoration programme was to return the Morant suite to its 1864 appearance. Wherever possible, the original work was to be conserved, but as the Octagon Room was to be occupied occasionally, elements in poor condition were to be restored. The materials chosen for use in the various treatments were selected for their compatibility of materials and/or appearance with the original materials. Once the programme began it was clear that the Morant suite retained most of its original material and that the balance of the brief had to be reassessed. The suggestion that the furniture should not be used was generally accepted, but the room would be used for receptions. Experience indicated that a comfortable buttoned chair would be sat on and its beautifully carved, gilt finish would be handled. It was agreed that the programme would continue as planned, but with a greater emphasis on conservation than was initially the case.

The objective of achieving a unified appearance for the Morant suite was an important consideration. The appearance of some pieces would have been distracting due to their degraded and faded appearance even after conservation treatment. This resulted in the decision to reproduce the pink/gold silk used for the top cover fabric and to replicate the most widely used scroll braid, the cord and the tufts. The second scroll braid, the fringe and the outer back wool found on the pair of corner sofas were all in good condition and were treated by the textile conservator.

8.3.1 Programming

At this stage the gilding, wood and upholstery conservators worked closely on the programme. As the three specialists would be working directly but separately with each object, the objects were graded according to the expected problems they would present for each conservator. Workshop space, budget balance, time and overall workload were also considered, as well as how to minimise the handling and moving of the objects.

This process started on the train journeys between London and Durham and continued by telephone; liaison with the textile conservator was by telephone as she lived in North-East England. Having examined and assessed the whole suite, the next consideration was how to treat each object. Each conservator described the probable treatment of each piece from their own point of view and then highlighted aspects of the other treatments that affected their specialism. The aspects discussed included: how much of the upholstery must be released or removed to give access to the frame for wood restoration; what effect would the removal and application of upholstery fixings have on the gilded finish; and, how to protect the upholstery from the materials used and dust generated during gilding conservation. As a result of this analysis the set was divided into five small groups. The first group contained the serpentine-backed sofa and the two matching armchairs; these were in the best condition, presented the fewest problems and would allow the effectiveness of the programme and proposed treatments to be tested. Groups 2–4 contained objects with increasingly difficult treatment problems; one less problematic piece formed the last group. Advice on the wrapping and handling of the objects was provided for the transporting company to complement their own procedures.

Table 8.1 Programme of co-ordinated treatment by the four conservation specialists*

	Conservation specialists			
Sequence of work for each group of seat furniture	**Upholstery conservator L.W.**	**Gilding conservator A.A.**	**Textile conservator C.R.**	**Wood/furniture conservator J.G.**
Pieces are delivered to upholstery studio, unwrapped and assessed	✓	✓		
Gilded finish is consolidated		✓		
Passementerie and top covers removed	✓			
Passementerie and top covers requiring textile conservation are moved to textile conservation studio for treatment			✓	
Surface cleaning of upholstery	✓			
Treatment proposal reviewed	✓			✓
Treatment of frame; this was mostly undertaken in upholstery studio†				✓
Treatment of upholstery foundation	✓			
Design and first fit of case covers	✓			
Pieces moved to gilding studio for treatment		✓		
Pieces returned to upholstery studio for application of new and conserved top covers and passementerie	✓			
Completion of case covers	✓			
Wrapping for storage and transportation	✓	✓		

*Each object was reviewed after each stage of treatment by the project manager (C.M.) to confirm that the treatment had been completed, thereby allowing an invoice to be raised.
†One object required major treatment to the wood frame and was therefore moved to the wood studio for treatment.

On arrival at the upholstery studio the pieces were unwrapped and assessed by the upholstery and gilding specialists. Delaminated areas of the gilded finishes were secured by the gilding conservator so that those top covers and passementerie identified for conservation treatment could be removed by the upholstery conservator and passed to the textile conservator for treatment. Surface cleaning of the upholstery was undertaken by the upholstery specialist, before the treatment proposal was reviewed jointly by the upholstery and wood specialists. Treatments to the wooden frames were then undertaken. Small works of gilding and wood restoration were undertaken by the gilding and wood specialists working in the upholstery studio. One object required a move to the wood studio for major treatment.

Treatment of the upholstery foundation and first fitting of case covers was undertaken by the upholstery specialist, before frames requiring gilding restoration were moved to the gilding studio. The furniture was then returned to the upholstery studio for the application of covers and passementerie, and including elements conserved by the textile conservator. Once the top covers were in place and the case covers completed objects were wrapped for transportation and storage by the upholstery and gilding conservators working together. All original elements were documented with notes, sketches and photographs. Each stage of treatment was recorded by the conservator concerned, and the object was reviewed by the project manager to confirm that each stage had been completed and to allow for an invoice to be raised. The latter point was an important factor for efficient cash flow given the five-year span of the project.

The timing between stages was quite generous to avoid disruption to each specialist's programme of work. The first group of three pieces was treated over four months and subsequent groups in three months. Table 8.1 summarises the programme developed for the co-ordinated treatment of the suite by the four conservation/restoration specialists involved. The whole programme ran over five years with the treatment over three years. Consistency was aided by extensive recording of each treatment in notes, sketches and photographs. Sketches were particularly helpful when communicating with each other. The intermittent involvement over three years might have caused problems. However, the similarity of materials and construction drew a common response from all the conservators, while the fact that no more than two pieces matched meant that there could also be a response to the individual piece. When reviewing the programme and treatment it was useful that each conservator could refer to conservation colleagues who had intimate knowledge of the piece and to the project manager to help interpret the overall brief.

8.3.2 Original techniques and materials

Investigations during treatment revealed that the original upholstery was intact on all pieces. It was built to a high standard and a wide range of techniques had been used in response to the variety of styles within the suite. There were sprung and unsprung seats, back pads with one or two layers of stuffing, with and without stitching. Springing and stitching techniques varied slightly. Generally there was continuity in the foundation materials, however there were some interesting variations. The materials used throughout were: black and white herringbone webbing 50 mm wide, black lacquered double cone springs, a plain-woven linen for the base cloth, curled horsehair fillings, fine linen scrim for the first stuffing covers and the dust covers (bottoming), and a layer of cotton wadding under the top cover. A brushed, twill-weave cotton was the most widely used second stuffing cover, while one pair of armchairs had a white cotton fabric with an abstract design printed in green. A third stuffing cover was found on one sofa; this was a finely printed linen fabric of a quality that would normally be on display. However, it had been applied before the bole and gilding and was part of the original upholstery, i.e. was not intended for display.

8.4 Upholstery treatment: general approach

The movement of an upholstery pad in response to use and gravity can be considered part of the history of a piece of upholstered furniture. Treatments intended to adjust its profile can therefore be viewed as unethical, an issue which attracts lively debate. In the case of the Octagon Room suite of upholstered furniture, no attempt was made to modify the softness of the upholstery.

The following treatment was common to all objects:

- The original silk cover and passementerie were removed. Small areas of silk around tack heads were left *in situ* on the seat and back stuffing rails. Samples of the silk covers, passementerie, wadding and fixings were taken for the report and the remainder was documented, wrapped and returned to the castle for storage.
- All surfaces were cleaned with vacuum suction.
- Frames were checked for insect infestation and stability.
- Applying pressure to the seat pad was the means used to assess the load-bearing capacity of each seat.
- The linen dust covers, which enclosed the underside of the seats, were historically significant, as they were printed with the Morant stamp. It was therefore considered important to maintain them *in situ*, yet without some intrusive investigation the condition of the springs could not be established. Therefore the dust covers were released, but only partially; at least one side of the tack fixings was left undisturbed. After vacuum cleaning the linen dust covers, they were supported with blotting paper and the heavily soiled areas were swabbed with distilled water to remove sooty black deposits. Small patches of new linen were stitched with linen thread to the dust cover to support the fixing points where the cover had degraded.
- The condition of the webbing and fixings was recorded, as was the arrangement, condition and fixing of the springs and the nature and condition of the base cover. Limited access made surface cleaning of the webbing and suspension systems difficult. A vacuum cleaner was modified with 2 metres of clear hose reducing the diameter of the hose from 25 to 12 mm; this was

manipulated into the spaces between the webs to clean the spring cavities and the upper side of the webbing where the layer of dust particles was thickest.
- All upholstery pads were surface-cleaned with vacuum suction through a net screen. The brushed surface of the stuffing covers was lightly sponged with industrial methylated spirits, wiped with fine cotton cloth and dried with warm air. Small areas were treated consecutively to minimise the penetration of the solvent into the hair pads. Although some of the brushed cotton twill stuffing covers were heavily soiled they provided a very effective dust barrier. In cases where they were released the reverse side was not soiled and pads that were investigated further were found to be very clean.
- New untreated cotton wadding[6] was fitted over the stuffing before application of the silk cover and passementerie.

8.5 Upholstery treatment: case examples

While some aspects of treatment were common throughout the suite, others varied from piece to piece. This was particularly apparent when assessing the implications of the removal and application of fixings. In some cases tacks could be lifted out of the gesso layers and in others the gesso would crumble in that area. The selection of appropriate fixings to secure fabrics to frames is a continuing topic of discussion for upholstery conservators; the problems were illustrated clearly in this project and choices were made on a case-by-case basis. This resulted in the use of a wide range of fixings to hold the fabrics to the frames. They were selected to ensure that each treatment was reversible and that evidence of the original treatment was preserved. Original tacks were supplemented with modern equivalents to fix original fabrics. In some cases modern upholstery tacks were used where replacement fabrics were fixed to the stuffing rails, in others stainless steel staples were used on the stuffing rails of fragile frames where the vibration from hammering was thought to endanger the gilded show-wood. Coloured gymp pins were used to fix the silk cover next to the gilding. These were preferred as a low corrosion fixing that would allow future removal with an extracting tool used parallel to the gilded surface. It was felt that in this case staples increased the problem of access to fixings next to the show-wood, especially where the rebate was narrow.

Having established a common general approach, objects were then treated case-by-case. Examples of three treatment approaches follow. They show that intervention was undertaken for a number of reasons: sometimes to monitor condition, sometimes to carry out remedial work and/or to meet cosmetic needs.

8.5.1 The serpentine-backed sofa and pair of chairs

Although these objects were of the same design the treatment varied in response to their condition. The sofa had three top covers of silk on the back and two on the seat, but was found to have the original seat borders intact (see Figure 8.4). The seat was webbed to the underside of the seat rail with 15 mm long, fine tacks and supported 20 springs. The seat pad was built with two layers of stuffing and had retained its shape, however it was very soft and the springs were noisy under pressure. The back pad was sound and maintained a fairly good profile (Plate 8.1).

The cleaning treatment described above was applied to the spring cavity, and cotton wadding was packed into some areas to reduce the noise from the springs. There was no intervention to the foundation upholstery. The original silk borders were intact but in fragile condition. Before further treatment, they were protected with a layer of silk crepeline held in place with stitches to the stuffing cover; this remained *in situ* when the new wadding and cover were applied.

One chair had a broken back rail. The stuffing cover was removed, and the curled hair pad and second stuffing were partially released to give access for the repair. Once the broken rail was repaired the pad was realigned and enclosed in the cleaned stuffing cover. The seat covers of both chairs were released and a small quantity of horsehair was added to the front edge to restore the seat profile.

8.5.2 Pair of armchairs with tufted backs

The most invasive upholstery conservation treatment undertaken on the Morant suite was undertaken on this pair of armchairs. The front leg of one chair was broken. Both chairs had three layers of silk on the inside back and replacement silk on the seat and outer back. The scroll gymp braid had been reapplied and supplemented with lengths of similar colour but of a different design. Under the silk was a printed cotton stuffing cover in good condition with some soiling. Traces of gold on this cover indicated that gilding was completed at this stage (as noted under Programming above). The sprung seats were soft and unstable. The back pads were soft, the additional covers had altered some of the tuft positions and stuffing had moved down and away from the tufts. The uneven pattern of tufting and the differences between the two chairs suggested that the tufts had been positioned by eye and possibly by different craftsmen.

Both chairs were given the same additional treatment. The outer back covers were released for access. The printed cover was removed from the inside back without disturbing the stitches joining the back and arms. New horsehair was used to fill areas around the tufting that had subsided before the stuffing cover was reapplied. The seat cover was removed; the first and second stuffings were removed in one piece to minimise disturbance of the layers. The base cover was released on all sides, leaving the stitches securing the springs in place. The spring cavity was vacuum cleaned. The springs were tied with laid cord in two directions to improve the stability of the seat and packed with cotton wadding to reduce noise. The seat pad was reinstated with some additional horsehair, and the printed cover was reapplied.

8.5.3 Pair of corner sofas

Due to the design and condition of the textiles on these objects it was possible to conserve and reapply the passementerie and outer back covers.

Both sofas were covered with the pink/gold damask on the inside back and the seat (see Figure 8.1). As they were positioned against the walls the outer back cover was plain, pink worsted. These were the only pieces with a heavy fringe and a scroll gymp braid of a different design from the remainder of the set. The braid was in excellent condition; the fringe was in good condition although heavily soiled. The upholstered pads were sound, fairly firm, but appeared to have some distortion to the profile.

The passementerie and outer back covers were removed and sent for textile conservation treatment. The stuffing covers were released, additional hair was used to adjust the profile of the back pads, particularly the top edge of the pads which would be seen in relief against the walls.

The bulbous seat profile was found to have only a slight forward movement of the second stuffing. The new silk covers were fitted; the worsted was sewn to the top edge and fixed through the original holes with both original and new tacks. The braid was reapplied with gymp pins through the original holes. As the original fixing of widely spaced brass pins was thought to offer insufficient support to the heavy fringe they were not reapplied. The fringe was held against the lower edge of the seat rail with a linen thread stitched through both the silk cover and the cotton stuffing cover (Figure 8.3).

8.5.4 Case covers

Case covers had been widely used within Raby Castle and two incomplete sets were found relating to the Octagon Room furniture. The earlier and most complete set was made from a fine woven cotton fabric 675 mm wide, printed with pink and brown arabesques (design repeat 330 mm) and lined with a plain, polished glazed cotton. The cover and lining were separately shaped to each piece of furniture, where a greater width of fabric was needed the panels were joined with running stitches parallel to the selvages and the simple seams opened to face the lining. The lining and cover were then joined together with the raw edges to the outside, held with whipping stitches and bound with a brown, grosgrain, silk ribbon 10 mm wide, secured with running stitches. All the covers were fairly loose fitting (Figure 8.4).

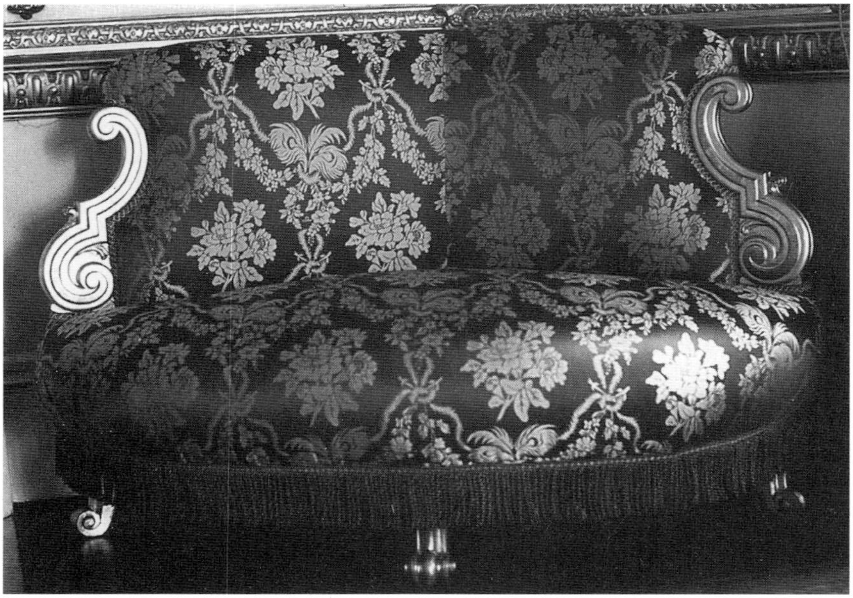

Figure 8.3 Corner sofa, after treatment

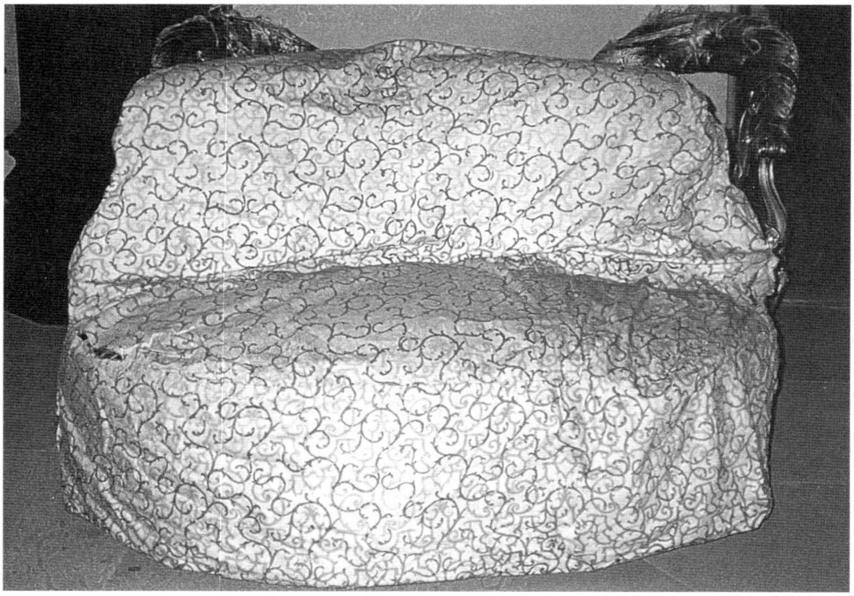

Figure 8.4 Corner sofa fitted with original case cover of printed cotton. The sofa with the serpentine back can be seen behind the corner sofa, before treatment

Some of the covers were fitted over the furniture, others had placket openings that were closed with buttons and hand-stitched buttonholes. The buttons were made by wrapping fabric round a brass ring and stitching the fabric in place; the rings were 15 mm in diameter and were placed 5 per opening. The placket opening was folded back and hemmed to the buttonhole side and an additional panel supported the buttons, when closed the fixing was concealed. These covers were extremely fragile. Both the printed and

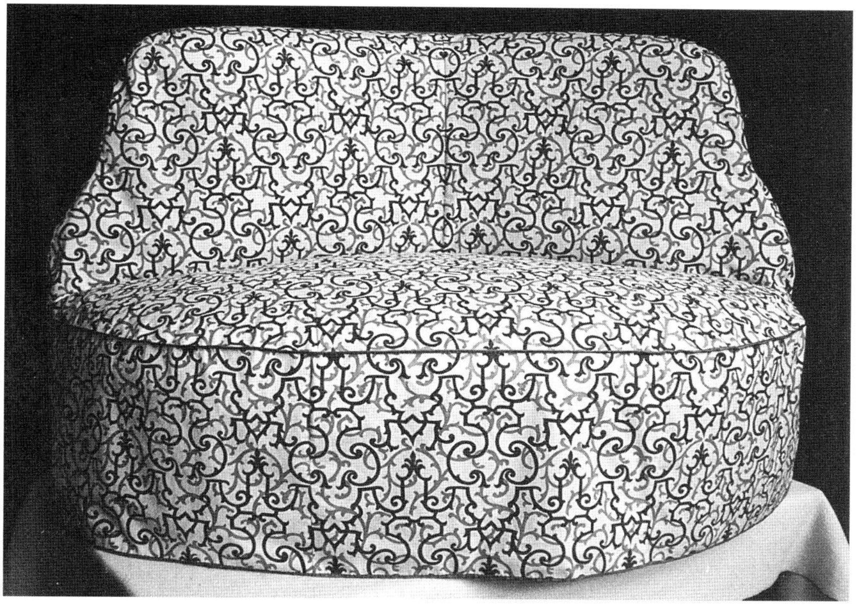

Figure 8.5 Corner sofa fitted with replica case cover of printed cotton

the lining fabric were so degraded that any handling caused damage. During the investigation period they were fitted onto the furniture and left in place to be wrapped and transported together.

A new set of covers was made following the original models. The pink/brown printed cotton was reproduced and a lightly glazed cream lining cotton selected (Figure 8.5). The brown silk ribbon binding was rewoven. The design and construction of the covers were reproduced in the studio, although the seams were machine stitched for economy, the covered buttons were copied and the buttonholes and ribbon binding were hand-stitched. Each cover was cut and fitted while the object was in the upholstery studio and then stored in the studio until the installation at Raby Castle. The original covers were labelled, wrapped in acid-free tissue, placed in archive boxes and returned to the Castle.

8.6 Installation

Throughout the programme objects were moved to storage when their treatment was completed so that the furniture could be installed as a group. All aspects of the installation and co-ordination with other programmes within the Castle were supervised by the project manager. The gilding and upholstery conservators worked on site to unwrap, check and position the furniture. Some damage to the giltwood had occurred during storage or moving and this was treated on site. Only two pieces, the corner sofas, had a known location. Other pieces, initially grouped around the fireplaces, were relocated when other objects were added to the room. The application of the case covers was demonstrated to the housekeeping staff.

8.7 Report

A report was prepared jointly by the gilding and upholstery conservators. The gilding and upholstery constructions found on the Morant furniture were described, and the policy and approach to treatment applied throughout was introduced. The main report on each object consisted of three pages: one page of text, one illustrated page each on the gilding and upholstery findings and treatment, and one photograph 'before' treatment and one 'after'. A single sheet was prepared to aid monitoring

OBJECT	UNDER REVIEW	AFTERCARE
Corner sofas	Monitor outer back cover which is fragile. Overall condition sound. Monitor the stability of the gesso layer, making note of all new signs of delamination.	When moving support the sofas from the outer back and under the seat rails, move the fringe aside taking care not to crush it, once moved check fringe is hanging correctly.
Sofa with curved back	Overall fair condition, back pad rather soft. Monitor the stability of the gesso layer, making note of all new signs of delamination. The sofa has a history of severe gesso delamination and loss.	Move by lifting from under the seat rail.
Sofa with back pad	Overall fair condition, monitor outer back. Monitor the stability of the gesso layer, making note of all new signs of delamination.	Consider sitting on this piece? Lift from underside of seat rail.
Sofa and armchairs with serpentine tufted back and arm pad	Fragile condition, seat soft, monitor underside of seat for spring movement and back to ensure tufts remain secure. Monitor the stability of the gesso layer, making note of all new signs of delamination. The sofa has a history of severe gesso delamination.	Disturb as little as possible, lift from under the seat rails.
Sofa with central back pad and two curved ends	Overall fair condition. The gilded finish has only received a partial conservation treatment. It should be monitored as all the other pieces.	When moving support well under seat rails.
Armchairs, diamond pattern tufted backs	Fragile condition, seats soft, monitor under-side of seats for spring movement and backs to ensure tufts remain secure. Monitor the stability of the gesso layer, making note of all new signs of delamination. The sofa has a history of severe gesso delamination. The legs on these chairs are very fragile.	Do not move by touching the back pad lift from under the seat rail. This style of chair is likely to be sat on, avoid if possible but if this happens the back and seat may need smoothing.
PLEASE NOTE:	Dusting may only be undertaken after carefully monitoring the condition of each piece and recording findings. A soft sable brush should be used, lightly flicking the dust from the gilded finish.	Keep handling to a minimum.
Case covers individually shaped for each piece	The use of case covers is recommended to protect the objects from light and dust. Originally they would have been in place for all but very special occasions. When removed after a period of use vacuum clean each cover before wrapping and storing.	Care must be taken, fit them gently so that they do not rub against the gilded surfaces. Some of the covers have back openings, others should be fitted onto the top of the back, drawn over the seat and arms, then down the back and side of the object.

Figure 8.6 Single-page monitoring advice prepared for the Morant suite at Raby Castle, Co. Durham, UK

of the suite (Figure 8.6). Each object was described on the checklist with aspects under review and notes on aftercare, this included advice for moving pieces, handling the case covers and aspects of each piece that were a cause for concern and would need particular monitoring. This concise form was thought more likely to be used as a reference than a more detailed report when non-specialist staff have a large and varied collection to maintain.

8.8 Evaluation

The installation of the Morant suite to the Octagon Room was well received (Cornforth, 1999). Evaluation was undertaken informally by the architect and conservators after installation, when the report was prepared. The aims of the project, the programme, choice of treatments and time management were jointly reviewed. At all stages the aim was to support and complement the original elements. The faded colour of the wall silk was particularly influential. The gold colour of the curtains was subdued. In the event the conservation of the gilding on the furniture revealed a very bright yellow/gold exactly matched by the gold in the original textile. This colour was considered too dominating when test samples were made. However, with that powerful thing hindsight, a brighter gold would have worked well on the furniture and not been distracting in the powerfully furnished room (Plate 8.1).

The overriding concern throughout treatment was the desire to balance the care of the original elements with the fact that such a detailed treatment was unlikely to be possible again and that the objects may be used; and in the longer term, it was acknowledged that they may be less protected. Elements that would be difficult to access, the frame and foundation upholstery, needed to be as stable as possible. Extensive records were made of the upholstery elements as they were uncovered, and the findings were fully documented in the conservation report. It is intended that eventually all the notes, photographs and sketches will be copied for the Raby Castle archive.

The Morant suite required close collaboration between conservators specialising in gilding, upholstery, wood and textiles and the long investigation period gave time for detailed planning. The programme ran well and all the conservators met the agreed dates. The only significant problem arose when a supplier did not meet delivery times. Although this affected completion of one group the buffer time between groups prevented delays in the overall programme.

Notes

1 For information on the castle and its occupants see *A Short Guide to Raby Castle* (Anon., n.d.), available from the castle.
2 William Burn (1789–1870) designed public buildings, churches and many country houses in Scotland and England (Colvin, 1995).
3 Caroline Rendell, Freelance textile conservator, Regional Conservator for the National Trust.
4 Annie Ablett, BAHons, DFPD, AMUKIC is an independent conservator of historic frames, combining special projects with the ongoing care of frames for national institutions and private collections.
5 Jonathan Garrard, HND is an independent furniture restorer working on objects in museums and private collections. He is Senior Lecturer and Co-ordinator of the Craft programme for Hammersmith & Fulham Community Service.
6 Cotton wadding produced for upholstery applications is now treated to improve its fire retardant qualities; there are concerns about the effects of this treatment on adjacent materials. The wadding selected for this project had not been treated in this way as it was produced for the application of surface finishes to wooden objects.

Acknowledgements

This study was prepared with the kind permission of the Lord Barnard. I should like to thank the colleagues named above for their knowledge and expertise so enthusiastically shared and to acknowledge the important contribution of the suppliers to the final appearance of the suite.

References

Anon. (n.d.) *A Short Guide to Raby Castle*. Barnard Castle: Teesdale Mercury Ltd.

Colvin, H.M. (1995) *A Biographical Dictionary of British Architects, 1600–1840*. London: J. Murray.

Cornforth, J. (1999) Raby recovers silken splendour, *Country Life*, 22 April, pp. 100–3.

Rogers, P. (1991) *Report on the Octagon Room, Raby Castle*. Unpublished internal report, English Heritage.

Part Two

Documentation: Case Studies

9

Seat furniture at the court of Henry VIII: a study of the evidence

Maria Hayward

9.1 Introduction

Probably the best known portrait of Henry VIII is the imposing standing figure recorded in the Whitehall cartoon drawn by Hans Holbein the Younger.[1] However, the image of the monarch seated in majesty was integral to the presentation of Tudor kingship, as it evoked the sacral nature of the sovereign and the monarch's role as law-giver, by recalling the coronation. Consequently, this image always appeared on the obverse of the great seal and was echoed in images like Holbein's group portrait of *Henry VIII and the Barber-Surgeons*.[2] Questions of precedence, social standing, wealth and simple comfort were also bound up with the significance of the chair in early sixteenth-century England.

The chair, like its counterpart the cushion, was symbolic of status and authority. Dependent upon the style and materials, a chair could accurately convey the wealth of its owner. Unfortunately, very little seat furniture has survived from the sixteenth century that can be studied and analysed and the percentage of pieces that have English royal connections is even smaller. In part the lack of objects can be countered by reference to written sources, but it is telling that Peter Thornton chose to write a history of seventeenth- rather than sixteenth-century interior decoration in Northern Europe (Thornton, 1978).[3] Simon Jervis summed up the problem with his title 'Shadows not substantial things' when he wrote about Charles I's furniture recorded in the Commonwealth Sale inventories of 1649.[4] In spite of the obvious difficulties, this chapter seeks to explore the available evidence, written and visual, to build up a picture of upholstered seat furniture at the court of Henry VIII. After considering whether the term and concept of upholstery are applicable, it will review the range of sources available to study English royal seat furniture in the first half of the sixteenth century.

9.2 Upholsterer and upholstery: sixteenth-century terms?

The 1542 inventory of the palace of Westminster records that Thomas Chapel, 'upholster' sold fifteen pieces of Normandy canvas to the King.[5] More interestingly, in January 1543 William Chapel of London, upholsterer, was paid for providing leather and feathers, as well as for making six cushions, faced with arras, which had been purchased separately from John Musteaner, the King's arras maker.[6] This example demonstrates that the term upholsterer (or upholder/upholster) was in use in the first half of the sixteenth century and that Chapel was working with materials that would be familiar to later upholsterers.[7] However, it was not an exclusive preserve and the work they did produce was very simple, with the main aim of providing a degree of comfort. It is also clear that they worked with other materials and on other projects which were more removed from the more traditional view of upholstery.

Other craftsmen were also working with these materials and techniques to produce chairs, namely coffer-makers. William Green, the King's coffer-maker, worked on a number of chairs for the Crown, making new chairs and recovering and repairing existing chairs (see below, also Hayward, 2000).[8] Other craftsmen employed in the production of the wooden frames were joiners, turners and carpenters, although the involvement of the latter was not so common. Peter Thornton had demonstrated the link between the development of quilted padding for seat furniture to the techniques used by saddlers working with leather in Italy and Sweden (Thornton, 1978: 216; 1991, 184–5). The saddles produced for Henry VIII were predominantly made from textiles over an under-structure, which indicates that they would have had common skills with craftsmen working on chairs.[9] In view of this diversity of craftsmen working in this area, it is perhaps not surprising that the Worshipful Company of Upholders was not granted a royal charter until 1626 (Beard, 1997: 4).

A range of seat furniture was recorded in sixteenth-century inventories: chairs, stools, benches, forms and the more private close stool, related in form and with a very specific function. This chapter will focus mainly on chairs and stools because they were more numerous. The main difference between a form and a bench is that the bench could have a back (Thornton, 1978: 182). While both could be a piece of wooden furniture, the seats, backs or both could be made more comfortable by the addition of fixed padding. By this period textile or leather coverings were often used to embellish the simple wooden frame. If these materials were used in conjunction with padding on the seat, back or arms, comfort was an added benefit. However, chairs and stools of this type were never referred to as 'upholstered' in royal inventories or accounts of this period. Descriptions were quite vague, ranging from 'a Cheire of cloth of golde tissued' (9301) to 'oone other old Chaier of wood covered with purple velvet pirled the Seate blewe velvet' (13963).[10]

The construction of the seat and back was very simple: each usually comprising two rectangular pieces of fabric stitched together and lightly padded. These were then nailed to the two upright struts of the back or the side batons of the seat. Quilting was sometimes used to ensure the even distribution of the stuffing materials. Some chairs had arms (or 'elbows'): these could be left plain, be covered

Table 9.1 Distribution and quantification of seat furniture and cushions recorded in the 1547–50 inventory

Location	Chairs	Cushions	Close stools	Footstools	Stools
Beddington	2	10	~	~	~
Greenwich	20	83	4	26	4
Hampton Court	39	95	5	41	4
The More	26	50	~	21	~
Newhall	~	~	~	~	~
Nonsuch	19	65	3	24	33
Nottingham	~	~	~	~	~
Oatlands	15	79	5	4	4
Removing wardrobe	12	26	~	~	~
Richmond	20	76	2	12	7
St James'	4	~	~	~	~
St Johns'	~	3	~	~	~
The Tower	11	59	~	~	~
Westminster	31	55	1	10	14
Windsor	22	48	~	6	~
Woodstock	10	36	~	20	6
Edward's wardrobe	8	15	~	~	~
Elizabeth's wardrobe	2	16	~	~	~
Mary's wardrobe	2	8	~	~	~
Total	**243**	**724**	**20**	**164**	**72**

For Westminster, Greenwich and Hampton Court only the wardrobe listings have been used. These figures only include chairs and stools that were upholstered.

with fabric or padded and then covered. A cushion could be used to provide additional comfort or, more simply, they could be used with a plain wooden chair or stool, which had been the norm in the fourteenth and fifteenth centuries. Cushions retained their importance in the sixteenth century as their numerical superiority relative to chairs indicates (see below and Table 9.1). In the seventeenth century, when seat furniture became more sophisticated, suites of matching chairs, stools and footstools still included cushions.[11] Those recorded in Henry VIII's inventories were predominantly rectangular and highly ornate:

> Item oone Cusshion of crymen golde tissue peced at eche end with richer like tissue/the backeside therof of cloth of gold reysid with great Rooses and smale of crymsen vellat frengid round aboute with a narrow frenge of venice/And iiij buttons with tasselles of venice golde and red silke [310].[12]

9.3 Inventories: a source of information

The most common use of inventories within the royal household was to record the objects placed in the charge of a particular official or keeper. They were financially liable for the goods in their care, so they either annotated the inventory or kept a book of issue to record when and why objects left their possession. When they were discharged from office, the documentation was checked against the objects for discrepancies. A number of inventories concerned with upholstered seat furniture, which was kept in one of the various 'wardrobes of the Beds', survive from Henry VIII's reign. The King's removing wardrobe of the Beds contained a group of furnishings that travelled with the monarch from one property to the next. By the sixteenth century it usually had a staff of four to six, and it complemented the standing wardrobes of the Beds that were based at a number of the King's houses.[13] This chapter focuses upon two of these documents. The first dates from 1542 and considers one place, the new palace of Westminster, or Whitehall as it was known, and the objects within the care of the keeper, Anthony Denny (Figure 9.1).[14] The objects are listed by type and this readily allows for some basic quantification of seat furniture to be undertaken. Although it must be borne in mind that items may have been omitted, so all figures should be treated with a degree of suspicion.

The second inventory dates from 1547–50 and is much broader in its remit.[15] This document was drawn up shortly after the accession of Henry VIII's son, Edward VI, who was a minor (see the family tree in the Appendix to this chapter). While there are some notable omissions, this document provides a detailed overview of the moveable goods that Henry VIII left to his son.[16] For this study the second section of the inventory is of particular interest as it concentrates on the contents of the wardrobes of the Beds at fifteen of the King's houses, the removing wardrobe and the wardrobes provided for Prince Edward and his half-sisters the Ladies Mary and Elizabeth. This inventory is a composite document made up of a series of smaller inventories, some of which list the items by type, others by the room they were found in. At three locations – Westminster, Greenwich and Hampton Court – a combination of both techniques is used.

The information recorded in these documents allows for the basic quantification of objects and for an idea of distribution, either between properties or within the rooms of a particular building (Table 9.1). This analysis reveals several points of interest. To consider the seat furniture first, chairs were more numerous than stools or footstools. Their distribution was quite uneven, with three properties having no chairs at all. It is not surprising that the most visited properties – Westminster, Hampton Court and Greenwich – had substantial numbers, along with the new developments at Oatlands and Nonsuch. The figure for Westminster is artificially low, reflecting the position after a number of items had been reallocated to other properties. Prior to Henry VIII's death, there were ninety-two chairs at this palace. The number of footstools is more than double the quantity of stools. This may be an indication of the relative unimportance of the stool in the royal household, where little seating provision was made for those not illustrious enough to be provided with a chair or cushion, or the number of footstools may have increased as a result of the King's need to support his bad leg.[17]

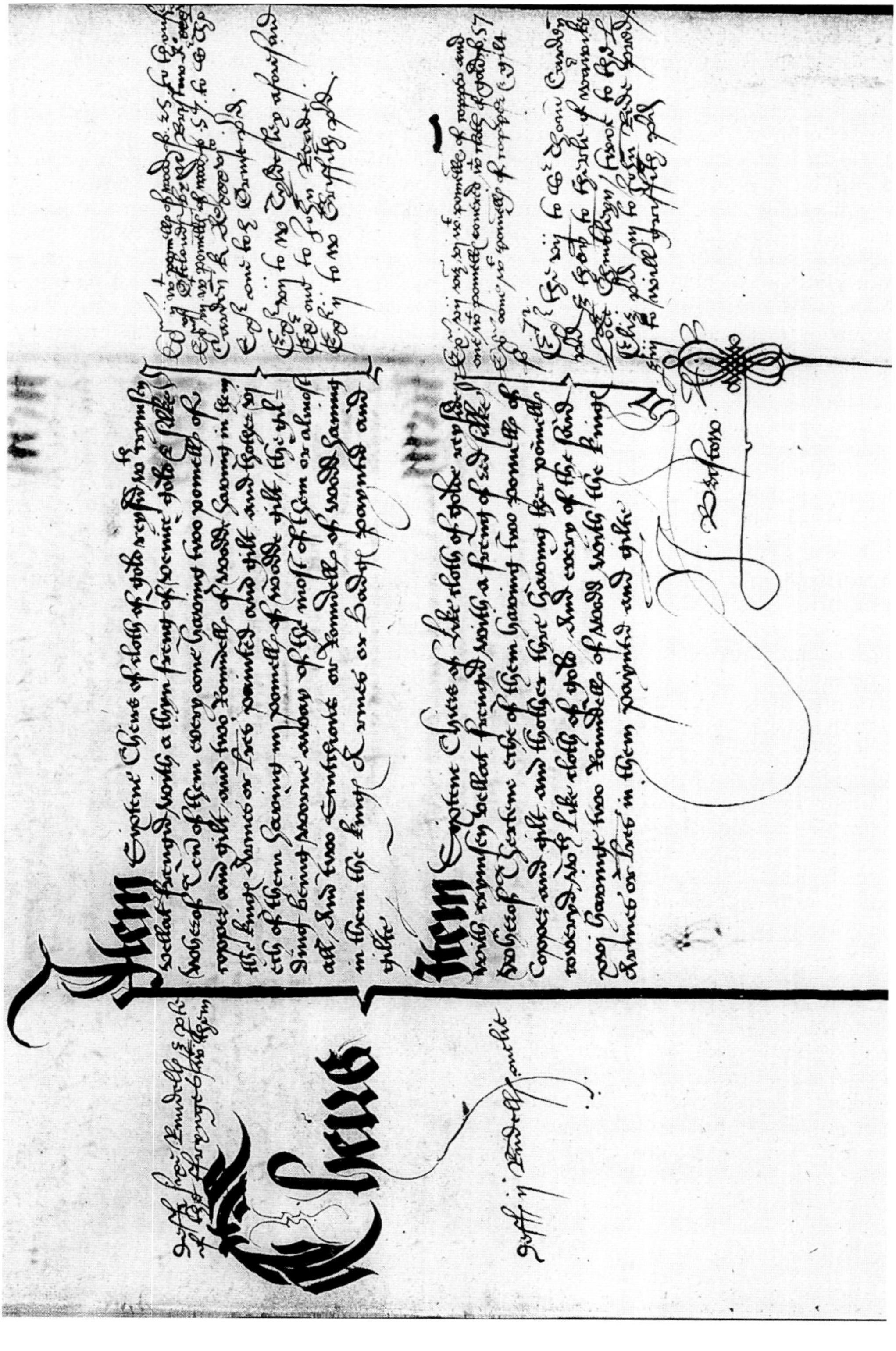

Figure 9.1 An extract from the 1542 inventory of the palace of Westminster describing two sets of chairs (Public Record Office. Reference number E315/160, f. 13). This inventory is unusual because of the quantity of marginal notation, generally placed to the right of the main text, which provides very useful details about how and when objects were removed from the palace. Most of the individuals mentioned in the marginal notes were keepers of standing wardrobes of the Beds at other royal properties: Sir Thomas Cawarden at Oatlands and Nonsuch, Humfrey Orme at the Tower of London, William Tildesley at Windsor Castle, John Reed at the palace of Westminster and William Griffiths at Richmond. Nicholas Bristow was clerk of the wardrobes of the Robes and Beds and it is most likely that he compiled this inventory. As a safety measure he checked the entries on each page against the objects and then signed the foot of the page to indicate that it was a true record.

The 1542 inventory acted as the book of charge for Anthony Denny, the keeper of the palace of Westminster, by recording all of the objects that he was responsible for. In addition he would have kept a book of issue or discharge, recording all of the objects passing out of his care. It is probable that the folio numbers given in the marginal notes relate to the point where a particular item was recorded as having left his possession. Dates are given in regnal years, which began on the day of the monarch's accession to the throne (Henry VIII's first regnal year ran from 22 April 1509 to 21 April 1510).

The two entries read as follows:

[Left Margin] Cheirs

Item Sixtene Cheirs of cloth of gold reysid with crymsen vellat frengid with a thyn freng of venice gold & silke wherof Ten of them every oone having two pomelles of copper and gilt/and two Roundelles of woode having in them the kinges Armes or lettres painted and gilt and thother vj ech of them having iiij pomelles of woode gilt/the gilding being worne away of the most of them or almost all/And two Scutchions or Roundelles of wodd hauing in them the kinges Armes or badges payntid and gilte. [238]

LM: deficiunt sixe Rundelles & parte of the Frynges with them.

RM: Ex' ij with pomelles of wood folio 25 to thouse of Otelondes by N. Bristow Anno xxxv^{to}.

RM: Ex' iij with pomelles of wood folio 57 to Sir Thomas Carden knight Anno xxxvj^{to}.

RM: Ex' one to H. Orme predicto.

RM: Ex' vij to W.Tyldesley aforesaid.

RM: Ex' one to John Reade.

RM: Ex' ij to W. Griffithe predicto.

Item Sixtene Chiers of like cloth of golde reyside with crymsen vellat frengid with a freng of red silke/wherof Thertene eche of them having two pomelles of Copper and gilt and thother thre having ther pomelles coveryd with like cloth of gold/And every of the said xvj havinge two Roundelles of wodd with the kinges Armes or Lettres in them payntid and gilte. [239]

LM: deficiunt ij Rundelles onelie.

RM: Ex' vij videlicet vj with pomelles of copper and one with pomelles couered with cloth of gold folio 57.

RM: Ex' oone with pomelles of copper & gilt folio 72.

RM: Ex' the vij to Sir Thomas Carden predicto & thone to therle of warwike Lorde Chamberleyn/twoe to the Lady Elizabeth predicto/iij to John Rede predicto/& iij to william griffith predicto.

N. Bristow

After modernising the spelling, numerals and capitalisation, the text reads as follows:

[Left Margin] Chairs

Item sixteen chairs of cloth of gold raised with crimson velvet fringed with a thin fringe of Venice gold & silk whereof ten of them every one having two pommels of copper and gilt/and two roundels of wood having in them the king's arms or letters painted and gilt and the other six each of them having four pommels of wood gilt/the gilding being worn away off the most of them or almost all/And two escutcheons or roundels of wood having in them the king's arms or badges painted and gilt. [238]

LM: deficient six roundels & part of the fringe with them.

RM: Ex' two with pommels of wood folio 25 to the use of Oatlands by N. Bristow year 35.

RM: Ex' three with pommels of wood folio 57 to Sir Thomas Cawarden knight year 36.

RM: Ex' one to H. Orme predicto (as previously mentioned, i.e. other items listed earlier in the inventory had also been delivered to Orme on this day).

RM: Ex' seven to W. Tildesley aforesaid.

RM: Ex' one to John Reed.

RM: Ex' two to W. Griffith predicto.

Item sixteen chairs of like cloth of gold raised with crimson velvet fringed with a fringe of red silk/whereof thirteen each of them having two pommels of copper and gilt and the other three having their pommels covered with like cloth of gold/And every of the said sixteen having two roundels of wood with the King's arms or letters in them painted and gilt. [239]

LM: deficient (i.e. missing) two roundels only.

RM: Ex' seven videlicet (namely) six with pommels of copper and one with pommels covered with cloth of gold folio 57.

RM: Ex' one with pommels of copper and gilt folio 72.

RM: Ex' the seven to Sir Thomas Cawarden predicto and the one to the Earl of Warwick Lord Chamberlain/two to the Lady Elizabeth predicto/three to John Reed predicto/& three to William Griffith predicto.

More obvious, however, is the fact that cushions outnumbered the chairs by almost three to one, indicating that this was still the chief way of providing comfortable seating. This was on a par with European trends (Thornton, 1991: 173–4). The difficulty in trying to assess how the cushions were used is that much of the plain wood furniture was omitted from the 1547–50 inventory because it formed part of the charge of the keeper of the houses not the wardrobe staff. However, at Oatlands, Sir Thomas Cawarden was keeper of both the house and wardrobe. Consequently, the inventory recorded thirty plain wooden forms (12846, 12851) and forty-five stools (12847, 12852–3). The number and distribution of the close stools raises a difficulty with this evidence. Each of the King's children would undoubtedly have had one or more close stools. The reason for them not being recorded here is that they came within the care of their grooms of the stool, whose remits were not covered by this inventory.

Dependent upon the level of detail provided within the individual entries, inventories can also be used to carry out a rudimentary qualitative assessment. Information about the materials used as top covers, the colour and the type of trimmings used can be extracted and analysed. The choice of fabric for covering of the frame and making the padded sections is of interest for several reasons (Tables 9.2a and 9.2b). Fourteen different materials, thirteen woven textiles and one example of leather, were recorded in the 1547–50 inventory. Of these, two textiles, velvet and cloth of gold, were predominant, with the others represented by a very small number of examples. In addition, the pattern on the cloth of gold was frequently woven as velvet. Velvet was highly prized in the sixteenth century and consequently it was used for furnishings in the inner chambers of royal lodgings throughout Europe. A good example is provided by a *sillón frailero* (friar's or monk's chair) with a walnut frame and crimson velvet used for the seat and back, made for the Escorial.[18]

In addition to the cloths of gold and silver, many of the other fabrics incorporated a high percentage of metal thread, such as tissue and tincel. Not surprisingly, these were favoured as an expression of wealth and the different cloths were ranked according to cost.[19] However, the correct interpretation of these terms can prove difficult, especially if the meaning of a word has changed over time, like tissue. When found in an eighteenth-century context, this word indicated a lampas silk but in the sixteenth century it was used as a blanket term covering all silk textiles with metallic weft loops, regardless of whether they were a velvet or lampas weave (Monnas, 1998). Practically all of the other textiles mentioned were silks, with the exception of one instance of fustian, one instance of cloth, which probably indicated wool, and a pair of references for both needlework and white

Table 9.2a The materials used for the top covers of the chairs recorded in the 1547–50 inventory: alphabetical order

Textile	**Occurrences**	
Baudekyn	2	(0.8%)
Cloth	1	(0.4%)
Cloth of gold	86	(35.5%)
Cloth of silver	4	(1.6%)
Fustian	1	(0.4%)
Leather	2	(0.8%)
Needlework	2	(0.8%)
New making silk	4	(1.6%)
Satin	7	(2.9%)
Tincel	1	(0.4%)
Tissue	18	(7.5%)
Velvet	111	(45.7%)
Velvet upon velvet	2	(0.8%)
White work	2	(0.8%)
Total	**243**	**(100%)**

Table 9.2b The materials used for the top covers of the chairs recorded in the 1547–50 inventory: numerical order

Textile	**Occurrences**	
Velvet	111	(45.7%)
Cloth of gold	86	(35.5%)
Tissue	18	(7.5%)
Satin	7	(2.9%)
Cloth of silver	4	(1.6%)
New making silk	4	(1.6%)
Baudekyn	2	(0.8%)
Leather	2	(0.8%)
Needlework	2	(0.8%)
Velvet upon velvet	2	(0.8%)
White work	2	(0.8%)
Cloth	1	(0.4%)
Fustian	1	(0.4%)
Tincel	1	(0.4%)
Total	**243**	**(100%)**

Table 9.3a The colour of the top covers used on chairs recorded in the 1547–50 inventory: alphabetical order

Colour	**Occurrences**	
Black	18	(7.5%)
Blue	7	(2.9%)
Carnation	3	(1.2%)
Crimson	103	(42.4%)
Gold	10	(4.1%)
Green	13	(5.3%)
Incarnate	1	(0.4%)
Murrey	5	(2.0%)
Purple	30	(12.4%)
Red	6	(2.5%)
Russet	6	(2.5%)
Tawny	7	(2.9%)
Two colours/metals	14	(5.7%)
Unspecified	10	(4.1%)
White	3	(1.2%)
Yellow	7	(2.9%)
Total	**243**	**(100%)**

Table 9.3b The colour of the top covers used on chairs recorded in the 1547–50 inventory: numerical order

Colour	**Occurrences**	
Crimson	103	(42.4%)
Purple	30	(12.4%)
Black	18	(7.5%)
Two colours/metals	14	(5.7%)
Green	13	(5.3%)
Gold	10	(4.1%)
Unspecified	10	(4.1%)
Blue	7	(2.9%)
Tawny	7	(2.9%)
Yellow	7	(2.9%)
Red	6	(2.5%)
Russet	6	(2.5%)
Murrey	5	(2.0%)
Carnation	3	(1.2%)
White	3	(1.2%)
Incarnate	1	(0.4%)
Total	**243**	**(100%)**

work. This emphasis on silk reflects the holdings of the Great Wardrobe and the separate silk store at Westminster, in the care of Anthony Denny.

Leather was much more popular in Spain, where there was a strong tradition of high-quality leather goods. Sets of wooden stools covered with leather (*banqueta de cordobán* – a leather covered stool) were made for the outer rooms of the Escorial, while stools with textile coverings were reserved for the more private chambers.[20] One interesting variant not recorded in either the 1542 or 1547–50 inventories was the use of carpet. The seat and back of a renaissance Italian chair in the Bernheimer Collection, Munich are covered with fragments of a small pattern Holbein carpet (King and Sylvester, 1983: 56).[21]

Some colours, such as purple, crimson and murrey (a shade of red), were more readily associated with monarchy than others. In sixteenth-century England this link between colour and social standing was reinforced by sumptuary legislation. Particular dyes (e.g. kermes) and dyeing processes (double dyeing to achieve black) were more costly and so indicated a higher level of disposable income in a society where conspicuous consumption was carefully observed. When the colours used on chairs were considered (Tables 9.3a and 9.3b) fourteen different colours were found and in a small group of instances, two or more colours were used, or the colour was not specified. A broad range of colours was referred to, including yellow, carnation and green. However, crimson was the most common colour, followed by purple. Variants of red were also numerous, including red, carnation, incarnate, murrey and russet. The preference for red noted in these documentary references is supported by dye analysis carried out on archaeological textiles dating from this period.[22]

Descriptions of chairs and stools rarely make a reference to the filling materials used in the seat, back or arm rests, so an entry which refers to 'twooe lowe stowles covered with lynnen clothe and stuffed with woole' (10833) is of particular interest. Often, it is only when there were structural problems relating to the upholstery that it is mentioned at all, as with 'twoe litle lowe ... nowe olde and brokin and vnstuffed' (11804). However, the range of filling materials available can be gleaned from the entries for mattresses and pillows. These were filled with down, feathers and, rather unusually, fox fur. There are no references within either the 1542 or 1547–50 inventories to other types of animal hair used in this context.[23]

Surface decoration was commonly used to ornament seat furniture produced for the social elite and a variety of techniques were used on the textile, wooden and metallic elements. These included embroidery, painting and gilding, in addition to the use of fancy trimmings. Much of the decoration was heraldic in origin, such as two low chairs 'having the kinges Armes crowned Joyned with tharmes of Cleveland and H. & A. enbraudred in the backe' [251]. However, there were a few examples of renaissance motifs, as with 'oone Cheir of wodde Antique worke percell gilt and walnuttre colour' [254]. The arms of France on the back of the chair suggest that it was a gift either from the French king, Francis I, or a French ambassador. Fringe was the most common form of trimming and it was made from silk or metal thread, or a combination of the two. While it could be the same colour as the top covers, it was often a contrasting colour or striped. A number of the chairs also had decorative finials or pommels that were usually made of wood, either painted or fabric-covered, but they could be made from gilded copper.

On first glance the bulk of the information relates to the materials, colour and the style and method of decoration. Closer reading reveals a range of other details. Distinct types of chair are mentioned, including Spanish chairs (e.g. 13828), Flemish chairs (e.g. 13799) and a church chair (13840). However, these pieces were all at St John's, a property that had been confiscated from the Knights of St John, so they are unlikely to reveal much about the King's taste. More interesting is the chair at St James' 'after the spanyshe fasshion with white bone the seate and backe parte therof of crymsen vellat with gilte nayles frengid with redd silke' (15349). St James' formed part of the new Palace of Westminster and its role was to house Henry VIII's male heir, initially his illegitimate son Henry Fitzroy and later Prince Edward (Thurley, 1993).

Occasionally, pieces were identified as being for a woman (e.g. 12968) or a child (9430). When no other details were given, the inference is that the small size distinguished them. Other specific types of chair were rarely highlighted and no pieces were identified as being used as a chair of estate. This makes the pair of chairs 'thone for the kinge having two knoppes of Copper and gilte thother for the quene havinge two knoppes of Ankomy silvered' (12728) at Oatlands most unusual. Even more interesting is the pair of invalid chairs that were made for Henry VIII in July 1544. They were described as

> Twoo Cheyres called trauewes for the kinges Majestie to sitt in to be carried to and fro in his galleries and Chambres couered with tawney vellat allouer quilted with a cordaunte of tawny silke with a halfe pace vnderethe euerie of the saide cheyres and twoo fotestoles standing vppon everies of the halfe paces enbrawdred vppon the backe of theym and the toppes of the twooe highe pomelles of euerie one a rose of venyce golde and frengid rounde aboute with tawnye silke (11798).[24]

Such chairs were not unique to Henry VIII (d. 1547), although his chair is one of the earliest. Variants on this theme were made for Philip II of Spain (d. 1598) and Charles X of Sweden (d. 1660).[25] Extensive quilting was used on the chairs for Henry VIII and Philip II for extra comfort. The back, seat and arms of Philip's chair were padded and quilted, while the back was hinged to make it adjustable and there was a footrest.

Where the 1547–50 inventory entries record the objects by room rather than by type, it is likely that these rooms were stripped down to the basic furnishings, suggesting that the details had been recorded when the houses were empty. Those chairs which were inventoried in these rooms appear to be wooden, without upholstery, e.g. 'a cheyre of joyned worke' (9599) in the closet over the waterstair and 'a Cheire of wallnuttre with dyuers devyses' (9531) in the King's gallery at Greenwich. An alternative explanation is that this was the normal decoration for such rooms and the upholstered furniture was reserved for more intimate rooms than these. However, the entries for the privy chamber and other rooms within the privy lodging at Greenwich and Hampton Court, also reveal a lack of upholstered seat furniture.

A number of the entries in the 1547–50 inventory contain incidental details about the objects, such as the donor or the condition. All of this helps to provide a fuller picture of the objects in general and upholstered furniture in particular. In contrast, the main text of the 1542 inventory includes no details of this kind. It is necessary to consult the marginal notation or the sections at the end of the inventory dealing with the purchases made by Anthony Denny between 1542–7.

While the 1547–50 inventory does not record the names of any craftsmen producing upholstered furniture for the royal household, it does reveal that a number of chairs and stools were given to the King as New Year's gifts. This choice is interesting because during Henry VIII's reign the most common presents were either pieces of plate or money. Gifts of furniture were divided fairly equally between male and female donors and they gave either one chair or two stools. The named donors were either high ranking, like John Russell, first earl of Bedford (12089) or members of the household like Sir Thomas Heneage (12076), the groom of the stool and Sir Thomas Cawarden (12075), master of the tents and revels. Such a gift was even acceptable for family members as the following piece given by Henry VIII's eldest daughter, the Lady Mary, demonstrates:

> one faire cheir of wood covreed with clothe of golde all over embraudered with grene vellat and Rooses with the Kinges Armes in the backe holden by his majesties beastes and fringed with venice gold silver and silke (12074).[26]

One final feature revealed by the 1542 inventory is that on occasion Henry VIII bought or commissioned suites of furnishings: 'oone Cheir of cloth of gold reysid with Rowes wherin ar flowers of blew vellat' [242], with a square stool [277] and one foot stool [289] to match. It is equally interesting to note that when the furnishings at the palace were reorganised shortly after his death, maintaining the integrity of the sets does not appear to have been a priority (Table 9.4). Of the twenty-one sets of chairs, 76 per cent were split up. As with the examples shown in Figure 9.1, the sets were not just split in two but distributed between a number of properties. This makes it appear to have been a conscious policy, where the emphasis had shifted from unity to diversity.

9.4 Inventories: a source of frustration

For all of their strengths, inventories also have demonstrable weaknesses for a study of this kind. While dimensions were given for bedsteads and most textiles, ranging from napery (table linen) to tapestries, they were not given for any of the seat furniture. This sort of information can only be gained from surviving examples and because so few pieces survive it is very hard to build up an accurate picture. The chair associated with Mary Tudor at Winchester cathedral is quite small, measuring just 938 mm in height, 600 mm in width and 413 mm in depth (Figure 9.2). This information can be used to reflect on other objects that were often poorly described in the documents. Leather or fabric cases, for use during storage or transportation, were provided for a number of objects but no dimensions were given. However, a range of possible dimensions could be proposed once the size of the chairs can be established.

The biggest difficulty with the two inventories under consideration here arises from the inconsistent recording of information by the clerks. This is most readily apparent in relation to the descriptions of chair frames. Details were either omitted or frustratingly vague. The inventory entries fail on two counts. First, there were two main types of chair, the rigid, upright frame, or back stool, and the x-frame, however this distinction was never made explicitly in either the 1542 or 1547–50 inventories.

Table 9.4 The reorganisation of the palace of Westminster in 1547: the impact on sets of seat furniture and cushions

Objects	Number of entries	Number of single items	Number of sets	Number/ % of sets kept intact		Number/ % of sets split up	
Chairs	30	9	21	5	(23.8%)	16	(76.2%)
Cushions	123	59	64	42	(65.6%)	22	(34.4%)
Footstools	4	1	3	2	(66.6%)	1	(33.3%)
Stools	18	6	12	6	(50%)	6	(50%)

This table is based on the marginal evidence found on the 1542 inventory, PRO E315/160.

Figure 9.2 The x-frame chair probably used by Mary Tudor at her wedding to Philip II of Spain celebrated in Winchester Cathedral in 1554 (Acc. no. 913; 938 × 600 × 413 mm) (photograph taken by John Crook). The wooden chair frame is covered with velvet, now greenish-blue in colour, and attached to the frame with gilt headed nails. The back panel is missing and the machine made webbing joining the uprights at the back is a later addition. The seat pad is also a later construction. The hexagonal finials on the uprights, which are decorated with foliate motifs and the sacred monogram (IHC), and the bronze medallions covering the intersection of the x-frame at the front and the back, are thought to be nineteenth-century additions

However, there may be an indirect indication of the frame type. A number of the surviving x-frame chairs have ornamented bosses or roundels covering the point where the two sections of the frame interlink. Such roundels are referred to in both inventories and may indirectly indicate the type of chair frame being described. If this is the case, sixty-four of the eighty-seven chairs listed in the main section of the 1542 inventory were probably of the x-frame type as they are described as having roundels and the remainder were upright chairs or back stools, as no roundels were mentioned.

Twelve of these chairs are described as having arms. However, as this reference is made only in relation to the padding on the arms, there is the possibility that other chairs had arms that were not upholstered.

Both styles of frame were originally designed to fold, making them easier to transport by a peripatetic household. The presence of cases for chairs and stools within the holdings of the wardrobes of the Beds suggests that most of Henry VIII's chairs could be folded for storage or transportation. Even so, only one or two entries refer to folding chairs (e.g. 9428), which suggests that either the majority of the frames were fixed by this point, or this quality was so obvious that the clerk did not feel it was worth recording.[27] Thirdly, there is very little detail given about the materials used. While most chairs and stools had wooden frames, the type of wood was rarely recorded. When the wood was identified, it was usually walnut. A few chairs had iron frames. Probably most unusual was the 'Cheir of wodde coverid over with plate of silver parcell gilt enbossed with Cardenall hattes and sondry wordes' [252]. The final elements of the frame were the decorative roundels and pommels. While these were often described in terms of materials, quantity and condition, their precise location was rarely recorded.

9.5 Accounts

Accounts, just like accountants, deal with specific information, focusing on names, dates, delivery points, quantities and most importantly, prices. Where sets of accounts relate to the objects recorded within an inventory, this extra, detailed information can be used to build on the more general picture developed so far. Unfortunately, it is unusual to have this combination of accounts and inventories because full sets of annual accounts rarely survive. Even so, because the royal household generated large quantities of documentation, enough has survived to be of relevance here. The accounts of the King's works and the Great Wardrobe, along with the *King's Book of Payments*, which detailed expenditure within the chamber, are valuable sources of information on furnishings. To cite one example: a set of building accounts for the palace of Westminster provides details about the craftsmen involved in making chair frames, the materials they were using and that furnishings were ordered for specific locations. Nicholas Starkey, a joiner, received 20d for 'wone pese of Sesoned Crabtre ... spente as in making of Cogges and pynnes For ... Chayres'. Robert Wilkins, turner, was paid for 'wode and Tornyng of viij pyllorse For ij Tornyng Chayres now In making To be sett upp In the low gallary' (Baker, 1947: 102, 108).

Another craftsman who appears in the Great Wardrobe accounts is William Green, the King's coffer-maker. The evidence reveals that he performed a range of tasks, from making new chairs in response to orders placed by warrant, to refurbishing and recovering existing chairs. In addition, Green also supplied some of the necessary materials, as well as protective leather cases, which were the mainstay of his trade (Hayward, 2000). The Great Wardrobe accounts for 1538 record the full range of Green's activities. He recovered two chairs with eleven yards of crimson velvet costing £14 13s 4d, for which he was paid 66s 8d. The chairs were trimmed with 4 lb of silk fringe bought from Robert Gower for £4 16s.[28] Green also charged 40s for two leather carrying cases lined with cotton that he had made for these chairs. For a separate project, he supplied a set of pommels costing 7s 6d for a chair he covered with five and a half yards of red velvet.[29] Such details provide a picture of how the royal household operated, maintaining and recycling furnishings to ensure that the King's possessions appeared at their best.

9.6 Household ordinances and etiquette

Tudor society was strictly hierarchical with the monarch at the apex. The royal household represented a microcosm of the country and everyone within it was governed by the need to show deference to their superiors. Consequently, the household ordinances required men to doff their hats to the chair and cloth of estate placed in the presence chamber, in acknowledgement of the King's authority in his absence. Equally, at dinner, precedence for seating arrangements was carefully observed. In a small drawing depicting Henry VIII dining in state in his privy chamber, the King is the only person seated, and indeed the only person eating.[30] For state banquets, such as that given for the French ambassador in July 1546, the seating arrangements were carefully planned. As always there was the difficulty of not enough space to accommodate those on the initial guest list. Not even a senior position within the household could guarantee a seat: Sir Anthony Denny, groom of the stool and first gentleman of the privy chamber, was one of twenty-eight people who was 'pricked not to sit'.[31]

The significance of seating arrangements within a domestic context is demonstrated by two group portraits. The first is the anonymous family portrait of Henry VIII, Jane Seymour and the three royal children. Henry's authority, as husband and father, was reinforced by his being the only seated figure.[32] The significance of Jane Seymour, as mother of the male heir, and Edward, as Henry's successor, was stressed by their proximity to the King. Distanced by physical space and illegitimacy were the standing figures of Henry's daughters, Mary and Elizabeth. The second is the portrait of Sir Thomas More's extended family, known from the preparatory sketch by Hans Holbein.[33] More and his father sat together on a bench or settle, with some of the younger men stood nearby. The women either stood or were seated on stools or cushions.

Returning to a royal context, a good example is provided by the chair associated with Mary Tudor. The chair was described by Lieutenant Hammond of the Norwich militia as being where 'Queen Mary did sit when she was marry'd to King Philip in his standing posture' (Hardacre, 1989: 83). Although Philip ruled equally with Mary, rather than acting as a consort, on this occasion he showed deference to her by standing while she was seated. This idea was continued in the joint portrait of Philip II and Mary I of 1557. Both were depicted with a x-frame chair beneath a cloth of estate but Philip stood while Mary was seated.[34]

Chairs, forms and stools can be seen as hierarchical. Communal seating was provided by the form and bench and it was less prestigious than individual seating. A chair with arms was preferable to one without. Such niceties were undoubtedly observed when the seating arrangements for the Somerset House Conference of 1604 were prepared and later recorded by an unknown artist.[35] Each chair was different and had arms, while those for the principal protagonists were richer in colour and ornament.

9.7 Visual sources

A number of visual sources have been cited already, indicating their value in a study of this kind. The range of visual evidence is quite broad but the quantities are limited and evidence of this type inevitably raises questions about the accuracy of depiction. That said, visual sources fall into two main groups. The first includes formal portraits and miniatures. Henry VIII envelops his chair in pictures such as Holbein's portrait of *Henry VIII and the Barber Surgeons.* In contrast, interesting chair details are often visible in the portraits of his daughter Mary. This is particularly true of the portrait painted by Antonio Mor in 1554 (Figure 9.3). The painted details, while not necessarily painted from life, are in keeping with the written description in Henry VIII's inventories. This is pertinent as Mary inherited her father's possessions from her late brother and their continued use reflected the quality of what he had bought as well as Mary's restricted finances.

Figure 9.3 Mary I painted by Antonio Mor, 1554 (by permission of the Isabella Stewart Gardner Museum, Boston, USA). Details of the chair's construction recorded by Mor include the x-frame, the metal thread embroidered decoration, the slightly spaced decorative nailing, the use of crimson velvet and the two gilded pommels on the uprights of the chair back. The choice of fabric and the colour both relate very well to the information drawn from the 1547–50 inventory

The second covers informal sketches. The drawing referred to earlier of Henry VIII dining in his privy chamber is problematic for several reasons. The rather sketchy nature of the drawing and its small size mean that relatively little detail of the King's chair can be seen. In addition, it has been suggested that the picture was drawn in the seventeenth-century. In contrast to this there is the small illustration of Henry VIII sitting reading in the King's psalter (Figure 9.4). This miniature depicts fairly accurately a x-frame chair. However, the artist's choice of blue for the textile elements is problematic as less than 3 per cent of the chairs in the King's possession at his death were that colour.

Potentially more useful, although at a slight tangent, is a set of late sixteenth-century drawings that accompany a wardrobe account in the Archivio di Stato (State archive), Florence. These are of interest because the clerk drew these sketches in order to work out the quantity of fabric required (Thornton, 1984). They include a sketch and calculations for twelve chairs covered with red leather, a set of walnut chairs 'in the Neopolitan style' with velvet backs and seats for a coach, which highlights the link between the skills required to make partially upholstered furniture and saddles. While this point is made by Peter Thornton, it is worth noting that Henry VIII's Great Wardrobe employed a series of saddlers, who appear to have worked exclusively on horse harness (Thornton, 1978: 217; 1991: 184).

BEATVS vir qui non abiit
in consilio impiorum, & in via
peccatorum non stetit, & in cathedra pe-
stilentiæ non sedit.

Figure 9.4 Henry VIII reading in his bed chamber, seated in an x-frame chair, from Henry VIII's psalter prepared by Jean Mallard (British Library Royal MS 2 A XVI, f. 3; by permission of The British Library). The chair is completely covered in blue fabric, probably velvet and it has been trimmed with fringe made from metal threads. The bed curtains are also in blue, possibly indicating a degree of co-ordination in the furnishings. While such a decorative scheme is possible, it is most unlikely that this illustration was based on a real interior

9.8 Material evidence

Very few pieces of seat furniture have survived from the early modern period and those that do are often highly problematic: original textiles and trimmings have often been lost, structural elements have been replaced or repaired and sets have been dispersed. The chair associated with Mary Tudor at Winchester cathedral has undergone a number of changes. The records of the cathedral's treasurer note that in 1819 a Mr

Godwin was paid £11 1s to repair and recover the chair (Hardacre, 1989: 83). Even without this confirmation, the attachment of the seat squab cushion is particularly unusual and suggests that Mr Godwin modified the original arrangement.[36] The colour of the current textile elements also poses a problem. Originally, the chair was covered in purple velvet, suited to a royal wedding; now it is blue/green in colour.[37] Whether Godwin used a different coloured cloth or it has radically faded and changed colour, the appearance is not as Mary had intended. In contrast it is thought that the x-frame chair in the treasury at York Minster may retain some of the original textiles and fringe (Rendell, 1990: 15–19). The seat appears to be almost complete and is made from silk velvet and a tabby woven linen, while the padding is cow body hair. Leather had been wrapped around sections of the wooden frame prior to it being covered with velvet. This chair, which is in a very delicate condition, has been associated with the enthronement of George Neville as archbishop in 1464 (Strange, 1928: 217).[38]

The x-frame chair continued in use well into the seventeenth century. Single examples survive, like the Juxon chair with its footstool in the Victoria & Albert Museum, but the best collection of individual pieces and sets of related pieces can be seen at Knole, Kent. While these are later in date than the period under consideration here, they are still relevant because many of the pieces were perquisites from the royal wardrobe. A number of the Knole chairs were stamped to denote royal ownership and to indicate the property that they belonged to. An x-frame chair of estate covered with red velvet in the Leicester Gallery has the Hampton Court mark and the date 1661, while two carved walnut chairs in the style of Thomas Roberts, displayed in the Brown Gallery, have an imperial crown carved on the front stretcher and the WP mark for Whitehall palace under the seat (National Trust, 1978: 19–20).

Brands with the broad arrow mark were used to identify royal military supplies in the Henrician period so it is possible that furniture was marked in this way. However, the recording of identifying marks was treated differently within the 1547–50 inventory dependent upon the type of object. Some plate marks were given, although without the opportunity to examine the plate it is not possible to tell how consistent this notation is. Equally, at some of the wardrobes of the Beds, letters were used to identify the sets of tapestries, whereas at other houses, the tapestries were identified by subject. The question of identifying marks on furniture is raised by surviving pieces but cannot be answered by the documentation analysed to date.

One surviving chair that was closely associated with Tudor kingship is St Edward's chair at Westminster Abbey. This chair was bound into the coronation ritual and is perhaps as close as it is possible to get to a Tudor throne. The chair was specially prepared on each coronation, as the Lord Chamberlain's accounts for 1547 indicate. A payment was made to William Green for covering St Edward's chair with eighteen yards of white baudekyn flowered with gold, trimmed with one ell, one ounce of white silk fringe and six ounces of penny breadth ribbon.[39] Without references of this type, it is very hard to imagine St Edward's chair in its full coronation glory by looking at its current bare wooden frame.

9.9 Conclusions

This study is very specific, concentrating on the luxury furniture that was produced for Henry VIII, his immediate family and the social elite at court. These furnishings were intended to make a striking visual impact, just as most of the written descriptions were aimed at wardrobe officers making a quick identification based on visual evidence. Quantitative and qualitative evidence about the type of seat furniture in use, its construction, decoration and materials is available in this context because two very rich inventories have survived: one valuable for the specific, additional details included in the marginal notation, the other for the breadth of its coverage. In spite of their strengths, this material is incomplete and open to a variety of interpretations. These documents were produced for the specific reasons described above, which did not require a detailed and uniform object record for each item. However, when inventories are studied in combination with other written sources, visual evidence and surviving objects, a richer insight into furnishings at the Tudor court is gained.

This combination of sources allows a more critical analysis of the material, with one source being used to question another. Only a detailed inventory or set of accounts could provide the specific information on the range of fabrics used on Henry VIII's chairs or the spectrum of colours but without the opportunity to study actual chairs or pictures there would be very little evidence as to how these fabrics were used. In the same way evidence from sumptuary legislation reveals the significance of certain colours, while household ordinances and books on etiquette explore the social significance of the chair or cushion that is missing from inventories and accounts. The caveats aside, the sources, both written and visual, are rich enough for Henry VIII's reign to provide a better understanding of luxury Tudor seat furniture and 'upholstery' practice.

Appendices

Glossary

Materials

BAUDEKYN: a rich figured silk; the name probably derives from Baldacco, the Italian name for Baghdad
CLOTH: a plain woven wool textile
CLOTH OF GOLD: a silk fabric with an additional weft of gold or silver-gilt metal thread (either a flat metal strip or a metal strip wound round a silk or linen core); the ground fabric in plain cloth of gold was yellow but it could be produced in a variety of colours
CLOTH OF SILVER: a silk fabric with an additional weft of silver metal thread; the ground fabric in plain cloth of silver was white but it could be produced in a variety of colours
FUSTIAN: a twill woven cloth with a linen warp and cotton weft, although some types included worsted thread; made in Norwich, Naples and Genoa
SATIN: a shiny silk fabric where the warp threads float over four or seven weft threads before binding
TINCEL: an expensive silk cloth incorporating silver or silver-gilt flat metal strips
TISSUE: the most expensive form of cloth of gold/silver; woven in the sixteenth century with raised loops of metal thread above a velvet ground
VELVET: a silk cloth with a short pile that was formed by placing the supplementary pile warp over rods introduced during the weaving process; the pile could be cut, uncut or a combination of the two; the best velvets came from Genoa, Florence and Lucca
VELVET UPON VELVET: velvet with two or more depths of pile

Colours

CARNATION: a pale pink, flesh colour
CRIMSON: a deep rich red dyed using kermes, derived from the wing cases of the *Coccus ilicis*
INCARNATE: a bright crimson
MURREY: a dull, purple red or mulberry colour
RUSSET: a red-brown colour
TAWNY: a colour made from red and yellow

Henry VIII and his children

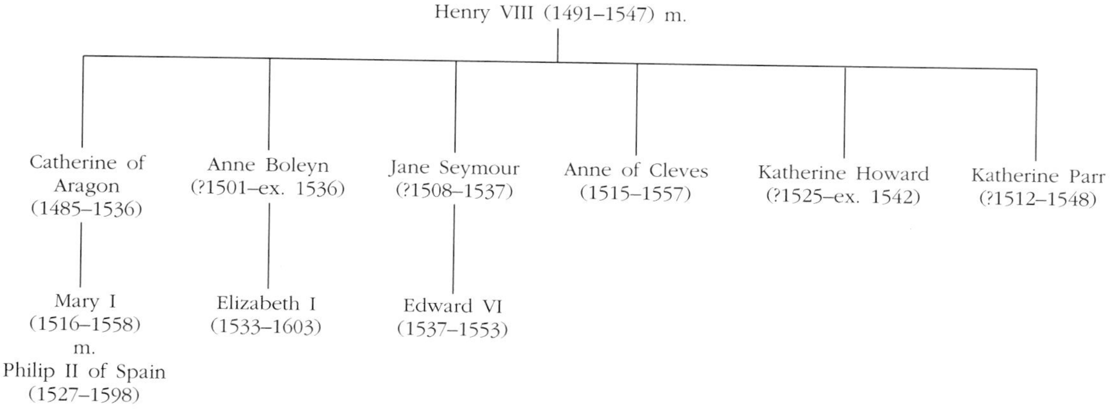

Notes

1 National Portrait Gallery, London, UK no. 4027.
2 Two versions of this picture survive. The original belongs to the Worshipful Company of Barber Surgeons, London, and the cartoon, which has been over-painted, belongs to the Royal College of Surgeons, London; see Strong, 1963.
3 As a counter, there is Peter Thornton's work on the Italian renaissance that draws on written and pictorial evidence rather than surviving pieces and covers the period under consideration here (see Thornton, 1991: 174–91).
4 Jervis (1989: 277) described his aims as being 'first a description and evaluation of the various types of furniture included in the inventories and second some remarks on their combination and arrangement, in so far as these can be reconstructed'. Simon Jervis is preparing a similar review of the furniture recorded in the 1547–50 inventory for a volume of specialist essays to be edited by David Starkey.
5 PRO E315/160, f. 120v. Anthony Denny made a number of purchases including chairs, stools and footstools but the suppliers were not recorded. This suggests that they were made within the Great Wardrobe.
6 British Library Additional MS 10109, f. 47v. The cushions were to furnish the new office for the staff of the King's Works, which was located next to the fish house at the old palace of Westminster. Additional purchases included matting for the floor, a green cloth for the table, a pair of bellows, fire shovels, tongues and a pair of creepers.
7 For one view of the upholsterer's craft during Henry VIII's reign see Beard, 1997: 20–22. Beard comments that 'the artificers of the Great Wardrobe included in their number what we now call "upholsterers" but in the Tudor period the description did not appear in wardrobe, or indeed other accounts'.
8 For a discussion of coffer terminology, see Hayward, 1997: 8–9. The terminology is not always used consistently in inventories but generally chests had flat lids, trunks and standards were similar to chests but larger and coffers had rounded lids.
9 As yet I have not found any links between saddlers and seat furniture in the early sixteenth-century English court context but that does not mean that they do not exist.
10 For an explanation of the inventory numbers and the sources of these quotations, see note 15.
11 In Dutch the phrase 'op het kussen ziten' (he who sits on a cushion) is used to indicate a person of high standing (see Thornton, 1978: 180).
12 In modern English this reads as 'Item one cushion of crimson gold tissue pieced at each end with richer like tissue/the back side thereof of cloth of gold raised with great roses and small of crimson velvet fringed round about with a narrow fringe of Venice gold/and four buttons with tassels of Venice gold and red silk'. For an explanation of the inventory numbers and the sources of these quotations, see note 14.
13 Organised on similar but smaller lines was the wardrobe of the Robes which was responsible for the King's clothes. For a discussion of the wardrobes of the Robes and Beds, see Hayward, 1998 (a and b).
14 Public Record Office (hereafter abbreviated as PRO) E315/160. This is being prepared for publication (see Hayward, 2001). Each entry in the inventory has been numbered and objects cited from the text will be referred to by this number given in square brackets [ ].
15 The inventory is split between two manuscripts: Society of Antiquaries MS 129 and British Library Harley MS 1419. The inventory has been transcribed and published (see Starkey, 1998). Each entry in the inventory has been numbered and objects cited from the text will be referred to by this number given in round brackets ( ).
16 The chief omission is the library at Westminster. However, it was documented in 1542 (see Hayward, 2001).
17 When Henry VIII hurt his foot playing tennis in 1527 and had to attend a dance wearing black velvet slippers, members of the court tactfully chose to wear the same so that the King should not look different. In the same way, it is likely that once the King needed a footstool, all new orders for chairs would include a footstool, so making this appear to be the norm.
18 This chair is illustrated in Rodríguez-Salgado, 1988: 96. The dimensions are given as 1080 × 620 × 490 mm.
19 Thornton notes that fabrics incorporating metal thread continued to be used as top covers in the seventeenth century but slipped out of use during the eighteenth century (1978: 221).
20 The dimensions given for one example cited but not illustrated in Rodríguez-Salgado, 1988: 96 are 550 × 535 × 225 mm.
21 The emphasis of the catalogue entry is on the carpet rather than its use on the chair frame. While the carpet and frame are approximately contemporary, it is not possible to assess when they were combined. For other uses of carpet, tapestry and turkey work, see Thornton, 1978: 220–1.

22 For example, see Walton 1984. A range of red related colours produced using madder, along with kermes and cochineal were the most common, while surprisingly little indigo/woad was found. A purple dye, possibly achieved using elderberries, was also identified.
23 A set of four padded forms owned by Cardinal Mazarin were described as 'enbourrées de crin courvertes de moquette' (stuffed with horsehair and covered with plush) (Thornton, 1978: 182). Philip II's invalid chair was also stuffed with horsehair (see below).
24 In modern English the entry is 'two chairs called traverses for the King's majesty to sit in to be carried to and fro in his galleries and chambers covered with tawny velvet all over, quilted, with a cordant of tawny silk with a half pace underneath every of the said chairs and two footstools standing upon every of the half paces, embroidered upon the back of them and the tops of the two high pommels of every one a rose of Venice gold and fringed round about with tawny silk'.
25 Two drawings of Philip II's invalid chair and the surviving chair of Charles X are illustrated in Thornton, 1978: 197, 199. A replica of Philip's chair is included in Rodríguez-Salgado, 1988: 970. The dimensions are given as 1610 × 780 × 940 mm.
26 In modern English the entry is 'one fair chair of wood covered with cloth of gold all over embroidered with green velvet and roses with the King's arms in the back held by his majesty's beasts and fringed with Venice gold, silver and silk'.
27 The evolution of the *faldestolium* (folding chair) to the rigid x-frame chair of the seventeenth century is described in Thornton, 1974.
28 PRO LC 9/51, f. 251v.
29 Ibid. f. 252r.
30 The drawing of Henry VIII dining by an unknown artist dating from the late sixteenth or early seventeenth century in the collection of the British Museum, 1854–6–28–74 (see Thurley, 1993: 138).
31 *LP* XXI.i, 1384.
32 The picture *The Family of Henry VIII* by an inknown artist, c.1545 is in the Royal Collection and is currently at Hampton Court Palace (see Thurley, 1993: 214–15).
33 Holbein's drawing *The Family of Sir Thomas More* is in the Kupferstichkabinett der Öffentlichen Kunstsammlung, Basle, 1662.31 (see Roberts, 1993: 26).
34 The picture, ascribed to Lucas de Heere, is at Woburn Abbey and a copy can be seen at the National Maritime Museum, Greenwich (BHC2952) (see Rodríguez-Salgado, 1988: 44).
35 National Portrait Gallery, London, UK no. 665.
36 I am very grateful to Kathryn Gill for discussing this point with me.
37 Personal communication, Alison Carter, curator of Art, Hampshire County Council Museums Service. Dye analysis might provide further information on this point.
38 I would like to thank Kathryn Gill for providing me with a copy of this article.
39 PRO LC2/3, p. 33.

Acknowledgements

First, I would like to thank Kathryn Gill and Dinah Eastop for asking me to contribute to their book and for all their help, suggestions and encouragement in the preparation of this paper. I am also most grateful to John Hardacre, curator of the Triforium Gallery, Winchester Cathedral, for allowing me to examine Mary Tudor's chair and to the Dean and Chapter of Winchester Cathedral for giving permission to reproduce the image in Figure 9.2. Thanks also to Alison Carter, curator of Art with Hampshire County Council Museums Service, for discussing the chair with me. In addition, I would like to thank Isabelle Eaton, Bob Smith, Lesley Miller and Peter Barber.

References

Baker, A.C. (1947) Extracts from royal accounts of Henry VIII. *London Topographical Record*, **19**: 100–16.

Beard, G. (1997) *Upholsterers and Interior Furnishing in England, 1530–1840*. London and New York: Yale University Press.

Brewer, J.S., Gairdner, J. and Brodie, R.H., eds (1861–3) *Letters and Papers Foreign and Domestic of the Reing of Henry VIII*. London: Longman, Green, Longman, Roberts and Green.

Hardacre, J. (1989) *Winchester Cathedral Triforium Gallery*. Winchester: Dean and Chapter of Winchester Cathedral.

Hayward, M. (1997) The packing and transportation of the goods of Henry VIII, with particular reference to the 1547 inventory. *Costume*, **31**: 8–15.

Hayward, M. (1998a) The possessions of Henry VIII: a study of inventories. Unpublished PhD thesis, University of London.

Hayward, M. (1998b) Repositories of splendour: Henry VIII's wardrobes of the robes and beds. *Textile History*, **29** (2): 134–56.

Hayward, M. (2000) William Green, coffer-maker to Henry VIII, Edward VI and Mary I. *Furniture History*, **36**: 1–13.

Hayward, M. (ed.) (2001) *The 1542 Inventory of the Palace of Westminster: The Curatorial Career of Sir Anthony Denny*. London: The Society of Antiquaries and The Westpark Press.

Jervis, S. (1989) 'Shadows not substantial things': Furniture in the Commonwealth Sale inventories. In A. MacGregor (ed.) *The Late King's Goods*. Oxford: Alistair McAlpine with Oxford University Press, pp. 277–306.

King, D. and Sylvester, D. (eds) (1983) *The Eastern Carpet in the Western World from the 15th to the 17th Century*. London: Arts Council of Great Britain.

Monnas, L. (1998) 'Tissues' in England during the fifteenth and sixteenth-centuries. *CIETA Bulletin*, **75**: 63–80.

National Trust (1978) *Knole*. London: National Trust.

Rendell, C. (1990) The Archbishop's chair, York Minster. In A. French (ed.), *Conservation of Furnishing Textiles*. Edinburgh: SSCR/UKIC pp. 14–20.

Roberts, J. (1993) *Holbein and the Court of Henry VIII. Drawings and Miniatures from the Royal Library Windsor Castle*. Edinburgh: National Galleries of Scotland.

Rodríguez-Salgado, M.J. (1988). *Armada 1588–1598*. Harmondsworth: Penguin.

Starkey, D.R. (ed.) (1998) *The Inventory of King Henry VIII. I: The Transcript*. London: Harvey Miller for the Society of Antiquaries.

Strange, E.F. (1928) The ancient chair at York Minster. *Old Furniture*. August issue (no issue number), 214–17.

Strong, R. (1963) Holbein's cartoon for the Barber Surgeon's group rediscovered. *Burlington Magazine*, **105**: 1–14.

Thornton, P. (1974) Canopies, couches and chairs of state. *Apollo*, **100**: 293–4.

Thornton, P. (1978) *Seventeenth-Century Interior Decoration in England, France and Holland*. New Haven and London: Yale University Press.

Thornton, P. (1984) Some late sixteenth-century Medici furniture. *Furniture History*, **20**: 1–9.

Thornton, P. (1991) *The Italian Renaissance Interior 1400–1600*. New York: H.N. Abrams.

Thurley, S. (1993) *The Royal Palaces of Tudor England*. New Haven and London: Yale University Press.

Walton, P. (1984) Dyes on medieval textiles. *Dyes on Historical and Archaeological Textiles*. Third meeting of the York Archaeological Trust, pp. 30–33.

10

Eighteenth-century close-fitting detachable covers preserved at Houghton Hall: a technical study

Kathryn Gill

10.1 Introduction

This case history focuses on the construction and method of attachment of tight-fitting, detachable covers preserved on three suites of important eighteenth-century furniture. This seat furniture forms part of a magnificent and well-documented private collection at Houghton Hall, Norfolk, UK. Houghton Hall is one of Britain's important stately homes. 'It was conceived, built and furnished between 1722 and 1735' for Sir Robert Walpole, Britain's first Prime Minister (Cornforth, 1996: 3). The history of Houghton Hall and its furnishings were the subject of a fascinating exhibition in 1996/7 (Moore, 1996; Shilling, 1997).

The velvet top covers of three suites of seat furniture at Houghton Hall were investigated in 1994 when researching designs for tight-fitting, detachable covers required to replace missing covers on two William Kent chairs at Chiswick House, West London (Gill and Eastop, 1997).[1] Two significant features revealed by this research are analysed.[2] The first is the apparently simple and effective way in which the covers have been constructed, achieving a remarkably close fit to the three-dimensional form of the upholstery. The second is the close affinity of these eighteenth-century covers with current conservation principles and practices, notably the use of readily reversible techniques that have the least damaging effect on the upholstered frames and textile elements of seat furniture.

Having examined each item from all three suites of furniture, two representative chairs from each suite were identified for closer study. Characteristic features of the chairs are described below. Due to the fragile condition of the covers, none of them was removed from its chair frame for examination. Access to the inner face of the covers was therefore restricted; for example, only those lower edges that could be safely turned back were examined. Consequently, areas of damage and wear, especially areas of loss which exposed underlying layers, became useful sources of information. Photographs and line drawings generated during that technical study illustrate this case study.

10.2 Green velvet covers on burr walnut and parcel gilt chairs

Each frame of the burr walnut and parcel gilt suite is covered in unpatterned, green, solid cut silk velvet, and is trimmed with a green silk, woven braid. This suite was supplied to Sir Robert Walpole as part of a large suite now comprising twenty-three chairs and two settees (Beard, 1997: 181, 149). The suite is

Figure 10.1 Side chair (c.1725–30) Houghton Hall, Norfolk. Part of a suite of 23 chairs and two settees. The burr walnut and parcel gilt frame displays a green silk velvet removable cover trimmed with green silk braid

thought to date to c.1725–30 (Beard, 1997) and is illustrated in Moore (1996: 131, 134) (Figure 10.1).

Two different shades of green velvet have been used to cover this suite. The reason for this is unclear. Cornforth suggests one possible reason: such large quantities of velvet were required to furnish Houghton (521¾ yards; approx. 407 metres) that the velvet had to be woven in at least two lots (Moore, 1996: 35). It is not known whether the colour difference was intentional. Interestingly, two different shades of green velvet were used to cover the headboard of the green state bed in the Green Velvet Bed Chamber, Houghton. The shades are alternated across the different segments of the scallop shell in a seemingly planned fashion.[3]

The removable chair cover comprises two main panels of fabric. The first panel, a green dyed solid cut silk velvet, covers the seat and inner back of the chair. The velvet panel is not joined at the juncture of the seat and inner back as the close fit around the three-dimensional upholstered form suggests on initial glance. It comprises one continuous panel with side inserts of matching velvet and two additional panels of matching velvet, each seamed along one of the two selvages of the panel's seat section, to accommodate the greater dimension of the seat. The width of velvet is 21–22 inches (550–560 mm). Chairs at Ham House provide another example of close-fitting covers with continuous inner back and seat panels (Beard, 1997: 183, fig. 179). The velvet panel of the Houghton cover is fully lined with an unbleached (and possibly glazed) linen (see Figure 10.5, item f). The linen lining provides support for the velvet and a means of concealing the selvages and raw edges of the velvet.

The second main panel, the outer back panel, is a green dyed wool fabric. The panel is not lined. Instead, a narrow linen tape, ½ inch (12 mm) wide, conceals and re-inforces its single-turned raw edge (see Figure 10.5, item j). The tape also eliminates the need for a double-turned edge to conceal the raw edge of the wool cloth. This extra turn would have created excessive bulkiness and spoiled the otherwise clean line of the chair's side profile.

The panels are joined together by a hand-stitched seam around the perimeter of the chair back. An additional row of stitching (close to and parallel with the outer back seam) serves to hold all seam allowances flat and in position, thus minimising bulkiness and disturbance to the line of the upholstery profile (see Figure 10.4, item g). The outer back seam is accentuated by a cord, ¼ inch (5 mm) in diameter stitched directly over the seam of the cover. The front and two sides of the lower edge of the seat cover and the cord are trimmed with a green silk braid which may not be the original to the covers.[4] The braid conceals the method of attachment of the covers to the front and side rails of the frame. The method of attachment comprises a row of eyelets which penetrate both the linen and the velvet layers. The perimeter of each eyelet is bound with overcast stitches worked in an unbleached

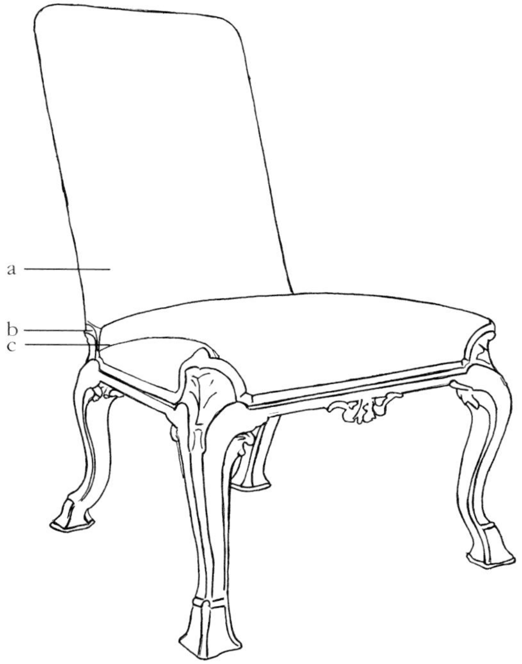

Figure 10.2 Line drawing of a three-quarter front view of the burr walnut and parcel gilt side chair illustrated in Figure 10.1 showing the removable velvet cover in position. Note that the inner back and seat comprise one continuous panel of velvet (a), with inserts one each side (b), and side panels seamed along the selvage to accommodate the wider dimension of the seat (c)

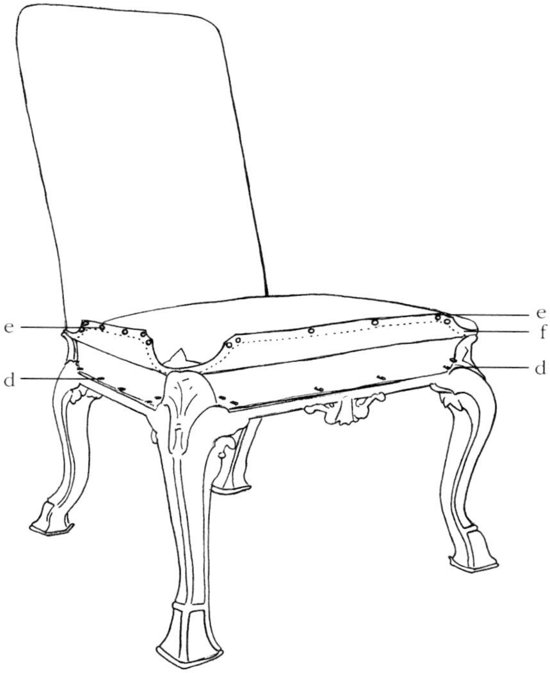

Figure 10.3 Line drawing of a three-quarter front view of the burr walnut and parcel gilt side chair illustrated in Figure 10.1. The lower edge of the removable cover is shown lifted upwards to illustrate the method of attachment to the frame. A single row of (20) metal pegs (d) protruding from the seat rails provide an anchoring point for the corresponding set of eyelets in the cover (e). The velvet panel is fully lined (f)

linen [?] stitching thread. The eyelets hook over a corresponding row of protruding metal pegs (in effect, 'headless nails') embedded into the seat rail. Although all eighteen metal pegs and eyelets, which are located at the front and two sides of the seat cover, are concealed by the braid, no attempt has been made to conceal the pegs and the eyelets along the lower edge of the outer back panel. Curiously, there are five eyelets along the lower edge of the outer back panel, but only two metal pegs in the frame, one at each corner. Furthermore, there is no evidence of corresponding metal pegs for these extra eyelets through the linen layer which covers the rear seat rail (see Figure 10.5). This was the case on nearly all the loose covers examined from this suite. Perhaps this is an indication that two pegs were found to be sufficient or that the underlying linen layer covering the seat rails is not original.

The means of fastening this cover to the chair requires only 20 headless nails. If these covers had been tacked directly to the frame it is estimated that at least three times the number of tacks would have been needed to anchor the cover to the frame.

To remove the cover from the frame would appear to have been a simple task: lifting the cover from the seat over the upholstered back unit, as shown in (Figures 10.2–10.5).

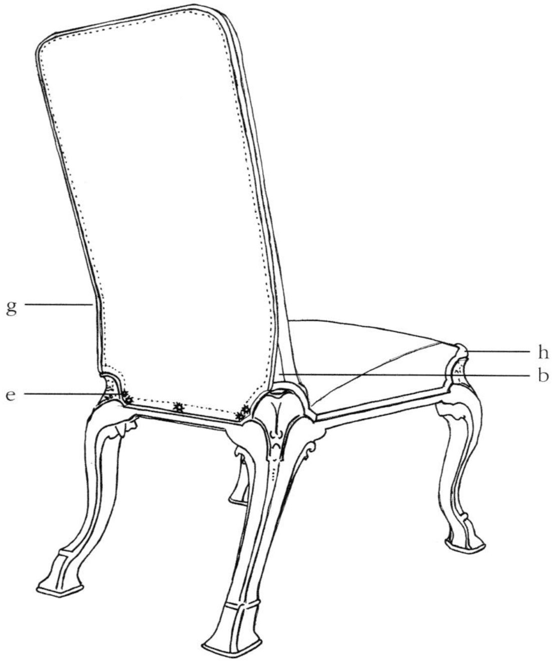

Figure 10.4 Line drawing of a three-quarter back view of the burr walnut and parcel gilt side chair illustrated in Figure 10.1 showing the removable velvet cover in position. The anchoring system for the outer back panel of green wool is the same as for the seat except that no attempt has been made to conceal the eyelets (e). The back seam is trimmed with a cord which has been covered by a green silk braid (g). The braid continues around the lower edge of the front seat rails (h). Note the velvet inserts (b)

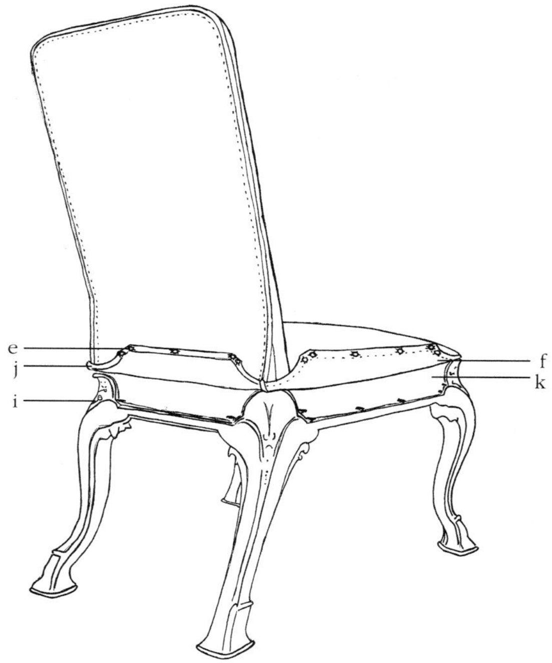

Figure 10.5 Line drawing of a three-quarter back view of the burr walnut and parcel gilt side chair illustrated in Figure 10.1. The lower edge of the removable cover is shown lifted upwards to illustrate the method of attachment to the frame. Curiously along the rear seat rail there are only two metal pegs (i) but five eyelets (e). Perhaps an indication that two nails were found to be sufficient, or that the underlying linen which shows no signs of extra tack holes, is not original. A narrow linen tape (j) conceals the raw edge of the unlined wool. The velvet is lined with linen (f); the fixed seat upholstery has a linen filling cover (k)

10.3 Green velvet covers on oil gilt and sanded walnut chairs

This suite has frames of oil gilt and sanded walnut, and is often referred to as the Satyr Mask suite because of the carved face on the apron of the frames; the suite is dated c.1731 by Edwards (Moore, 1996: 126). Like the previous example, the suite is covered in removable covers of an unpatterned, green solid-cut silk velvet and wool fabric; some of the covers are trimmed with a silver-gilt thread braid. The large suite, which now comprises thirty-three chairs, two settees and four stools, was supplied to Sir Robert Walpole for use in three rooms at Houghton (Edwards in Moore, 1996: 126–7) (Figure 10.6). The suite is illustrated in Moore (1996: 126, 128, 134).

The covers of this suite are of very similar materials and construction as those of the burr walnut suite; compare, for example, the two wing chairs, one from each suite, illustrated in Moore (1996: 134). Both sets of covers are made from more than one type of green velvet. The width of the velvet fabrics is 21.5 inches (540–550 mm). In addition, the outer back panel of green wool fabric is similar to that used on the burr walnut suite. However, although some covers are trimmed with a green silk braid, like the burr walnut suite, others are trimmed with a silver-gilt thread braid (1 inch; 25 mm wide). The metal thread braid is probably original.

Figure 10.6 Side chair (c.1731) Houghton Hall, Norfolk. Part of a suite of 33 chairs, two settees and four stools. The chair displays a green silk velvet removable cover with gold plated metal thread braid. The frame is of oil gilt and sanded walnut

Furthermore, the same simple principle has been used in the construction of the covers, a single panel of velvet with side inserts and two additional panels of velvet, each seamed along one of the two selvages of the panel's seat section, to accommodate the greater dimension of the seat (Figure 10.7). Possible reasons include economy (as less yardage is required), and limiting bulkiness, as the absence of seams at the juncture of the inner back reduces bulk. The velvet panel covers the seat and the inner back of the chair. It is fully lined with linen like the burr walnut chair. However, unlike the burr walnut chair cover, the outer back panel of green wool is lined. As with the cover on the burr walnut chair, the panels are joined together by a hand-stitched seam around the perimeter of the chair back. An additional row of stitching close to and parallel with the outer back seam serves to hold all seam allowances flat and in position, thus minimising bulkiness and disturbance to the line of the upholstery profile.

The fastening method of metal pegs and corresponding eyelets (concealed by the braid) is the same as that used on the burr walnut suite. The braid conceals the method of attachment of the covers to the front and side rails of the frame; it comprises a row of six eyelets

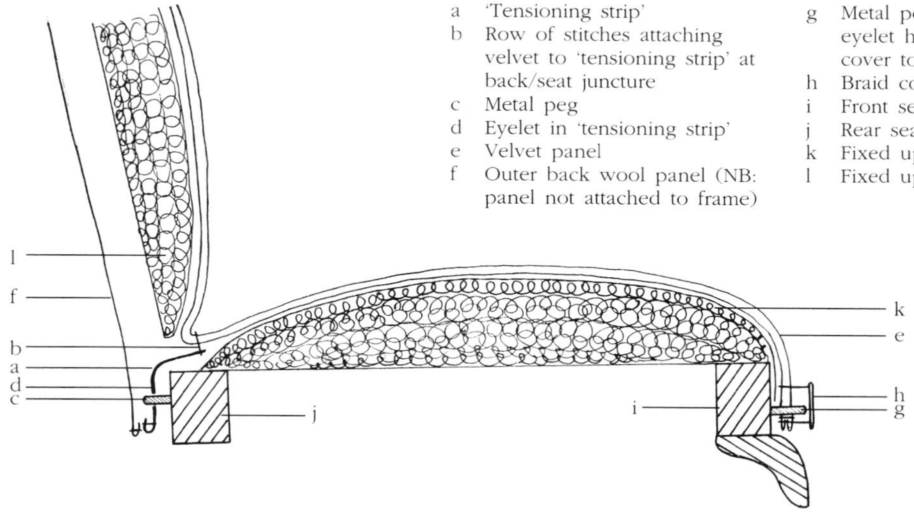

- a 'Tensioning strip'
- b Row of stitches attaching velvet to 'tensioning strip' at back/seat juncture
- c Metal peg
- d Eyelet in 'tensioning strip'
- e Velvet panel
- f Outer back wool panel (NB: panel not attached to frame)
- g Metal peg and corresponding eyelet holding seat section of cover to the frame
- h Braid concealing metal peg
- i Front seat rail
- j Rear seat rail
- k Fixed upholstered seat unit
- l Fixed upholstered back unit

Figure 10.7 Line drawing of a cross-sectional view of the oil gilt and sanded walnut chair frame to show the method of attachment of the cover to the frame. The 'tensioning strip' (a) is attached along the full width of the velvet panel at the seat/back juncture with a row of stitches (b). The 'tensioning strip' is held under the required tension by three metal pegs (c) and matching eyelets (d), to keep the velvet in position over the three-dimensional form of the chair seat (k)

which penetrate the velvet and its linen lining. The edges of each eyelet are bound with overcast stitching worked in an unbleached linen [?] stitching thread.[5] The eyelets hook over a corresponding row of protruding metal pegs, embedded into the seat rail.

The main difference between the sets of green velvet covers on the burr walnut chairs and the satyr mask chairs occurs along the lower edge of the outer back panels. The outer back of the burr walnut chair cover is anchored with two pairs of eyelets to metal pegs in the seat rail (see Figures 10.4 and 10.5). In contrast, the lower edge of the outer back cover of the oil gilt chair is not attached to the frame (Figure 10.7). To compensate for this apparent lack of tensioning, concealed beneath the outer back is a tensioning strip of green wool cloth which has been sewn along the full width of the reverse side of the velvet cover at the inner back and seat juncture. This tensioning strip, held under the required tension by three metal pegs and matching eyelets, keeps the velvet cover stretched in position over the 3-D form of the chair seat and back (Figure 10.7).

Other details of interest are the numbers embroidered on the understructure upholstery; these numbers correspond to numbers embroidered on the covers. Since none of the covers was removed from the frames for examination, due to their fragile condition, it was not possible to adjust the cover sufficiently to photograph these embroidered numbers. However, a clear view of a numbered cover from this suite is illustrated by Beard (1997: 182–4).

Quite remarkably, the means of fastening this cover to the chair requires only nine metal pegs, half the amount used for the burr walnut and parcel gilt chair cover. The main reason for this is that the lower edges of all four sides of the seat cover are straight and therefore require fewer points of contact to hold the covers close to the upholstered frame. In contrast, the lower edge of the burr walnut chair cover is shaped to follow the rising contours around the legs; these contours account for six of the extra metal pegs.

10.4 Crimson velvet covers on gilt gesso chairs

This suite comprises carved and gilt gesso frames covered in crimson velvet of Genoese manufacture: a crimson cut and uncut (*ciselé*) voided velvet on a ground of cream silk and metal thread (Plate 10.1). The suite is dated c.1715–20 (Beard, 1997: 176) and so predates the building of Houghton Hall. The suite is thought to have been made by the cabinet maker James Moore for James Brydges, the owner of Cannons in Middlesex (Jackson Stops, 1985: 154, 223; Beard, 1997: 176). The contents of Cannons was sold in 1747; the suite was not recorded at Houghton until the mid-nineteenth century, and is currently shown in the Marble Parlour. The suite now comprises eight side chairs and two armchairs[6] and is illustrated in Moore (1996: 139).

A side chair and an armchair were selected for examination and comparison. The construction of the side chair and the armchair covers is the same with the exception of obvious adaptations to accommodate the differences in the shape and dimensions of the frames. Although the same simple principle of a single panel of velvet and a single panel of wool has also been used in the construction of the removable covers for this suite (Plate 10.1), the covers and upholstered frames are quite different from the other two covers in a number of respects. For example, although the seat understructure upholstery is fixed to the main chair frame, the back upholstered unit is *a chassis* (see Figure 10.10). Brass swivel 'buttons' hold the back unit in place; these buttons can be turned to release the chair's back unit (Figures 10.8 and 10.9).

As is the case for all three suites, in the crimson cover the back and seat comprise one continuous panel of velvet (see Figure 10.12). The width of the velvet fabric is 22–3 inches (570 mm). In this case, one advantage would be no break in the large pattern of the crimson velvet, in addition to economy and limiting bulkiness.

The second main panel, the outer back panel, is a red dyed wool fabric.[7] Both the crimson velvet and the red wool panels are fully lined with linen. Furthermore, the lower edge of the lined outer back is reinforced with a narrow linen tape (½ inch; 15 mm), not unlike that used on the unlined panel of the parcel gilt chair cover. The lower edge of the covers is bound with a woven metal thread tape (Plate 10.1).

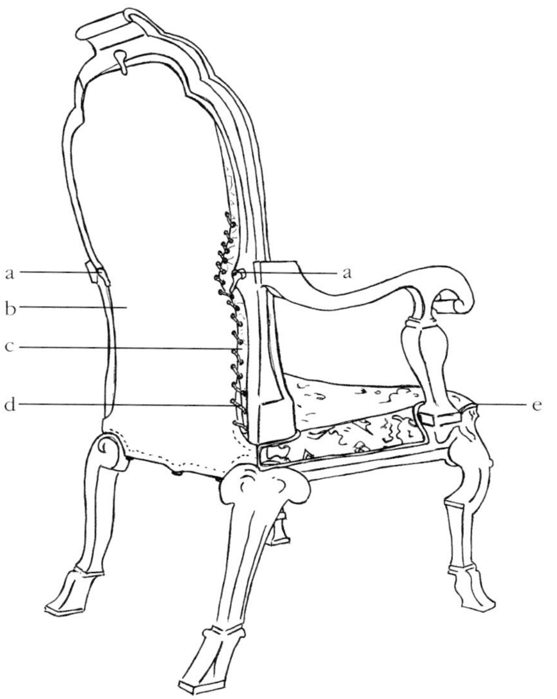

Figure 10.8 Line drawing of a three-quarter back view of the gilt gesso armchair illustrated in Plate 10.1. Three 'swivel' buttons (a) hold the chassis back unit to the main chair frame. The red wool panel (b) and silk velvet panel (c) have a laced closing (d). The edges of the seat section are bound with a metal thread tape (e)

a 'Swivel' button fastening system
b Outer back panel of red wool
c Inner back and seat panel of crimson velvet
d Laced fastening of silk cord along one vertical side of the back unit
e Binding of woven metal thread tape

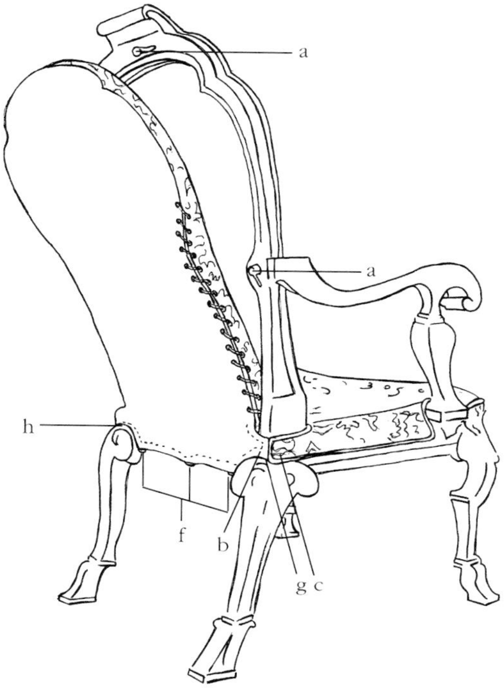

Figure 10.9 Line drawing of a three-quarter back view of the gilt gesso armchair illustrated in Plate 10.1. The 'swivel' buttons (a) are shown released causing the back to tilt out in readiness for the covers to be removed. Three linen tabs (f), located along the width of the outer back, are secured onto metal pegs located on the underside of the seat rail. Each rear corner of the panels (b) and (c) is held together with two pairs of hooks and eyes (g). A row of stitching holds the linen tape to the inner face of the lower edge of the lined panel (h)

a 'Swivel' button fastening system
b Outer back panel of red wool
c Inner back and seat panel of crimson velvet
f Linen tab fastening system
g Hook and eye fastening system
h Outer back panel

With the exception of one vertical side, the panels are joined together by a hand-stitched seam around the perimeter of the chair back. The unseamed section is left open for a laced closure. The closing on the armchair cover documented here is on the proper right side, in contrast to the proper left closing of the side chair cover. Presumably the choice of which side to place the closing depended on the positioning of the chair in the room, the laced side being on the less prominent aspect. The silk lacing cord is threaded through approximately 15 pairs of eyelets and tied off level with the juncture of the seat rail and back unit. Each end of the cord is tipped with a metal tag (*aiguillette*) (Plate 10.3). The lower edge of the outer back is held in position by linen tabs with stitched eyelets that hook over metal pegs nailed into the underside of the rear seat rail (Figures 10.10 and 10.11). The lower sides of the outer back are held to the corresponding side edges of the velvet seat panel with hooks and eyes.

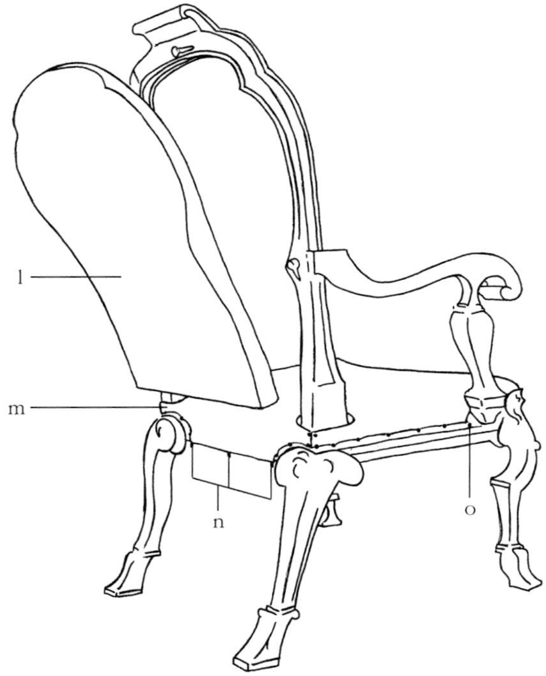

Figure 10.10 Line drawing of a three-quarter back view of the gilt gesso armchair illustrated in Plate 10.1. The chair is shown after the cover has been removed, and the independent upholstered back unit (l) and the fixed upholstery on the seat (m) are exposed. The metal pegs (n) which hold the linen tabs (f) (illustrated in Figure 10.11) are shown, as is one of the drilled holes in the seat rail (o)

l Independent upholstered back unit
m Fixed seat upholstery
n Metal peg fastening system
o Drilled holes in the seat rail

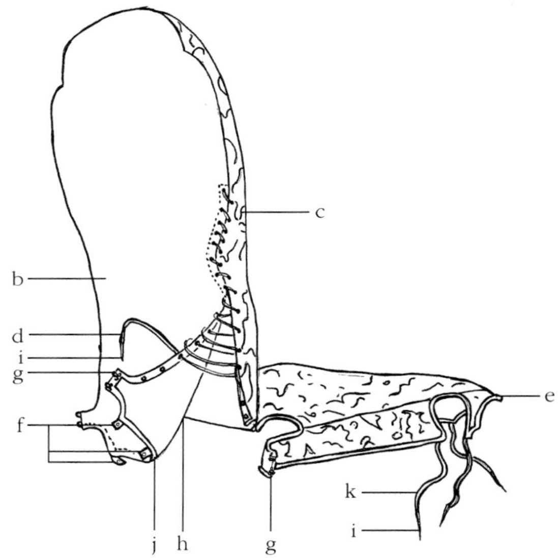

Figure 10.11 Line drawing of a three-quarter back view of the crimson velvet cover shown removed from the gilt gesso armchair illustrated in Plate 10.1. The linen tabs (f) have been unhooked from the metal pegs. The hooks and eyes (g) have been undone and the lacing (d) has been loosened. The seat rail lacing (k) has been untied and released. The independent upholstered back unit (l) (illustrated in Figure 10.10) is pulled downwards (out of the cover), and the remaining section of the cover is lifted from the seat (m) (illustrated in Figure 10.10)

b Outer back panel of red wool
c Inner back and seat panel of crimson velvet
d Laced fastening of silk cord along one vertical side of the back unit
e Binding of woven metal thread tape
f Linen tab fastening system
g Hook and eye fastening system
h Outer back panel
i Metal tip (*aiguillette*) covering ends of each length of silk lacing cord
j Narrow woven tape of unbleached linen
k Seat rail lacing of silk cord

The lower front and side edges of the armchair seat cover are held closely to the frame by a very simple and effective technique. Eight silk cords (of the same type as that used for the laced closure on the back unit), each anchored with stitches between the lining and the velvet at eight different points, are threaded through eight corresponding holes in the seat rail. Each cord is secured by tying to the cord hanging from the adjacent hole (Plate 10.3). The cords are located at points where the cover has been cut to follow the acute angles of the seat rail contours, namely either side of each arm base, each front corner and either side of the central cartouche of the front seat rail (Figures 10.11 and 10.12).

As with the other two suites, due to the fragile nature of the suite it was decided not to remove the covers at this stage of the examination/photo-documentation process. Line drawings were prepared to illustrate how the covers would be removed and reapplied to the frame (Figures 10.8–10.14). A three-quarter back view of the chair as seen on

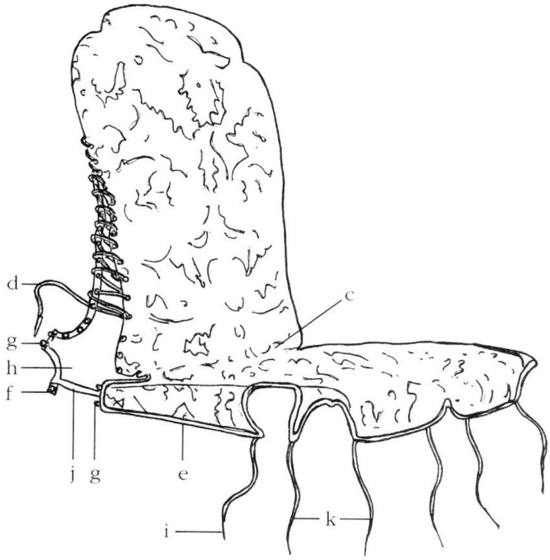

Figure 10.12 Line drawing of a three-quarter front view of the crimson velvet cover shown removed from the gilt gesso armchair illustrated in Plate 10.1. The seat rail lacings (k) are more visible

c Inner back and seat panel of crimson velvet
d Laced fastening of silk cord along one vertical side of the back unit
e Binding of woven metal thread tape
f Linen tab fastening system
g Hook and eye fastening system
h Outer back panel
i Metal tip (*aiguillette*) covering ends of each length of silk lacing cord
j Narrow woven tape of unbleached linen
k Seat rail lacing of silk cord

display is shown in Figure 10.8. The 'swivel' buttons have been turned and the back unit released in Figure 10.9.

The upholstered chair as it would have appeared once the covers were removed, showing the independent back unit, is illustrated in Figure 10.10. A three-quarter back view of the cover removed from the frame is shown in Figure 10.11. To release the cover the linen tabs would have been unhooked from the metal pegs, the hooks and eyes released, the lacing loosened, and the seat rail lacing untied and released. The upholstered back unit would have been pulled downwards, out of the cover to release the cover from the frame. A three-quarter front view of the cover as shown removed from the frame illustrates the construction of the inner face of the outer back panel and the continuous panel which comprises the back and seat cover (see Figure 10.12). To re-attach the cover to the frame the steps outlined above would have been followed in reverse order, as illustrated in Figures 10.13 and 10.14, showing three-quarter front views of the chair with the back in tilted and upright positions.

This loose-cover design is based on a very simple principle; it is very effective and beautifully executed. A total of three headless nails, three 'swivel' buttons and eight small holes in the seat rail secure the entire cover to the frame. Knowledge of the eighteenth-century covers at Houghton Hall and current conservation practices were combined with experience in cover construction to produce a set of replica covers for the contemporary chairs at Chiswick House. There was no evidence of either metal pegs or drilled holes in the frames of the Chiswick House chairs, so the replica covers were attached with hook and loop contact fastener (Velcro™) to customised sub-frames, which rested on the seat rail section of the main frame. The back unit covers were stitched to themselves around the upholstered frame. Details of this project have been published elsewhere (Gill and Eastop, 1997; see also Eastop, 1998).

10.5 Conclusion

Although the close-fitting, removable covers at Houghton Hall were initially examined with a view to providing models for replication, documentation of the covers highlights three points of general significance for the conservation of the upholstery. First, the examination and documentation of such rare specimens provides detailed information which contributes to the understanding of techniques, materials, structures and use of upholstered furniture. Such documentation provides a useful tool for interdisciplinary collaboration, essential for projects involving the re-interpretation of surviving elements and the re-building of missing elements. Secondly, informed examination, documentation and analysis of such textile furnishings can provide

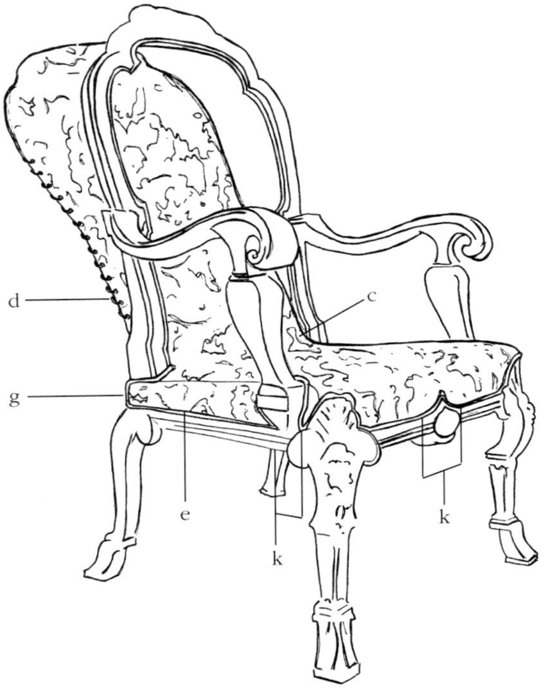

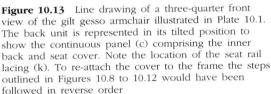

Figure 10.13 Line drawing of a three-quarter front view of the gilt gesso armchair illustrated in Plate 10.1. The back unit is represented in its tilted position to show the continuous panel (c) comprising the inner back and seat cover. Note the location of the seat rail lacing (k). To re-attach the cover to the frame the steps outlined in Figures 10.8 to 10.12 would have been followed in reverse order

c Inner back and seat panel of crimson velvet
d Laced fastening of silk cord along one vertical side of the back unit
e Binding of woven metal thread tape
g Hook and eye fastening system
k Location of seat rail lacing cords

Figure 10.14 Line drawing of a three-quarter front view of the gilt gesso armchair illustrated in Plate 10.1. The back unit is represented in its upright position. It should be noted that the upper section of the back unit is held to the main frame with 'swivel' buttons, unlike the lower edge which appears to rely completely on the two fastening systems illustrated in Figures 10.10 and 10.11, namely the hooks and eyes, the tabs and metal pegs

clues for understanding and possibly 'reconstructing' the changing sequence and fashions of decorative schemes and other alterations. Finally, such records provide models for current preventive conservation practice, such as that implemented at Chiswick House. The Houghton Hall covers manifest a minimally intrusive approach to upholstery conservation, and can be understood as exemplary models of traditional practices of preventive conservation. This case example shows that examination, documentation and analysis are essential stages in the preservation and presentation of upholstered artefacts and related decorative schemes. Another excellent example of such analysis was undertaken by Gentle (1990).

Notes

1 In 1995, Kathryn Gill was runner-up in the UK National Award for Conservation for the treatment undertaken on a pair of William Kent chairs (specially commended for innovative treatment). The award was sponsored by the Jerwood Foundation and administered by The Conservation Unit of the Museums and Galleries Commission.
2 'A Technical Study of 18th Century Close-fitting Covers: Early Examples of Minimally Intrusive Upholstery Techniques', conference paper presented by Kathryn Gill at 'Uncovering the Past:

New Research on Historic Upholstery, 1600–1850', Bard Graduate Centre for Studies in the Decorative Arts, New York, 16–17 October, 1998.

3 A clear view of the alternating bands of each shade of green velvet on the headboard is illustrated by Beard (1997: 186, figs 92 and 93).

4 On some chairs the braid extends to the lower edge of the outer back and is glued in place. The braid covering the cord and the braid binding the edges of the back seams are different. It is unlikely that these trimmings are original to the covers.

5 Sampling for fibre identification was not possible on any of the covers examined.

6 Some pieces from this suite were included in a sale at Christie's, and are illustrated in Christie's Houghton Catalogue, 8 December 1994 (for example, an armchair, lot 135).

7 Although the outer back panels on all the chairs in this suite are of red wool, several different red wool fabrics (with different thread counts) were noted.

Acknowledgements

I am pleased to acknowledge the Marquess of Cholmondeley of Houghton Hall and Nell Hoare of the Textile Conservation Centre for permission to publish and Sheila Stainton, conservation advisor for Houghton, and Geoffrey Beard for their help and encouragement. Thanks are also due to English Heritage (in particular former Assistant Curator, Sebastian Edwards) and to Susan Cleaver.

References

Beard, G. (1997) *Upholsterers and Interior Furnishings in England, 1530 to 1840*. London and New York: Yale University Press.

Christie's (1994) *Works of Art from Houghton*. Sales Catalogue. London: Christie's.

Cornforth, J. (1996) *Houghton Hall Guidebook*. Norwich: The Marquess of Cholmondeley and Jarrold Publishing.

Eastop, D. (1998) Decision making in conservation: determining the role of artefacts. In: A. Tímár-Balázsy and D. Eastop (eds), *International Perspectives on Textile Conservation*. Papers from the ICOM-CC Textiles Working Group Meetings, 1994 and 1995. London: Archetype, 43-46.

Gentle, N. (1990) Conservation of the Dolphin chairs at Ham House. In: A. French (ed.), *Conservation of Furnishing Textiles*. Postprints of the conference held at the Burrell Collection, Glasgow, 30–31 March 1990, Edinburgh: SSCR/UKIC, 30-40.

Gill, K. and Eastop, D. (1997) Two contrasting minimally interventive upholstery treatments: different roles, different treatments. In: K. Marko (ed.), *Textiles in Trust*. Proceedings of the Symposium held at Blickling Hall, Norfolk, September 1995, London: Archetype Publications and the National Trust, pp. 67–77.

Jackson Stops, G. (ed.) (1985) *The Treasure Houses of Britain*. Exhibition Catalogue. Washington, DC: National Gallery of Art.

Moore, A. (1996) *Houghton Hall. The Prime Minister, Empress and The Heritage*. London: Philip Wilson and Norfolk Museum Service.

Shilling, M.E. (1997) Houghton Hall Exhibition at Kenwood. *Furniture History Society Newsletter*, 127, August 1997, pp. 17–18. (With additional information from Dinah Eastop and Kate Gill.)

11

Evidence from artefacts and archives: researching the textile furnishings of a Victorian bedroom at Brodsworth

Crosby Stevens

11.1 Introduction

Detailed research into the historic textile furnishing of Bedroom 14[1] at Brodsworth Hall in South Yorkshire, UK, was commissioned by English Heritage[2] in 1998. This work was part of a broader project to research the printed textiles of the house. The aim was to provide historical information needed for the presentation of three bedrooms, including Bedroom 14, to the public for the first time, and to reassess other rooms already displayed. A careful study of the half-tester bed found in Bedroom 14 (Figure 11.1) when the house was taken over in 1990 revealed two layers of printed cotton fabric. Research in the archive of the house, which contains a number of relevant bills, inventories and photographs, and in commercial textile archives followed. Information from these sources led to the close examination of other historic artefacts from different parts of the house now found to have been associated with Bedroom 14, and to a study of how they were inter-related. Thus there was a 'dialogue' in information between objects and documents as the research progressed through a number of stages: the documentation of objects from Bedroom 14, archival research, the collating of evidence found, the identification of contradictions and anomalies, and the further documentation of other objects in the Brodsworth collection. This chain of research produced a probable chronology for the furnishing of the room.

The resulting understanding of items found in Bedroom 14 and of pieces in store and on show elsewhere in the house will be valuable to English Heritage curators and conservators. It will assist them in choosing which objects to display on the first floor and how they will be shown, including deciding priorities and methods for conservation.

This paper outlines the background to the project and the current display ethos at Brodsworth Hall in order to show how English Heritage will use the research in future. It then traces the steps in the research into the history of the textile furnishing of Bedroom 14 and presents the evidence used to construct the suggested chronology.

11.2 Background

Brodsworth Hall was built between 1861 and 1863 by Charles Sabine Augustus Thellusson and was subsequently continuously occupied by one family. The last occupant was Mrs Sylvia Grant-Dalton, the widow of a Thellusson cousin. She died at the house in 1988.[3]

Charles Thellusson had used the London firm of Lapworth Brothers[4] to provide most of the carpets, soft furnishings and furniture for the new house.[5] Through the ensuing decades a variety of new objects was gradually added to the contents while other pieces were repaired or discarded. Rooms were redecorated

Figure 11.1 View of the East wall of Bedroom 14 taken in May 1990 shortly after the house was acquired. This photograph shows the half-tester bed, and one of the set of mahogany side chairs (EHIN 9000 8618), with a mid-twentieth-century loose case cover (in a plain covered fabric) on the seat

periodically and furniture reupholstered. Many items, including pieces of upholstered furniture, were moved from their original positions of 1863 and were mixed with the newer acquisitions. This movement was most marked from the 1930s onwards, and there was a period of extensive reordering after 1988 as the family prepared to hand the house over to English Heritage. Some of the damaged, unfashionable or surplus pieces including older curtains, case covers and bed hangings, were stored over time in cupboards and in abandoned rooms, and the history of the contents of the house became difficult to trace.

English Heritage took over Brodsworth Hall in 1990. Gradually a display policy evolved. The presentation of the house was guided by how individual rooms were used by Mrs Grant-Dalton in her later years. They showed the accumulation of objects and decorative schemes over time and the general decline of the house. Pragmatic considerations were taken into account: visitor access, security, the condition of pieces too fragile for open display or too expensive to conserve immediately. Also, some flexibility was allowed in the selection of artefacts so that pieces of particular interest were shown if not in their 'as found' position of 1990 then at least in a room appropriate to their known function or another phase of their history. This approach remained broadly the same as new pieces were put on show after the opening of the house, and it is likely to guide the presentation of Bedroom 14 in the future.

Considerable research into the collection was undertaken before the house was opened to the public in 1995.[6] None the less, it was clear that several areas of the collection required more attention. As a matter of priority a greater understanding of the history of the printed textiles was needed before they could be appropriately and safely displayed, particularly in the bedrooms. One hundred and ten designs of printed textile associated with furnishing have been identified in the collection at Brodsworth Hall, and documentary evidence suggests that there were once more designs, now lost. Printed textiles were used for upholstery, loose case covers, bedhangings and curtains in the house at various times between 1863 and 1990. Many objects were in sets evidently intended for use together in single rooms or in suites of rooms. Some fabrics, like those found on the Bedroom 14 bed, were found together in layers of fixed upholstery coverings[7] on beds and furniture where new fabrics had been applied without stripping off the old. Several loose case covers of the same dimensions were found in more than one pattern. These varied in date indicating a chronological sequence of covers for the same or similar furniture (and much of this furniture was evidently still in the collection). Indeed, some seat furniture was being used by 1990 with two or three loose case covers on top of each other.

Unfortunately the poor condition of most of the printed textiles still in use in the house in 1990 precluded their immediate display. This created display and conservation problems. Bedrooms that were presented to the public in 1995 when the house was opened looked more sparsely furnished than they had at any point in their history. For instance, none of the bedrooms had window curtains sufficiently robust to rehang. Likewise the upholstered pieces that had been protected from light, dust and abrasion by their degraded loose case covers were now exposed to those dangers when the covers were removed from display.

It was decided that research into the history of the artefacts made wholly or partly of printed textile (the subject of this chapter) was needed in order to understand the history of the rooms and their furnishings and resolve the conservation and display issues. This would be followed by a survey of their condition, and then a review of the options for their display and conservation. Ideas for consideration in the review would include replacing items in poor condition that were recently in use with others in the collection in better condition; rotating objects between the store and the display areas; adding items of historical significance to particular rooms or taking away pieces considered of less relevance; and the use of appropriate reproduction fabrics for case covers and curtains to complete the displays and offer protection to other historic artefacts. The review would apply to the printed textiles from the whole house, but the alteration and expansion of displays would necessarily be phased over a number of years.

11.2.1 The bedrooms on the West corridor

The programme for the continued development of the displays at Brodsworth Hall includes work toward the opening of three further bedrooms, Bedrooms 13, 14 and 15, all on the West corridor. (Figure 11.2) These rooms were probably among those intended by Charles Thellusson for his children (the youngest would still have slept in the night nursery in 1863).[8] The bedrooms on the West corridor were used in the mid- and later twentieth century as guest rooms, but by 1990 they were in a dilapidated condition and had become a repository for a variety of objects including bolsters, mattresses, bed linen and clothing (Figure 11.1). It was decided that one useful early focus for the research would be the textiles found and previously used in these three bedrooms. The evidence for Bedroom 14 proved to be particularly plentiful and it contributed to an understanding of the textile furnishing of several other rooms.

11.3 Research into the history of the printed textiles from Bedroom 14

Printed cotton fabrics in eight designs were found in Bedroom 14 (see Table 11.1). The bed was the starting point for research.

11.3.1 The bed

The bed found in Bedroom 14 (see Figure 11.1) is a half-tester, comprising a carved wooden footboard, wooden side rails, a wooden slatted base, an upholstered wooden headboard,[9] an upholstered wooden backboard,[10] and an upholstered wooden half-tester with a curtain

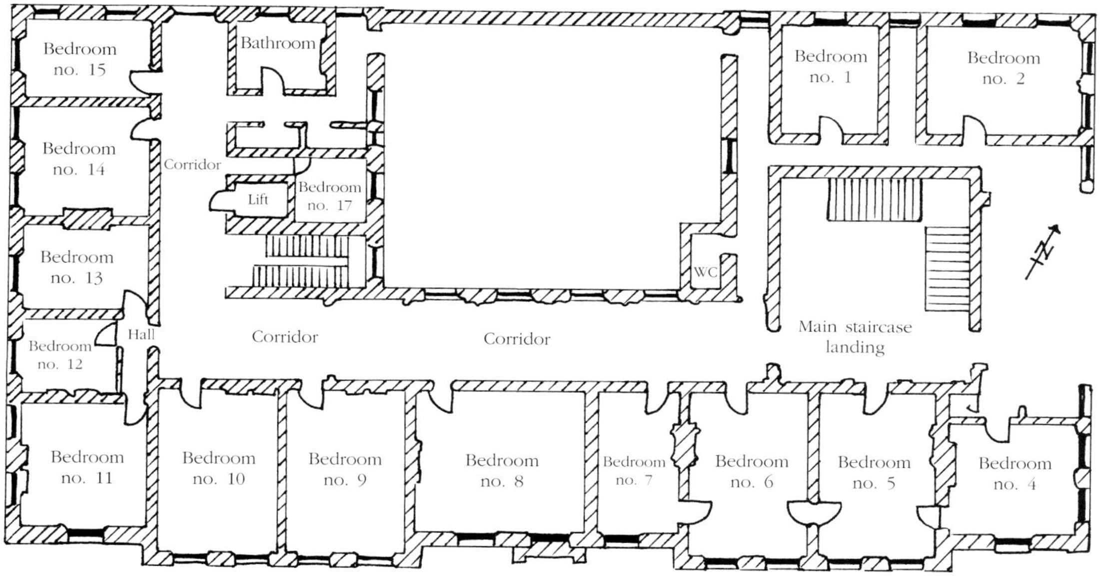

Figure 11.2 Room location plan of some of the first floor family bedrooms at Brodsworth Hall, showing Bedroom 14; Bedroom 17 was altered in 1951 for the installation of a lift

Table 11.1 Artefacts with printed textiles found in Bedroom 14 in 1990

Design	See Figure	Artefact	EHIN
Garland and ribbon design (Pattern 1)	11.24	Cushion cover	9000 2050
Rose on a seaweed ground design (Pattern 2, glazed version)	11.3	Valance	9000 4111 9000 4112
Rose and phlox design (Pattern 6)	Plate 11.3	Fixed upholstery covering on armchair	9000 8576
Lavatera design (Pattern 11)	11.15	Mahogany side chair with buttoned fixed upholstery covering	9000 8618
Floral design (Pattern 21)	11.11	Fixed upholstery covering on drop-on seat, on a rosewood side chair	9000 8674
Arborescent design (Pattern 32)	11.5	Fixed upholstery coverings on backboard, headboard and half-tester of bed	9000 8603 9000 8602 9000 8604
		Bed curtains	9000 4099 9000 4100
		Window curtains	9000 4103 9000 4104 9000 4107 9000 4108
Fruit design (Pattern 38)	11.22	Loose case cover on armchair	9000 8577 9000 8576
Brown slash design (Lining Pattern 10)	11.10	Fixed upholstery covering on backboard and headboard of half-tester bed	9000 8603 9000 8602

Figure 11.3 Detail of a loose case cover (EHIN 9000 2380) in the design of rose on a seaweed ground (Pattern 2, the glazed version). The ground design is severely faded. This was used for patches on the Lapworths' armchair (9000 8576), and for base valances found in 1990 on the half-tester bed in Bedroom 14. It is not known in which bedroom the design was originally used

Figure 11.4 Photograph of 1910 from an album (EHIN 9001 1728) celebrating the wedding anniversary of Charles and Constance (née Philips) Thellusson, showing the Library. The loose case covers are in the rose on a seaweed ground design (Pattern 2, unglazed version). This fabric was probably supplied by the furnishing company Hall and Armitage of Wakefield in 1904

Figure 11.5 Loose case cover for the seat of one of the mahogany side chairs in the arborescent design (Pattern 32) on a brown fleck ground (EHIN 9000 6321). This artefact is probably made from a later twentieth-century printing. Other pieces in the design in the collection, including bed hangings, window curtains and a cover for a Lapworths' armchair, have a white ground and were probably made c.1900. Fabric in this design was probably used for upholstery and curtains in Bedroom 14 and another unidentified bedroom

rail.[11] It has a blue checked divan that is possibly of the same date as the bed, and a later mattress. In 1990 the bed was hung with two base valances[12] in a glazed cotton fabric printed in a rose design with a seaweed ground (Pattern 2)[13,14] (Figure 11.3). This same rose design with seaweed ground was in use in the Library in 1910 (Figure 11.4). The base valances were pinned to the divan. However, there were also a pair of bed curtains[15] in a different arborescent design (Pattern 32).[16] A loose case cover in this design is shown in Figure 11.5. These curtains are made from an unglazed ribbed cotton and they match the fabric on the canopy, headboard and backboard of the bed, and the two pairs of window curtains[17] found in the room.

The backboard of the bed provided a first step towards understanding the chronology of furnishing in the room. It is composed of a wooden frame with a wooden inverted 'T' shaped support structure (see Figures 11.6, 11.7, 11.8 and 11.9). Two metal plates are fixed to the reverse at the top edge and these receive metal bars on the half-tester. Metal brackets on the East wall in Bedroom 14 fit

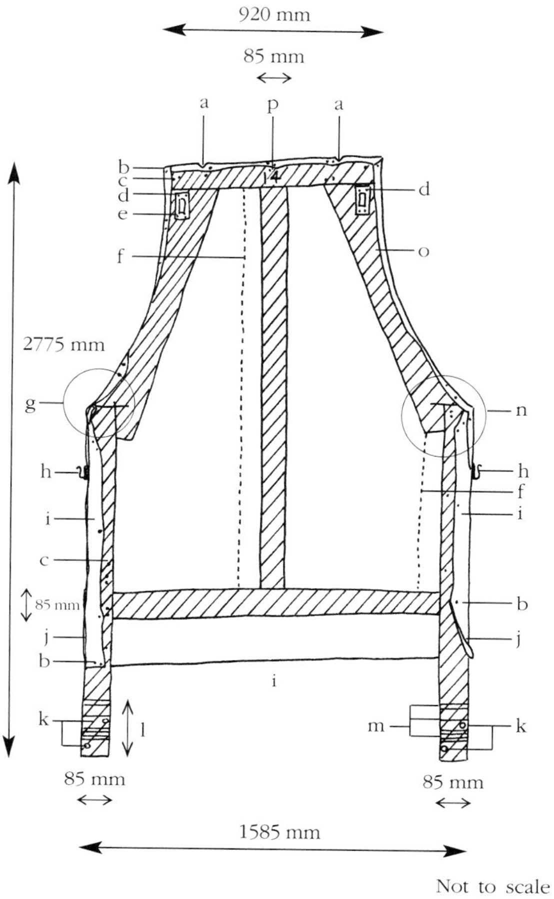

Figure 11.6 Reverse of the backboard of the Bedroom 14 half-tester bed showing construction and dimensions

- a Notch to receive metal bracket on the wall
- b Tack
- c Tack hole
- d Metal receiving plate for bracket on the half-tester
- e Screw
- f Seam joining pieces of Undyed Cloth 1
- g For detail, see Figure 11.10
- h Cleat hook for bed curtains
- i Undyed Cloth 2
- j Edge of panel of arborescent design (Pattern 32)
- k Holes to receive screws for attachment to the wall
- l Tapered in steps from 35 mm depth to 10 mm depth
- m Grooves in the wood to fit the skirting board of the wall
- n For detail see Figure 11.7
- o Wood
- p Pencil inscription probably referring to Bedroom 14

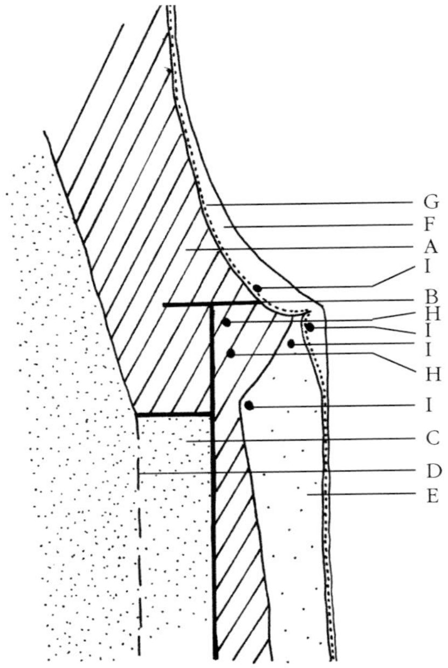

Figure 11.7 Detail of reverse of backboard of the Bedroom 14 half-tester bed showing construction and dimensions

A Wood frame
B Join between two pieces of wood
C First lining of plain weave undyed cotton cloth, Undyed Cloth 1
D Seam in first lining
E Second lining of plain weave undyed cotton cloth, Undyed Cloth 2
F Second top cover of unglazed printed cotton, arborescent design (Pattern 32)
G Stitching securing a cotton tape to the edge of the second top cover
H Tack hole
I Tack

(the first top cover of glazed printed cotton, the brown slash design (Lining Pattern 10) is concealed between Undyed Cloth 1 and Undyed Cloth 2)

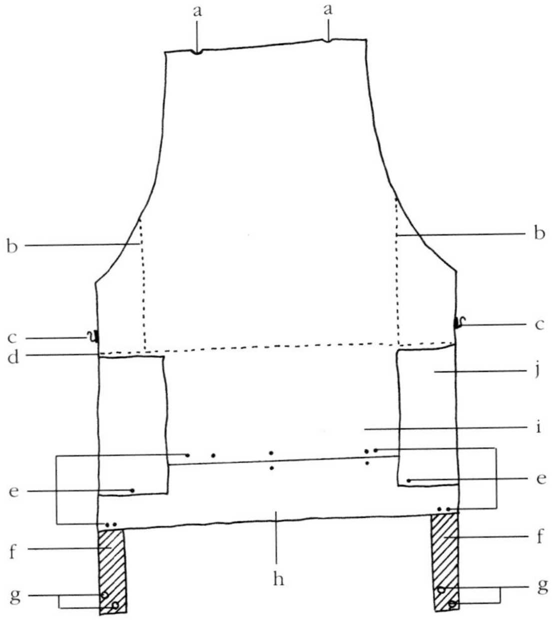

Figure 11.8 Obverse of the backboard of the Bedroom 14 half-tester bed showing construction

a Notch to receive metal bracket on the wall
b Seam joining pieces of arobescent design (Pattern 32) to Undyed Cloth 3
c Cleat hook for bed curtains
d Seam joining pieces of arborescent design (Pattern 32) to Undyed Cloth 3
e Tacks
f Wood
g Holes to receive screws for attachment to the wall
h Undyed Cloth 2
i Undyed Cloth 3
j Panel of arborescent design (Pattern 32) fabric hand sewn over Undyed Cloths 2 and 3

into notches at the top of the backboard to secure it to the wall. In addition, screws pass through holes in the legs of the backboard to attach them to the skirtings of the wall.

Four layers of fabric are stretched over the obverse of the wooden frame and fixed to the reverse with metal tacks. Nearest to the wood are a pair of fabrics, evidently a lining and top cover cut to the same size: a plain-weave undyed cotton cloth (Undyed Cloth 1) and a glazed cotton fabric printed with a design of small brown slashes (Lining Pattern 10) (Figure 11.10).[18] These textiles were apparently left undisturbed when the backboard was reupholstered so that they are almost entirely covered by two further layers: another lining and top cover. These are a second plain-weave undyed cotton cloth (Undyed Cloth 2), and the unglazed cotton fabric printed with an arborescent design (Pattern 32) (see Figure 11.5) in five pieces. A third plain-weave undyed cotton cloth was used for an inserted panel sewn to the arborescent design fabric. This created, as an economy measure, an unpatterned area hidden by the headboard when the bed was assembled.

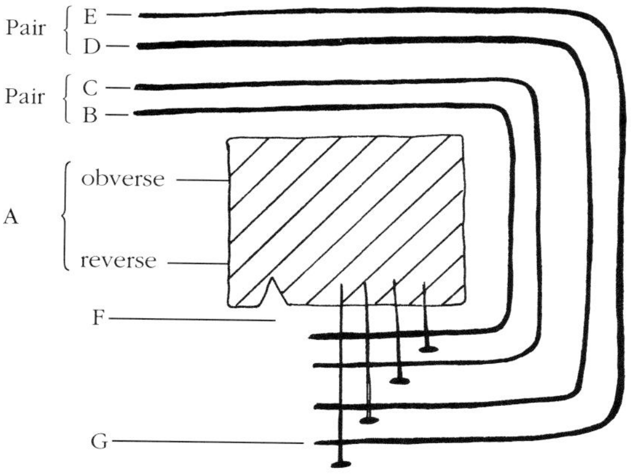

Figure 11.9 Cross-section diagram to show the layers and pairing of fixed upholstery coverings on the backboard of the Bedroom 14 half-tester bed

A Wood frame
B First lining of plain weave undyed cotton cloth, Undyed Cloth 1
C First top cover of glazed printed cotton, brown slash design (Lining Pattern 10)
D Second lining of plain weave undyed cotton cloth, Undyed Cloth 2
E Second top cover of unglazed printed cotton, arborescent design (Pattern 32)
F Location of additional tack holes
G All textile layers attached to wood frame with tacks

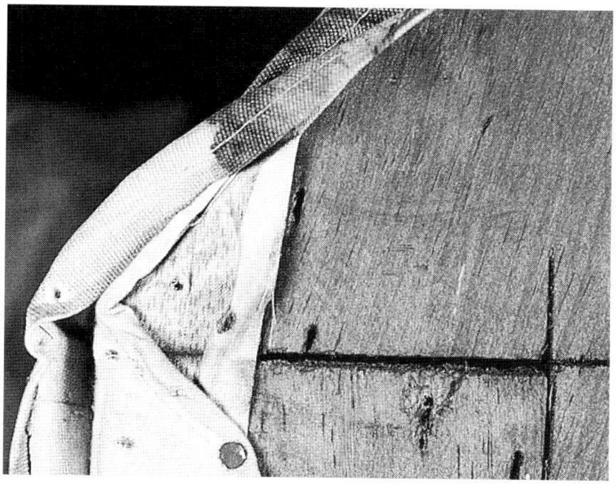

Figure 11.10 Detail of fixed upholstery coverings on the reverse of the backboard of the half-tester bed from Bedroom 14. The photograph shows, in order from the wood, tack holes, the brown slash design (Lining Pattern 10), Undyed Cloth 2, a tack and the arborescent design (Pattern 32)

There are tack holes on the reverse of the backboard frame. These appear to be in either one or two sets. Some lie below the arborescent design and associated covering, Undyed Cloth 2. However some are on the wood beyond all the textiles (Figure 11.10). Some, if not all, of them are probably from an earlier attachment of the arborescent design and Undyed Cloth 2; both textiles have small holes with rust stains along the edges suggesting they have been removed and reattached. It may be that both coverings shrank during laundering and so had to be reattached nearer to the edge of the backboard. This would account for the uncovered tack holes. However there may none the less have been one or more additional fixed upholstery coverings now missing. Thus there were several possibilities for the sequence of the upholstery: the brown slash design fabric over its associated lining certainly pre-dates the arborescent design fabric with its lining. However, any missing covering or coverings might pre- or post-date the brown slash design.

The headboard was studied for further evidence of the chronological order of the textile furnishing. It has a loose case cover in the arborescent design over two fixed upholstery coverings: a top cover in the brown slash design (Lining Pattern 10) and, below that, an associated lining in an undyed cotton cloth. There are tack holes on the frame of the headboard beyond the lower edge of the brown slash design fabric that may correspond with that top cover or may indicate a missing layer or layers of textile. However, the brown slash design fabric cannot be fully examined until the headboard receives conservation treatment. The brown slash design fabric is fragmented and in poor condition and the loose case cover in the arborescent design is so tightly fitted that it cannot be safely removed for research. Thus the evidence of the tack holes on the headboard appeared to correspond with that of the tack holes on the backboard but this could not be regarded as conclusive. None the less, it was reasonable to assume that the headboard had been covered in the same sequence as the backboard.

Further confirmation could not be gained from the half-tester either because it, by contrast, had been completely stripped of all earlier textiles before the arborescent design fabric was applied. However, multiple tack holes confirmed that it too had been covered several times and again the same sequence of coverings was assumed.

11.3.2 The fabric designs

Research into the two printed fabrics revealed probable dates for their application. The design of brown slashes (Lining Pattern 10) was found to be the ground design for a glazed printed floral fabric in the collection (Pattern 21) (Figure 11.11).[19] The same roller was probably used for both fabrics and they were probably intended to be used together. Some of the draperies on the half-tester bed may thus have been made in the floral design instead of the brown slash design. The floral design fabric has been used for the drop-on seats of four rosewood side chairs in the collection (Figure 11.12), one of which was found in Bedroom 14.[20] It has also been used for a cushion cover, a chair seat cover and an upholstered armchair. Evidence from the Warner Fabrics Archive showed that the floral design was produced through the wholesale and manufacturing company David Walters of Braintree, Essex as a special one-off commission for a single unknown customer between 1870 and 1890. It was printed at Clarkson and Turner of Carlisle, Cumbria.[21] The Stead McAlpin Archive holds the original design on paper for the fabric, dated 1873.[22]

Information again from a commercial textile archive concerned the arborescent design fabric (Pattern 32). This was first printed in c.1900 by Ramm, Son and Crocker.[23] The design is in current production by the same company and may have been reproduced many times.[24] Thus the fabric on the Bedroom 14 bed could be later than c.1900 but not earlier. As we have seen, the design was used at Brodsworth Hall for the fixed upholstery coverings and bed hangings on the Bedroom 14 half-tester bed and two pairs of window curtains found hanging in that room, and also for loose covers for two chair seats and one armchair, and for a further set of window curtains in the collection. Because the arborescent design has been produced a number of times since 1900 it is possible that the artefacts from Brodsworth Hall in the design are from a later printing. However, examination of other items in the collection suggests that except for one chair seat loose case cover[25] this is probably not true.

First, the artefacts in the arborescent design are probably related to two green curtains with a woven design in the collection.[26] These are trimmed with a cord that is very similar, though in a different colourway, to the cord found on all the curtains in the arborescent design. These green curtains have not been

Figure 11.11 Detail of an armchair probably supplied by Lapworth Brothers (EHIN 9000 8659), showing the fixed upholstery covering in the floral design (Pattern 21). Fabric in this design is known to have been printed by Clarkson and Turner and supplied to an unknown single customer by David Walters between 1870 and 1890. It was probably bought by the Thellussons as a special commission and used by Maple and Co. to refurnish Bedroom 14 in 1886

Figure 11.12 One of the set of rosewood side chairs with drop-on seats (EHIN 9000 8476), probably dating to c.1845. The top fixed upholstery covering is in the floral design (Pattern 21)

firmly dated, but from design and construction are probably from the turn of the century. Second, the ground cloth of the arborescent design fabric of the majority of the artefacts is very similar in weight and weave count to the ground cloth of another textile in the collection which has a design of urns and swags (Pattern 28). This was used to make window curtains and loose covers and to dress another one of the half-tester beds.[27] This again has not been firmly dated, but the design, and the construction of the relevant artefacts, suggests that it is from c.1890. These two associations lend weight to the view that all except one of the pieces in the arborescent design (Pattern 32) are from an early printing of the design, produced in 1900 or soon after.

11.3.3 Historic photographs

A photograph in an album from c.1878–80 in the Brodsworth Hall Archive shows Constance Thellusson seated in an armchair in Bedroom 14 (Figure 11.13).[28] The armchair and the seat of the side chair behind it are covered with loose case covers. These are in a lace design fabric found elsewhere in the house (Pattern 19) (Figure 11.14).[29] In addition, the photograph shows the edge of a bed's footboard. This could be the footboard of the bed found in Bedroom 14 or either one of two similar though slightly wider half-tester beds in the Brodsworth collection.[30]

This photographic evidence shows that at least two pieces of furniture in Bedroom 14 had loose case covers in the lace design fabric in c.1878–80. These following questions now arose: whether the lace fabric was used on the bed as well as the chairs in c.1878–1880; whether the lace design was supplied by the company Lapworth Brothers who organised the furnishing of the house in 1863; if so whether they supplied it for Bedroom 14; whether the bed found in Bedroom 14 had been there since the house was built; whether, then, the lace design was used on the backboard and headboard of the bed and so was the possible missing layer (or one of the missing layers) indicated by the tack holes; and, if this was the case, when exactly the lace design on the bed was replaced by the first remaining design, the brown slashes.

11.3.4 Documentary evidence

Bills and inventories in the Brodsworth Hall archive provided the next steps in answering these questions.

The c.1878–1880 photograph of Constance Thellusson in Bedroom 14 (Figure 11.13) does not include a view of the bed hangings to see whether they matched the chairs. However, the textiles first used in that room were almost certainly a set. Lapworths submitted a detailed bill in 1863 that included charges for sets of cotton covers and curtains for Bedrooms 9 to 15 (Table 11.2). It was assumed from this that in 1863 the textile coverings, both loose and fixed, of the furniture and bed in Bedroom 14 matched. If it could be established that the lace design in the c.1878–80 photograph was the design used by Lapworths in that room it

Figure 11.13 Photograph (EHIN 9001 1732.005) of c.1878–80 attributed to Peter Thellusson showing his sister Constance Thellusson seated in Bedroom 14. The armchair and the side chair against the wall have loose case covers in the lace design (Pattern 19). The footboard of one of the half-tester beds in the Brodsworth Hall collection is on the right

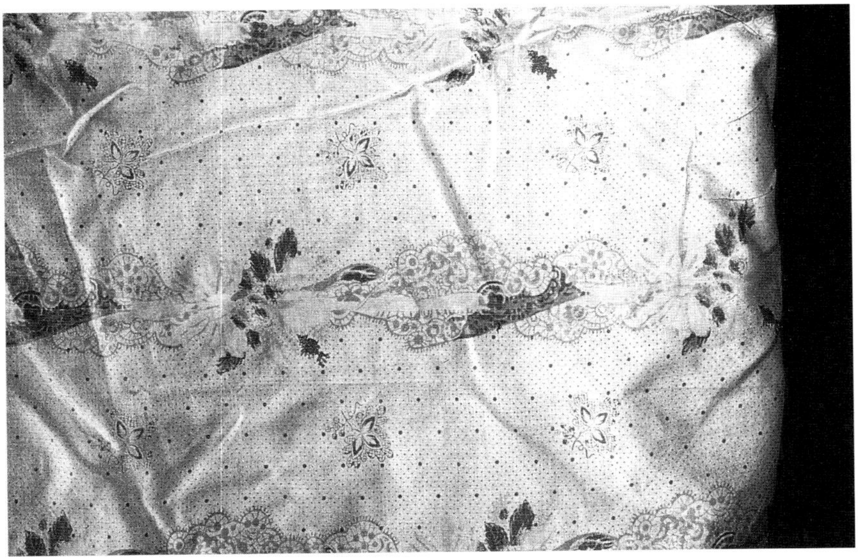

Figure 11.14 Detail of loose case cover (EHIN 9001 7627), showing lace design (Pattern 19). Some of the colours are severely faded. Fabric in this design was probably supplied by Lapworth Brothers for Bedrooms 14 and 15

would be highly likely that the bed in the room in 1863 was upholstered in that design (and probably also, according to the bill, with a complementary design).

The Lapworths bill specified for Bedrooms 14 and 15[31] a 'Super French Chintz' (probably the same as a 'Mauve [?] Stripe' fabric also in the bill for the same rooms) used with 'a Lilac Spot Lining', 'White Binding', 'Chintzed Fringe' and a 'White Lining'. The lace design (Pattern 19) is the nearest of the designs in the Brodsworth collection to this description. The lace design is probably French, though exact details of origin were not found. It is glazed and might be described as a chintz. The pattern is arranged in vertical stripes. It originally depicted bright purple strips of twisted lace with posies of multicoloured flowers at intervals, on a ground of grey dots with small purple lace motifs.[32] There are strong similarities in the colours and severe fading between this lace design and a design of Lavatera (Pattern 11) in the collection which was probably supplied by Lapworths in 1863 (Figure 11.15).[33] Loose case covers in the lace design have white linings, white binding tape and piping covered in the same lace design fabric. And there are side chairs and an armchair in the lace design that also fit the description in the bill.

However, uncertainties remained. First, the illegible word in the bill describing the ground was assumed to be an adjective describing colour – it was read as 'mauve', which would fit the dominant purple of the lace design, but it could equally have been, for example, 'marone', 'maroon' or 'marine'.

Second, there were difficulties in establishing that the half-tester bed found in Bedroom 14 had been there in 1863. It was not certain either that the three similar half-testers in the collection were in the house in 1863 or that the bed found in Bedroom 14 was the exact one in the c.1878–80 photograph rather than one of the two similar beds. Lapworths did not specify a half-tester bed for the room. Instead it charged for supplying an 'Arabian' bed for either Bedroom 14 or 15 (and it left out the second bed for this pair of bedrooms).[34] A close look at the Lapworths' bill for all the family bedrooms and an investigation of the beds remaining in the collection suggested that Lapworths did not supply all the beds in the house in 1863, and that beds were replaced at intervals in the ensuing twenty years.[35]

An important document for the history of the textile furnishings is the inventory of Brodsworth Hall made in 1885[36] on the death of Charles Augustus Sabine Thellusson, who built the house. This shows for Bedroom 14 a five foot mahogany half-tester bed 'with cretonne furniture complete' as well as a mahogany frame easy chair and three mahogany chairs all in chintz.[37] (The term

Figure 11.15 Detail of the fixed upholstery covering on the boat bed (EHIN 9000 8520), from Bedroom 13, showing the lavatera design (Pattern 11), probably supplied by Lapworth Brothers for Bedrooms 11, 12, 13 and 17

Table 11.2 Extracts from the bill of 1863 from Lapworth Brothers charging for textiles, upholstery work and beds supplied for Bedrooms 9 to 15

Bedroom	Item supplied	Price per unit (£.s.d.)	Price charged (£.s.d.)
Bedrooms 9 and 10	195yds Superfine Chintz	2/9	16.16.3
	204½yds Spotted Lining	10	8.10.5
	11½yds Heading Gimp	2/9	1.11.8
	73yds Chintzed Paris Binding	4	1.4.4
	35yds Fine twine fringe	2/6	4.7.6
	8 Super Curtain Holders	9/6	3.16.0
	4 Super Bell Pulls	12/6	2.10.0
Bedroom 9	A Chintz Bed furniture for your own bedstead		
	129yds Super Chintz	2/9	17.14.9
	110yds Crimson Chintz Binding	4	1.16.8
	71yds Spotted Lining	10	2.19.2
	9yds Fine twine fringe	2/6	1.2.6
	4¾yds Chintz rope	3/6	16.8
	Upholsterers time cutting out & making up Do		2.15.0
Bedroom 10	Upholsterers time cutting out & making Bed furniture for No 6 Room [Bedroom 10] same Chintz as in No 7 Room [Bedroom 9]		1.14.0
	A 5.6 Spanish Mahogany Arabian stuffed headboard, shaped and carved footboard with birch double screw frame		22.10.0
	An easy Chair spring stuffed and covered in Chintz		5.3.6
	A Loose Chintz Cover for Do		1.13.6
	4 Spanish mahogany Chairs in Chintz	37/6	7.10.0
	4 loose Chintz cases for Do	6/6	1.6.0
	2 Chintz Toilet Draperies		
	Containing 50yds Super Chintz	2/9	6.17.6
	32yds Lining	10	1.6.8
	100yds Crimson Chintz Binding	4	1.15.4
Bedrooms 11, 12 and 13	102yds Super French Chintz	2	10.4.0
	107yds Drab French Lining	15	6.13.9
	132yds Green Paris Binding	3	1.13.0
	27yds Chintzed Fringe	2/6	3.7.6
	6 Curtain Holders	10	3.0.0
	6 Bell Pulls	16/6	4.19.0
	Upholsterers time cutting out & making up curtains		5.4.0
	A 5.6 Spanish Mahogany Canopy Bedstead Double screw frame stuffed headboard. Carved and shaped footboard		22.10.0
	Furniture for Bed		
	Containing 89yds French Chintz	2	8.18.0
	121yds Scroll Lining part of which has been used for other Chintz	15	7.11.3
	7yds Green Paris Binding	3	18.0
	Upholsterers time cutting out & making up		1.18.6
Bedroom 12	2 Spanish Mahogany ?Lamp back chairs in Chintz	37/6	3.15.0
	2 Loose Chintz cases for Do	5/9	11.6

Table 11.2 continued

Bedroom	**Item supplied**	**Price per unit (£.s.d.)**	**Price charged (£.s.d.)**
Bedrooms 11 and 12	2 Spring Stuffed Easy Chairs tight stuffed in Chintz		10.0.0
	2 Loose Chintz Covers for Do	1.8.6	2.17.0
	7 ?Linup back Spanish Mahogany Chairs in Chintz	40	14.0.0
	7 Loose Chintz Covers for Do	6	2.2.0
Bedroom 17 and Bathroom	69yds Super French Chintz	2	6.18.0
	64yds Green Watered Lining	15	4.0.0
	48yds Paris Binding	3	12.0
	171yds Chintzed fringe	2/6	2.3.9
	4 Curtain Holders	9/6	1.18.0
	3 Bell Pulls	12/6	1.17.6
	Upholsterers time cutting out & making curtains		
Bathroom	8yds Super French Chintz	2	16.0
	9yds of lining for Do	1/3	11.3
	Upholsterers time making up and oilproofing Do		14.6
	3 Mahogany ?Linup Backed Chairs Stuffed in Chintz	37/6	5.12.6
	3 Loose Chintz Covers for Do	5/9	17.3
Bedrooms 14 and 15	112yds Super French Chintz	2/3	12.12.0
	80yds Do filling	2/3	18.0
	130½yds Lilac Spot Lining	10½	5.14.2
	108yds White Chintz Binding	4	1.16.0
	27yds Chintzed Fringe	2/6	3.7.6
	9yds Gimp	2/6	1.2.6
	6 Curtain Holders	9/6	2.17.0
	4 Bell Pulls	12/6	2.10.0
	Upholsterers time cutting out & making up Curtains etc.		6.12.0
	A 5.0 Spanish Mahogany Arabian Bedstand. Prices Double screw framed stuffed headboard carved and shaped footboard		21.10.0
	Mauve stripe Bed furniture		
	Conts. 58yds	2/3	6.10.6
	46yds Lining	10½	2.0.3
	156yds Chintzed Paris Binding	4	2.12.0
	Upholsterers time cutting out and making up		1.13.6
Bedroom 14	An easy Chair spring stuffed in Chintz		5.0.0
	A loose Chintz Cover for Do		1.5.6
	4 Mahogany Chairs tight stuffed in Chintz	37/6	7.10.0
	4 loose Chintz Covers for Do	5/9	1.3.0
Bedroom 15	A Toilet Drapery of Chintz		
	18yds Chintz mauve Stripe	2/3	2.0.6
	13 3/5yds White Lining	10	11.6
	108yds White Chintz Binding	4	1.16.0
	4 Mahogany Chairs in Chintz	37/6	7.10.0
	4 Loose Chintz Cases for Do	5/9	1.3.0

Table 11.3 Extract from the bill from Maple & Co. of 1886 describing upholstery work and textiles supplied

Date	Item supplied	Price per unit (£.s.d.)	Price charged (£.s.d.)
1886			
July 6	85yds Brussels carpet	3/6½	15.1.6½
	85yds Making	3	1.1.3
	85yds Packing		2.0
		For 2 Rooms	
	Upholsterers rail conveyance and expenses to measure for curtains etc.		1.17.1
July 17	24yds satteen	10½	1.1.0
July 29	215½yds Cream Ground rose dimity	1/2½	13.0.4½
	259yds Lining	5½	5.18.8½
	186yds Cord	5¾	4.9.1½
	35yds Fringe	1/9½	3.2.8½
	4 doz Binding	1	4.0
	5 prs Loophooks	9	3.9
	Rings and Heading		7.9
	Buckram		18.0
	7yds Calico for head & tester of bed	4	2.4
	Cutting out & making 5 sets curtains 3 widths lined and corded	8/6	2.2.6
	Do 5 sets Bands	1/6	7.6
	Do 1 Set Curtains 3 widths lined and corded for bed		8.6
	Do 1 Bed furniture with shaped buckram valance lined and trimmed fringe & frill heading curtains corded		14/6
	Do 3 shaped buckram valances lined and trimmed fringe & frill heading		1.5.6
	Do 1 Do Do		16.0
	Packing		2.6
Aug 24	2 Bell ropes	4	8.0
Aug 17	30yds dimity	1/2½	1.16.3
	40yds lining	5½	18.4
	33yds Cord	5¾	15.10
	6yds Fringe	1/9½	10.9
	2 prs loophooks	9	1.6
	Rings & heading		1.0
	Cutting out & making 1 set curtains 3 widths lined and corded		8.6
	Do 2 sets Bands Do	1/6	3.0
	Do 1 shaped valance lined and trimmed fringe		7.6
Aug 9	42yds paper	2	7.0
Aug 4	43yds dimity	1/2½	2.11.11½
Aug 14	Upholsterers time covering head board of bedstead fixing canopy bed furniture, poles, curtains, valances etc.		1.7.0
	Rail conveyance and expenses		1.19.6
	30yds Calico	4	10.0
	Cutting out & making loose covers in own material lined & flounced for 2 Easy Chairs	7/6	15.0
	12 small chairs	1 1/3	15.0
Aug 25	1½yds Brussels carpet		5.3½

'cretonne' commonly referred to unglazed cotton, or cotton and linen mix, upholstery fabrics.) It seems likely that the bed seen in Bedroom 14 in the photograph of Constance Thellusson seated, c.1878–80 (Figure 11.13) was the bed mentioned in the 1885 inventory because the description is close and the interval was only about five to seven years. However, it cannot at present be proved that this bed was put in the room in 1863. It could be a bed bought between 1863 and c.1878–80, possibly to replace the 'Arabian' bed of the Lapworths' bill if indeed that was put in Bedroom 14 not Bedroom 15. Certainly the style of the bed is consistent with beds known to date to the later 1870s and early 1880s.[38] In any case, whether it dated from 1863 or slightly later, it may have had cretonne hangings in c.1878–80 when the photograph of Constance seated was taken, as described in the inventory of 1885, despite the continuation in the use of the loose case covers in the lace design (Pattern 19).[39] Thus a cretonne (not identified in the collection) might have been a missing textile indicated by the tack holes on the backboard and headboard.

If the bed dates from 1863, the lace design fabric or the complementary 'lilac spot' design described in the 1863 bill (now probably no longer in the collection)[40] could also have been a missing fixed upholstery covering, and a cretonne (design not identified) could have succeeded it at some point before the 1885 inventory was taken. However, if the bed is slightly later it is possible that only one layer preceded the brown slash design, and this would probably have been the cretonne described in the 1885 inventory.

The question of when the bed was covered in the brown slash design (Lining Pattern 10) and floral design (Pattern 21) remained. A bill of 1886 in the Brodsworth Hall Archive from the London furnishing shop Maple & Co. provided a possible answer[41] (Table 11.3). This bill appears to refer to sewing and upholstery work using fabric supplied by another company or charged separately. It could have referred to the floral design (Pattern 21) (see Figure 11.11), which, as we have seen, was probably produced as a special order for Brodsworth Hall. This possibility was strengthened by a study of the side chairs from the bedrooms at Brodsworth and associated loose case covers.

11.3.5 The mahogany and rosewood side chairs and the Lapworths' armchairs

The sets of objects in the lace design fabric (Pattern 19) (see Figure 11.14), the floral design fabric (Pattern 21) (see Figure 11.11) and the arborescent design (Pattern 32) (see Figure 11.5) were examined for any further evidence of links to the Lapworths' or Maples' bills (see Tables 11.2 and 11.3).

Two sets of bedroom side chairs (with related loose case covers) were identified in the collection (Table 11.4). The first was a set of seventeen identical mahogany side chairs with fixed buttoned upholstery in various fabrics (Figure 11.16).[42] These date to c.1860 and are likely to have been among the mahogany chairs supplied by Lapworths and mentioned in the

Figure 11.16 One of the set of mahogany side chairs (EHIN 9000 8173), probably supplied by Lapworth Brothers in 1863. The buttoned fixed upholstery covering is in the lace design (Pattern 19)

Table 11.4 Designs of fixed upholstery coverings found on the sets of mahogany and rosewood side chairs

Mahogany side chairs with buttoned fixed upholstery coverings, supplied by Lapworth Brothers (see Figure 11.16)

No. of chairs	EHIN	Outer fixed covering design	Concealed fixed covering design	Tack holes indicating missing covering or coverings	See Figure/ Plate
2	9000 3617 9000 7785	Pattern 6: Rose and phlox design	—	—	Plate 11.3
5	9000 7784 9000 8013 9000 8109 9000 8171 9000 8618	Pattern 11: Lavatera design	—	—	11.15
6	9000 3618 9000 8015 9000 8018	Pattern 19: Lace design	—	—	11.14
	9000 8107 9000 8110 9000 8173		—	—	—
3	9000 8111	Red wool damask			
	9000 8112		—	Possible – no access to the wood under the textile covering	—
	9000 8113				
1	9000 8106	Later twentieth-century fabric woven design			
Total 17					

Rosewood side chairs with drop-on seats covered with fixed upholstery coverings, probably c.1845 (see Figures 11.12 and 11.17)

No. of chairs	EHIN	Outer fixed covering design	Concealed fixed covering design	Tack holes indicating missing covering or coverings	See Figure
4 complete chairs	9000 8474 9000 8475 9000 8476 9000 8674	Pattern 21: Floral design	Pattern 31 – Diamond design	Yes	11.11 and Plate 11.2
4 complete chairs	9000 7315 9000 7634 9000 8473 9000 8676	Pattern 30: Leaf design	Pattern 31 – Diamond design	Yes	Plate 11.1 and Plate 11.2
2 seats without accompanying chairs	9000 4640 9000 8477	Pattern 30: Leaf design	Pattern 31 – Diamond design	Yes	Plate 11.1 and Plate 11.2
Total 10					

1863 bill. The second set was of eight rosewood side chairs with cane seats and upholstered drop-on seats, plus two drop-on seats of the set that had lost their accompanying chairs[43] (see Figure 11.12). These drop-on seats have fixed upholstery coverings in two designs, the floral design (Pattern 21) and a leaf design (Pattern 30) (Plate 11.1).[44] There are tack holes on the underside of the drop-on seats suggesting there was once a further layer or layers of fixed upholstery coverings. The chairs probably date from c.1845 and were assumed to have already belonged to the Thellusson family in 1863. A diamond design fabric (Pattern 31)[45] (Plate 11.2) was found under the floral and leaf design fabrics. The diamond design was difficult to date as similar geometric designs were produced throughout the nineteenth century and no record of the design has been found. However, these hidden fixed upholstery coverings appear to be original to the rosewood chairs.

Both sets of side chairs, in mahogany and rosewood, have fixed upholstery coverings and loose case covers in several designs of fabric. Many of the loose case covers were found in 1990 in cupboards in the house, separated from their associated chairs. An attempt was made as part of this research to match covers to chairs and these artefacts to the relevant documents.

The following evidence emerged:

- The lace design (Pattern 19) had been used for chair seats in the mahogany set (as described in the Lapworths' bill) (see Figures 11.13 and 11.16). However, the surviving loose case covers in the design fit only the rosewood set (not mentioned in the bill). No loose case covers in this design survive for the mahogany set (Table 11.5).
- The rosewood set, as we have seen, has fixed covers in the floral design (Pattern 21) (see Figure 11.12) and the leaf design (Pattern 30) (Plate 11.1) but it had none in any of the Lapworths' designs. However the survival of Lapworths' lace design loose case covers suggests that the rosewood chairs may have had different fixed upholstery coverings in 1863. There is additional evidence for this. A second photograph of Constance Thellusson of c.1878–80, which shows her standing at an easel, includes one of the rosewood side chairs with a rose and phlox design (Pattern 6) loose case cover[46] (Figure 11.17). The rose and phlox design was probably supplied by Lapworths for Bedrooms 9 and 10 (Plate 11.3).
- Only eight rosewood side chairs survive, although they are carved underneath the side rails with Roman numerals up to ten suggesting that there were originally at least ten chairs. Two drop-on seats from the set with no accompanying chairs survive as confirmation. It is possible, however, that there were originally two more. Two loose case covers[47] for the drop-on seats in the collection are in a magnolia design (Pattern 16) (Figure 11.18).[48] Curtains in the magnolia design have a lining in a blue squiggle design (Lining Pattern 3). Curtains in a rose design with damask ground (Pattern 20) have a lining in the design in a red colourway (Figure 11.19). Thus the magnolia and rose with damask ground designs are probably

Table 11.5 Artefacts in the main designs associated with Bedroom 14 remaining in the Brodsworth Hall collection

Artefact	Pattern 19: Lace design	Pattern 21: Floral design	Pattern 32: Arborescent design	Lining Pattern 10: Brown slash design
Fixed upholstery covering on mahogany side chair	6	—	—	—
Loose case cover to fit mahogany side chair	—	—	2[a]	—
Fixed upholstery covering on rosewood side chair	—	4	—	—
Loose case cover to fit rosewood side chair	3	1	—	—
Fixed upholstery covering on Lapworths armchair	—	1	—	—
Loose case cover to fit Lapworths armchair	1	—	1	—
Fixed upholstery covering on backboard of half-tester bed	—	—	1	1
Fixed upholstery covering on headboard of half-tester bed	—	—	—	1
Loose case cover on headboard of half-tester bed	—	—	1	—
Fixed upholstery covering on half-tester bed	—	—	1	—
Bed curtains	—	—	2	—
Cushion cover	—	1	—	—
Window curtains	—	—	6	—

[a]One may be in a later twentieth-century reprinted version of the design.

Figure 11.17 Photograph (EHIN 9001 1732.010) of c.1878–80 attributed to Peter Thellusson showing his sister Constance Thellusson standing at an easel. The painting is a copy of 'The Music Lesson', a late seventeenth-century picture, possibly by De Hooch, known to have been at Brodsworth Hall. The photograph shows one of the set of rosewood side chairs with a loose case cover in the rose and phlox design (Pattern 6)

Figure 11.18 Detail of a curtain (EHIN 9000 5850), in the magnolia design (Pattern 16) possibly supplied by Maple and Co. in 1886

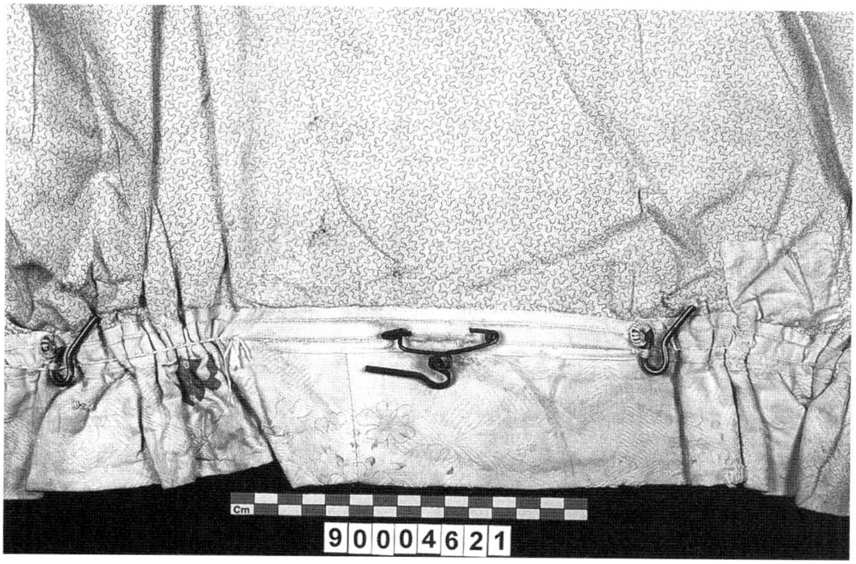

Figure 11.19 Detail of the reverse of a curtain (EHIN 9000 4621), in the rose with damask ground design (Pattern 20) showing the lining (Lining Pattern 3), in a red colourway. The same design in a blue colourway was used to line curtains in the magnolia design (Pattern 16). All of these fabrics may have been supplied by Maple and Co. in 1886

linked. The curtains in the rose with damask ground design appear to be those described in the Maples' bill of 1886 as made from a 'cream ground rose dimity' (Table 11.3). As will be further discussed below, the same Maples' bill records the covering of twelve chairs. If there were once two more this could refer to the rosewood side chairs, and the two chairs that are now missing might have been covered with the magnolia design.

- Seventeen identical mahogany side chairs survive. However the Lapworths bill charged for twenty-four mahogany chairs for the Bedrooms 8 to 15, plus four for the schoolroom. Some were described in the bill as 'tight stuffed', others as 'sweep back', and some had illegible descriptions (?'linup' or ?'lamp' back) or no description beyond 'mahogany chair in chintz' (Tables 11.2 and 11.4). It is unlikely that all twenty-four were identical as Lapworths charged three different prices for them: seventeen cost 37s 6d each, seven cost 40s each (these were for Bedrooms 11 and 13) and four cost 38s 6d each (for the schoolroom on the ground floor).

The best explanation is, as for the beds, that the Lapworths' bill does not give a complete picture of the furniture in the house in 1863. The rosewood side chairs may have been additional to the chairs in the bill. They probably belonged to the Thellusson family before 1863 when they were used with the diamond design fabric (Pattern 31) fixed upholstery covers that remain as the first textile layer on the chair seats. Tack holes under the drop-on seats indicate a missing layer or layers of fabric and this is likely to be evidence for reupholstery by Lapworths (possibly as well as other phases of reupholstery). Lapworths applied fixed upholstery coverings to several pieces of older furniture for the new house including a set of side chairs in a glazed cotton associated with the Library (also not shown specifically in the 1863 bill).[49] The seventeen identical mahogany chairs in the collection are probably those that cost 37s 6d each. The others in the bill may have been in a different style, though also of mahogany. However those have not been identified as surviving in the collection.

The stripping of the Lapworths fabrics from the rosewood side chairs to put on the floral fabric (Pattern 21) would be consistent with the stripping of the Bedroom 14 half-tester bed at the same time to apply the brown slash design fabric (Lining Pattern 10) if this had originally been hung with the lace design. If the Maples' bill of 1886 refers to reupholstery in Bedroom 14 using the floral design fabric

(Pattern 21), as has been argued above for the bed, and if there were originally twelve rosewood side chairs, then the recovering of twelve small chairs, mentioned in the same Maples' bill, would fit. Some of the set could have been covered in the floral design, others in the leaf and magnolia designs. This theory is supported by close similarity in the way the floral and leaf design fabrics have been applied to the drop-on seats. Both fabrics have been positioned under the seats with a turned allowance so that they sit against two metal pegs which insert into holes at the back and front of each fixed chair seat to keep the drop-on seat in place. It seems from the lace design (Pattern 19) loose case covers for these chairs, which make no allowance for a peg, that the pegs were added after 1863. It is probable the pegs had already been put in before the seats were recovered in the floral design fabric as on one seat the leaf design fabric covers a broken peg.[50]

Figure 11.20 Armchair (EHIN 9000 8659), probably supplied by Lapworth Brothers in 1863. The fixed upholstery covering in the floral design (Pattern 21) may have been applied by Maple and Co. in 1886

An anomalous piece of evidence emerged from the study of the chair and seat covers in the arborescent design (Pattern 32). The armchair loose case cover in this fabric was not found on the armchair with a fixed upholstery cover in the floral design fabric (Pattern 21) (Figure 11.20), as might be expected from the reupholstery sequence suggested above for the Bedroom 14 bed. Instead, it was found on a similar armchair (reupholstered possibly in the 1960s or 1970s) in another bedroom, Bedroom 12. This prompted a closer examination of the four similar armchairs in the collection[51] and the covers that fit them (Tables 11.6 and 11.7).

The Lapworths' bill specifies five 'easy chairs' upholstered in chintz (see Tables 11.2 and 11.6). It shows the room each chair was made for, the number and price of associated loose covers and the prices of the armchairs. It appears that Lapworths supplied four identical armchairs costing £5 0s 0d each and one slightly more expensive one at £5 3s 6d. Each chair had one loose case cover, probably in the same chintz used for the fixed upholstery of the chair. (The cost of making the case covers varied even among the armchairs of the same price possibly indicating a difference in construction.) Four armchairs that may be among those referred to in the bill remain in the collection (Tables 11.6 and 11.7). Three are identical (though with fixed upholstery covers in different designs), one has a slightly different leg shape. They cannot be matched to the bill exactly, however. The chair with the fitted upholstery cover in the rose and phlox design (Pattern 6), which has a rough patch in the rose and seaweed design (Pattern 2), is one of the three identical chairs in the collection, not the exception, the more expensive chair, as would be expected from the entry in the bill for Bedroom 10 (Figures 11.21 and 11.22).

Likewise, it is not clear why the armchair with the fixed upholstery cover in the floral design (Pattern 21) is the chair with the variation in the leg shape. It is likely that this chair was in Bedroom 14 with the half tester bed when this was reupholstered in the floral design (Pattern 21) and the brown slash design (Lining Pattern 10). If the armchair had been in that bedroom since 1863 (and was therefore probably the chair on which Constance

Table 11.6 Armchairs listed in the bill from Lapworth Brothers of 1863

Number of chairs	Bedroom	Probable design of both fixed upholstery covering and loose case cover	Price (£.s.d.)
1	Bedroom 8	Not established	£5.0.0 chair £1.5.6 loose case cover
1	Bedroom 10	Pattern 6: Rose and phlox design	£5.3.6 chair £1.13.6 loose case cover
1	Bedroom 11	Pattern 11: Lavatera design	£5.0.0 chair £1.8.6 loose case cover
1	Bedroom 12	Pattern 11: Lavatera design	£5.0.0 chair £1.8.6 loose case cover
1	Bedroom 14	Pattern 19: Lace design	£5.0.0 chair £1.5.6 loose case cover
Total 5			

Table 11.7 Armchairs with fixed upholstery coverings and associated loose covers that were probably supplied by Lapworth Brothers in 1863 and remain in the Brodsworth Hall collection

Number of armchairs	Number of loose case covers	Design of fixed upholstery covering	Design of loose case cover	Probable original position	EHIN
1	—	Pattern 6: Rose and phlox design	—	Bedroom 9 or 10	9000 8576
1	—	Pattern 11: Lavatera design	—	Bedroom 11, 12, 13 or 17	9000 7678
1	—	Original fixed covering not known. Recovered in a later twentieth-century woven fabric	—	Not known	9000 8142
1	—	Pattern 21: Floral design	—	Bedroom 14	9000 8569
—	1	—	Pattern 19: Lace design	Bedroom 14	9000 7627
Total 4	**Total 1**				

Thellusson sat in the photograph of c.1878–80 (see Figure 11.13) it would have been, according to the 1863 bill, one of the four armchairs bought for an identical sum. It is therefore strange that it should be the chair with the variation in the shape of the legs.

Once again the bill may not be giving the full picture. It is possible that there were more armchairs in the family bedrooms in 1863 than the five in the 1863 Lapworths' bill, and these could also have been covered in the Lapworths' chintzes. The chair with the fixed upholstery in the floral design may in this case not be specified in the bill, although it was in the bedroom from 1863 and had a case cover in Pattern 19. An alternative possibility is that the two styles of armchair remaining in the collection cost the same amount: in this case, the more expensive armchair in the rose and phlox design (Pattern 6) mentioned in the bill may not be the chair that survives with a fixed upholstery cover in that design in the collection. It may be a chair of a different style that has not been identified as surviving in the collection. It is also possible that the bill was not entirely accurate regarding the rooms into which the chairs of the same cost were placed. Thus the armchair in the rose and phlox design that survives could have been one of these of the same cost, put into Bedroom 10 or indeed Bedroom 9, which was given the same rose and phlox design but had no armchair mentioned in the bill.

Despite the difficulties in matching the Lapworths' bill to the armchairs that survive in the collection, there is enough evidence to

Figure 11.21 Armchair (EHIN 9000 8576), probably supplied by Lapworth Brothers in 1863. The fixed upholstery top covering nearest the wood is in the rose and phlox design (Pattern 6), probably applied by Lapworths to match textiles in Bedrooms 9 and 10. The armchair also has rough patches in the rose on a seawood ground design (Pattern 2, glazed version) and fragments of a fixed upholstery covering in the fruit design (Pattern 38)

Figure 11.22 Armchair (EHIN 9000 8576), with a loose case cover in the fruit design (Pattern 38), from the later twentieth century

construct a likely history for the armchair with the fixed upholstery cover in the floral design (Pattern 21). If it is assumed that this chair was for many years in Bedroom 14, then it was probably first covered with the Lapworths' lace design fabric (Pattern 19) and was used in the early years with a matching case cover (probably the cover seen in the photograph of Constance Thellusson seated, and the cover still in the collection)[52] (Figure 11.23). The armchair was probably stripped and given its current fixed cover in the floral design (Pattern 21) after c.1878–80 (when the photograph of Constance seated was taken) and before 1890 (the latest date given by the Warners Archive for the special commissioning of the printing of the floral design), possibly in 1886 by Maples. This chronology broadly follows that for the Bedroom 14 half-tester bed. There may have been a matching case cover for the armchair in the floral design, now missing, as the Maples' bill of 1886 also charges for 'making loose covers in own material lined and flounced for two easy chairs'. Then, in 1900 or soon after, when the room was furnished with the arborescent design (Pattern 32), the armchair was probably used with a new arborescent design case cover (still in the

Figure 11.23 Loose case cover (EHIN 9001 7627), in the lace design (Pattern 19), which fits the four bedroom armchairs in the Brodsworth Hall collection probably supplied by Lapworths in 1863. This may be the cover on the armchair seen in the photography of Constance Thellusson of c.1878–80 in Bedroom 14 (see Figure 11.13)

collection)[53] without stripping off the fixed upholstery covering in the floral design fabric. This was still in good condition even in 1990, so it is possible that there was felt to be no need to change the fixed upholstery when a new loose case cover would suffice to complete the arborescent design scheme. It was probably only in Sylvia Grant-Dalton's time, when there was extensive rearranging of furniture in the house, that the arborescent design cover became detached from the Bedroom 14 armchair and was moved onto another armchair of the same size.

11.3.6 Other printed fabrics found in Bedroom 14

A likely chronology of upholstery for Bedroom 14 had begun to emerge, then, from the research described above (summarised in the Appendix below). However, several further designs were found in Bedroom 14 in 1990, and it was of interest in presenting and conserving the contents of the room to know something of the history of all these pieces (Table 11.1). These were researched through a similar pattern of investigation for other rooms in the house.

Research into the Lapworths' bill and an examination of artefacts found in other bedrooms and in cupboards established that the rose and phlox design (Pattern 6) (Plate 11.3) that was found in Bedroom 14 was probably associated with Bedrooms 9 and 10. It was also established that the lavatera design which was used for the buttoned fixed upholstery covering on one of the mahogany side chairs[54] found in Bedroom 14 was probably also supplied by Lapworths in 1863 but for Bedrooms 11, 12, 13 and 17.

Several pieces of evidence linked the garland and ribbon design (Pattern 1) (Figure 11.24) to Bedroom 8 and established the likely date for its introduction to Brodsworth Hall as 1904. An entry in a bill of 1904 from the Wakefield furnishing company Hall and Armitage charged for curtains and loose case covers for Bedroom 8 and mentioned darkening the flowers of the frieze on the walls in that room to match new chintz.[55] The dominant colour in Pattern 1 is a dark purple. Also, a curtain in the Brodsworth collection in

Figure 11.24 Detail of a loose case cover (EHIN 9000 4611) showing the garland and ribbon design (Pattern 1). Fabric in this design was possibly supplied by Hall and Armitage for Bedroom 8 in 1904

the design fits brass poles associated with a large boat bed in Bedroom 8. This curtain has pinched pleats typical of c.1900.[56] And finally, the design was identified at the Warner Fabrics Archive as a design first printed at Wardles in Derbyshire in 1895.[57] It is likely that it remained available in 1904.

The rose design on a seaweed ground (Pattern 2) was found in Bedroom 14 as a rough patch over the armchair upholstered in the rose and phlox design (Pattern 6) (Figure 11.21) and was the fabric of the valances pinned to the half-tester bed. Further examination of all the pieces in the collection in the rose design with seaweed ground (Pattern 2) revealed that there were two versions at Brodsworth: one the lighter-weight glazed fabric found in Bedroom 14, and a heavier, unglazed fabric.[58] The sizes of loose case covers and curtains and the pattern of tack holes on a tester valance, all in the glazed version, as well as the fixed upholstery covering on a bed backboard in the collection, show that it was certainly used for hangings and fixed upholstery coverings on one of the two larger (5 ft 6 in) half-tester beds in the collection that resemble the Bedroom 14 bed.[59] No further information was found, however, to show in which bedroom it was used.

No evidence was found to suggest that the valances and the patch on the armchair in the rose on a seaweed ground design found in Bedroom 14 had any strong connection with that room. They were probably introduced there as part of the wider movement of objects and a series of crude repairs in the mid- and later twentieth century.

None the less, there was good evidence for the history of the unglazed version and it is possible that the glazed version was bought at the same time. A photograph of the Library at Brodsworth Hall of 1910[60] shows the rose design on a seaweed ground (Pattern 2) used in the Library, and surviving loose case covers which fit furniture that remained in the Library to 1990 show that this was in the unglazed version.[61] The 1904 Hall and Armitage bill charged for supplying cretonne covers for the Library and these are likely to be those seen in the photograph taken only six years later.

Finally, little was discovered about the fruit design (Pattern 38) (Figure 11.22),[62] which was used for a loose case cover and fragments of a fixed upholstery covering on the armchair probably supplied by Lapworths in 1863 that was found in Bedroom 14. However, the design almost certainly dates to Sylvia Grant-Dalton's later years and may have been used in more than one bedroom.

11.4 Research summary

The pieces found in Bedroom 14 were from various dates from 1863 onwards and included pieces originally from different bedrooms.

No piece in the lace design (Pattern 19) was found in the room, although this was probably the fabric used by Lapworths to cover the furniture and dress the windows in 1863. It is possible there was a different bed in Bedroom 14 in 1863 and that the half-tester found there dates from the late 1870s. However this is not certain. The mahogany side chairs and the armchair loose case cover in the lace design (Pattern 19) found elsewhere in the house probably came from Bedroom 14 and Bedroom 15. The existence of three loose case covers in the lace design fitting the rosewood side chairs suggests that at least three chairs in this set were also given fixed upholstery coverings in the lace design by Lapworths and placed in these bedrooms.

The rosewood side chair with a fixed upholstery covering in the floral design (Pattern 21) found in Bedroom 14 was related to the half-tester bed found in that room through the brown slash design fabric on the headboard and backboard. These fabrics were probably printed as a special commission and may have been applied by Maples in 1886. The leaf design (Pattern 30) and the magnolia design (Pattern 16) may have been applied to the side chairs in the rosewood set at the same time. There may originally have been twelve of these chairs. All the pieces in the collection in the floral design (Pattern 21) may have been in Bedroom 14 in 1886.

The textiles in Bedroom 14 were probably last replaced in 1900 or soon after when the arborescent design fabric (Pattern 32) was acquired. There is no evidence to show that any seat furniture was given a fixed cover in the arborescent design although loose covers in the design for a Lapworths armchair and two mahogany side chairs (one of which is made from a later printing) remain in the collection. The design may have been used in a second room as well, as a third pair of window curtains in the arborescent design survives.

The garland and ribbon design (Pattern 1) and the rose design with seaweed ground (Pattern 2, glazed version) may both have been supplied by Hall and Armitage in 1904 for Bedroom 8 and an unidentified bedroom respectively. The addition of pieces in these designs and in the fruit design fabric (Pattern 38) to Bedroom 14 probably occurred during the occupancy of Sylvia Grant-Dalton.

11.5 The contribution of the research to the review of options for the display and conservation of the printed cottons

The research into the historic textile furnishing of Bedroom 14 will be useful to English Heritage in planning future displays and conservation. It has shown that the lace, floral and arborescent designs (Patterns 19, 21 and 32 and Lining Pattern 10) in the collection were probably fabrics used in consecutive refurnishings of the room.

Various display possibilities might arise from this information within the context of the display policy at Brodsworth Hall:

- There is scope for distributing the rosewood and mahogany side chairs and the Lapworths armchairs with their assorted case covers of differing dates among the bedrooms. They could be placed according to the known position of designs at various times.
- There are duplicate chairs and covers within sets which might be rotated on display for conservation reasons.
- It would be an option to introduce an object in the lace design (Pattern 19) into Bedroom 14 to show the fabric probably supplied by Lapworths for that room.
- Reproduction fabrics in any of the four main designs (Patterns 19 and 21, Lining Pattern 10, and Pattern 32) would be appropriate for Bedroom 14 and there is considerable evidence from surviving pieces for the construction of window curtains, bed hangings and case covers if these were to be copied.

The historical research may also contribute to conservation recommendations in a number of ways. As every period from 1863 is considered important in the presentation of the house, all the layers of printed textile discovered on the bed and chairs found in Bedroom 14, and all the case covers found there, are significant to the history of the room and should be carefully conserved. It has become clear that these printed textile artefacts can best be understood alongside pieces from other parts of the house. The research has therefore highlighted the importance of documenting and preserving all the layers of fabric on the furniture, and the tack holes, during conservation, and retaining access to them. It has also shown how pieces can be grouped according to date, room, supplier and design and this points to issues of consistency in the conservation techniques chosen. Likewise, the fading of the dyes in some pieces has been noted and this points up the importance of light management and monitoring colour changes.

11.6 Conclusion

Brodsworth Hall has a remarkably complete collection of the printed textiles used in its furnishing from 1863 to 1990, including fabrics remaining in layers of fixed upholstery coverings, and loose case covers for furniture. A greater understanding of the history of the collection has been achieved through close documentation of the furniture and other textile items, archive research into the designs, and a study of photographs and documents from the house. This integrated approach has allowed mutually supporting evidence to emerge. While ongoing research will undoubtedly add further information, it has proved possible to propose a likely chronology for the textile furnishing of Bedroom 14. Printed fabrics were a prominent part of the successive design schemes in this room as in all the family bedrooms, and the greater understanding of them that has been achieved will make an important contribution to display and conservation planning at Brodsworth Hall.

Appendix: The probable chronology of textile furnishing in Bedroom 14

1863

Bedroom 14 was probably furnished by Lapworth Brothers in the lace design (Pattern 19) as a pair with Bedroom 15. Items in the design are likely to have included bed hangings (the style of the bed in Bedroom 14 is not certain), an armchair with matching case cover, mahogany and rosewood side chairs with matching case covers for the seats, and window curtains with a lilac spotted lining.

1886

The Thellusson family probably engaged Maple & Co. to redecorate Bedroom 14, supplying the new textiles themselves. They may have directly commissioned Clarkson and Turner to produce a special printing at David Walters printing works of an 1873 floral design with a brown slash roller-printed ground (Pattern 21). Maples probably used this fabric to reupholster a Lapworth's armchair and at least four rosewood side chairs, and, together with a complementary fabric of the brown slashes only (Lining Pattern 10) to reupholster the half-tester bed. In all cases the earlier textiles were stripped off. It is likely that window curtains were made in the floral design to match.

c.1900

Bedroom 14 was probably re-furnished with the arborescent design (Pattern 32) by an unknown upholsterer, possibly as a pair with another bedroom. The brown slash design on the headboard and backboard of the half-tester bed was covered over without being stripped off. Case covers were made for a Lapworth's armchair and at least two rosewood side chairs, probably without new fixed upholstery coverings. Window curtains in the arborescent design were also made.

c.1900–1990

The arborescent design remained the main furnishing fabric in Bedroom 14 until the death of Mrs Grant-Dalton in 1988 and the acquisition of the house by English Heritage in 1990. Indeed, one loose case cover for a chair seat may have been made from a version of the design bought in the later twentieth century. None the less, pieces were mixed between bedrooms at unknown times. Items in the arborescent design were found in Bedrooms 11 and 12 and in cupboards in 1990. Likewise, by then items in the ribbon and garland design (Pattern 1), the rose on a seaweed ground design (Pattern 2, unglazed version), the rose and phlox design (Pattern 6) and the fruit design (Pattern 38) had been brought into Bedroom 14.

Notes

1 The numbering of bedrooms at Brodsworth Hall has changed several times. This bedroom was called Bedroom 2 in 1863 when the rooms were counted from West to East, but at the turn of the century became known as Bedroom 14 when the order was reversed. The latter system has been chosen here because the room has been known as Bedroom 14 for most of its history (see Figure 11.2).

2 English Heritage (The Historic Buildings and Monuments Commission for England) is the lead body in England concerned with the conservation of the built environment. Its principal activities include the management and conservation of over 400 ancient monuments and historic properties in its direct care, the awarding of conservation grants to assist owners of ancient monuments and historic properties, and the provision of advisory and education services, including statutory advice to the government.

3 Much of the research on the historic documents regarding the history of the family and the contents of the house referred to in this paper was done by Caroline Carr-Whitworth, Regional Curator. The following provide useful information on the building, the history of the family, the contents of the house and the display policy (Allfrey, 1999; Carr-Whitworth, 1995a; Carr-Whitworth, 1995b; Girouard, 1979; Gordon-Smith, 1997; Hall, 1995; Read, 1989; Smith and Handley, 1996).

4 Lapworth Brothers owned the Wilton carpet factory and by the 1860s was a general furnishing company with offices in Bond Street, London.

5 Some furniture in the house is known to have come from an older Thellusson house near Brighton in Sussex. The Lapworth Brothers bill of 1863, West Yorkshire Archive Service, held by the Yorkshire Archaeology Service, Leeds, DD 168/7/1/4 charges for carrying goods from another house to Brighton. It also includes £54 5s 0d paid to the Brighton Railway Company for taking the goods from Brighton to London, and £5 0s 0d for time spent at Brodsworth unpacking. Thus Lapworths were closely involved with the introduction of the older furniture.

6 For further information on the textile collection at Brodsworth Hall and its conservation see Berkouwer (1994); Berkouwer and Church (1993); Berkouwer and Stevens (1999).

7 Fixed upholstery coverings are defined as textiles tacked to wooden frames.

8 Charles and Georgiana Thellusson had six children: Peter 1850–99, Herbert 1854–1903,

Aline 1856–1880, Constance 1858–1893, Charles 1860–1919, Augustus 1863–1931.

9 English Heritage Inventory Number 9000 8602.
10 EHIN 9000 8603.
11 EHIN 9000 8604.
12 EHIN 9000 4111 and 9000 4112.
13 The weave count is 24 warps per centimetre and 27 wefts per centimetre. The pattern repeat is length 525 mm, width 780 mm. Block and roller printed. The fabric width is 810 mm.
14 The numbering of the designs was devised by Inga Gamble, Regional Curator during the initial cataloguing of the collection between 1990 and 1995. The list was subsequently expanded as more designs were identified. See Stevens, 1999.
15 The cloth on which the arborescent design Pattern 32 (the c.1900 version) is printed is cotton with 24 warps per centimetre and 12 wefts per centimetre. The pattern repeat is length 620 mm, width 1255 mm. The design is block printed. The fabric width is 1235 mm.
16 EHIN 9000 4099 and 9000 4100.
17 EHIN 9000 4103, 9000 4104, 9000 4107, 9000 4108.
18 The cloth on which Lining Pattern 10 is printed is cotton with 29 warps per centimetre and 31 wefts per centimetre. The pattern repeat is length 65 mm, width 8 mm. The design is roller printed. The fabric width is 660 mm.
19 The cloth on which Pattern 21 is printed is cotton with 29 warps per centimetre and 31 wefts per centimetre. The pattern repeat is length 360 mm, width 450 mm. The design is block and roller printed. The fabric width cannot be determined from the pieces in the collection.
20 EHIN 9000 8474, 9000 8475, 9000 8476, also 9000 8674 which was found in Bedroom 14.
21 Information courtesy of Warner Fabrics: Sue Kerry, Archivist, Warner Fabrics, Milton Keynes, UK. For background information on the Warner Archive, see Bury, 1981; Schoeser and Rufey, 1989; Victoria & Albert Museum, 1970.
22 Information supplied by Dennis Irwin, Archivist, Stead McAlpin Archive, Carlisle, UK, branch of the John Lewis Partnership. Stead McAlpin reference K/5259. For examples of mid-nineteenth-century English glazed cottons including some produced at Bannister Hall near Preston, Lancashire, UK, and at Stead McAlpin, see Victoria & Albert Museum, 1960: 56–62.
23 Information supplied by Keith Lambourne, Managing Director, Ramm, Son and Crocker, High Wycombe, UK. The design, called 'Latimer' is still produced by the company, now by the Galee printing method on linen union cloth.
24 EHIN 9000 6321, 9000 8626, 9000 8143, 9000 4119, 9000 4120.
25 The chair seat cover EHIN 9000 6321 has a brown fleck woven in the ground. This is in much better condition than the other pieces in the same design and is probably a single item made from fabric printed in the later twentieth century.
26 EHIN 9000 5301 and 9000 5298.
27 EHIN 9000 4159, 9000 4160, 9000 4161, 9000 4163, 9000 4164, 9000 4165, 9000 4166, 9000 4169, 9000 4170, 9000 4173, 9000 4645, 9000 4776, 9000 4777, 9000 4791, 9000 5972, 9000 7890.
28 EHIN 9001 1732.005. The photograph has been attributed to Constance's brother Peter Thellusson. For the collection of photographs at Brodsworth Hall, see Carr-Whitworth (1999).
29 The cloth on which Pattern 19 is printed is cotton with 27 warps per centimetre and 28 wefts per centimetre. The pattern repeat is length 242 mm, width 290 mm. The design is roller and block printed. The fabric width cannot be determined from the pieces in the collection.
30 The three similar half-tester beds in the collection are in two sizes. One bed, the Bedroom 14 bed, is 15 240 mm (5 ft) wide. The other two are 16 764 mm (5 ft 6 in) wide. The EHIN of the parts of the latter two beds are 9000 8103, 9000 8151, and 9000 7889, 9000 7987, 9000 7890.
31 The lace design (Pattern 19) may have been used also in the Governesses' bedroom, Bedroom 1, as the fabric specified by Lapworths in the bill of 1863 was a 'super chintz' at 2s 3d a yard, the same price as the fabric used in Bedrooms 14 and 15.
32 Dye analysis by Penelope Rogers, Textile Research in Archaeology, York, UK, showed the purple and pink colorants in the design to be synthetic dyes. These colours are now severely faded except in areas screened from light.
33 The lavatera design (Pattern 11) was identified by Jean-Francois Keller of the Museé de L'Impression sur Étoffes, Mulhouse, France (which holds the original document) as a design of 1861 produced by Steinbach Koechlin. This was probably supplied for Bedrooms 11, 12, 13 and 17 together with a grey scroll design (Lining Pattern 5) complementary fabric.
34 A note on the front of the bill states that the final instalment was paid on 11 April 1864, apparently without amendment. It is likely, then, that a bed at the price charged was supplied.
35 Account books of the Thellusson Estates from the later 1860s to 1870s written by the family's London solicitors give figures for expenditure on Brodsworth Hall. They show that the family continued to spend large sums on repairs and probably also on additions to the contents. For

example, payments included in 1869 £89 5s 1d to Lapworths; in 1870 £130 0s 0d to Maples; in 1872 £84 10s 4d again to Lapworths, £351 13s 10d to Mawe and Son of Doncaster (which in other bills supplied textile furnishing fabrics, and repaired furniture), and a further £166 12s to Maples. However it is not known what was bought for these sums and no entry in the accounts or bill was found to specifically show the purchase of beds. WYA DD168/1/1-45.

36 The 1885 Inventory of Brodsworth Hall, WYA DD BROD 13/2.

37 The 1885 inventory shows a number of brass beds not mentioned in the Lapworth's bill of 1863, possibly bought to replace beds that were put in the house when it was first furnished.

38 The three similar half-tester beds in the collection resemble beds in the catalogue of Heal and Son (1878: 79–81). Also designs for beds by C.&R. Light of 1881 and G. Maddox of 1882 in Joy, 1977: 12–13.

39 The 1885 Inventory also notes '2 flowered cretonne valances and 2 pairs of curtains' for Bedroom 14. It is not clear whether these matched the textiles on the bed.

40 There are two purple star designs in the collection which might loosely be described as spotted: Lining Pattern 2 and Lining Pattern 15. However neither has a likely association with the lace design (Pattern 19).

41 The bill from Maples & Co. from 1886, WYA DD BROD 12/4. For background information on Maples, see Barty-King, 1992.

42 EHIN 9000 3617, 9000 3618, 9000 7784, 9000 7785, 9000 8013, 9000 8015, 9000 8018, 9000 8106, 9000 8107, 9000 8109, 9000 8110, 9000 8111, 9000 8112, 9000 8113, 9000 8171, 9000 8173, 9000 8618.

43 EHIN 9000 7315, 9000 7634, 9000 8473, 9000 8474, 9000 8475, 9000 8476, 9000 8674, 9000 8676. The detached seats are 9000 4640 and 9000 8470.

44 This design, called 'The False Acacia', was first printed in England in 1848 at Bannister Hall for Swainson and Dennys. The Stead McAlpin Archive holds the original document reference C/7895. The pink dye was analysed by Textiles in Archaeology and found to be similar to synthetic alizarin, which may date the fabric to after 1869.

45 The design is printed on cotton cloth. The pattern repeat is length 26 mm, width 22 mm. The design is roller printed. The fabric width cannot be determined from the pieces in the collection.

46 EHIN 9001 1732.010. The photograph has been attributed to Constance's brother Peter Thellusson. For the paintings at Brodsworth Hall, see Dars and Watkinson (1993).

47 EHIN 9000 5833, 9000 5855.

48 The design was dated from information at the Stead McAlpin Archive to c.1850. The pattern repeat is length 880 mm, width 440 mm. The design is block printed. The fabric width is 650 mm.

49 This is a design of entwined ribbons (Pattern 24) found in two colourways in the collection. The pattern repeat is length 880 mm. The design is block printed. The fabric is 650 mm wide. The design was first produced in 1842 at Bannister Hall and was printed for Swainson and Dennys. Stead McAlpin hold the document, reference C/7566. This is probably a reprinting of the design produced in 1863. A photograph in an album of 1910, EHIN 9001 1728, shows the entwined ribbon design also used for loose case covers on side chairs, dated to the early part of the nineteenth century, in the hall outside the Drawing Room. These may be among the covers in the design that remain in the collection.

50 EHIN 9000 4640.

51 EHIN 9000 7678, 9000 8142, 9000 8576, 9000 8659.

52 EHIN 9001 7627.

53 EHIN 9000 8143.

54 EHIN 9000 8618.

55 Bill of 1904 from Hall and Armitage, WYA DD BROD 13/3.

56 Date attributed by Mary Schoeser, Consultant Textile Historian. For more information on pleats in curtains in this period, see Schoeser and Rufey, 1989: 135.

57 The pattern repeat is length 580 mm, width 410 mm. The design is block printed. The fabric width is 850 mm.

58 The heavier version appears to be unglazed, but 9000 8575 may have been starched in laundering.

59 EHIN 9000 4125, 9000 4126, 9000 4154, 9000 4623, 9000 7624.

60 EHIN 9001 1728.

61 EHIN 9001 2386, 9001 2387, 9001 2388, 9001 2389, 9001 2390. These have been crudely overdyed in red at some point in their later history.

62 Possibly screen printed. Three seat covers in the design: EHIN 9000 8577, 9000 8675, 9000 8677 fit the rosewood side chairs.

Acknowledgements

I have a number of debts for information regarding the designs: to Dennis Irwin, Archivist at Stead

McAlpin branch of the John Lewis Partnership; Sue Kerry, Archivist at Warner Fabrics; Jean-Francois Keller, Curator at the Musée de L'Impression sur Étoffes; Keith Lambourne, Managing Director of Ramm, Son and Crocker; Linda Parry, Acting Chief Curator, Lucy Pratt, Curator, and Paul Harrison, Curator, of the Textiles and Dress Department at the Victoria & Albert Museum; and Mary Schoeser, Consultant Textile Historian. I am likewise grateful to Mary Brooks, Head of Studies and Research at the Textile Conservation Centre, University of Southampton for encouragement and information, and to Penelope Rogers of Textile Research in Archaeology for the dye analysis.

I have had valuable support from Martin Allfrey, Caroline Carr-Whitworth, Andrew Morrison, Bob Smith and Rosalyn Thomas of the curatorial team of the Northern regions of English Heritage, including assistance with photography, production, background information and guidance in using the Brodsworth Hall archive. And I would like to thank Dinah Eastop and Kate Gill for their contribution as editors.

Thanks are also due to English Heritage and the Pasold Research Fund for financial support. The copyright of all photographs included belongs to English Heritage Photo Library.

References

Allfrey, M. (1999) Brodsworth Hall: the preservation of a country house'. In: G. Chitty and D. Baker (eds), *Managing Historic Sites and Buildings: Reconciling Presentation and Conservation*. London: Routledge, pp. 115–27.

Barty-King, H. (1992) *Maples Fine Furnishers: A Household Word for 150 Years 1841–1991*. London: Quiller Press.

Berkouwer, M. (1994) Freezing to eradicate insect pests in textiles at Brodsworth Hall. *The Conservator*, **18**: 15–22.

Berkouwer, M. and Church, D. (1993) Textiles at Brodsworth Hall. *Conservation Bulletin*, **19**: 12–14.

Berkouwer, M. and Stevens, C. (1999) Conservation treatment of 19th century silk damask fixed wall coverings at Brodsworth Hall. In: S. Howard (ed.), *Solutions – The Influence of Location on Treatments*. Conference Postprints. London: United Kingdom Institute for Conservation, pp. 21–30.

Bury, H. (1981) *A Choice of Design, 1850–1980: Fabrics by Warner and Son Limited*. Exhibition Catalogue. Purley: Purley Press.

Carr-Whitworth, C. (1995a) *Brodsworth Hall*. London: English Heritage.

Carr-Whitworth, C. (1995b) Remembrance of things past. *Conservation Bulletin*, **27**: 3–4.

Carr-Whitworth, C. (1999) Fleeting images: the Brodsworth Hall photograph collection. *Collections Review*, **2**: 109–12.

Dars, C. and Watkinson, T. (1993) Brodsworth Hall. In: C. Dars and T. Watkinson (eds), *Catalogue of Paintings in British Collections*. London: Visual Arts Publishing, pp. 21–46.

Girouard, M. (1979) *The Victorian Country House*. New Haven, CT: Yale University Press.

Gordon-Smith, P. (1997) Charles Sabine Augustus Thellusson and Italianate Buildings on the Brodsworth Estate. In: B. Elliot (ed.), *Aspects of Doncaster*. Barnsley: Wharncliffe Publishing, pp. 75–86.

Hall, M. (1995) Brodsworth Hall, Yorkshire. *Country Life*, 29 June, pp. 60–5.

Heal and Son. (1878). *Illustrated Catalogue of Bedsteads and Bedroom Furniture*. London: Printed shop catalogue.

Joy, E. (ed.) (1977) *Pictorial Dictionary of British 19th Century Furniture Design*. Woodbridge, Suffolk: Antique Collectors' Club.

Read, B. (1989) Vintage Victoriana. *Country Life*, 8 June, pp. 314–17.

Schoeser, M. and Rufey, C. (1989) *English and American Textiles from 1790 to the Present*. London: Thames and Hudson.

Smith, B. and Handley, M. (1996) *Brodsworth and Pickburn: A Tale of Two Villages*. Doncaster: Brodsworth and Pickering Local History Society.

Stevens, C. (1999) The Printed Textiles of Brodsworth Hall. Unpublished research report: held at Brodsworth Hall.

Victoria & Albert Museum (1960) *Catalogue of a Loan Exhibition of English Chintz: English Printed Furnishing Fabrics from Their Origins until the Present Day*. London: V&A.

Victoria & Albert Museum (1970) *A Century of Warners Fabrics, 1870–1970*. London: V&A.

Appendices

Upholstery Documentation

Appendix I

Documenting upholstery: a guide for practitioners

Sherry Doyal

I.1 Introduction

Why should we engage in the analysis and documentation of upholstered objects? An important reason is that so much information on the history and technology of upholstery has already been lost. This information is especially important when the survival of the object cannot be assured (for instance objects in private use or objects made up of unstable materials). Upholstery is rather like archaeology in this respect; when a layer is removed or disturbed it is never quite the same.

Information collected during examination and treatment may be used to interpret the object or other similar objects. These interpretations exchanged and shared by conservators/restorers, curator/collectors, students and the public increase interest in the subject. This increased interest may accelerate the rate at which upholstery is preserved.

As a conservator one can aim for the ideal, that is preserving both the object and the information it contains; indeed the ethics of the profession insist on this. However, it would be naively optimistic to expect all persons to whom the care of upholstered objects falls to be willing or able to do this. Detailed documentation and analysis may be uneconomic or impossible in some circumstances. Simple documentation can be applied in most circumstances.

I.2 Written documentation

The first step towards clarity in written documentation is an unambiguous use of language. This may be achieved by reference to an agreed terminology or a glossary of terms. These may be provided by reference to publications. For woven textiles there is an agreed terminology accepted by the International Councils for Museums; it would be beneficial to work towards such agreements in other areas.

The length of a report relates to its purpose. A report may be very brief, perhaps as a concession to time constraints or as part of a large survey. A detailed written report may form part of an extended documentation of a particularly interesting, rare, or important item. A format with headings, key words or multiple choice answers is time-effective. Direct entry into a computer or word processor 'shell' (template) makes future access and comparisons simple. Checklists, summaries and formats have been developed by various institutions and individuals in response to the demands of their work (be that museum, conservation agency or private workshop).

To summarise, a written report should record the following information: a description including outside dimensions (remember that an object is usually described proper left and right not visual left and right); materials and techniques used in construction; a technical analysis of the materials; description of condition; requested treatment or aim of treatment; a treatment proposal; a treatment report and recommendations for future care, storage and display.

I.3 Visual recording

Upholstered structures can be complex. Diagrams can simplify both the keeping of records and their interpretation. A picture really can be worth a thousand words. Cross-section diagrams are particularly useful and colour is required for clarity.

To produce quick, clear diagrams or drawings, photographs are used. Tracings made from photocopies on a light box or from projected slides are within the capabilities of the least artistic among us. Such a tracing may then be photocopied and used several times to make different points clear.

Technical drawings give accurate information about dimensions and construction. A local draughtsman can be asked to produce the drawings – the cost of hire being more efficient than the frustrated erasings of a conservator/restorer.

Diagrams and drawings are used in publications and lectures. To make overhead projection transparencies, the information may be photocopied onto acetate sheets. To project as slides, the information can be recorded on reverse-text transparency film.

At its most basic, a photographic record may consist of a simple identification photograph. For conservation purposes a series of photographs is required recording the condition of an object before, during and after treatment. In an extended documentation, many photographs may be taken. A 'ripping down' series (not to be taken literally) and a profiles series of seven photographs (based on a third-angle projection technical drawing) have been found useful by the author.

The photographic record is only as good as its labelling. Time is wasted trying to identify slides and photographs unless information is recorded in the photograph. It is suggested that a scale, colour tiles and/or a grey scale, an identification number for the object and some indication of the stage of treatment be included.

The end use of photographs may influence the choice of black and white or colour photography. If a permanent archival record is required, black and white photographs, archivally processed and stored, are needed. For presentations and publicity, colour transparencies may be used to produce brochures, posters, case histories and lectures. If budgets allow, both black and white and colour records complement each other. In the event that an accident should befall one, the other acts as a fail safe record. Special lenses, lights and films may be used as required (to produce close detail, photomicrographs and ultra-violet examination records, for instance).

I.4 Sample records

During the course of conservation or restoration treatments, upholstery features may be exposed or removed. Valuable study collections of upholstery materials have been built up by retaining this material and recording details of the position, provenance and date of the source. Upholsterers in private practice and upholstery technique tutors have made great contributions by donating interesting stitched edges, filling materials, tacks/nails and fabrics or trimmings to study collections or museums. Museum staff may also visit private workshops to examine and record particularly interesting or rare examples of work.

It is not always possible or desirable to retain all of the material removed from an object. In such instances small samples may be retained on file. These samples can be examined in future. Fine acrylic sheet bags or envelopes are the best form of storage for these materials; non-archival quality materials such as some plastics or papers may degrade and affect the samples. Samples must also be clearly labelled.

I.5 Technical analysis

The technical analysis of an object is a look in detail at the materials and techniques of construction of the constituent parts. Upholstery is a multi-media subject. The examiner must be familiar with upholstery techniques; leather technology; rush and cane work; textile technology; cabinet making; finishing techniques; metals technology and plastics technology. The skills of examination are rarely (if ever) embodied in one individual. There are few conservators trained in this field as a speciality; those who have been are still actively researching their subject. More trained upholstery conservators are required. In practice, conservators call upon the skills of colleagues or specialists. Ideally, one has the opportunity to study each area. Such study may be limited in its scope but should provide a sound vocabulary for discussions with others or for informed reading and research.

When an upholstery conservator is not available for consultation, fruitful partnerships have been formed between upholsterer, conservator and curator.

Leather conservation is also an emerging field with few specialists as yet. Conservators working in related fields may be approached. Book conservators, textile conservators, ethnographic conservators and archaeological conservators all invariably have some experience in the identification and treatment of leathers.

Textile conservators can give valuable insight into the fabric and fibre content of an upholstered object. Non-destructive analysis of weaves and fibres can be made with equipment as simple as a thread counter or a hand-held microscope. Small samples may be removed to facilitate the use of wet chemical tests (using a binocular microscope) for finishes, dyes and adhesives.

Furniture conservators can advise on construction, woods, adhesives and finishes employed in an upholstered framework. Woods may be sampled for identification. Computer wood analysis programs may be utilised. Metals may be identified by wet chemical techniques. X-radiography and ultraviolet inspection techniques can be used to examine the structure; such examination may prevent the unnecessary removal of existing upholstery.

Plastics conservation is a field that has only been developing since the 1980s; the amount of synthetic materials represented in collections is limited at present but is increasing.

Synthetic filling materials for upholstery are particularly at risk; conservation solutions are being researched now.

The conservation scientist plays an important role in technical analysis. The more complex analytical techniques include: thin-layer chromatography (used to identify dyestuffs); gas chromatography (used to identify natural finishes and adhesives); infra-red spectrometry, preferably Fourier transform infra-red spectrometry (used for the identification of synthetic and semi-synthetic finishes, adhesives and fillings) and energy dispersive X-radiography (used in the identification of metals in threads, finishes and hardware). Although many conservators have a working knowledge of these techniques, in practice they may best be employed by a consulting scientist. The very small sample size preferred by both conservators and curators often give results which are difficult to interpret by any but the most experienced eye. Deterioration changes the characteristics of materials and complicates identification. Conservation scientists are few in number and will be extremely specialised; when approaching a consultant, allowances should be made; an expert in organic materials identification will not always be able to identify dyestuffs, for example. With the constraints on sampling imposed by conservation, analysis may still result in a qualified answer to the question 'What is it?'

Large institutions may have both expensive equipment and the specialist staff required to employ the equipment. Other conservators may have access to this expertise through professional courtesy, by access to the equipment and staff of regional conservation guilds and associations or access to the expertise located in conservation training programs or universities. Local industries or hospitals may also help. It is important to stress that even in well-equipped institutions, simple tests using simple equipment are the most frequently used! Some of these techniques may be taught to non-conservators.

Collated information is interpreted by conservation and curatorial staff. Without the important contributions on historic and documentary evidence supplied by curatorial colleagues, valuable conclusions may be missed. The interpretations presented to the public promote the subject; this is crucial to research in this field.

I.6 Conclusion

This Appendix broadly outlines the range of options available and offers some simple practical guidelines. The funding for training in documentation for non-conservators working on historic upholstery is to be encouraged. Conservators always document artefacts. When asked, upholsterers and restorers are often willing to document objects for their clients. However, the client must place enough value on the history an object contains to pay for the time required to recover and record it. The loss of this history is to be regretted by us all. Degrees of documentation must of necessity vary; some is always better than none.

Note

This is an abridged version of a paper first presented at the Upholstery Conservation Symposium held at Colonial Williamsburg in 1990 and published as: Doyal, S. (1990) The analysis and documentation of upholstered objects. In: M.A. Williams (ed.), *Upholstery Conservation*. Preprints of a Symposium held at Colonial Williamsburg, 2–4 February 1990. East Kingston, NH: American Conservation Consortium Ltd, pp. 42–54.

Appendix II

Example of cross-section diagrams to document changes to upholstery layers before and after conservation treatment

Kathryn Gill

This brief account of the information revealed during the preliminary investigations of the Lawrence Alma-Tadema settee, Metropolitan Museum of Art (Acc. no. 1975.219; refer to Chapter 2 of this book) includes four cross-section diagrams which document changes to upholstery layers before and after conservation treatment.[1]

The Metropolitan Museum of Art settee 1975.219 has an upholstered back and seat. All the original back upholstery understructure was intact. However, some of the seat structure was missing or had been replaced.

In addition, the following fragments of the original top covers were located embedded under a number of tack heads in various locations around the frame or mingled in the re-teased hair from the second filling in the seat:

- top cover, inner back and seat – green dyed warp faced silk (approx. 100 warps/10 mm, each warp comprises 2 non-plied filaments; approx. 16 wefts/10 mm, each weft comprises more than 2 non-plied filaments;
- decorative panel – linen backed, black-purple silk satin with evidence of embroidery;
- embroidery yarn – yellow, cream, turquoise and red dyed silk threads (2 'Z' ply)
- gimp – white, green and yellow dyed silk, with 2 supplementary wefts of yellow, silk wrapped cotton cord (12 mm wide);
- top cover – outer back green dyed figured silk.[2]

The diagrams (Figures III.1–III.4) record the location, function, type and order of application of each layer of upholstery comprising the seat and the back units before and after the 1991 treatment.

Notes

1 This preliminary investigation was undertaken by Kathryn Gill when Associate Conservator in charge of upholstered works of art 1984–91.

2 Due to its fragile condition this entire panel was removed in 1981.

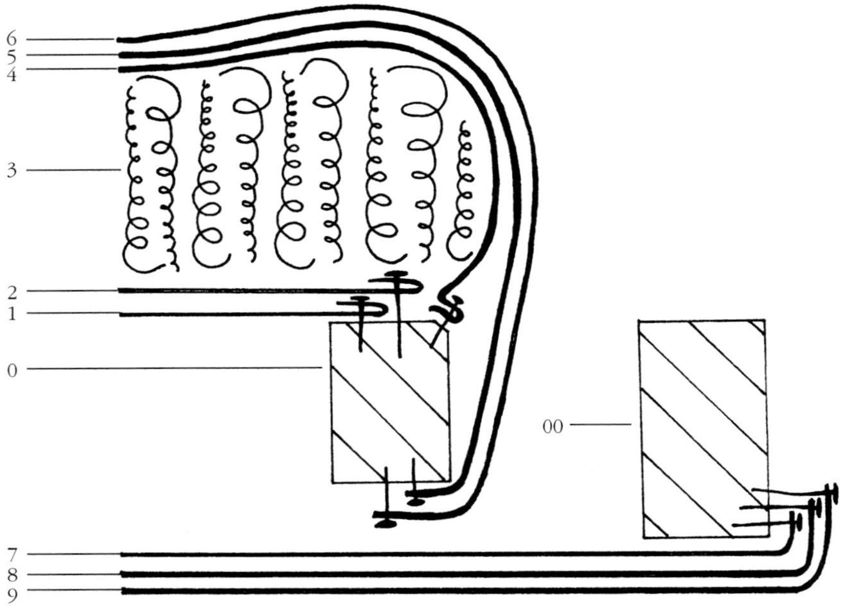

Figure II.1 Cross-section of settee back – lower rail, and seat frame – rear rail, before 1991 treatment

Numbers denote individual upholstery layers:

6 Top cover – silk, warp stripe: dyed green satin, dyed cream satin, floral brocatelle – not original, nailed
5 First filling cover 2 – cotton, brushed one side, twill weave other side, nailed
4 First filling cover 1 (not accessible for examination) – nailed
3 First filling (not accessible for examination) – black curled hair [?] – original
2 Base cloth (partially accessible for examination) – unbleached linen [?] – original, nailed (evidence of stuffing ties and/or 'bridal' stitching through base cloth and webbing)
1 Webbing (partially accessible for examination) – unbleached linen [?], brown and white striped warp chevron twill weave (55–60 mm wide) – original, nailed
0 Frame – wood (lower back rail)
00 Frame – wood (rear seat rail)
7 Base cloth (outer back) – linen [?], open even plain weave – original, nailed
8 Interlining (outer back) – cotton, dyed grey brushed plain weave – original, nailed
9 Top cover (outer back) – cotton, dyed cream sateen – not original, was nailed, (original removed previously, now in Museum storage)

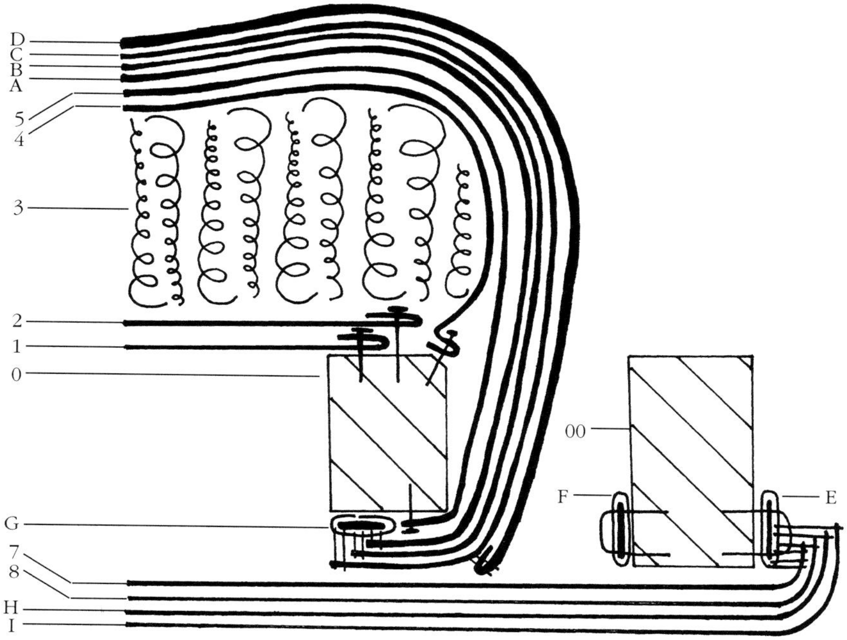

Figure II.2 Cross-section of settee back – lower rail, and seat frame – rear rail, after 1991 treatment

Numbers denote individual upholstery layers, letters denote conservation and replica materials:

D Decorative panel – silk-screened, replica, stitched
C Top cover – silk, dyed green rep, replica, stitched
B Cotton, brushed plain weave, stitched
A Needle punched felt, polyester, stitched
5 First filling cover 2 – cotton, brushed one side, twill weave other side, nailed
4 First filling cover 1 (not accessible for examination) – unbleached linen[?], nailed
3 First filling (not accessible for examination) – black curled hair[?] – original
2 Base cloth (partially accessible for examination) unbleached linen[?] – original, nailed (evidence of stuffing ties and/or 'bridal' stitching through base cloth and webbing)
1 Webbing (partially accessible for examination)– unbleached linen[?], brown and white striped warp chevron twill weave (55–60 mm wide) – original, nailed
0 Frame – wood (lower back rail)
00 Frame – wood (rear seat rail)
E Cotton covered acid-free card strips (for outer back attachments), stapled
F Cotton covered acid-free card strips (for seat layer attachments), stapled
G Cotton covered acid-free card strips, stapled
7 Base cloth (outer back) – linen[?], open even plain weave – original, nailed
8 Interlining (outer back) – cotton, dyed grey brushed plain weave – original, nailed
H Cotton (outer back) – brushed plain weave, stitched
I Top cover (outer back) – silk, dyed, replica, stitched

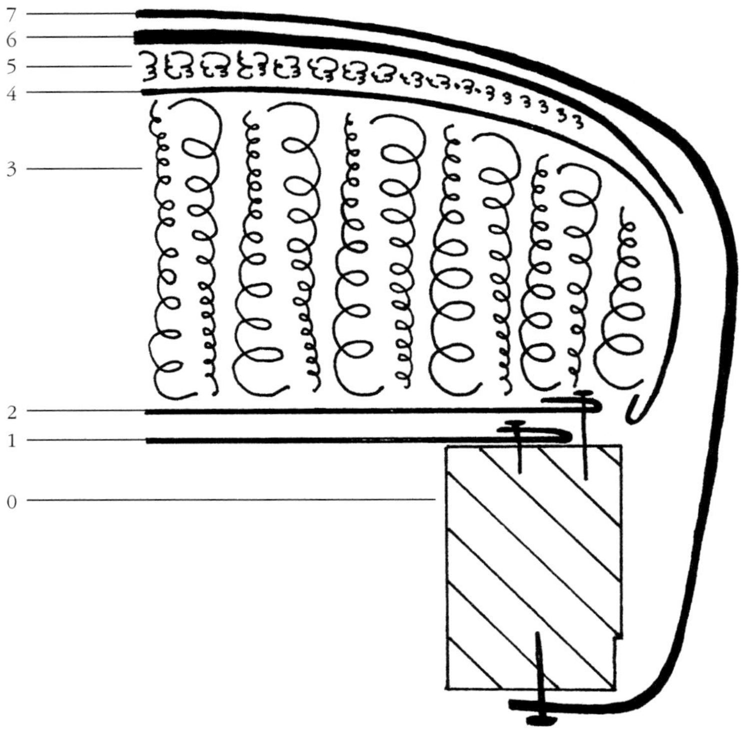

Figure II.3 Cross-section of settee seat – front seat rail, before 1991 treatment

Numbers denote individual upholstery layers:

7 Top cover – silk, warp stripe: dyed green satin, dyed cream satin, floral brocatelle – not original
6 Skimmer layer – cotton felt – not original
5 Second filling – black curled hair (possibly re-teased) – original
(second filling cover, top cover, trimming – missing)
4 First filling cover – linen/hemp open even plain weave top stitched (single row) roll edge on either short side of the seat unit – original
3 First filling – black curled hair [horse?] – original
2 Base cloth – jute, open even plain weave – not original
1 Webbing, jute, unbleached with dyed red warp stripe, plain warp faced weave (75 wide) – original
0 Frame – wood

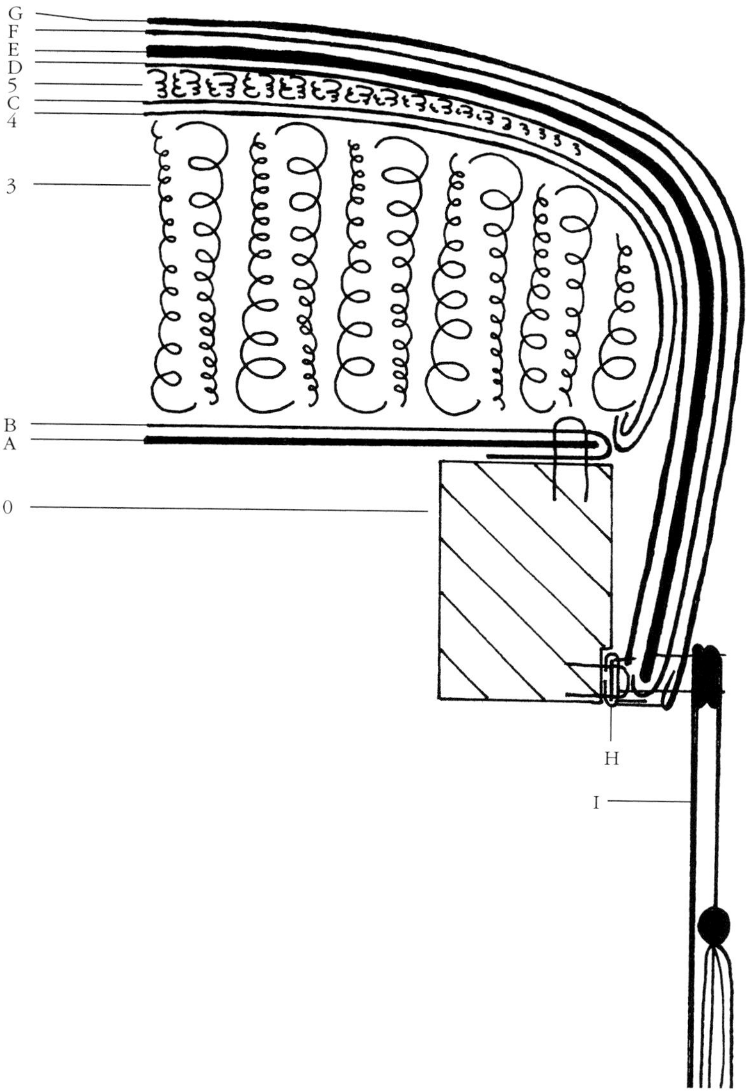

Figure II.4 Cross-section of settee seat – front seat rail, after 1991 treatment

Numbers represent individual upholstery layers, letters denote conservation and replica materials:

G Decorative panel – silk screened, replica, stitched
F Top cover – silk, dyed green rep, replica, stitched
E Cotton, brushed plain weave, stitched
D Needle punched felt, polyester, stitched
5 Second filling – black curled hair (possibly re-teased) – original
C Net – nylon, stitched
4 First filling cover – linen/hemp open even plain weave top stitched (single row) roll edge on either short side of the seat unit- original
3 First filling – black curled hair [horse?] – original
B Net – nylon, stitched
A Mesh – polypropylene, covered with linen, open even plain weave, stapled
0 Frame – wood
H Cotton covered acid-free card strips, stapled
I Fringed trimming – silk and wooden beads, replica, stitched

Appendix III

A brief object record: the Brooklyn Museum of Art easy chair

Kathryn Gill and Sherry Doyal

III.1 Introduction

In 1991, two upholstery conservators (Sherry Doyal and Kathryn Gill) spent one day examining an eighteenth-century New England easy chair at the Brooklyn Museum of Art (Acc. no. 32.38). The main purpose of the visit was to see how much information could be gained by a detailed examination of the chair. Non-intrusive examination techniques enabled a great deal of information to be recorded about the construction, materials and techniques of the chair's upholstery. All material identification was by 'naked eye' only: no materials were removed, no samples were taken, no analytical techniques were applied.

III.2 The examination

Due to the unstable condition of the upholstery, movement of the chair had to be kept to a minimum. Consequently, access to certain sections of the chair was limited. Throughout the examination process the chair remained upright on a mobile bench with locking wheels allowing safe transportation between the gallery and the examination room.

The tools and equipment used to assist in the examination comprised a magnifying lens (×10), thread counter, tweezers, spatula, probes, tape measure, two cameras (one with black and white film, the other with colour slide film) and an X-radiograph machine with a Polaroid camera attachment.

Since none of the upholstery was to be removed, the underlying upholstery structure and obverse faces of individual layers were observed through partially detached and missing areas. In most instances, only small sections were accessible. Many exposed sections were too small to undertake either weave analyses or accurate thread counts. Inaccessible sections of the chair were examined and recorded using X-radiography. As expected the X-rays revealed construction joints in the wood frame, and the location, shape and number of concealed metal fasteners. Unexpectedly, in some instances, individual textile and filling layers were also recorded on the X-ray plate (see Figure III.3).

The following information was recorded: depth of stuffing, warp direction, order of application of different panels, and detailed dimensions of frames. The majority of this information was recorded in a series of line drawings (e.g. Figure III.1), photographs (e.g. Figures III.2 and III.5), X-ray plates (e.g. Figure III.3) and written notes. A copy of the brief examination report, recording individual layers of the upholstery structures and metal fasteners, is reproduced in Figure III.4.

The amount of information generated using this range of examination techniques and equipment is largely dependent on the condition of the object and the degree of access to individual layers, the level of understanding of upholstery materials and structures, and experience of object documentation and analyses.

Figure III.1 Line drawing of a three-quarter front view of the easy chair illustrated in Figure III.2 to show upholstery construction

Inner back

1 Trim: flat tape binding cord – wool and silk
2 Top cover – wool
3 Second filling cover – [linen?]
4 Second filling –animal hair
5 First filling cover – [if present]
6 First filling – straw
7 Base cloth – [linen?]
8 Webbing – [linen?]
9 Wood frame

Inner wing/arm

10 Trim: flat tape binding cord – wool and silk
11 Top cover – wool
12 Second filling cover – [linen?]
13 Second filling – curled hair
14 First filling cover – [linen?]
15 First filling – straw roll
16 Bare cloth – [linen?]
17 Wood frame

Seat

18 Trim: flat tape – wool and silk
19 Top cover – wool
20 Second filling cover – [linen?]
21 Second filling – [straw?]
22 First filling cover – [linen?]
23 First filling – straw roll
24 Base cloth – [linen?]
25 Webbing – [linen?]
26 Wood frame

Loose seat cushion

27 Trim: flat tape binding seamed edge – wool and silk
28 Top cover – wool
29 Inner case – [linen?]
30 First filling – feather and down

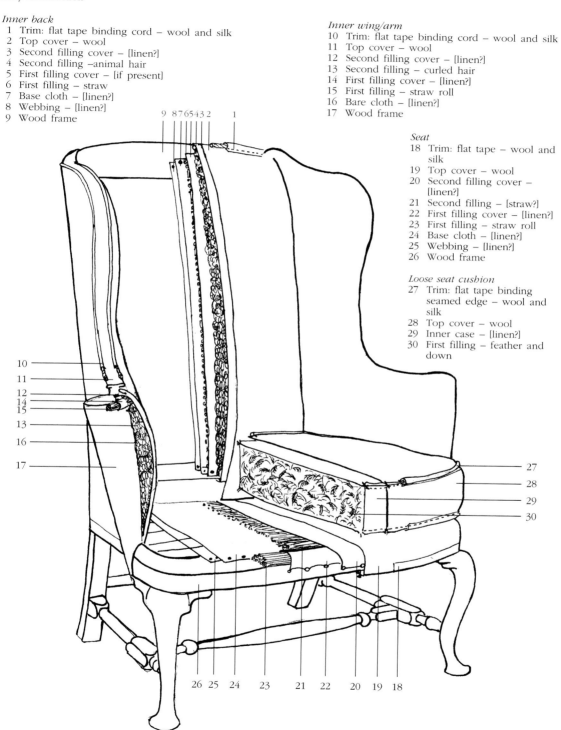

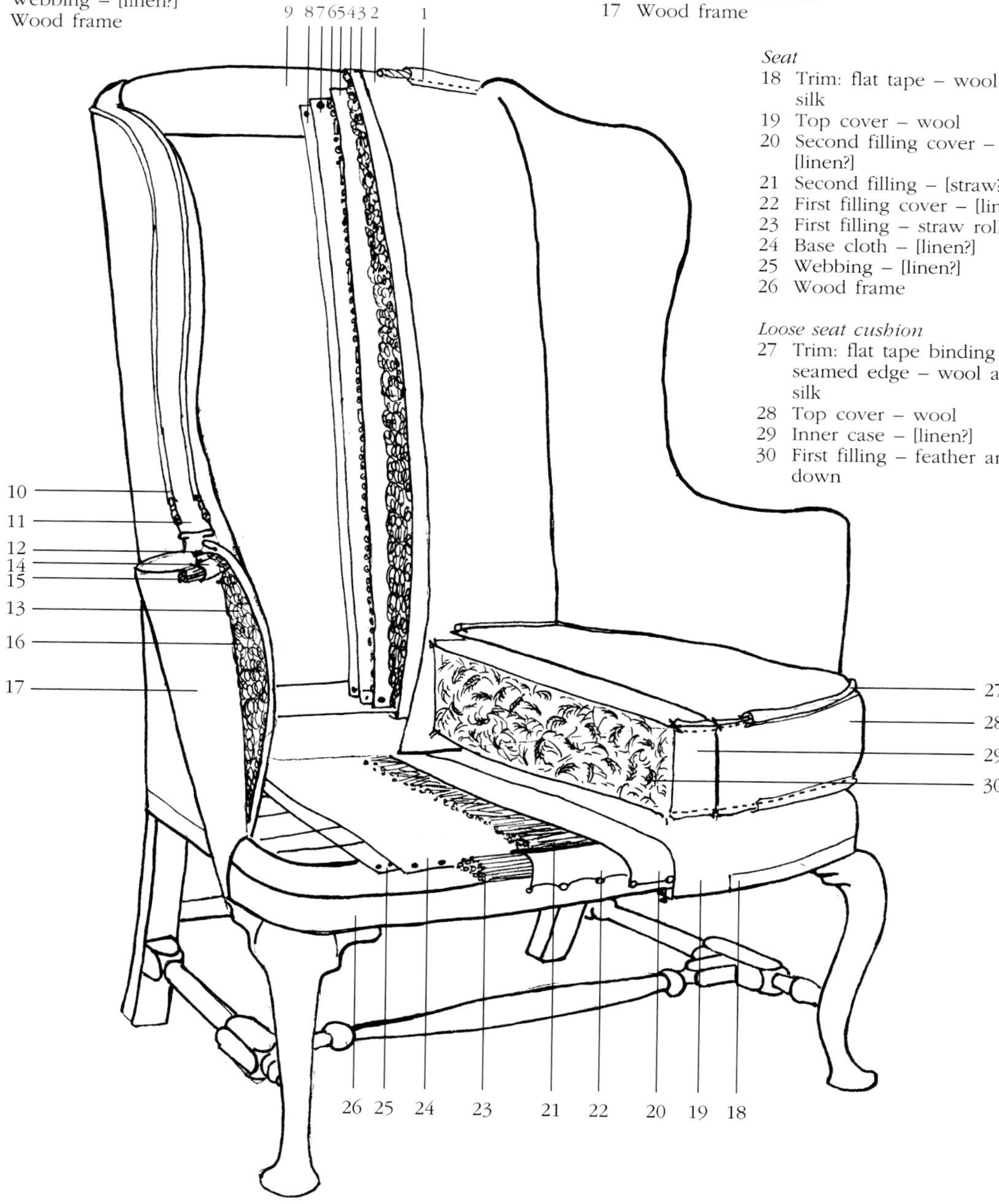

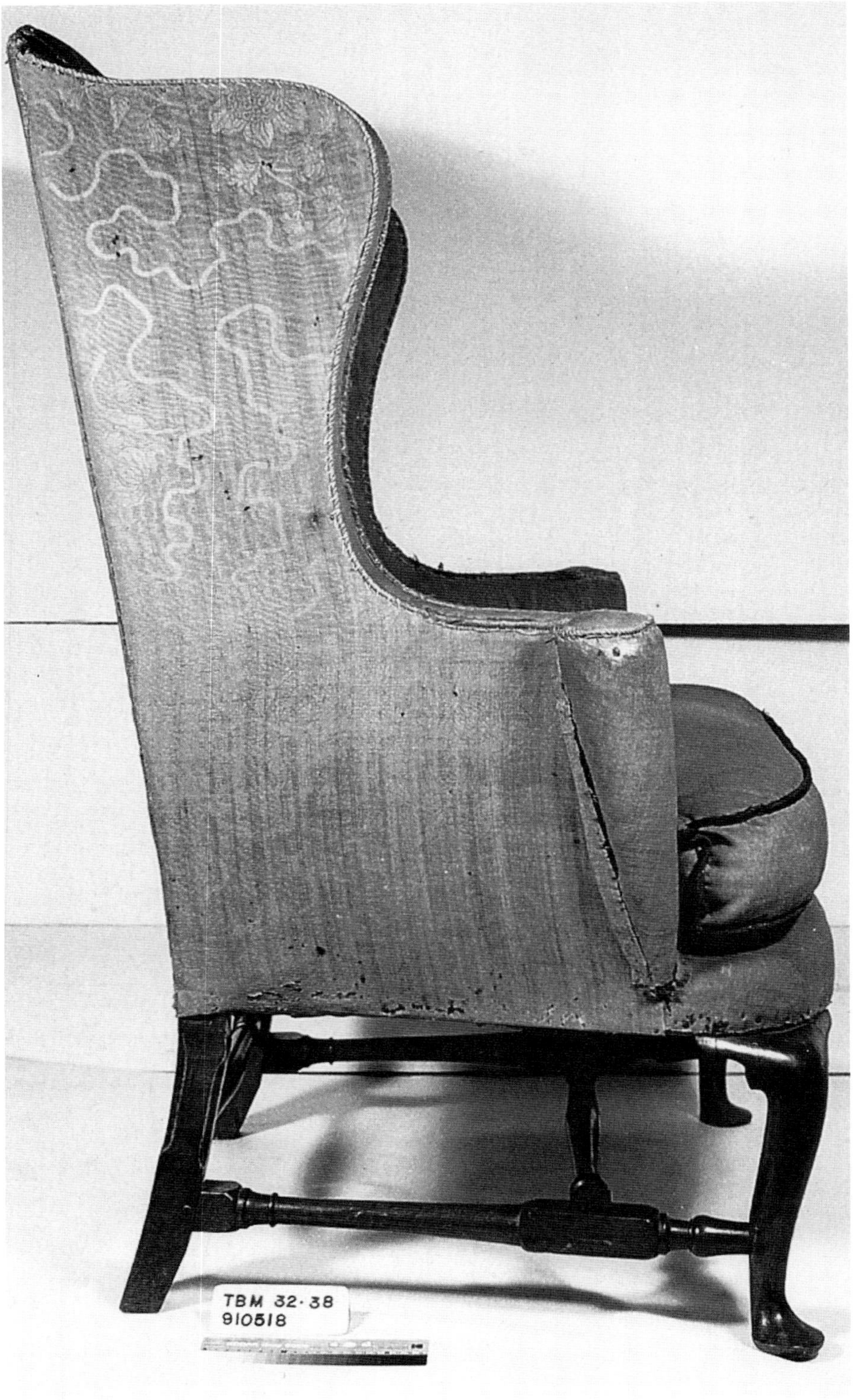

Figure III.2 Side view of an easy chair: American (New England), 1730–90; walnut, wool upholstery. (The Brooklyn Museum of Art, 32.38. Henry S. Batterman Fund; Carll H. DeSilver Fund; Maria L. Emmons Fund; and Charles S. Smith Memorial Fund)

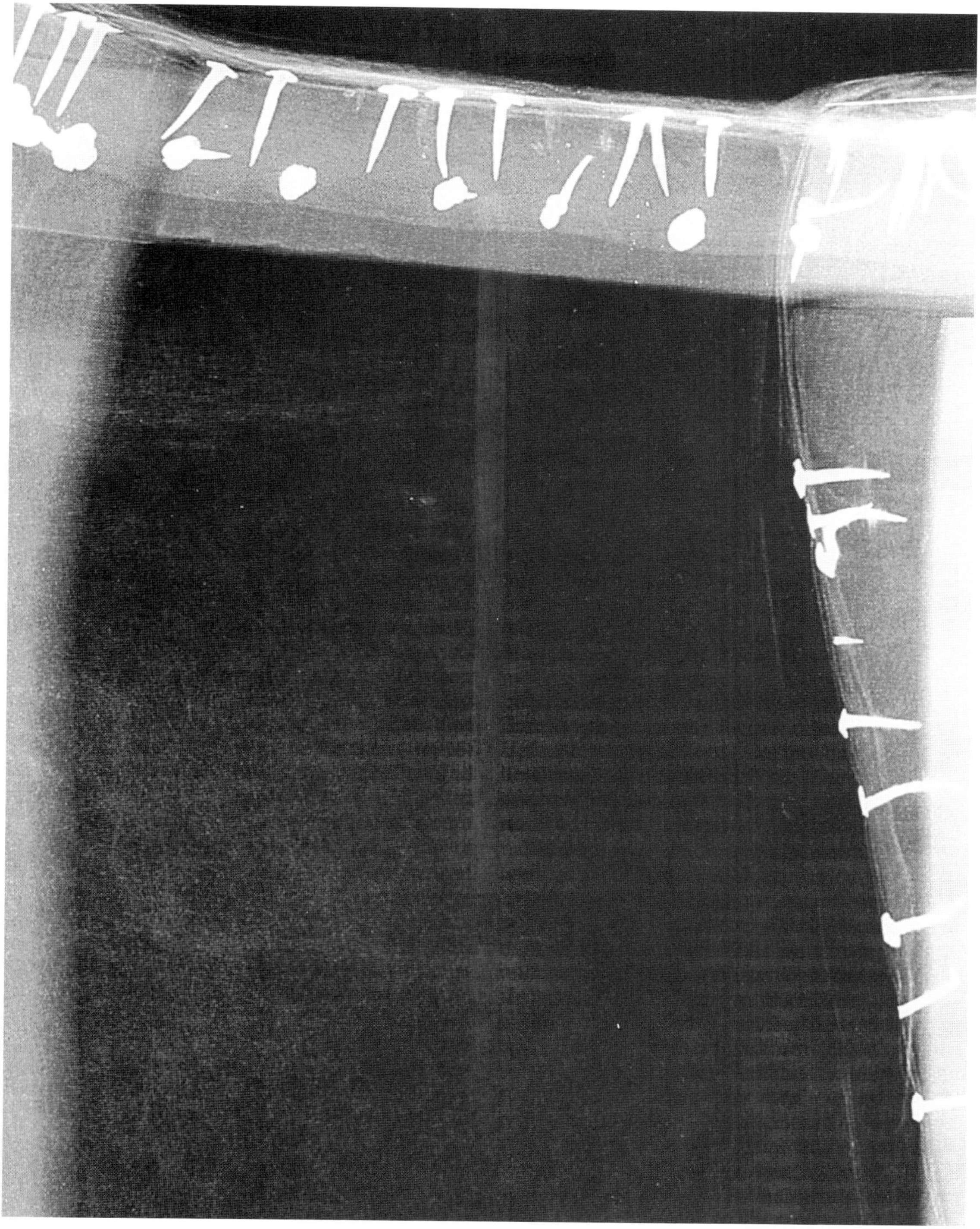

Figure III.3 X-radiograph of the arm section of the easy chair illustrated in Figure III.2, revealing both organic and inorganic components

Examination Report

Acc. or Loan No. 32.38 Department: Decorative Arts

Owner: Brooklyn Museum of Art, New York

1. Object and Type: Upholstered Easy Chair
2. Provenance and/or date: Massachusetts 1730–90
3. Size: overall height: 1180 mm (46½ inches)
   overall depth: 635 mm (25 inches)
   seat height: 356 mm (13 inches)
   seat width: 772 mm (30⅜ inches)
   seat depth: 562 mm (22⅛ inches)

---

4. Photographs: B/W neg. nos. 88192-1/-2 [Metropolitan Museum of Art]
   Colour file nos. TBM 3238
5. X-rays: Dates and nos. 91.05.17-1: front seat rail
   91.05.17-2: back stuffing rail
   91.05.17-3: proper left arm
6. Materials and techniques of construction:

UPHOLSTERED LAYER DOCUMENTATION – SEAT

<u>Webbing type 1:</u> Warp – unbleached mid-brown, dark brown and cream linen; weft – unbleached mid-brown linen; plain weave; 9 warps per 10 mm (23 per inch); 3 wefts per 10 mm (9 per inch); warp single Z twist; weft single Z twist; selvages present; width 45 mm (1¾ inches); attached with hand wrought tacks – unable to examine fully but X-ray indicates ferrous metal, width of head 1.5 mm (1/16 inch); 4 tacks at each end about 13 mm (½ inch) apart in a single row; other comments: the webbing arrangement is open interlace comprising 3 strips of webbing running from back to front and 3 from side to side.

<u>Webbing type 2:</u> Fibre, colour and weave are the same as webbing type 1 with warps 7 per 10 mm (20 per inch), 5 wefts per 10 mm (14 per inch); twist and ply the same as type 1; selvages present; width the same as type 1; attached with hand wrought tacks the same as type 1.

<u>Base cloth:</u> Warp – unbleached mid-brown linen; weft – unbleached mid-brown linen; plain weave; 9 warps per 10 mm (24 per inch); 9 wefts per 10 mm (24 per inch); warp single Z twist; weft single Z twist; selvages not seen; width not less than 508 mm (20 inches); attached with hand wrought tacks – unable to examine fully but X-ray indicates ferrous metal, width of head (15 mm, 1/16 inch); about 64 mm (2–2½ inches) apart and 14–38 mm (½–1½ inches) from front edge of seat rail; other comments: no stuffing ties present in this layer.

<u>Roll edge which consists of a first filling and cover:</u> Unable to examine visually but X-ray and touch by fingers indicate straw filling; linen cover; width of roll 89 mm (3½ inches); depth of roll 19 mm (¾ inch); attached with hand wrought tacks to outside front seat rail and possibly sewn (not accessible for examination) to base cloth; ferrous tacks, width of head 7 mm (¼ inch); length of shank 19 mm (¾ inch), about 64–76 mm (2½–3 inches) apart on front top edge of seat rail.

<u>Second filling:</u> Examined through a hole in the top cover; straw filling laid in the well formed by the edge roll (visually inaccessible but probably extends across the entire seat); depth does not exceed 19 mm (¾ inch).

<u>Second filling cover:</u> Examined through a hole in the top cover; warp – unbleached mid-brown linen; weft – unbleached mid brown linen; plain weave; 10 warps per 10 mm (27 per inch); 8 wefts per 10 mm (20 per inch); warp single Z twist; weft single Z twist; selvages not seen; attached with hand wrought tacks – unable to examine fully but X-ray indicates ferrous metal, width of head 7 mm (¼ inch); length of shank 16 mm (½ inch); about 51–89 mm (2–3½ inches) apart on the front face of the rail.

<u>Top cover:</u> Warp and weft – bluish-red piece dyed wool; applied decoration of moiré and floral stamping; design of centralised spray of peonies alternating with a spray of chrysanthemums with offset smaller sprigs of roses, lillies, carnations and iris[?]; English provenance [?]; plain weave; 18 warps per 10 mm (45 per inch); 12 wefts per 10 mm (27 per inch); warp single Z twist; weft single Z twist; selvages present (outer back bottom pr. right); width 650 mm (25⅝ inches); seat width 772 mm (30⅜ inches); attached with hand wrought ferrous tacks and stitched; width of head 4–6 mm (⅛–¼ inch); tacks located along vertical edge of rear arm support, above legs (concealed by tape) and underside of seat rail between legs; about 32 mm (1¼ inch) apart above legs; about 45–50 mm (1¾–2 inches) apart on underside of seat rail; other comments: the weave count on the outer back panel differs (the weave is more open, due to over stretching and/or degradation[?]) except where the fabric has been protected by trimming.

Flat tape: Warp – red dyed wool, yellow dyed silk; weft – red dyed wool; complex twill weave, diaper pattern; 16 warps per 10 mm (42 per inch) (NB: warps fragmentary); 18 wefts per 10 mm (48 per inch); warp single loose S twist; weft 2 S ply, Z twist; selvages present, width 22 mm (⅞ inch); attached with stitches over areas or cording, adhered over nails [original?]; other comments: originally the tape was applied flat around all four sides of the lower edge of the seat rail, rear of arm support and back uprights and over cording on arm and wing face, crest rail and probably – though now missing – was used to bind the raw seams on the cushion cover.

UPHOLSTERED LAYER DOCUMENTATION – BACK

Webbing: Description based on X-ray interpretation only; width 52 mm (2¹⁄₁₆ inch); attached with hand wrought ferrous tacks; width of head 5–7 mm (¼ inch); 4 tacks observed across full width of webbing; 6–19 mm (¼–¾ inch) apart, tacked to the mid rail; other comments: only one vertical strip or webbing visible on X-ray.

Base cloth: Description based on X-ray interpretation: attached by hand wrought ferrous tacks; width of head 5–7 mm (¼ inch;) 35–54 mm (1⅜–2⅛ inches) apart.

First filling: Examined through holes in lower corners; straw filling; where visible the filling is laid laterally in a vertical position; other comments: It is assumed that this layer is continuous on the back; it is not clear if a filling cover separates this layer from the second filling.

Second filling: Examined through small hole in top cover; black, grey and chestnut curled hair.

Second filling cover: Examined through small hole on top cover; warp – unbleached mid brown linen; plain weave; warp and weft 8 per 10 mm (23 per inch); selvages not seen; attached with hand wrought ferrous tacks.

Top cover: See 'Top cover – seat' entry for details; other comments: attached with hand wrought ferrous tacks.

Welting cord: Unbleached mid brown vegetable fibre: 3 Z ply, 6 S twist; width 6 mm (¼ inch); other comments: in those areas exposed, the tape is held down with large overcast stitches – probably not original.

Flat tape: See 'Flat tape – seat' entry for details.

UPHOLSTERED LAYER DOCUMENTATION – INNER ARMS AND WINGS

Base cloth: Observed through small hole in top cover; warp – unbleached mid-brown linen; weft – unbleached mid-brown linen; plain weave; 7 warps per 10 mm (19 per inch); 8 wefts per 10 mm (22 per inch); warp single Z twist; weft single Z twist; selvages not seen; X-ray indicating textile is attached with hand wrought ferrous tacks; width of head 7 mm (¼ inch); about 25–38 mm (1–1½ inches) apart along lower edge of arm.

First filling: Observed through small hole in top cover; black, grey and chestnut curled animal hair.

First filling cover: Warp – unbleached mid-brown linen; weft – unbleached mid-brown linen; plain weave; 12 warps per 10 mm (32 per inch); 9 wefts per 10 mm (24 per inch); warps single Z twist; wefts single Z twist; selvages not seen; X-ray interpreted textile to be attached with hand wrought ferrous tacks; width of head 8 mm (¼ inch); length of shank 16 mm (½ inch); about 25–50 mm (1–2 inches) apart in top face of arm.

Top cover: See 'Top cover – seat' entry for details.

Welting cord: See 'Welting cord – seat' entry for details.

Flat tape: See 'Flat tape – seat' entry for details.

UPHOLSTERED LAYER DOCUMENTATION – OUTER BACK AND SIDES

Outer back and outer sides consist of top cover and flat tape only – see entries for seat; other comments: top cover attached with tacks and by stitching; tape attached with animal glue; all raw edges of lower edges of outer panels are folded in before tacking; orientation of top cover design of one outer panel is inverted – probably deliberate to gain maximum use of yardage.

UPHOLSTERED LAYER DOCUMENTATION – LOOSE CUSHION

First filling: Based on observations made on samples trapped in seams; white and brown feathers and down.

First filling cover: Observations made through small hole in top cover; warp – bleached and unbleached linen with occasional blue linen warp; weft – bleached and unbleached linen; twill variation, herringbone effect; 20 warps per 10 mm (50 per inch); 20 wefts per 10 mm (50 per inch); warp single Z twist; weft single Z twist; selvages not seen; sewn in running stitch with 2 S ply Z twist thread.

Top cover: See 'Top cover – seat' entry for details; other comments; top cover seams sewn wrong sides together with raw edges facing outward.

Flat tape: See 'Flat tape – seat' entry for details; other comments: the flat tape binds the seamed raw edges; the cushion appears to have been partially or totally dismantled and reconstructed; one of the rear seat panels is of a different red wool fabric; the flat tape used to bind the edges of the seam is not the same as that found on the rest of the chair – possibly a later addition.

Figure III.4 Written documentation sheet recording individual layers of the upholstery structures and metal fasteners on the easy chair illustrated in Figure III.2

Figure III.5 Detail of the proper left side seat rail (cushion removed) of the easy chair illustrated in Figure III.2 showing the original flat tape and stamped wool moiré top cover. (The Brooklyn Museum of Art, 32.38. Henry S. Batterman Fund; Carll H. DeSilver Fund; Maria L. Emmons Fund; and Charles S. Smith Memorial Fund)

Acknowledgements

The authors would like to thank the Brooklyn Museum of Art for permission to publish this work. Special thanks are due to Kevin Stayton, Curator of Decorative Arts and to the Conservation Department, especially Kenneth Moser, Vice Director for undertaking and processing the X-rays.

References

Abbreviations

AIC	American Institute for Conservation of Historic and Artistic Works
CIETA	Centre International d'Etude des Textiles Anciens
IIC	International Institute for the Conservation of Historic and Artistic Works.
SSCR	Scottish Society for Conservation and Restoration
UKIC	United Kingdom Institute for Conservation

Adams, W. B. 1971 [1837]. *English pleasure carriages*. Bath: Adams and Dart.

Allfrey, M. 1999. 'Brodsworth Hall: The Preservation of a Country House'. In: G. Chitty and D. Baker (eds.) *Managing Historic Sites and Buildings: Reconciling Presentation and Conservation*. London: Routledge, pp. 115–127.

American Art Association 1927. *Sales Catalogue*. New York: 15 October 1927.

American Art Association/Anderson Galleries 1903. New York, 23–31 January 1903, Marquand sales catalogue.

Anon. (n.d.). *A short guide to Raby Castle*. Barnard Castle: Teesdale Mercury Ltd.

Anon. 1825. Inventaire après le décès de M. le Baron Denon. *Archives Nationale, Paris*. MN Etude VC 1541.

Anon. 1885. Furniture for New York Millionaires, from London Truth, *Cabinet Making and Upholstery* (New York), September (1885), 104.

Anon. 1911. Furniture of the XVII & XVIII Centuries: Furniture at Hampton Court, near Leominster – I. *Country Life* (November 18, 1911) Vol. **30**, 750–753.

Anon. 1911. Furniture of the XVII & XVIII Centuries: Furniture at Hampton Court, near Leominster -II. *Country Life* (November 25, 1911) Vol. **31**, 788–791.

Anon. 2000. Advertisement placed for a Furniture Upholstery Conservator within the Master of the Household's Department, Windsor Castle. *Grapevine Supplement* (UKIC), January 2000, **66**, 4.

Appelbaum, B. 1997. Some Thoughts on Conservation Literature and the Publication of Treatments. *AIC News* **22** (6), 1–2.

Aslin, E. 1962. *Nineteenth Century English Furniture*. London: Faber and Faber.

Bacchus, H. (Forthcoming, 2002). Single image, changing contexts: understanding a rare 18th century Chinese embroidered thangka (working title). In: M.M. Brooks and M. Hayward (eds.) *Textile Strands: Images and Values in Textiles*. Edited papers from the Textile Strand of the Association of Art Historians' annual conference, 'Images and Values', held at the University of Southampton, 1999.

Baker, A. C. 1947. Extracts from royal accounts of Henry VIII. *London Topographical Record*, **19**, 100–16.

Balfour D., Metcalf S. and Collard F. 1999. The first non-intrusive upholstery treatment at the Victoria and Albert Museum. *The Conservator*, **23**, 22–29 & 46.

Barty-King, H. 1992. *Maples Fine Furnishers: A Household Word for 150 Years 1841–1991*. London: Quiller Press.

Beard, G. 1997. *Upholsterers and Interior Furnishings in England, 1530–1840*. London and New York: Yale University Press.

Beard, G. and Westman, A. 1993. A French Upholsterer in England: Francis Lapiere, 1653–1714. *The Burlington Magazine*, August, CXXXV, 515–524.

Berkouwer, M. 1994. Freezing to Eradicate Insect Pests in Textiles at Brodsworth Hall. *The Conservator*, **18**, 15–22.

Berkouwer, M. and Church, D. 1993. 'Textiles at Brodsworth Hall'. *Conservation Bulletin*, **19**, 12–14.

Berkouwer, M. and Stevens, C. 1999. Conservation Treatment of 19th Century Silk Damask Fixed Wall Coverings at Brodsworth Hall. In: S. Howard (ed.) *Solutions – The Influence of Location on Treatments* (Conference Postprints). London: UKIC, pp. 21–30.

Blair. C. 1958. *European Armour*. London: B.T. Batsford Ltd.

Blyton, E. 1937. *The Adventures of the Wishing Chair*. London: Mammoth.

Bourdieu, P. 1984. *Distinction: A Social Critique of the Judgement of Taste*. London: Routledge.

Bourdieu, P. 1977. *Outline of a Theory of Practice.* Cambridge: Cambridge University Press.

Brewer, J.S., Gairdner, J. and Brodie, R.H., eds. 1861–3. *Letters and Papers Foreign and Domestic of the Reign of Henry VIII.* London: Longman, Green, Longman, Roberts and Green.

Brooks, M. 1990. The Conservation of a Textile Covered Bed Cornice from Harewood House. In: A. French (ed.) *Conservation of Furnishing Textiles.* London: UKIC Textile Section, pp. 49–57.

Buck, S.L. 1991. A Technical and Stylistic Comparison of Twelve Massachusetts State House Chairs. In: AIC, *Wooden Artefacts Group Preprints.* Washington, DC: American Institute for Conservation, 22pp.

The Building News and Engineering Journal. 1885a. **49** London 24 July.

The Building News and Engineering Journal. 1885b. **49** London 31 July.

Burges, W. (n.d.). *Furniture Album.* Victoria and Albert Museum, Prints and Drawings Department, Album 93.E.8.

Burges, W. 1865. Furniture. In: W. Burges, *Art Applied to Industry: a series of lectures.* Oxford and London: John Henry and James Parker, pp. 69–82.

Burgess, J. W. 1881. *A practical treatise on coach-building.* London: Crosby Lockwood & Co.

Bury, H. 1981. *A Choice of Design 1850–1980: Fabrics by Warner and Son Limited.* Exhibition Catalogue. Purley: Purley Press.

Calnan, C. (ed.) 1991. *Conservation of leather in transport collections.* Papers given at a UKIC conference Restoration '91, London October 1991. London: UKIC.

Carr-Whitworth, C. 1995a. *Brodsworth Hall.* London: English Heritage.

Carr-Whitworth, C. 1995b. Remembrance of Things Past. *Conservation Bulletin,* **27**, 3–4.

Carr-Whitworth, C. 1999. Fleeting Images: The Brodsworth Hall Photograph Collection. *Collections Review,* **2**, 109–112.

Chambers, E. 1738. *Cyclopaedia; or, an Universal Dictionary of Arts and Sciences.* Second Edition. 2 vols. London: D. Midwinter, J. Senex, *et al.*

Christie, Manson and Woods 1917. *Catalogue of Objects of Art Porcelain Old English and Other Furniture being a portion of the Hope Heirlooms Removed from Deepdene, Dorking.* (Sale: July 18th). London: Christie, Manson & Woods.

Christie's. 1994. *Works of Art from Houghton,* Sales Catalogue. London: Christie's.

Clinton (White), L. 1979. The State Bed from Melville House. *Victoria and Albert Museum Masterpieces* – Sheet 21.

Collard, F. 1985. *Regency Furniture.* Woodbridge, Suffolk: Antiques Collectors' Club.

Colvin, C. (ed.) 1971. *Maria Edgeworth Letters from England 1813–44.* Oxford: Clarendon.

Colvin, H.M. 1995. *A Biographical Dictionary of British Architects 1600–1840.* London: J.Murray.

Conway, H. 1982. *Ernest Race.* London: The Design Council.

Cooke, Jr., E.S. (ed.) 1987. *Upholstery in America & Europe from the Seventeenth Century to World War I.* Paris, W. W. Norton & Company.

Cornforth, J. 1973a. Hampton Court, Herefordshire – I. *Country Life* (22 February 1973) 450–453.

Cornforth, J. 1973b. Hampton Court, Herefordshire – II. *Country Life* (1 March 1973) 518–521.

Cornforth, J. 1973c. Hampton Court, Herefordshire – III. *Country Life* (8 March 1973) 582–585.

Cornforth, J. 1986. British State Beds. *Magazine Antiques* (February) 392–401.

Cornforth, J. 1992. Velvet Stamp Duty. *Country Life* (1 October 1992) 76–77.

Cornforth, J. 1996. *Houghton Hall Guidebook.* Norwich: The Marquess of Cholmondeley and Jarrold Publishing.

Cornforth, J. 1999. Raby Recovers Silken Splendour, *Country Life* (22 April 1999) 100–103.

Dars, C. and Watkinson, T. 1993. Brodsworth Hall. In: C. Dars and T. Watkinson (eds.) *Catalogue of Paintings in British Collections.* London: Visual Arts Publishing, 21–46.

Davies, V. and Doyal, S. 1990. Upholstered Mattress Construction and Conservation. In: A. French (ed.) *Conservation of Furnishing Textiles.* Postprints of the conference held at the Burrell Collection, Glasgow, 30–31 March 1990. Edinburgh: SCCR/UKIC, 58–67.

Denon D.V. 1802. *Voyage dans la Basse et la Haute Egypt, pendant les Campagnes du Gënéral Bonaparte.* Paris: P. Didot.

Digby (Wingfield), G. F. 1939. Damasks and Velvets at Hampton Court, *Connoisseur* (January-June 1939) **103**, 248–253.

Doyal, S. 1982a. *Daybook.* Unpublished records. Property of the author.

Doyal, S. 1982b. *Conservation Report 0432a.* Unpublished Report, The Textile Conservation Centre.

Doyal, S. 1990. The Analysis and Documentation of Upholstered Objects. In: M.A. Williams (ed.) *Upholstery Conservation.* Preprints of a Symposium held at Colonial Williamsburg, February 2–4, 1990. East Kingston, New Hampshire: American Conservation Consortium, Ltd., 42–54.

Dubios, L. J.-J. 1826. Description des objets d'art qui composent le cabinet de feu M. le Baron V. Denon: estampes et ouvrages à figures, par Duchesne âiné. In: L.J-J. Dubois (ed.) *Monuments Antiques, Historiques, Modernes; Ouvrages Orientaux, etc.* (Vol. III). Paris: Imprimerie d'Hippolyte Tilliard.

Eastop, D. 1998. Decision making in conservation: determining the role of artefacts. In: A. Tímár-Balázsy and D. Eastop (eds.) *International Perspectives on Textile Conservation.* Papers from the ICOM-CC Textiles Working Group Meetings 1994 & 1995. London: Archetype, 43–46.

Eastop, D. 2000. Textiles as multiple and competing histories. In: M.M. Brooks (ed.) *Textiles Revealed: Historic Costume and Textiles in Object-based Research.* London: Archetype Press.

Elias, N. 1978. *The Civilising Process. The History of Manners.* Oxford: Basil Blackwell.

Farr, W. and Thrupp, G. A. 1998 [1888]. *Handbook of coach trimming.* West Yorkshire: William Binns.

Felton, W. 1996 [1794–5]. *A treatise on carriages.* Mendham, New Jersey: Astral Press.

Ffoulkes, C. 1988 [1912]. *The Armourer & his Craft.* New York: Dover Publications, Inc.

Fiell, C. and Fiell P. 1997. *1000 Chairs.* Köln: Taschen.

Fishlock, M. 1992. *The Great Fire at Hampton Court.* London: The Herbert Press.

Flury-Lemberg, M. 1988. Hangings of a State Bed. In: M. Flury-Lemberg, *Textile Conservation and Research*. Bern: Abegg-Stiftung, 148–153.

Gentle, N. 1990. *Conservation of the Dolphin Chairs at Ham House*. In: A. French (ed.) *Conservation of Furnishing Textiles*. Postprints of the conference held at the Burrell Collection, Glasgow, 30–31 March 1990. Edinburgh: SCCR/UKIC, 30–40.

Gill, K. 1990. Approaches in the Treatment of 20th-Century Upholstered Furniture. In: M.A.Williams (ed.) *Upholstery Conservation*. Preprints of a symposium held at Colonial Williamsburg, February 2–4, 1990. New Hampshire: American Conservation Consortium, Ltd, 305–22.

Gill, K. 1991. *Report on the treatment of the Alma-Tadema settee*. Unpublished treatment report, Sherman Fairchild Center for Objects Conservation, The Metropolitan Museum of Art, accession number 1975.219.

Gill, K. 1999. *Interim Report on Oral History Account of Foam Production*. Unpublished report, The Textile Conservation Centre, University of Southampton.

Gill, K. 2000. A 1950s upholstered chair: combining the conventional and the innovative in both manufacture and conservation. In: *Tradition and Innovation: Advances in Conservation*. Summaries of the Posters at the 18th International Congress of IIC, Melbourne 2000, p.11.

Gill, K. & Boersma, F. 1997. Solvent Reactivation of Hydroxypropyl Cellulose (Klucel G) in Textile Conservation: Recent Developments. *The Conservator* **21**, 12–20 and i.

Gill, K. and Eastop, D. 1997. Two Contrasting Minimally Interventive Upholstery Treatments: Different Roles, Different Treatments. In: K.Marko (ed.) *Textiles in Trust*. Proceedings of the 'Textiles in Trust' Symposium held at Blickling Hall, Norfolk, September 1995, London: Archetype Publications and the National Trust, 67–77.

Girouard, M. 1979. *The Victorian Country House*. New Haven: Yale University Press.

Gordon-Smith, P. 1997. Charles Sabine Augustus Thellusson and Italianate Buildings on the Brodsworth Estate. In: B. Elliot (ed.) *Aspects of Doncaster*. Barnsley: Wharncliffe Publishing, 75–86.

Grier, K.C. 1988. *Culture and Comfort. People, Parlors, and Upholstery 1850–1930*. Rochester, New York: The Strong Museum in association with the University of Massachusetts Press.

Hall, M. 1995. Brodsworth Hall, Yorkshire. *Country Life* (June 29 1995) 60–65.

Handley-Read, C. 1963. Notes on William Burges's Painted Furniture. *Burlington Magazine*, **CV**, 496–509.

Handley-Read, C. 1966. Aladdin's Palace in Kensington. *Country Life* (17 March 1966) 600–604.

Hardacre, J. 1989. *Winchester Cathedral Triforium Gallery*. Winchester: Dean and Chapter of Winchester Cathedral.

Hayward, M. 1997. The packing and transportation of the goods of Henry VIII, with particular reference to the 1547 inventory. *Costume*, **31**, 8–15.

Hayward, M. 1998a. *The Possessions of Henry VIII: A Study of Inventories*. Unpublished PhD thesis, University of London.

Hayward, M. 1998b. Repositories of splendour: Henry VIII's wardrobes of the robes and beds. *Textile History*. **29** (2) 134–56.

Hayward, M. (2000). William Green, coffer-maker to Henry VIII, Edward VI and Mary I. *Furniture History*. The Journal of the Furniture History Society, **36**, 1–3.

Hayward, M. (ed.) 2001. *The 1542 Inventory of the Palace of Westminster: The Curatorial Career of Sir Anthony Denny* (Provisional title). London: The Society of Antiquaries and The Westpark Press.

Heal and Son. 1878. *Illustrated Catalogue of Bedsteads and Bedroom Furniture*. Shop catalogue. London.

Hobbs, J. 1999. The 'restore or conserve' dilemma. *Old Glory* **113** (July 1999). Surrey: CMS publishing.

Hodgkins, V. and Bloxham, C. 1981 [1980]. *Banbury and Shutford Plush*. Oxford: Banbury Historical Society/Oxford Museum.

Horie, C.V. 1987. *Materials for Conservation: Organic Consolidants, Adhesives & Coatings*. London: Butterworths.

Howitt, F.O. 1948. *Bibliography of the Technical Literature on Silk*. London: Hutchinson's Scientific and Technical Publications.

Jackson Stops, G. (ed.) 1985. *The Treasure Houses of Britain*. Exhibition Catalogue. Washington, D.C.: National Gallery of Art.

James, D. 1990. *Upholstery: A Complete Course*. London: The Guild of Master Craftsman Publications.

James, D. 1994. *Traditional Upholstery Workshop*. Part 1. Drop-in and Pinstuffed Seats. Part 2. Stuffover Upholstery. London: The Guild of Master Craftsman Publications.

James, D. 1997. *Upholstery Restoration*. London: The Guild of Master Craftsman Publications.

Javér, A., Eastop, D. and Janssen, R. 1999. A sprang cap preserved on a naturally dried human head. *Textile History*, **30** (2) 135–154.

Jervis, S. 1983. A Painter as a Decorator: Alma Tadema. Rediscovering a Victorian artist's quirky designs. *House and Garden* (USA), **155** (11) November 1983, 142–147, 201 & 206.

Jervis, S. 1989. 'Shadows not substantial things': Furniture in the Commonwealth Sale inventories. In: A. MacGregor (ed). *The Late King's Goods*. Oxon: Alistair McAlpine with Oxford University Press, 277–306.

Jones, O. 1856. *The Grammar of Ornament*. London: Messrs Day & Son.

Jourdain, M. 1922. *English Furniture of the Later XVIIIth Century*. London: B.T. Batsford Ltd.

Joy, E. (ed.) 1977. *Pictorial Dictionary of British 19th Century Furniture Design*. Woodbridge, Suffolk: Antique Collectors' Club.

Kerr, N. and Batcheller, J. 1993. Degradation of Polyurethanes in 20th century museum textiles. In: D. Grattan (ed.) *Saving the Twentieth Century: The Conservation of Modern Materials*. Proceedings of the Symposium '91, Ottawa, Canada, 189–212.

King, D. and Sylvester, D. (eds.) 1983. *The Eastern Carpet in the Western World from the 15th to the 17th Century*. London: Arts Council of Great Britain.

Kisluk-Grosheide, D. O. 1994. The Marquand Mansion. *Metropolitan Museum Journal* **29**, 151–181.

Kopytoff, I. 1986. The cultural biography of things: commoditization as process. In: A. Appadurai (ed.) *The Social Life of Things*. Cambridge: Cambridge University Press, pp. 64–91.

Lloyd, H. 1997. The Role of Housekeeping and Preventative Conservation in the Care of Textiles in

Historic Houses. In: K. Marko (ed.) *Textiles in Trust.* Proceedings of the Symposium 'Textiles in Trust' held at Blickling Hall, Norfolk, September 1995. London: Archetype Publications and the National Trust, 40–53.
Lopez, M.G. 1997. *Urbino Palazzo Ducale. Testimonianze inedite della vita di corte.* Urbino: Soprintendenza per i Beni Artistici e Storici delle Marche.
Medlam, S. 1993. The Decorative Art Approach: Furniture. In: D. Fleming, C. Paine and J.G. Rhodes (eds.) *Social History in Museums. A Handbook for Professionals.* London: HMSO, 39–41.
Miller, D. 1987. *Material Culture and Mass Consumption.* Oxford: Blackwell.
Monnas, L. 1998. 'Tissues' in England during the fifteenth and sixteenth-centuries. *CIETA Bulletin,* **75**, 63–80.
Montgomery, F. M. 1984. *Textiles in America 1650–1870.* New York: Norton & Co.
Moore, A. 1996. *Houghton Hall. The Prime Minister, Empress and The Heritage.* London: Philip Wilson and Norfolk Museum Service.
Mordaunt Crook, J. 1981a. *William Burges and the High Victorian Dream.* London: John Murray (Publishers) Ltd.
Mordaunt Crook, J. (ed.) 1981b. *The Strange Genius of William Burges, 'Art-Architect', 1827–1881.* A catalogue to a Centenary Exhibition organised jointly by the National Museum of Wales, Cardiff, and the Victoria and Albert Museum, London. Cardiff: National Museum of Wales.
Moyr Smith, J. 1889. *Ornamental Interiors Ancient and Modern.* London.
Mucci, P.E.R. 1997. Rapid identification of plastics using external beam mid-infrared spectroscopy. In: *Proceedings of the Royal Society of Chemistry Symposium. Chemical Aspects of Plastics Recycling.* University Manchester Institute of Science and Technology, Manchester (1996). Cambridge Royal Society of Chemistry Information Services, 53–70.
Murphy, E. A. 1966. Some Early Adventures with Latex. *Technology* **39** (3 June 1966) lxxiii–lxxxiv.
Museums and Galleries Commission 1998. *Standards in the Museum Care of Costume and Textiles.* London: HMSO.
National Trust 1978. *Guidebook to Knole.* London: National Trust.
Nicholson, C. 1997. The Care of the National Trust's Carriage Collections. In: K. Marko (ed.), *Textiles in Trust.* Proceedings of the Symposium 'Textiles in Trust' held at Blickling Hall, Norfolk, September 1995. London: Archetype, 59–66.
Oddy, W.A. (ed.) 1994. *Restoration: Is it acceptable?* London: Britsh Museum.
Ossut, C. 1994. *Le Siege et sa Garniture.* Dourdan, France: Editions H. Vial.
Ossut, C. 1996. *Tapisserie D'Ameublement.* Dourdan, France: Editions H. Vial.
Pallot, Bill G.B. 1989. *The Art of the Chair in Eighteenth-Century France.* Paris: ACR-Gismondi Editeurs.
Philipson, J. 1994 [1897]. *The art and craft of coachbuilding.* Warwickshire: TEE Publishing.
Philp, P. 1980. The Empire Style. In: N.Riley (ed.) *World Furniture.* London: Octopus Books Ltd, pp. 141-159.
Pullan, R. P. (ed.) 1885. *The House of William Burges, ARA.* London.
Read, B. 1989. Vintage Victoriana. *Country Life* (June 8 1989) 314–317.
Rendell, C. 1990. The Archbishop's chair, York Minster. In: A. French (ed.) *Conservation of Furnishing Textiles.* Postprints of the conference held at the Burrell Collection, Glasgow, 30–31 March 1990. Scotland: SSCR, 14–20.
Rivers, S. and Umney, N.D. (eds.) (forthcoming) *Conservation of Furniture.* Oxford: Butterworth-Heinemann.
Roberts, J. 1993. *Holbein and the Court of Henry VIII. Drawings and Miniatures from the Royal Library Windsor Castle.* Edinburgh: National Galleries of Scotland.
Rodríguez-Salgado, M. J. 1988. *Armada 1588–1598.* Harmondsworth: Penguin.
Rogers, P. 1991. *Report on the Octagon Room, Raby Castle.* Unpublished internal report, English Heritage.
Sandwith, H. and Stainton, S. 1991 [1984]. *The National Trust Manual of Housekeeping.* London: Penguin Books.
Schoeser, M. and Rufey, C. 1989. *English and American Textiles From 1790 to the Present.* London: Thames and Hudson.
Shilling, M.E. 1997 (With additional information from Dinah Eastop and Kate Gill). Houghton Hall Exhibition at Kenwood. *Furniture History Society Newsletter* **127** (August 1997) 17–18.
Simpson, J.A. and Weiner, E.S.C. (eds.) 1989. *Oxford English Dictionary.* 20 vols. Oxford: Clarendon Press.
Smith, B. and Handley, M. 1996. *Brodsworth and Pickburn: A Tale of Two Villages.* Doncaster: Brodsworth and Pickering Local History Society.
Starkey, D. R. (ed.) 1998. *The Inventory of King Henry VIII.* I. The Transcript. London: Harvey Miller for the Society of Antiquaries.
Stevens, C. 1999. *The Printed Textiles of Brodsworth Hall.* Unpublished research report: held at Brodsworth Hall.
Strange, E. F. 1928. The ancient chair at York Minster. *Old Furniture.* August issue (no issue number) 214–7.
Stoughton-Harris, C. 1993. Treatment of 20th-century rubberised multimedia costume: conservation of a Mary Quant raincoat (ca. 1967). In: D.W.Grattan (ed.) *Saving the Twentieth Century: The Conservation of Modern Materials.* Ottawa:CCI, pp. 213–221.
Strong, R. 1963. Holbein's cartoon for the Barber Surgeon's group rediscovered. *Burlington Magazine,* **105**, 1–14.
Swain, M. 1997. Loose Covers, or Cases. *Furniture History.* The Journal of the Furniture History Society, **XXXIII**, 128–33.
Swanson V. G. 1990. *The biography and catalogue raisonne of the paintings of Sir Lawrence Alma-Tadema.* London: Garton & Co.
Thomerson, C. 1980. *Report on the investigation of the tub chair, Mus.ref. W.25.1980.* Unpublished investigation report, Dept. of Furniture and Woodwork, Victoria and Albert Museum.
Thornton, P. 1974. Canopies, couches and chairs of state. *Apollo,* **100**, 293–4.
Thornton, P. 1978. *Seventeenth-Century Interior Decoration in England, France and Holland.* New Haven CT and London: Yale University Press.
Thornton, P. 1984. Some late sixteenth-century Medici furniture. *Furniture History.* The Journal of the Furniture History Society, **20**, 1–9.
Thornton, P. 1991. *The Italian Renaissance Interior 1400–1600.* New York: H. N. Abrams.

Thornton, P. 1993 [1984]. *Authentic Decor. The Domestic Interior 1620–1920.* London: Weidenfeld and Nicolson.

Thornton, P.K. and Tomlin, M.F. 1980. *The Furnishing and Decoration of Ham House.* London: The Furniture History Society.

Thurley, S. 1993. *The Royal Palaces of Tudor England.* New Haven and London: Yale University Press.

Thurley, S. 1997. A Conflict of Interest? Conservation versus Historic Presentation, a Curatorial View. In: K. Marko (ed.) *Textiles in Trust.* Proceedings of the Symposium 'Textiles in Trust' held at Blickling Hall, Norfolk, September 1995. London: Archetypes Publications and the National Trust, 20–4.

Timár-Balázsy, A. & Eastop, D. 1998. *Chemical Principles of Textile Conservation.* Oxford: Butterworth-Heinemann.

Tortora, P. G. and Merkel, R.S. (eds.) 1996. *Fairchild's Dictionary of Textiles.* New York: Fairchild Publications.

Victoria and Albert Museum. 1960. *Catalogue of a Loan Exhibition of English Chintz: English Printed Furnishing Fabrics From Their Origins Until the Present Day.* London: V&A.

Victoria and Albert Museum. 1970. *A Century of Warners Fabrics* 1870–1970. London: V&A.

Wainwright, R. 1981. Pre-Raphaelite Furniture. In: J. Mordaunt Crook, J. (ed.) 1981b. *The Strange Genius of William Burges, 'Art-Architect', 1827–1881.* A catalogue to a Centenary Exhibition organised jointly by the National Museum of Wales, Cardiff, and the Victoria and Albert Museum, London, pp. 67–70.

Walker, S. 1986. Investigation of the properties of Tyvek, pertaining to its use as a storage material for artifacts. *IIC-CG Newsletter*, September 1986, 21–25.

Walton, K. 1973. *The Golden Age of English Furniture Upholstery 1660–1840.* Leeds: Temple Newsam House (Exhibition Catalogue).

Walton, P. 1984. Dyes on medieval textiles. *Dyes on Historical and Archaeological Textiles.* Third meeting of the York Archaeological Trust, 30–33.

Watkinson, R., c.1979. *William Morris as Designer.* London: Studio Vista.

Westman, A. 1994. Splendours of State. The textile furnishings of the King's Apartments. *Apollo,* **CXL** (390) (New Series) August 1994, The King's Apartments Hampton Court Palace (William III 1689–1702), 39–45.

White, L. 1982. Two English State Beds in The Metropolitan Museum of Art. *Apollo* (August) 84–87.

Williams, M.A. (ed.) 1990. *Upholstery Conservation.* Preprints of a Symposium held at Colonial Williamsburg, February 2–4, 1990. East Kingston, New Hampshire: American Conservation Consortium, Ltd.

Wilson, L. 1999. Foams in Upholstered Furniture. In: D.A. Rogers and G. Marley (eds.) *Modern Materials – Modern Problems.* Postprints of the Conference, Modern Materials, Modern Problems, organised by the UKIC, 17 April 1999. London: UKIC, 19–25.

Wilson, L. & Balfour, D. 1990. Developments in Upholstery Construction in Britain during the First Half of the 20th Century. In: M.A.Williams (ed.) *Upholstery Conservation.* Pre-prints of a Symposium held at Colonial Williamsburg, February 2–4, 1990. New Hampshire: American Conservation Consortium, Ltd, 136–48.

Wylie, A. and Singer, P. 1997. The Resurrection of the Uppark State Bed. In: K. Marko (ed.) *Textiles in Trust.* Proceedings of the Symposium 'Textiles in Trust' held at Blickling Hall, Norfolk, September 1995, 118–127.

Select bibliography

Abbreviations

AIC American Institue for Conservation of Historic and Artistic Works
IIC International Institute for the Conservation of Historic and Artistic Works
SSCR Scottish Society for Conservation and Restoration
UKIC United Kingdom Institute for Conservation

Walton, K. 1973. *The Golden Age of English Furniture Upholstery 1660–1840.* Leeds: Temple Newsam House (Exhibition Catalogue).

White, E. 1990. *Pictorial Dictionary of British 18th Century Furniture Design. The Printed Sources.* Woodbridge, Suffolk: The Antique Collectors' Club.

White, A. & Robertson, B. 1990. *Furniture & Furnishings: A Visual Guide.* London: Studio Vista.

Upholstery history

Anderson, M. & Trent, R.F. 1993. A Catalogue of American Easy Chairs. In: L. Beckerdite (ed.) *American Furniture.* Hanover and London: Chipstone Foundation in association with the University Press of New England, 212–234.

Beard, G. 1997. *Upholsterers and Interior Furnishing in England, 1530–1840.* London and New York: Yale University Press.

Cooke, Jr., E.S. (ed.) 1987. *Upholstery in America & Europe from the Seventeenth Century to World War I.* New York: Norton.

Fiell, P. & Fiell, C. 1997. *1000 Chairs.* Köln: Taschen.

Fowler, J. & Cornforth, J. 1986. *English Decoration in the 18th Century.* London: Barrie & Jenkins.

Grier, K.C. 1988. *Culture and Comfort: People, Parlours and Upholstery 1850–1930.* Rochester, New York: The Strong Museum in association with the University of Massachusetts Press.

Jackson Stops, G. (ed.) 1985. *The Treasure Houses of Britain.* Exhibition Catalogue. Washington, D.C.: National Gallery of Art.

Joy, E. 1986 [1977]. *Pictorial Dictionary of British 19th C Furniture Design.* Woodbridge, Suffolk: Antique Collectors' Club.

Passeri, A. & Trent, R. 1983. Two New England Queen Anne Easy Chairs with Original Upholstery, American Classics No. 5. *Maine Antique Digest, II* (4) April 1983, 26A–28A.

Thornton, P. 1978. *Seventeenth Century Interior Decoration in England, France and Holland.* New Haven and London: Yale University Press.

Thornton, P. 1993 [1984]. *Authentic Décor: The Domestic Interior 1620–1920.* London: Weidenfeld and Nicholson.

Thornton, P. & Tomlin, M.F. 1980. *The Furnishing and Decoration of Ham House.* London: The Furniture History Society.

Upholstery conservation/interpretation

Andersch, T. 2001. Die Restaurerung einer Stahlrohrmöbelgruppe mit Stuhlrohrgeflecht nach einem Entwurf Ludwig Mies van der Rohes von 1927. *Arbeitsblätter für Restauratoren,* **1**, 171–180.

Anderson, M. 1988. A non-damaging system applied to an 18th century easy chair. In: *Wooden Artefacts Group Preprints.* AIC 16th Annual Meeting held in New Orleans, Lousiana, 5 June 1988. Washington DC: AIC, pages not numbered.

Anderson, M. 1989. New Applications of Non Damaging Upholstery. In: *Wooden Artifacts Group Preprints.* Papers presented at the Wooden Artifacts Group Speciality session, June 4, 1989, AIC Annual Meeting, Cincinnati, Ohio. Washington, D.C.: AIC, pages not numbered.

Angst, W. 1979. The conservation of an upholstered chair reputed to be the one in which President Madison died. *Proceedings of AIC 7th Annual Meeting, Toronto.* Washington, D.C.: AIC, 1–9.

Balfour, D., Metcalf, S., Collard, F. 1999. The first non-intrusive upholstery treatment at the Victoria and Albert Museum. *The Conservator,* **23**, 22–29 & 46.

Battram, A. 1994. Diverse solutions from the upholstery lab at SPNEA. *The Textile Speciality Group Postprints (AIC),* **4**, 17–25.

Berkouwer, M. 1994. Freezing to Eradicate Insect Pests in Textiles at Brodsworth Hall. *The Conservator,* **18**, 15–22.

Blank, S. 1990. An introduction to plastics and rubbers in collections. *Studies in Conservation,* **35** (2), 53–63.

Britton, N.C. 1994. Basket cases: Two upholstery treatments composed of plant materials. *The Textile Speciality Group Postprints* (AIC) **4**, 27–38.

Buck, S.L. 1991. A Technical and Stylistic Comparison of twelve Massachusetts State House Chairs. *Wooden Artefacts Group Preprints.* Washington D.C.: AIC, 22 pp.

Calinescu, I. & McLean, C. 1995. Low interventive upholstery conservation at LACMA – A crash course. *Textile Conservation Newsletter*, **29**, Fall 1995, 10–19.

Calnan, C. (ed.) 1991. *Conservation of leather in transport collections*. Papers given at a UKIC conference Restoration '91, London in October 1991. London: UKIC.

Doyal, S. 1996. The treatment of the Wellington Museum Apsley House hall porter's chair. A case study of the treatment of coated fabric. *The Conservator*, **20**, 77–86.

Eastop, D. 1998. Decision making in conservation: determining the role of artefacts. In: A. Tímár-Balázsy and D. Eastop (eds.) *International Perspectives on Textile Conservation*. Papers from the ICOM–CC Textiles Working Group Meetings 1994 & 1995. London: Archetype, 43–46.

Fairbairn, G. 1987. Creating the right impression — reproducing textured finishes. In: *Wooden Artifacts Group Preprints*. AIC 15th Annual Meeting held in Vancouver. Washington D.C.: AIC, pages not numbered.

Fiell, C. & Fiell, P. 1997. *1000 Chairs*. Köln: Taschen.

French, A. (ed.) 1990. *Conservation of Furnishing Textiles*. Postprints of the conference held at the Burrell Collection, Glasgow, 30–31 March 1990. Edinburgh: SSCR.

Gentle, N. 1990. Conservation of the Dolphin Chairs at Ham House. In: A. French (ed.) *Conservation of Furnishing Textiles*. Postprints of the conference held at the Burrell Collection, Glasgow, 30–31 March 1990, Edinburgh: SSCR/UKIC, 30–40

Gill, K. 1988. Upholstery conservation. In: *Wooden Artefacts Group Preprints*. AIC 16th Annual Meeting held in New Orleans, Lousiana, 5 June 1988. Washington DC: AIC, pages not numbered.

Gill, K. 1992. Upholstery conservation. In: K. Bachman (ed.) *Conservation Concerns. A Guide for Collectors and Curators*. Washington, D.C. and London: Smithsonian Institution Press, 111–114.

Godla, J. & Hanlon, G. 1995. Some applications of adobe photoshop for the documentation of furniture conservation. *JAIC*, **34** (3), 157–172.

Landi, S. 1992 [1985]. Chapter 13, Upholstery. In: *The Textile Conservator's Manual*. London: Butterworth-Heinemann, 248–276.

McGiffin, R.F. 1983. *Furniture Care & Conservation*. Tennessee: The American Association for State & Local History.

Marko, K. (ed.) 1997. *Textiles in Trust*. Proceedings of the Symposium 'Textiles in Trust' held at Blickling Hall, Norfolk, September 1995. London Archetype and N.T.

Munn, J. 1989. Treatment techniques for the Vellum-covered Furniture by Carlo Bugatti. In: *Wooden Artifacts Group Preprints*. Papers presented at the Wooden Artifacts Group Speciality session, June 4, 1989, AIC Annual Meeting, Cincinnati, Ohio. Washington, D.C.: AIC, pages not numbered.

Neher, A. & Rogers, D. (eds.) 1996. *Pest Attack & Control in Organic Materials*. Postprints of the Conference held by UKIC Furniture Section at the Museum of London, November 1996. London: UKIC.

Orlofsky, P. & Trupin, D. 1993. The role of connoiseurship in determining the textile conservator's treatment options. *Journal of the American Institute for Conservation* (AIC) **32**, 109–18.

Paepke, K. & Hassell, M. 1993. *Textile Kosbarkeiten in Sanssouci bewahrt*. Potsdam: Stiftung Schlösser und Gärten Potsdam–Sanssouci.

Rogers, D.A. & Marley, G. (eds.) 1999. *Modern Materials—Modern Problems*. Postprints of the Conference, 'Modern Materials, Modern Problems', organised by UKIC, 17 April, 1999. London: UKIC.

Sandwith, H. & Stainton, S. 1991 [1984]. *The National Trust Manual of Housekeeping: A new edition of the practical guide to the conservation of old houses and their contents*. London: Penguin Books.

Sheetz, R. 1989. Conservation of Russian Artifacts from Sitka, Alaska. In: *Wooden Artifacts Group Preprints*. Papers presented at the Wooden Artifacts Group Speciality session, June 4, 1989, AIC Annual Meeting, Cincinnati, Ohio. Washington, D.C.: AIC, pages not numbered.

Thornton, P. 1977. Fringe Benefits. *The Connoisseur*, September, p. 2.

Trupin, D.L. 1994. Upholstery conservation in New York State historic sites: case studies of problems and solutions. In: *La Conservation des Textiles Anciens*. Journées d'Etudes de la SFIIC, 265–275.

Twitchell, J. 1991. Non-invasive foundations for re-upholstery. In: *Wooden Artifacts Group Preprints*. Papers presented at the Wooden Artifacts Group Speciality session, AIC 19th Annual Meeting. Washington, D.C.: AIC, pages not numbered.

Williams, M.A. 1988. *Keeping it All Together: The Preservation & Care of Historic Furniture*. Ohio: Ohio Antique Review Inc.

Williams, M.A. (ed.) 1990. *Upholstery Conservation*. Preprints of a Symposium held at Colonial Williamsburg, February 2-4, 1990. East Kingston, New Hampshire: American Conservation Consortium, Ltd.

Upholstery technique

Bast, H. 1948. *New Essentials of Upholstery*. Milwaukee, USA: Bruce Publishing Co.

Hayward, C.H. (ed.) 1981. *The Woodworker's Pocket Book*. London: Evans Brothers Limited.

James, D. 1990. *Upholstery: A Complete Course*. London: The Guild of Master Craftsman Publications.

Ossut, C. 1994. *Le Siege et sa Garniture*. Dourdan, France: Editions H. Vial.

Ossut, C. 1996. *Tapisserie D'Ameublement*. Dourdan, France: Editions H. Vial.

Palmer, F. 1983 [1921]. *Practical Upholstering and the Cutting of Loose Covers* (3rd impression). London: Herbert Press.

Robinson, T. 1983. *A Guide to Recognition in 18th Century Upholstery Substructure*. USA: unpublished notes.

Stenberg, B. & Åkervall, T. 1989. *Möbelstoppning Som Hantverk*. Stockholm: Sveriges Tapetseraremästares Centralförening.

Van Blitterswijk, J. 1944. *Binnenhuis-Materialen*. Amsterdam: Uitgave Holdert & Co.

Upholstery understructure materials

Bast, H. 1948. *New Essentials of Upholstery*. Milwaukee, USA: Bruce Publishing Company, 248–292.

Bodey, H. 1983. *Nail Making*. Shire Album **87**, Haverfordwest, UK: C.I. Thomas & Sons.

Bradley Smith, H.R. n.d. *Chronological Development of Nails*. Supplement to Blacksmiths' and Farriers' tools at Shelburne Museum – A History of their Development from Forge to Factory. Museum Pamphlet series, No. 7. Shelburne, Vermont, USA: The Shelburne Museum, pages not numbered.

Holley, D. 1981. Upholstery springs. *Furniture History*. The Journal of the Furniture History Society, **17**, 64–67.

Milnes, E.C. 1983. *History of the Development of Furniture Webbing*. Leeds: Private publication.

Nelson, L.H. 1968. Nail Chronology as an Aid to Dating Old Buildings. *History News*, Vol. 24, No. 11. American Association for State and Local History: Technical Leaflet 48, pages not numbered.

Thornton, P. 1978. *Seventeenth Century Interior Decoration in England, France and Holland*. New Haven and London: Yale University Press.

Thornton, P. 1991. *The Italian Renaissance Interior 1400–1600*. New York: H.N. Abrams.

Thornton, P. 1993 [1984]. *Authentic Décor. The Domestic Interior 1620–1920*. London: Weidenfield and Nicolson.

Traupel, B. 1955. Jute manufacturing industries. *CIBA Review*, February 1955, **108**, 3911–3916.

Velterli, W. 1951. Rubber in the textile industry. *CIBA Review*, August 1951, **87**, 3157–3159.

Walton, K. 1973. *The Golden Age of English Furniture Upholstery 1660–1840*. Leeds: Temple Newsam House (Exhibition Catalogue).

Webster & Parkes. 1845. *Domestic Economy*. New York: Harper & Brothers.

Furnishing textiles

Clabburn, P. 1988. *The National Trust Book of Furnishing Textiles*. London: The National Trust.

Montgomery, F.M. 1984. *Textiles in America 1650–1870*. New York: Norton & Co.

Nylander, J.C. 1990. *Fabrics for Historic Buildings* (4th rev. edition). Washington, D.C.: The Preservation Press.

Schoeser, M. & Rufey, C. 1989. *English and American Textiles from 1790 to the Present*. London and New York: Thames & Hudson.

Upholstery trimmings

Musée d'Arts Decoratifs. 1973. *Des Corelotiers Aux Passementerie*. Paris: Musee d'Arts Decoratifs.

Index

This index has been designed to encourage exploration of the principles and practices of upholstery conservation. In selecting key words, the aim has been to link important concepts with case histories, and visa versa. A three-part division (top cover, understructure and trimming) has been adopted for 'upholstery'. The term intervention has been employed as a key word in the index, rather than treatment, as it encompasses investigation as well as both preventive and interventive conservation. Generic terms are privileged; thus, for example, staples are found under fastener, and Velcro™ under hook and loop fastener.

Note: **bold** indicates key page(s), *italic* indicates Plates.